DISCIPLES OF CHRIST IN

Georgia

DISCIPLES
OF CHRIST
IN
Georgia

By J. Edward Moseley

THE BETHANY PRESS
St. Louis, Missouri

To
THE HEROIC PIONEERS
Unorthodox Critics of Tradition
in Things of the Spirit
but Steadfast of
Christian Purpose
This Book
Is Gratefully Dedicated

Preface

This book describes the chronological origin and development of the Georgia Disciples of Christ, known locally as the Christian churches or Churches of Christ. In 1949, a century after the first State Convention of this Protestant body, 156 churches survived while 170 congregations, and more perhaps, failed to overcome the ravages of time.

Numerically small for many years, the movement thrived on opposition from orthodox religious neighbors. Despite inadequate missionary aid from their own agencies, the Disciples grew and became, even with constant dissension and division, a force to be reckoned with in the state.

The history, full of dramatic interest, was enlivened by colorful personalities. There was James Jenkins Trott, missionary to the Cherokee Indians, who demonstrated that he could die at his post, but would not desert it. The influence of the generosity of Mrs. Emily H. Tubman for Christian stewardship is felt even today. Some of the strongest congregations in the state owe their beginnings to the evangelistic labors of the pioneers. Erastus Lamar Shelnutt, who established more congregations of Disciples in Georgia than any other person, was arrested for his religious convictions.

These and numerous others left a glorious heritage. The record reveals enterprise, courage, sagacity, much struggle. They described issues in terms of what they felt obliged to preach, not what they were permitted to say. Therefore, they pronounced their unpopular heresies which proved so disturbing to current religious ideas and practices.

7

The preparation of this volume, really started more than fifty years ago, was a much bigger task than anyone ever thought it was going to be. Mrs. B. O. Miller began the collection and writing of the material about 1901. It was resumed in earnest in the 1940's. At that time much material and a balance of $2,070.11 from the treasury of the Woman's Society for Georgia Missions was conveyed to the Christian Board of Publication at the request of the women who earned the money. Others who subsequently shared in collecting, preserving, and transmitting the unfinished manuscript included Mrs. Lane Mitchell, Mr. and Mrs. John H. Wood, Miss Mattie Mitchell, and Bruce Nay.

The material that was sent to the publisher several years ago contained many gaps and almost nothing about the work since 1900. Many details were inaccurate and objectivity was lacking. What was considered an editorial assignment, therefore, developed into a major research and writing task. It thus became the point of no return for me. This history, developed chronologically rather than topically, which ends with 1949, is the result.

Actually one needs to be a detective to write church history. A motto for the church historian might well be, *sed ultra quaero*—but I seek further. Diligent research to discover original source material was the order of many days. Dusty volumes often yielded unsuspected treasures. All data, gathered from many sources, was winnowed and evaluated for its possible significance. Unquestioned "facts" often proved to be mere legends or fables.

The search for primary source materials led to private and public collections of Discipliana. Rare items discovered included diaries, letters, newspaper clippings, tracts, sermons, periodicals, books, pamphlets, convention minutes, reports, and theses. Some of the material was published, much of it unpublished. This history is more comprehensive because such documents were preserved.

The people with the foresight to write, to collect, or to preserve such material deserve medals of honor. May their tribe increase!

Permission was granted for unrestricted use of the unpublished biography of Dr. Daniel Hook which was written by his daughter, Mary D. (Mrs. Clark) Howell. The manuscript is unquestionably one of the most valuable primary sources on the struggles of the pioneer Disciples in Georgia. Miss Sue Steiner Hook, granddaughter of Dr. Hook, and her niece, Beverly Hook (Mrs. Jack) Frierson, his great-granddaughter, kindly permitted use of the only copy of the manuscript. Because of its importance, permission was given to deposit a typescript with The Disciples of Christ Historical Society in Nashville, Tenn. It is hoped that the manuscript may eventually be edited and published.

Librarians of several libraries containing valuable historical collections granted use of materials and aided the necessary research in various ways. I gratefully acknowledge such assistance from the following: Carolina Discipliana Library, Atlantic Christian College, Wilson, N. C.; The Disciples of Christ Historical Society, Nashville, Tenn.; Butler University School of Religion, Indianapolis; The College of the Bible, Lexington, Ky.; Philip Fall Memorial Library of the First Christian Church, Frankfort, Ky.; George Pepperdine College, Los Angeles; Historical Foundation of the Presbyterian and Reformed Churches, Montreat, N. C.; Georgia State Library, Atlanta; Indiana State Library and the Library of The United Christian Missionary Society, Indianapolis; Joint Universities Library, Nashville, Tenn.; University of North Carolina, Chapel Hill, and the Georgia Historical Society, Savannah.

Unpublished graduate theses treating history of the Georgia Christian churches afforded important clues for additional research. My appreciation for this help goes to the following: Lenton L. Poss, Brite College of the Bible, Texas Christian University; James Harkness Barfield, Sr., Vanderbilt University School of Religion; A. Goff Bedford, West Virginia University; and Jack Mathews Daniell, The College of the Bible.

I am grateful for assistance and encouragement, frequently and generously offered, by Dr. Robert W. Burns, pastor of the Peachtree Christian Church, Atlanta, and by my wife, Louise Lomax Moseley. Both read the manuscript, chapter by chapter, and made helpful suggestions when impatience with the slow progress might have been expressed. Their understanding of the difficulties encountered is appreciated.

Other persons rendered worth-while counsel in libraries and through correspondence. The number included the following: Dr. Charles C. Ware, Claude E. Spencer, Dr. Charles W. Ross, Mrs. Ada M. Mosher, Lorenzo J. Evans, Dr. Howard E. Short, Dr. Ronald E. Osborn, Mrs. Robert Richardson Gum, Dr. T. H. Spence, Jr., Henry King Shaw, Mrs. J. Lloyd Sanders, E. G. Orahood, Dr. Myrddyn W. Jones, J. Randall Farris, and Mrs. Lilla M. Hawes. Some of these read part or all of the manuscript. A number of Georgians much interested in the publication of a creditable manuscript, read a processed copy of the book before it was issued in the present form. I am grateful for all such assistance.

The following publishers granted permission to quote copyrighted material: American Baptist Publication Society, Bobbs-Merrill Co., Broadman Press, Byrd Printing Co., Continental Book Co., Culver-Stockton College, Edwards and Broughton Printing Co., Foote and Davies Co., Franklin Printing and Publishing Co., Henry Holt & Co., Indiana University Press, Rinehart & Co., Inc., Fleming H. Revell Co., The University of Chicago Press, the University of Georgia Press, and the University of North Carolina Press.

The question of inadequate space to cover the fascinating story was always a paramount one. That is the only explanation possible to those who may, after reading the following pages, feel that some churches or preachers received insufficient recognition. It was necessary to be selective in using so much material. Consequently, much detail and many gems of human interest had to be deleted from succeeding drafts of the manuscript in the tedious rewriting that was required. Really a history is like an iceberg, showing just a small portion of the material that went into the composition. Yet the unseen part is what provides solidity and conviction.

Many expectant persons who paid for copies of the book a long time ago were quite patient. It is my hope and that of the publisher—who is making a considerable contribution to the publication—that the volume proves worth the long wait.

I tried to be accurate,—I first learned the importance of this in my newspaper and magazine editing—, objective, and fair in controversial matters discussed in the book. Opinions expressed and conclusions reached herein are mine. They were based on my interpretation of the many records that were thoroughly examined. Therefore, the elements of human error and prejudice must be considered.

The heritage of the Georgia Disciples of Christ is certainly worth preservation. It should provide stimulation and hope for the present and succeeding generations. The pioneers accomplished much, but they did not finish anything, as Seneca, the Roman philosopher, said long ago.

My own understanding and appreciation of the heritage claimed by the Disciples was enhanced by this study. Now that the unfinished manuscript is written and ready for publication, I am confident that in writing history one does not count the cost of the laborious research and writing. All must be regarded as fun or no sensible person would engage in it!

J. EDWARD MOSELEY

Contents

CHAPTER I

The Religion of a Chosen People

Georgia, the last English colony established in America, was designed to be different. It was unique as a New World Utopia in that the religious role was paramount. Since it was considered the noblest social and philanthropic experiment of the colonial period, more attention was given to Georgia by the English than to any other colony.

Part of the vast domain of the Creek and Cherokee Indians, Georgia had Catholic missions established by Spanish Franciscans as early as 1566. When the Carolina English colonists drove the Spaniards farther south, the missions decayed with the ravages of time. The explorer Hernando de Soto had visited the area in 1540 while searching for gold. In 1663 and 1665 the land was given to eight lords' proprietors of Carolina. By 1729 the undeveloped region was returned to the English Crown. After being partitioned into North and South Carolina, the southern section was retained for future disposal.

In 1732, when that southern frontier of Colonial America was a recurring danger, King George II granted a charter for the new colony. No English colony had been established in America for fifty years, since Pennsylvania was settled in 1682. The name of the new colony, Georgia, for King George I (according to a plat of 1715),[1] was derived from a Greek word meaning agriculture.

[1] Clark Howell, *History of Georgia* (4 vols.; Chicago-Atlanta: S. J. Clarke Publishing Co., 1926), I, 31.

15

The expression of religion and philanthropy originally guided the founders of Georgia in providing a refuge for indigent persons and persecuted European Protestants. However, the Crown was not unmindful of the strategic importance of trade and military defense for the struggling frontiersmen, already residing in the Carolinas, from invasion by the Spaniards of Florida and the French of Louisiana.

General James Edward Oglethorpe, youthful, Oxford-educated, Member of Parliament (elected at the age of 24) in February, 1728, was named chairman of a committee of Parliament. This group was authorized to investigate conditions of debtors in the wretched jails. A debtor could be imprisoned for years by a penurious creditor and thus rendered unable to earn the money needed to pay the debt. This committee secured the redress of many grievances. Oglethorpe and a few friends, however, sought to get at the roots of the situation by providing the distressed people with new opportunities for earning a living as well as with a refuge from persecution.

In seeking this haven, Oglethorpe and his friends decided to found the colony in Georgia. Struggling in behalf of others was a characteristic of the General's faith.

In this connection the Rev. Thomas Bray had for years emphasized improved moral conditions for England and the American colonies. He organized two imposing alphabetical agencies for this purpose. One was the Society for the Propagation of the Gospel in Foreign Parts (SPG). The other was the Society for the Promotion of Christian Knowledge (SPCK). After Bray's death in 1730, Oglethorpe was a trustee for the estate.

John Lord Viscount Percival, later the first Earl of Egmont, was a friend of Oglethorpe's and associated with Bray's philanthropic causes. Discussion of a colony for unfortunates resulted in Oglethorpe and Percival securing initial funds to launch the project. The two were joined by nineteen other citizens, including Members of Parliament, in petitioning King George for American land on which to establish a new colony.

The charter authorizing the founding of Georgia was granted on June 9, 1732. The document, providing for twenty-one trustees, was to expire in twenty-one years. No trustee could own any of the colonial land or receive pay for his services. The enterprise was for the welfare of oppressed people. Oglethorpe remained a trustee throughout the colonial experiment.

Five clergymen were among the first trustees. English preachers and churches raised money for the colony while Parliament made a grant of 10,000 pounds. Contributions also included Bibles and many hundreds of other books, plants, seeds, and military weapons.

Selection of the first settlers required four months. Hundreds of applications were received and the applicants thoroughly investigated. There was no welcome for criminals, deserters of dependents, or debtors without consent of creditors. Always, the needy received prior consideration. Those whose applications were approved received free passage to Georgia, 50 acres of land, farming tools, seeds, and cattle. Also, subsistence was provided until houses could be built and land cleared. The trustees recognized from the beginning that the moral vigor of the settlers was essential for a successful colony. So while many persons applied, only a few were chosen. The religious faith and practices of those cosmopolites are the concern of this chapter.

Oglethorpe's idealism was tinged with imperialism when he and 35 families, or more than 100 persons, sailed on the "Anne" for Georgia in November, 1732. Public prayers were offered twice daily during the two-month voyage. On Feb. 12, 1733, after ascending the Savannah River for 18 miles, the settlers landed on a high bluff. An agreement for the site was reached with the Yamacraw Indians, an outlawed Creek tribe, and their kindly chief, Tomo-chi-chi, "earliest of the great Georgians." The settlement was named Savannah.

Religion was recognized as a necessity in the establishment of the colony. The early settlers had several clergymen in their groups. The Rev. Henry Herbert, Anglican clergyman, accompanied the original cargo. A temporary site for worship was quickly selected at Savannah and the first congregation was called Christ Church. Herbert was soon succeeded by the Rev. Samuel Quincy.

Persons in desperate need received first consideration from the trustees. So the persecuted Protestants of Europe were invited to join the new colony of chosen people in the land of Georgia. Lutherans in Austria's province of Salzburg suffered persecution from Catholic clergymen. Even prior to the founding of Georgia, thousands of those victims sought refuge in other European countries. Bray's SPCK and the German Evangelical Lutheran Church helped to defray the costs of the emigration of the Salzburgers. Under the spiritual leadership of the Rev. John Martin Bolzius, 42 families of Salzburgers began Georgia's Ebenezer settlement in 1734 and established the Jerusalem Evangelical Lutheran Church in Effingham County. In 1742 they welcomed the Rev. Heinrich Melchior Muhlenberg as a colonial missionary. He lived to become the patriarch of American Lutherans. Within a few years more than 1,000 God-fearing Salzburger Lutherans had established residence in Georgia.

What did the new settlers think of Georgia? Their deep thanksgiving upon seeing the land for the first time was recorded by the master of the sailing vessel that brought the first Salzburgers to Georgia. He wrote:

God blessed us this Day with the Sight of Our Country, our wish'd for *Georgia,* which we saw at ten in the Morning; and brought us unto the *Savannah* River, and caused us to remember the Vows we had made unto him, if He did through his infinite Goodness bring us hither.[2]

---

[2]Commissary Von Reck, *An Extract of the Journals of Mr. Commissary Von Reck, Who Conducted the First Transport of Saltzburgers to Georgia: and of the Reverend Mr. Bolzius, One of their Ministers* (London: The Society for Promoting Christian Knowledge, 1734), p. 9.

An indication of the devout faith of the early colonists, who established a pattern for generations to come, was evidenced by the Rev. Mr. Bolzius in his diary, thus:

Last Night we Prayed on shore for the first time, in the *English* Chapel, made of Boards, and used for divine Worship, till a Church can be built; the Use of which is allowed us, during our Stay here. The Inhabitants join with us, and shew much Devotion. The *Jews* likewise, of which there are 12 families here, come to Church, and seem to be very devout: They understand the *German* Tongue. Though the Chapel is but of Boards, it is very convenient, and pleases the Salzburgers.[3]

More oppressed European Protestants, that time the Moravians, entered Georgia in 1735 and 1736 on condition that they should not be forced to bear arms and thus desecrate their pacifist confession of faith. With their minister, the Rev. Gottleib Spangenberg, they remained in or near Savannah. They began an Indian mission school at Irene. When the Moravians, "who had a faith above fear," refused to participate in military drill, resentment against them by other Georgians became merciless. So within a few years all of the Moravians migrated to Pennsylvania or elsewhere. One third of the approximately 600 white inhabitants of Georgia in the first part of 1736 came from Germany.

When the threat of an attack by the Spaniards of Florida became more dangerous, the trustees of the Georgia colony recruited Highland Scotsmen. Nearly 200 fighting men, with their wives and children, arrived in Georgia in 1735. They settled at Darien, sometimes called New Inverness. The Rev. John McLeod was their spiritual advisor, "but the parsons never held sway here as extensively as in Ebenezer,"[4] where the devout Salzburgers resided.

Upon Oglethorpe's return to England in 1734 he was accompanied by Tomo-chi-chi and other Indians. The chief's nephew could repeat the Lord's Prayer in Eng-

---

[3] *Ibid.*, p. 20.

[4] E. Merton Coulter, *Georgia: A Short History* (Chapel Hill: University of North Carolina Press, 1947), p. 31.

lish as well as in his own tongue. Their visit created a sensation and included audiences with the King and the Archbishop of Canterbury. In 1735, sailing for Georgia again, Oglethorpe brought additional settlers. Included were more Salzburgers and Moravians, and the versatile brothers, the Revs. Charles and John Wesley, then of the Church of England. Oglethorpe and the Rev. Samuel Wesley, father of the brothers, were friends. That likely caused the brothers to make the long voyage to Georgia. All concerned soon learned that the brothers were unfortunate misfits on the American frontier.

For a short time Charles was Oglethorpe's secretary at Fort Frederica on St. Simon's, one of the coastal islands. Since Charles was tactless he was soon at loggerheads with the colonists. He suffered miserably under the colonial privations. After complaining incessantly, he went back to England within a few weeks.

The Rev. John Wesley became rector of Christ Church at Savannah. While in that settlement he organized America's first Sunday school. He translated hymns and assisted the Indian missionary work of the Moravians, but he was unable to learn the Indian language. "The austerity of his maxims involved him in controversies"[5] and made him unpopular. Incurring the wrath of the local rulers, he was indicted on ten counts for interfering with the colony's secular affairs. After trying in vain to clear his reputation in the court, he slipped away from Savannah one night in 1737 to return to England.

Oglethorpe returned to England again, in 1737, to obtain financial support for the adequate military defense of Georgia. Parliament consented for him to assume responsibility for the protection of the colony. His return to Georgia the next year was followed by a regiment of troops. The struggling colony continually faced war or

---

[5]George Bancroft, *History of the United States of America, From the Discovery of the Continent* (New York: D. Appleton and Co., 1884), II, 288.

the threat of it with the Spaniards. However, friendly relations were maintained with the Indians and when Chief Tomo-chi-chi died about 1738, he was buried at Savannah near his white friends.

The Rev. George Whitefield, who became renowned for his persuasive exhortations throughout the American colonies, arrived at Savannah in May, 1738. He soon returned to England to seek funds for the establishment of an orphanage and to receive ordination as an Anglican clergyman. When he rejoined the colonists in 1740, he had obtained 1,000 pounds and a grant of 500 acres of land, the latter from the Georgia trustees.

The orphanage-school was named Bethesda in the hope that "it would be a house of mercy to many souls."[6] Permanent quarters for the new institution were erected about 10 miles from Savannah. James Habersham recruited and taught the children religion and other subjects until 1744.

Passionately devoted to Bethesda, Whitefield subsequently made five voyages to England and numerous itinerant preaching tours in the colonies, all to enlist support. His fervent sermons helped to launch the Great Awakening, which emphasized the common elements of Christianity, beginning about 1740. He later bought a South Carolina plantation and used the income, made by slave labor, for Bethesda. An account of Whitefield's preaching and its effect was related by Benjamin Franklin, as follows:

... I happened soon after to attend one of his sermons, in the course of which I perceived he intended to finish with a collection, and I silently resolved he should get nothing from me. I had in my pocket a handful of copper money, three or four silver dollars, and five pistoles [obsolete gold coins, then worth about $4.00 each] in gold. As he proceeded I began to soften, and concluded to give the coppers. Another stroke of oratory

6Quoted in Lucian Lamar Knight, *Georgia's Landmarks, Memorials and Legends* (2 vols.; Atlanta: Byrd Printing Co., I, 1913; II, 1914), I, 82.

made me asham'd of that and determin'd to give the silver;
and he finish'd so admirably, that I empty'd my pocket wholly
into the collector's dish, gold and all.[7]

Other spiritual ministers who served in Georgia during the colonial days included the Revs. Thomas Bosom-
worth, William Metcalf, William Norris, Christopher
Orton, and Bartholomew Zouberbuhler, the latter a Swiss
clergyman and one of the ablest identified with the colony.

The trustees of Georgia did not permit Roman Catholics to enter the colony as settlers when the experi-
mental Utopia was launched. As time passed, however,
the prohibition against Catholics was ignored and they
were brought over by plantation owners and others.

Opposition to Catholics in Georgia was based on a fear
that they would be disloyal to England in a crisis. Some
of the troops brought over in Oglethorpe's 1738 flotilla
included Romanists who denied King George's authority and were spies for Spain. Many events of the colonial period encouraged anti-Catholicism. "Catholics
were granted no liberty of conscience," Ray Ellen Billington stated in *The Protestant Crusade,* "and oaths
denouncing transubstantiation were required of all officeholders after 1743. Virginia, with less excuse than
Georgia, showed similar alarm."[8]

The first Jews to settle in Georgia in July, 1733, hailed
from Spain and Portugal. As displaced persons they
lived awhile in Holland before coming to America. The
group was increased later by some German Jews who
entered as charity dependents of Oglethorpe. Some of
the early Jewish settlers finally migrated to South Carolina.

Before the end of the colonial period of Georgia, however, the last English colony in America had ceased be-

[7]Benjamin Franklin, *Autobiography of Benjamin Franklin.* Edited
from his manuscript with notes and an introduction by John Bigelow
(Philadelphia: J. B. Lippincott & Co., 1868), pp. 254 f.

[8]Ray Allen Billington, *The Protestant Crusade, 1800-1860* (New York:
Macmillan, 1938), p. 10.

ing a refuge for the oppressed peoples of Europe. It gradually became instead a stronghold against the Spaniards of Florida. Oglethorpe, prior to his final departure for England in 1743 at the age of forty-six, had, in fact, fortified the colony's defenses extensively. As the key leader of Georgia colonists for ten years, Oglethorpe helped, perhaps unknowingly, to establish several different Protestant bodies. Some of these later spread from their Georgia beginnings and became major American religious denominations.

When Oglethorpe left Georgia permanently, a governing body had to be set up since he had been the civil supervisor. A council with a president and five councilors became the civil governing body under the colony's trustees.

By 1742 the Georgia trustees began to sanction violation of the rum law because of its widespread popular disapproval. Nonobservance of the law caused juries to refuse to convict persons for violations.

When the Georgia colony was founded, the immigration and use of Negro slaves were forbidden. That act made the colony different from the other English colonies in the New World. The reason for that prohibition was described in an early journal thus:

There are five Negroes to one White, and there are imported generally 3000 fresh Negroes every Year. There are computed to be 30,000 Negroes in this Province, all of them Slaves, and their Posterity for ever: They work six Days in the Week for their Masters without pay, and are allowed to work on *Sundays* for themselves. Baptism is rarely here administer'd to the Children of the Negroes, and Marriage is not in use amongst them; but they are suffer'd promiscuously to mix, as if they were a Part of the Brute Creation. Being thus used, lays amongst them a Foundation of Discontent; and they are generally thought to watch an Opportunity of revolting against their Masters, as they have lately done in the Island of St. *John* and of St. *Thomas,* belonging to the *Danes* and *Sweeds;* and it is the Apprehension of these and other Inconveniences, that has induced the Honourable Trustees for *Georgia,* to prohibit the Importation and Use of Negroes within their Colony.[9]

[9]Von Reck, *op. oit.,* p. 9.

Oglethorpe never became concerned about the Negro slaves like he did the impecunious debtors of England and the oppressed Protestants of Europe. In fact, he profited from the slave trade, being a director of the slave-trading Royal African Co. Influential churchmen like Whitefield and the Lutheran Salzburgers eventually urged the adoption of slavery in Georgia. In addition, sufficient white labor was not available and the desire for profit from slaveholding increased. Since slavery existed across the Savannah River in nearby South Carolina, Georgians began to smuggle slaves into their colony.

So the trustees allowed limited slavery in 1749 with certain restrictions. Slaveholding soon became widespread throughout the colony. Within two years after the ban against slavery was lifted, more than 1,000 Negro slaves were brought into Georgia.

The other policy of Georgia which had set it apart from the other English colonies was altered in 1750 when the population was slightly more than 3,000 persons. That was the change of the rules to make it possible for colonists to buy, sell, or inherit land. The colonists had been increasingly irked by land restrictions.

Colonial hardships in Georgia were described by the poet Oliver Goldsmith in his "Deserted Village." Additional financial aid for desperate needs of the sorely tried colony was denied by Parliament and the King in 1752. Since the colony was anything but flourishing and the trustees were weary of increasing complaints, they surrendered the charter to the Crown on June 23, 1752. That was a year in advance of the time designated in the document. However, provision was made in the yielding of the charter that Georgia would continue to remain a distinct colony.

More than 2,100 persons arrived in Georgia via philanthropies while the colony was supervised by the trustees under the spell of Oglethorpe's promotional techniques.

Slightly more than 1,000 of those were persecuted European Protestants. Perhaps two-thirds of the colonists aided by charitable funds finally abandoned Georgia, for various reasons, and migrated elsewhere.

A ROYAL PROVINCE BEFORE THE REVOLUTION

Georgia became a royal province similar to the other English colonies in America in 1754. John Reynolds was appointed the first of three successive governors. The mother country continued to levy taxes and fix punishments. With the change in government the Christian motives that guided the founders of Georgia in their noble experiment yielded to the stronger military and commercial impulses of the colonists.

Those governmental changes brought about certain policy alterations. Ownership of the land was made absolute for the individual. The laws which forbade slavery and the importation of rum were abrogated. Those three changes and subsequent governmental inducements brought an influx of emigrants from the Carolinas, Virginia, and other colonies to Georgia.

Changes taking place in Georgia were reflected by some New England Puritans who entered the colony, following a stay in the Carolinas, in 1752. They settled below Savannah "midway" between the Savannah and Altamaha Rivers. The Congregational Church which they established became known as the Midway Church[10] and strengthened both the moral and intellectual standards of the colony. Those Puritans brought 1,500 slaves with them.

---

[10]The present Midway building, erected in 1792, still stands with the slave gallery and high pulpit intact. Among distinguished Americans to come from the Midway settlement were two signers of the Declaration of Independence, one American President (Theodore Roosevelt), three United States Senators (John Elliott, Alfred Iverson, and Augustus O. Bacon), four Governors of Georgia, and 82 clergymen (Presbyterian, Baptist, Episcopalian, and Methodist). Abiel Holmes, father of Oliver Wendell Holmes, the New England poet, was an early pastor at Midway (Knight, *op. cit.*, I, 739, 743).

The Presbyterians organized the Independent Presbyterian Church[11] at Savannah in 1755. The congregation has existed ever since, independently in name and fact, as a branch of the Scottish Presbyterian Church, free of any American connection. The Rev. John J. Zubly, native of Switzerland, was the first minister.

Georgia officially organized the Church of England within the province in 1758. Taxes were imposed for clerical salaries and a charitable fund instituted for the poor. While there was no compulsion on the colonists to become Anglican communicants, yet no one was exempt from the religious tax. By 1762 compulsory attendance at religious worship was required of all colonists. That was one of many efforts to keep Sundays holy. Religious freedom was extended to all faiths except that the Roman Catholic Church was explicitly banned.

When Sir James Wright became the last of Georgia's royal governors in 1760, the colony "was languishing under the accumulated mismanagement of the former Trustees, and the more recent Governors; but his zeal and efforts soon changed its aspect to health and vigor. . . . The few years of his administration were the only happy ones Georgia had enjoyed."[12] In 1766, Governor Wright wrote that Georgia was "the most flourishing colony on the continent."[13] In that same year he estimated that Georgia's population was 10,000 white persons and 7,800 Negroes.

In addition to farming, livestock raising, and lumbering, the colonists engaged in the fur trade and some shipping for their livelihood. In 1763, Georgia's first newspaper, the *Georgia Gazette,* was published at Savannah.

---

[11]In the manse, now replaced, Miss Ellen Louise Axon, granddaughter of Pastor I. S. K. Axon and daughter of the Rev. and Mrs. S. E. Axon, became the first wife of Woodrow Wilson on June 28, 1885. She died in the White House on Aug. 6, 1914.

[12]*History of the Baptist Denomination in Georgia: With Biographical Compendium and Portrait Gallery of Baptist Ministers and Other Georgia Baptists.* Compiled for the *Christian Index* (Atlanta: Jas. P. Harrison & Co., 1881), p. 7.

[13]*Loc. cit.*

The French and Indian Wars, with Spain on the tag end of the fighting, ended in 1763 with Florida ceded to England. So Georgia became much safer for its settlers.

Several Baptists resided in the Savannah settlement from its start. A number of white Baptist families, coming from England and the other colonies, existed in various parts of Georgia prior to the Revolutionary War.

Nicholas Bedgewood, an agent of Whitefield's Bethesda orphanage-school, became a Baptist at Charleston, S. C., in 1757. He was ordained to the ministry in 1759. He baptized several persons residing at or near Bethesda in 1763. When they received the emblems of the Lord's Supper, "to the no small annoyance of Whitefield,"[14] it was the first Baptist communion observance in Georgia.

The first Baptist church in Georgia was organized in 1772 by Daniel Marshall on the banks of the Kiokee near Appling and not far from Augusta. He had preached in Georgia since 1771 when he arrived from South Carolina. The church was incorporated by the state in 1789. By the outbreak of the Revolutionary War, there were three or four Baptist churches in Georgia, all near Augusta. The first Georgia Baptist Association was formed in 1784 and 1785 with six congregations as members.

Persecution of Negro Baptists stopped soon after the war ended and peaceful conditions returned. When the Savannah Baptist Association was formed in 1802, two small white churches, with the Negro one of Savannah, composed its membership. Two other Negro churches joined the association as full-fledged members the next year. The Baptist historian Newman stated that the white churches had 84 members while there were 850 Negro Baptists.[15]

[14] Albert Henry Newman, *A History of the Baptist Churches in the United States* (6th ed.; Philadelphia: American Baptist Publication Society, 1915), p. 316.

[15] *Ibid.*, p. 323.

The first periodical published by Baptists in America was the *Analytical Repository,* issued at Savannah, 1802-1803, by Henry Holcombe, Baptist pastor there from 1795 to 1811.

As the Negro slave population of Georgia increased, after 1749, white Christian missionaries entered to convert the slaves. Negroes became members of white congregations as the churches became stronger. The slaves worshipped with their masters. Segregated Negro congregations were suspected of rebellious tendencies.

In 1773 white members of the Silver Bluff Baptist Church near Augusta moved to a new building. The Negro slaves, permitted to worship in the old structure, organized the Springfield Baptist Church of Augusta. This is considered the first Negro congregation of Baptists to be formed in America. Though scattered during the Revolutionary War, the Negro church was reorganized in 1793 at Augusta.

It was in 1775 that a slave, Andrew Bryan, began holding prayer meetings in a barn on the Brampton plantation of his master, Jonathan Bryan, near Savannah. He and his wife Hannah had been baptized by George Leile, another converted slave. Leile was licensed to preach by a Baptist church and had been freed by his master, Henry Sharp. Their Christian witness and its result, as set forth in Baptist history, follows:

. . . Although persecuted by wicked and cruel white people, who thus sought to interrupt their worship and put a stop to their religious meetings under a pretence that they were plotting mischief and insurrection, they were sustained by Chief Justices Henry Osburne, James Habersham and David Montague, Esquires, after an examination. Permission to worship in the day was given them. A barn, for a house of worship, was granted them at Bramton, by Jonathan Bryan, the master of Andrew and his brother Samson. A number of respectable and influential people befriended them, and by *well-doing* they at length disarmed and silenced their bitterest persecutors. Andrew learned to read, and for two years preached to great numbers without interruption, in his master's barn, although neither licensed nor ordained; and converts began to increase. Their condition, as being destitute of any one qualified to administer the ordinances, became known at a distance, and they were visited by Rev. Thomas Burton, an aged Baptist minister, who baptized eighteen converts. In 1788, Rev. Abraham Marshall, of Kiokee church, visited them, in company with Jesse Peter, a young colored minister of Augusta, baptized forty-five more, and on the 20th of January organized them into a church, and ordained Andrew Bryan to the ministry, as their pastor. Thus was Andrew Bryan fully authorized to preach and administer the ordinances, and his church, at length, properly organized. Permission was granted them to build a house of worship, in the suburbs of Savannah.[16]

Andrew Bryan was set free in 1789 by Jonathan Bryan's son, William, who then owned the Negro. Andrew Bryan's estate, after his death on October 12, 1812, was valued at $3,000. His immediate successor in the ministry of this congregation was a nephew, Andrew Marshall, slave, too, who nevertheless became a powerful and influential pastor, serving until his death in 1856.

A small Quaker community was established on a grant of land alongside the Little River, not far from Augusta, in 1770 by Joseph Matlock. The town was called Wrightsboro in honor of James Wright, colonial Georgia's most distinguished governor.

Across the years the ties of the Georgians with the other early Americans had grown stronger. The Georgians, therefore, revolted against England as much because of their sympathies for the other colonies as for a redress of their own grievances.

. . . Beginning with objections to the Stamp Act, which called into existence the ''Liberty Boys,'' the province became more and more agitated from 1766 until the storm of revolution burst forth in 1775. . . . there were many respectable citizens in Georgia who inclined to royalty, but the majority sided with the State and aided in achieving independence.[17]

The peculiar, chosen people of Georgia were finding that they were no different from the other colonists as

---

[16]*History of the Baptist Denomination in Georgia* . . . , *op. cit.*, p. 48.
[17]*Ibid.*, p. 7.

they became obsessed with the desire for independence. That fervent desire, however, forced their religion into a secondary position in their lives. "Interest in religion, which climbed to a high pitch in the American colonies at the time of the Great Awakening after 1734, had declined by the time of the War for Independence."[18]

After some misunderstanding, which included a "ban of colonial nonintercourse," Georgians accepted their obligations in the increasing movement for independence. The Rev. John Joachim Zubley was one of the delegates seated in the Continental Congress that met in Philadelphia in 1775. The three Georgians who voted for independence with the other colonists and who signed America's Declaration of Independence were Button Gwinnett, Lyman Hall, and George Walton. The historic document was read enthusiastically and approved throughout Georgia. With a letter from John Hancock, the transcribed document was received by Archibald Bulloch at Savannah, Aug. 10, 1776, from the courier who rode horseback from Philadelphia. Bulloch read the Declaration to the Georgia Provincial Congress and later to a mass assembly of the people.

Guerrila fighting chiefly characterized the participation of Georgians in the Revolutionary War which began in 1775. The first warfare on Georgia soil occurred in 1778. By the end of 1779, the British had overrun the state and captured almost every strategic settlement.

Religion and property of the churches suffered as much in Georgia during the War for Independence as other aspects of the state's life. Not only were church buildings used as barracks and for other military purposes, but they were abandoned and destroyed. Congregations were dispersed. Even churchyards became scenes of battle. According to a Salzburger Lutheran historian, the church of the Lutheran was "first used as

18R. Carlyle Buley, *The Old Northwest, Pioneer Period, 1815-1840* (Bloomington: Indiana University Press, 1951), II, 420.

a hospital, and afterwards as a stable, by the British.''[19]
The Bethesda school and orphanage were temporarily
abandoned after an accidental fire.

RELIGION ADJUSTS TO THE STATE

The churches in Georgia were weak in both numbers
and influence in the confusion that existed at the end
of the Revolutionary War following the surrender of
Cornwallis, Oct. 19, 1781. A South Carolina minister,
stopping at Savannah en route to Scotland, wrote in
1784 that he had been informed ''there is not an ordained minister in the whole State.''[20]

The orderly processes of daily life had first to be restored with peace. Liberty ruled supreme instead of
the saints who were dethroned when the old state par-
ishes were voided. The tax for the church was removed
and all clergymen were forbidden membership in the
Legislature. The Christian forces rebuilt the worship
centers from the ruins and reorganized the congregations. Both Governor Lyman Hall and the Legislature
urged the Georgians to meet for worship and to resume
religious activities. State authorities soon learned, however, that it was a mistake to grant aid to stricken
churches because it violated the principle of separation
of church and state.

By 1785 American Methodists, acting on the Rev. John
Wesley's written suggestions, seceded from the Church
of England by declaring their independence and adopt-
ing the name, Methodist Episcopal Church. Wesley
claimed that one of the triple sources of Methodism's
origin was at Savannah in 1736 when ''twenty or thirty
persons'' met in his home. That, like the Oxford source
of 1729, was the beginning of an effort to create an Anglican revival of religion.

---

[19]P. A. Strobel, *The Salzburgers and Their Descendants* (Baltimore:
T. Newton Kurtz, 1855), p. 206.

[20]Quoted in James Stacy, *A History of the Presbyterian Church in
Georgia* (Elberton, Ga.: Press of the *Star*, 1912), p. 5.

It is of interest in this connection to recall that of the several Oxford students who finally left the Anglican Church to become Methodists, four—the Wesleys, Whitefield, and the Rev. Benjamin Ingham—located in Georgia with three of them guiding colonial churches. In 1785, after the founding of Methodism, the first preacher in Georgia to proclaim that faith was Beverly Allen. Others included the "weeping prophet," John Major, and Thomas Humphries. However, the Rev. Hope Hull (1763-1818) is called the "Father of Georgia Methodism." Barton W. Stone, who helped originate the movement that became known as the Disciples of Christ, taught in Hull's Academy near Washington, Ga., in 1795.

The first Methodist church in Georgia was organized in 1787, five miles east of Washington. In 1788 the first Methodist Conference in the state's history was convened by Bishop Francis Asbury. The roaming bishop vigorously protested such artificial attractions for churches as steeples, bells, and organs.

Presbyterianism in Georgia was stimulated when John Newton, missionary, moved to the state in 1785 or 1786. The first Presbyterian ordination took place under a large poplar tree at Washington, Ga., in 1790. The candidate was John Springer, later an influential friend of Barton W. Stone. Georgia's original Hopewell Presbytery first met in 1797.

. . . Liberty church where the Presbytery met was so called because allowed to the use of other denominations, and selected on account of its central position. It was a rough house built of logs and located in the South-western part of Wilkes county, about fourteen miles from Washington, and seven from Woodstock, . . . Rev. John Springer was the first regular minister.[21]

The new Georgia constitution of 1799 eased somewhat the restrictions on Catholics in the state. However, a small Roman chapel existed at Savannah in 1792. In 1796 new residents from Maryland formed a Catholic church at Locust Grove near Washington. That slow

21*Ibid.*, p. 14.

beginning was due no doubt to the prevalence of bitter anti-Catholicism among the citizens generally. It was a bigotry that was recognized, too, in official actions:

Anti-Catholicism in America was too deeply rooted to expire even under the influence of the French alliance and the liberal spirit of the Declaration of Independence. Protestants might be willing to admit that the 300,000 Catholics in the country could do them no harm, but the state constitutions which were adopted during the Revolution showed them still wary. The New Jersey constitution of 1776 contained a safeguarding clause that no Protestant could be denied enjoyment of his civil rights because of religion and barred Catholics from state offices. . . . The North Carolina constitution of the same year contained a similar provision in respect to officeholders, as did that of Georgia. . . . By the end of the Revolution seven states, Massachusetts, New Hampshire, New Jersey, Connecticut, North Carolina, South Carolina and Georgia specified Protestant officeholders and other states inflicted additional liabilities on Catholics in their constitutions. . . .

Before the turn of the century Delaware enfranchised every free white male inhabitant of the state regardless of creed, and Georgia did away with its religious test for officeholders.[22]

William Few and Abraham Baldwin were the two Georgians who signed the Constitution of the United States following its drafting and adoption by the Philadelphia Constituting Convention of 1787. Four Georgia delegates of the six chosen attended the sessions and almost invariably gave their support to the measures needed to strengthen the fledgling national government. Georgia, last of the original thirteen colonies to be founded, became the fourth state of the Union, on January 2, 1788, to ratify the Federal Constitution and one of only three states that did so unanimously. George Washington, the nation's first President, was inaugurated on April 30, 1789. A State Constitution for Georgia had been adopted in 1777; it was revised in 1789. An entirely new State Constitution was adopted in 1798.[23]

[22]Billington, op. cit., pp. 21 f.
[23]The present Georgia Constitution was ratified in 1945.

It was in 1785 that John Adams was received by England's King George III as the first Ambassador from the United States of America. Three days after that historic event, another, of singular significance, occurred when General Oglethorpe called on Minister Adams. The visit was returned by the new American representative and he talked with the veteran founder of Georgia for more than two hours. Oglethorpe was forty-six years old when he ended his colonial career in 1743. In the meantime, he had become an eminent figure along with Samuel Johnson, lexicographer; Oliver Goldsmith, poet; Joshua Reynolds, artist, and Edmond Burke, orator. The old General died in 1785 when he was probably about ninety years of age.

An important step for Georgians was the granting of the charter by the Legislature for the founding of the University of Georgia at Athens. This act in 1785 made it the oldest chartered state educational institution in America. The University was opened in 1801.

Following the Revolutionary War the culture of tobacco was introduced into Georgia at Augusta by settlers from Virginia. This was supplanted in a few years by cotton because of the invention of the cotton engine—soon contracted to gin—by Eli Whitney near Savannah in 1793. That invention riveted slavery on the southern states for many years, changing Georgia's economic pattern and affecting that of the entire nation. Growing cotton on large plantations became immensely profitable and more and more was planted for many years. Slavery, which had almost disappeared during the war, increased quickly because it provided the vast numbers of laborers essential to low production costs.

The increase in Georgia's population from 82,548 in 1790 to 162,680 in 1800 was doubtless caused by the cotton gin as much as anything else. In 1791 a total of 1,000 bales of cotton was grown in the state. By 1800 that had increased to 20,000 bales. The rise in the number of bales continued to 701,000 in 1860. The population of Georgia showed an increase in every decade after 1790. In 1830 it was 516,823 and shortly afterward the Disciples began their century and more of Christian service in Georgia. In 1860 it passed one million for the first time at 1,057,286. In 1900 it was 2,216,331 and in 1950, at 3,444,578 it passed the three-million mark for the second consecutive time. It was during those years, up to 1860, that the plantation owners of Georgia wielded a tremendous influence with their wealth.

INTO THE NINETEENTH CENTURY

The American Revolution not only broke down political sovereignty, but also aroused the spirit of religious liberty; and much dissatisfaction arose among the sects on account of the iron clad rules and severe exactions concerning the faith and practice of each denomination.[24]

The religious witness of Disciples of Christ in Georgia began in the early years of the nineteenth century from one of several sources that contributed to the movement nationally. Various efforts seeking more Christian liberty and reform within existing churches emerged in several areas, mainly on the frontier, and from at least three denominations. The leaders of those renewals, aimed at infusing new life into the churches, held essentially common conclusions about Christian errors and ways to correct such evils.

In New England the advocates of reform were Baptists—Abner Jones (1772-1841) and Elias Smith (1769-1846). The revolters in the southern states of Virginia, North Carolina, and Kentucky were Methodists—Rice Haggard (1769-1819) and James O'Kelly (1735?-1826). Another revivalist was a Presbyterian, in Kentucky—Barton Warren Stone (1772-1844). The other reformer was a Presbyterian too—Thomas Campbell (1763-1854) in southwestern Pennsylvania.

---

[24]Mrs. B. O. Miller, "*Antioch*," the Mother Church of the Disciples in Georgia (Atlanta: E. W. Allen & Co., 1904), pp. 5 f

O'Kelly, of the several reformers, merits attention here in this historical statement of the background of the Georgia Disciples of Christ.

Before hostilities broke out in America's War for Independence in 1775, O'Kelly was a lay preacher in North Carolina for the Methodists. Shortly after the founding of American Methodism in 1784, he helped to lead a secession from the new church that had withdrawn from the Church of England. He was the principal Methodist to disagree with the dictatorial tactics of Bishop Francis Asbury and in opposing life-tenure for superintendents and centralized control of the churches. It was a break caused, not by doctrinal divergence, but by dissatisfaction with Methodist administration and administrators. O'Kelly stood firm for his convictions. How the schism occurred was briefly set forth in *The Disciples of Christ: A History,* as follows:

At the first Methodist General Conference, in 1792, O'Kelly presented a resolution demanding the right of appeal to the conference by preachers who felt themselves unjustly treated in their assignments by the bishop. The resolution was voted down. O'Kelly and a number of other preachers thereupon withdrew from the conference. But most of those who had joined with O'Kelly in his earlier protests now yielded to Asbury and the majority. This break in the Methodist ranks is commonly referred to as the "O'Kelly secession."

The following year those who had seceded organized the Republican Methodist Church. Several of their congregations adhered to this new organization, which is said to have had, at this stage, about thirty ministers (mostly lay preachers) and 1,000 members—though these figures may be too large. But the movement remained in this transition stage, as a group of separated Methodists, only about seven months.

At a conference held at Old Lebanon Church, in Surry County, Virginia (just across the James River from Williamsburg), on August 4, 1794, the Republican Methodist Church adopted as its new name, the "Christian Church," and declared that the Bible should be its only creed. It resolved that there should be complete equality among all the preachers, with no bishops or superintendents or presiding elders in the Methodist fashion, and that ministers and laymen alike were to enjoy the fullest liberty in interpreting Scripture. The principle of congregational independence was to be fully applied. Conferences would be only advisory, and every church would "call its own pastor and enjoy the greatest freedom." As one of them stated it, "the primitive church government, which came down from heaven, was a republic, though 'Christian Church' is its name." The adoption of this name was suggested by Rice Haggard, who had been a Methodist lay preacher and one of O'Kelly's supporters in his long campaign of protest against the autocratic control of preachers and churches by "superintendents."[25]

The first "Christian Church" of the O'Kelly group was established near Chapel Hill, N. C.[26] The O'Kelly movement later merged with a similar one in New England to form the "Christian Connexion," now a part of the Congregational Christian Church.

The influences of those nineteenth century American religious movements, even of those groups now essentially lost to all but historians, were widespread, particularly among the Disciples of Christ. In his Yale Lectures, the late Peter Ainslie wrote, "It is only when movements lose themselves in the bosom of Christianity that their influences strike the deeps and leave their pulse beats on all shores."[27]

Georgia became a religious frontier for the Disciples of Christ in the early part of the nineteenth century. Adherents of the religious reform teachings of O'Kelly, Barton W. Stone, Thomas Campbell and his son, Alexander, were mainly proselytes from schisms among Republican Methodists, Presbyterians, and Baptists. It was about 1807 that "O'Kellyites" migrated to Georgia from North Carolina.

The struggles of Georgia Disciples of Christ from their polygenetic beginnings in the nineteenth century to 1950 will be chronicled in the following pages as fully as the known facts permit. Surely the "pulse beats" set reverberating more than a century ago have left significant influences.

---

[25]Winfred Ernest Garrison and Alfred T. DeGroot, *The Disciples of Christ: A History* (St. Louis: Christian Board of Publication, 1948), pp. 85 f.

[26]Winfred Ernest Garrison, *Religion Follows the Frontier; A History of the Disciples of Christ* (New York: Harper & Bros., 1931), p. 61.

[27]Peter Ainslie, *The Message of the Disciples for the Union of the Church* (New York: Fleming H. Revell Co., 1913), p. 94.

CHAPTER II

A Heritage of Freedom of Opinion

Disciples of Christ tend to regard themselves as peculiar and different from other Christians. They were labeled from their beginnings, for better or for worse, by characteristics of a spiritual heritage which brought freedom from religious strait jackets. How Georgia Disciples acquired those telltale markings will be discovered by briefly investigating the beliefs and teachings of the founding fathers.

The mold of the revolutionary movement in America was cast during the first third of the nineteenth century by bitter controversies, prophetic utterances, and the self-righteous fervor of proclaiming evangelists. They made simple words, with new ideas for the release of men's minds and spirits, come alive.

In addition to James O'Kelly and his Republican Methodists, Georgia Disciples trace their beginnings to the influence of Barton W. Stone and Thomas and Alexander Campbell. Both Stone and the Campbells were big men who adhered to free trade in the big ideas which guided them. What they believed and taught and how they affected the struggles of the reforming Christians in Georgia are the concern of this chapter.

Late in 1794, at the age of 21, Stone left Guilford County, N. C., where he awaited licensing as a Presbyterian minister. Embarrassed by debts and with only 15 dollars to his name, he decided to visit his brothers in Georgia. Matthew Stone resided near Lexington, Oglethorpe County, and Thomas, the other brother, lived in adjoining Wilkes County. Riding alone on horseback,

Barton was overcome with a "violent fever" en route. He was ill for several months after arriving at Matthew's farm home.

According to Barton Stone's autobiography, "about the beginning of 1795," with the help of his brothers, he was appointed language teacher at a Methodist school (the first in Georgia) in Wilkes County. That was Succoth Academy, three and one-half miles southeast of Washington. The school opened in January, 1795. The principal was the Rev. Hope Hull, one of the founders of Methodism in Georgia and of the University of Georgia, who had been assisting the Rev. John Springer (1745?-1798) with his academy.[1]

It was Hull who issued the state's first religious hymnal on a Washington press. Five miles east of Washington was located Georgia's first Methodist church where Bishop Francis Asbury, a friend of Hull's, often preached. Hull, in Georgia since 1788, attended the Baltimore Methodist Conference of 1792. There he supported O'Kelly's resolution protesting autocratic power for bishops, but Hull did not follow O'Kelly and leave Methodism.

There is no record that Stone had anything to do with the Baptists at or near Washington. Yet it would have been strange if he did not. Rev. Jesse Mercer (1769-1841), one of the state's most influential Baptists, resided near Washington then. From 1833 to 1840 he issued a Baptist periodical, *The Christian Index*,[2] from Washington. Mercer and Rev. John Springer, with whom Stone became "warmly attached," were intimate friends despite the religious bigotry of the times.

---

[1] John Rogers, *The Biography of Eld. Barton Warren Stone*, Written by Himself: With Additions and Reflections (5th ed.; Cincinnati: J. A. & U. P. James, 1847), p. 15. Addison W. Simpson, *Life and Service of Reverend John Springer*, Including Some Early History of the Presbyterian Church in Northeast Georgia (Washington, Ga.: N. P., July, 1941), p. 33. Reba Carolyn Strickland, *Religion and the State in Georgia in the Eighteenth Century* (New York: Columbia University Press, 1939), pp. 172 f.

[2] Established in 1821 at Philadelphia, moved to Georgia in 1833, it is now the oldest continuously published religious journal in the South, edited by John Jeter Hurt, Jr., in Atlanta.

Succoth Academy had 70 pupils, more or less, when
Stone began teaching there. It was not to be the last
time that he relied upon that means of earning money
with which to pay his obligations. He wrote of his
Georgia teaching days, as follows:

> . . . I exerted myself to fill the appointment with honor to
> myself and profit to my pupils, and had the unspeakable satis-
> faction of receiving the approbation of the trustees of the in-
> stitution, and of the *literati* of the country. Men of letters
> were few at that time, especially in that part of the world, and
> were regarded with more than common respect. The marked
> attention paid me by the most respectable part of the community,
> was nearly my ruin. Invitations to tea parties and social
> circles were frequent. I attended them for a while, until I
> found that this course would cause me to make shipwreck of
> faith and a good conscience. Though I still maintained the
> profession of religion, and did not disgrace it by improper
> conduct, yet my devotion was cold, and communion with God
> much interrupted. Seeing my danger, I denied myself of these
> fascinating pleasures, and determined to live more devoted to
> God.[3]

During the months that Stone was teaching in Georgia,
Rev. John Springer, 400-pound Presbyterian minister
and schoolmaster, became a close and influential friend.
It was Springer who was set aside to the ministry under
a Washington poplar tree in 1790 to become the first
Presbyterian minister ordained in Georgia. He had
been graduated from Princeton University in 1776. In
1788, he located five miles north of Washington. Rev.
Jesse Mercer, the Baptist, was a student of Springer's
for two years. Stone's biographer, C. C. Ware, declared
that "the influence of John Springer on Barton Stone
was decisive."[4]

As a result of Springer's talks, either from the pulpit
or with Stone in conversation, perhaps both, Stone began
to "feel a very strong desire again to preach the

---

[3]Rogers, *op. cit.*, p. 15.

[4]Charles Crossfield Ware, *Barton Warren Stone:* Pathfinder of Christian
Union, A Story of His Life and Times (St. Louis: Bethany Press, 1932),
p. 42.

gospel.''[5]   It was in 1793 that Stone, along with his friend, Samuel Holmes, later president of the University of North Carolina, had become a ministerial candidate of the Orange Presbytery in North Carolina.   Theological study, however, along with other factors, depressed Stone.   So he moved to Georgia, having decided to forego preaching.   In Georgia, then, his significant final decision to dedicate himself to the Christian ministry took place during the formative months while he was teaching and learning firsthand just what religious tolerance and freedom of understanding mean.   He wondered, later, about his ministerial qualifications, but he never reversed his Georgia decision committing himself to the ministry.

Georgia, too, provided Stone with an opportunity to broaden his knowledge.   That was in addition to the cultural and religious advantages provided for the maturing young man.   He merely suggested in one paragraph what happened, as follows:

About this time, a great many Frenchmen, who had fled from the reign of terror in France, landed in Georgia.   Washington was full of them.   The trustees of the academy employed one of them, Francois Aubir, to teach the French language.   With him I learned the language more perfectly, having acquired some knowledge of it before, with a certain Doct. Hale, of North Carolina.[6]

Stone's spiritual growth was furthered during the winter of 1795-96 when he accompanied Hull and other preachers to a Methodist Conference at Charleston, S. C. Upon his return to Washington, Stone continued to teach until the spring of 1796.   He described his departure thus:

. . . Then, having resigned my professorship to the trustees, I started back to North Carolina, with a determination to receive from Orange Presbytery a license to preach.   I had now more than enough of money to discharge all my debts.   The day of my departure was a day of sorrow.   I bade an affectionate farewell to my pupils and numerous friends, and hurried off alone.

[5]Rogers, op. cit., p. 14.
[6]Loc. cit.

Nothing of moment occurred in my solitary journey, till I arrived at the Presbytery. Here I met with many of my warm friends, and our joyful salutation was mutual.[7]

The spring meeting of the Orange Presbytery was held at the Hawfields Presbyterian Church, four miles southwest of present-day Mebane, N. C. Stone and two others were licensed to preach. It was not long until Stone traveled the Wilderness Road to the western frontier of Tennessee and Kentucky. Had he not received the Bible that April day when he was licensed with the charge, "Go ye into all the world, and preach the gospel to every creature"?

Late in 1796 Stone was located with the Cane Ridge and Concord Churches in Bourbon County, Ky., as the settled minister. He learned that winter, by trial and error that his "rambling course of preaching" was of little value either to him or to the people who looked to him for spiritual guidance. So he applied himself to "reading and study" and "witnessed the good effects of this procedure."

While he was not ordained to the ministry until nearly two years later, yet Stone was already bothered by certain theological issues. Questions began to arise in his mind before he went to Georgia the first time. "My mind was embarrassed with many abstruse doctrines, which I admitted as true; yet could not satisfactorily reconcile with others which were plainly taught in the Bible,"[8] he wrote. He realized that he would be examined prior to ordination. So, much thought and study in a renewal of his mind and spirit were necessary before that eventful date. Presbyterian ministers were among the best educated persons of the American frontier. Stone was to prove that he could keep pace mentally with any of them.

"Some unsettled business in Georgia," however, demanded his return to the state where he had taught so happily for 15 months. So, in the autumn of 1797, Stone

---

[7]*Ibid.*, p. 16.

[8]*Ibid.*, p. 14.

left Cane Ridge and Concord for Georgia and a visit to his mother in Virginia. He had been commissioned, too, by the Translyvania Presbytery to visit Charleston, S. C., in search of funds with which to launch a college in Kentucky.

Travel in those days was no picnic for preachers or others. The danger of an attack by Indians always threatened. It doubtless provided excellent training and developed one's mettle for the furious religious battles ahead. Stone left a graphic description of what he and his companion went through in the following words:

Marauding parties of Indians still infested travelers in the wilderness between Kentucky and Virginia, so that travelers always went in companies prepared for defence. In the fall of 1797, I left Caneridge for Georgia, in company with Henry Wilson, who, with a led horse packed with silver, was going to Virginia on land business. Having repaired to the house of rendezvous for travelers at Crab Orchard, we learned that a company had just left that place two hours before, with intention to encamp at Hazlepatch [east of the present Stanford in Lincoln County] that night. We instantly followed at a quick pace, determined to ride late and overtake them. About 10 o'clock we came to the Hazlepatch, but to our distress we found no one there. My companion being an early settler of Kentucky, and often engaged in war with the Indians, advised to turn off the road some distance, and encamp till day. Having kindled a fire, supped, hobbled our horses, and prayed together, we laid down in our blankets to rest. But we were soon aroused from our slumbers by the snorting and running of our horses. We sprang up, and saw a fire about 150 yards below us, and in a moment it was pulled asunder; as quickly did my companion pull ours apart also. He whispered to me, "they are Indians after our horses." We laid down again, not to sleep, but to consult the best method of escape. We soon distinctly heard an Indian cautiously walking on the dry leaves towards our camp, about fifty yards off. Fearing he might shoot us in our blankets, without noise we crept into the bushes. Becoming very chilly there, and contrary to advice, I returned to my blanket, and was followed by my companion. A short time after we heard the Indian walk off in the same cautious manner. We concealed the bag of money, and most valuable goods, and hung up our blankets and bags of provision over our camp, and cautiously went towards the course our horses had gone. When it was day, we found their trace and overtook them about 8 o'clock, and rode back very watchfully to our camp. When we came near it, with difficulty we compelled our horses to advance, they frequently snorting and wheeling back. Every moment we expected to be fired upon, but were mercifully preserved. We packed up very quickly, and swiftly pursued the company, and late in the day came up with them. They informed us that when they came to the Hazlepatch the evening before, they found a camp of white people, just before defeated, several lying dead and mangled in Indian style; that they pushed forward and traveled late at night. We clearly saw the kind hand of God in delivering us.[9]

The autobiography of Stone had little to tell of what he did while in Georgia on that trip. He wrote thus:

. . . After having settled my business, visited my relations, and preached throughout the country for several weeks, I started alone to Charleston. Nothing of note happened in my journey, except that by my caution, and the fleetness of my horse, I escaped a band of robbers, who attempted to stop me. I had been previously warned of the danger in those dismal swamps between Augusta and Charleston, and was therefore continually on my guard.[10]

His reference to the "dismal swamps" suggested a less favorable impression, and more maturity, than when he had traversed them approximately two years before. For on that trip with Hope Hull and the other Methodist preachers, Stone referred to the journey as a "pleasant" one. Also, he had added that the "road from Black Swamp to Charleston was surpassed by none in the world for beauty and goodness."

The more important reference from Stone's 1797 visit to Georgia was that he "preached throughout the country for several weeks." The significance of that, in terms of the beginnings and development of Georgia Disciples of Christ, will be discussed later.

ANOTHER DECLARATION OF INDEPENDENCE

Stone was formally ordained to the ministry at Cane Ridge by the Transylvania Presbytery on Oct. 4, 1798.

[9]*Ibid.*, pp. 26 f.
[10]*Ibid.*, p. 27.

As the date approached, he continued to be troubled, especially about adherence to the Westminster Confession of Faith. Two days before the rites, a committee examined him in the languages, sciences, and, as might be expected, in church history and government. The presbyterial minutes indicated that members of the committee "were fully satisfied with his examination. The Presby. agreed to accept the report."[11]

During that time, however, Stone considered requesting that the service be postponed. He expressed that view to two influential leaders of Kentucky Presbyterianism, James Blythe and Robert Marshall. Writing about the experience, Stone stated:

. . . They labored, but in vain to remove my difficulties and objections. They asked me how far I was willing to receive the confession? I told them, as far as I saw it consistent with the word of God. They concluded that was sufficient. I went into Presbytery, and when the question was proposed, "Do you receive and adopt the Confession of Faith, as containing the system of doctrine taught in the Bible?" I answered aloud, so that the whole congregation might hear, "I do, as far as I see it consistent with the word of God." No objection being made, I was ordained.[12]

As Stone's ministry with the Cane Ridge and Concord congregations proceeded, he became concerned with the prevailing religious apathy. So, hearing about the revival under way in Logan County, in south-central Kentucky, he went to see and hear for himself. The preacher was James McGready whose preaching had affected Stone earlier in North Carolina. Stone was gripped by the enthusiasm engendered by the revival, following a careful analysis of the results. Sweeping ahead like a forest fire, the meetings penetrated the Bluegrass country and attracted thousands of persons early that summer. A protracted meeting at Concord, Stone wrote, brought "multitudes of all denominations."

---

[11]Quoted in William Warren Sweet, *Religion on the American Frontier*, 1783-1840, *The Presbyterians* (Chicago: University of Chicago Press, 1936), II, 180.

[12]Rogers, *op. cit.*, p. 29 f.

Not many weeks thereafter, in August, 1801, the spectacular Cane Ridge camp meeting was held in the little log building which still stands and throughout the surrounding area. Stone helped to prepare for the revival. Preaching was mainly in the open air of the nearby woods. Stone reported that "the roads were literally crowded with wagons, carriages, horsemen, and foot men."[13] The crowd of perhaps 20,000 or more persons listened to sermons, often preached simultaneously, by Presbyterians, Methodists, and Baptists. That was truly the climax of all the Great Western revivals.

In the tremendous excitement many unusual and disorderly manifestations of religious hysteria occurred in the emotional upheaval. Stone admitted the numerous eccentricities and fanatacisms of the revival, but contended that the meeting "promoted unity for awhile."[14] Christian unity, demanded by the people, was evidenced by the singing of the same gospel songs, uniting in prayer, and sermons on the same appealing theme of salvation by faith and repentance.

However, many orthodox Presbyterians did not approve of the revivals, either the techniques or the sermonic content. Stone and the other liberal reformers, though, became convinced that the simple presentation of the universal Christian message, in biblical terms, was desperately needed. Stone and his cohorts, called heretics by the more orthodox, argued too, that creeds were divisive and unscriptural.

So in September, 1803, Barton W. Stone and four other Presbyterian ministers withdrew from the Kentucky Synod, but not from the Presbyterian Church at that time. In their declaration of independence they claimed the right to interpret the Bible without restrictions of doctrinal uniformity required by human creeds and confessions. After a futile attempt to win their allegiance again, the five men were suspended by the Synod.

13*Ibid.*, p. 37.

14*Ibid.*, p. 42.

Stone and the others constituted the independent Springfield Presbytery. That "organization," if such it was, did not prove permanent, however, for within less than a year the Springfield Presbytery was dissolved. That action was expressed on June 28, 1804, by the issuance of *The Last Will and Testament of the Springfield Presbytery*. The earliest of the fundamental religious charters of the Disciples of Christ, it was one of the first statements of religious freedom proclaimed in the Western Hemisphere.

The document willed the dissolution of the Springfield Presbytery so that it could "sink into union with the Body of Christ at large."[15] It sought to institute scriptural practices, appealed for the universal church of Christ with individual allegiance to Christ and with the Bible as sole authority. It also sought to encourage one Christian name, banned the use of the title "Reverend," and urged the automony of local congregations.

Publication of *The Last Will and Testament* was Preceded by a booklet, *An Apology for Renouncing the Jurisdiction of the Synod of Kentucky. To Which Is Added, a Compendious View of the Gospel, and a Few Remarks on the Confession of Faith*. It was a lengthy statement of objections to the Confession of Faith, announced abandonment of creeds and confessions, and stated that the Bible alone would become the dissenters' rule of life and work. The volume, which was first published by the Springfield Presbytery in January, 1804, at Lexington, Ky., was quickly reprinted, Stone stated, by the Methodists in Virginia except for the remarks on creeds. It was reprinted in Georgia too, he said in a letter to Richard McNemar, dated Apr. 2, 1805. It is not known who issued the Georgia reprint and no copy is known to exist now. Also, in 1805, there were reprints by George Kline at Carlisle, Ky., and by S. Engles at

---

[15]*Ibid.*, p. 51.

Philadelphia Pa.[16] The various printings indicated the wide circulation of the *Apology* and suggested why it made "zealous advocates" for the cause of the reforming liberals.

During the short but historic existence of the Springfield Presbytery, Rice Haggard arrived in Kentucky. In 1794 he was the one who suggested the name Christian to O'Kelly's Republican Methodists. He made the same suggestion when the Springfield Presbytery was dissolved. Stone wrote that he "had lately united with us."[17] The name Christian was accepted on both occasions.

The question of baptism was not raised at first. In a few years Stone accepted the validity of believers' immersion as scriptural baptism. That view was gradually accepted by his followers in Kentucky and elsewhere. While Stone immersed converts in 1807, he was not immersed until later.

The seceding preachers were followed by their congregations. By 1804 eight Kentucky churches and seven Ohio ones were adhering to the new Christian Church. Converts were made by the appeal of the name and other attractive apostolic simplicities. Churches, however, as well as families, were disrupted in the resulting confusion. That distress, wrote Stone, was "not produced by the Bible; but by human authoritative creeds, supported by sticklers for orthodoxy."[18] It was ever thus and likely always will be.

Stone's followers began to be dubbed "Stoneites" and "New Light Christians," among other things, and it was years before the appelations were discontinued.

---

[16]Richard McNemar, *The Kentucky Revival* . . . (Cincinnati: Printed; Albany: Reprinted by E. & E. Hosford, 1808), p. 79. Robert Davidson, *History of the Presbyterian Church in the State of Kentucky* (New York: Robert Carter; Lexington, Ky.: Charles Marshall, 1847), p. 195 fn. Joseph Sabin, *A Dictionary of Books Relating to America* . . . (29 vols.; New York: J. Sabin's Son, 1885), XV, 422. Ware, *op. cit.*, p. 137. Sweet, *op. cit.*, p. 897.

[17]Rogers, *op. cit.*, p. 50.

[18]*Ibid.*, p. 48.

Indeed, those Christians "became a by-word and laughing stock" to their religious neighbors with many predictions of an early end to the movement.

Yet from that time the excommunicated Stone[19] dated the beginning of the New Reformation that resulted in a great religious fellowship, enlisting thousands, known as the Disciples of Christ. He was the only one of the original five nonconformists who withdrew from the Synod because of heresy charges and who remained faithful to the movement which they originated together.

The new movement grew rapidly, especially in Kentucky, Ohio, and Tennessee. Migrating frontiersmen from those states took the new ideas with them when they moved. Zealous traveling evangelists proclaimed the biblical message and condemned sectarian division. Some of those, preaching on numerous occasions in Georgia, left many "Stoneites," often unorganized perhaps. It was thus that the liberalizing influence of Barton W. Stone's teachings spread to Georgia, apparently before any of the frontiersmen had opportunity to learn of the teachings of Thomas and Alexander Campbell.

Controversy Exposes Sin of Division

The Campbells were both natives of Ireland. Thomas, the father, was educated at the University of Glasgow and had a complete seminary course. A teacher and Seceder Presbyterian preacher, he migrated to America in 1807, at the age of 44, and soon became a circuit-riding dissenter in southwestern Pennsylvania.

He was unhappy about the disunity of Seceder Presbyterianism and had struggled in vain, before coming to the United States, to resolve factional differences. Four months after his arrival in America, he was charged with heresy in his presbytery. That was caused by his desire

---

[19]In October, 1808, the Synod of Kentucky, according to its minutes, finally officially deposed Stone and his four colleagues, thus severing them completely from the Presbyterian Church (Sweet, *op. cit.*, pp. 371 f.). Ware, *op. cit.*, pp. 145 f., questioned the 1808 date, maintaining that the final severance occurred earlier.

for closer relations with other Christians and a growing conviction that creeds and other barriers that fenced the Lord's Table and denied Christian fellowship were not essential, but actually divisive. In addition, he claimed the Bible as final authority, resented clerical domination of the church, and taught that all persons had a common right to salvation. Such challenges of Presbyterian doctrine were too much for his orthodox colleagues. Consequently, the presbytery upheld the heresy charges, rebuked and suspended Thomas Campbell from the ministry.

He appealed to the Presbyterian Synod and a formal trial ensued with Mr. Campbell being "rebuked and admonished by the moderator." In September, 1808, he renounced the jurisdiction of both presbytery and synod. He was later officially deposed by both groups.

Though officially defrocked, Mr. Campbell continued to preach his convictions whenever and wherever opportunity permitted. That was generally in the homes of friends. Gathering followers, he organized the Christian Association of Washington, Pa., on Aug. 17, 1809. The group, not a congregation actually, but rather a society, accepted his slogan which later became widely known and quoted: "Where the Scriptures speak, we speak; where the Scriptures are silent, we are silent."

As a result of the censure and suspension by the Presbyterian bodies, Mr. Campbell was moved to write the *Declaration and Address*. It was approved by the Christian Association on Sept. 7, 1809 and ordered printed. A prophetic document, it became one of the major charters in the heritage of the Disciples of Christ.

The *Declaration and Address* consisted of four parts: 1) The formal Declaration which asserted the purposes and methods of the Christian Association; 2) The Address, which advocated Christian unity and enunciated ways to restore that unity; 3) An Appendix, "to prevent mistakes," by explaining in detail certain parts of the Address and answering expected objections; and 4) A

Postscript, written more than three months later, that set forth promotional methods for the new movement.

The document essentially urged Christian unity and the restoration of apostolic Christianity. Human opinions were rejected as tests of fellowship and all Christian ideas were to be measured by biblical standards. The Address set forth 13 propositions as a means to the restoration of apostolic life and work. The first of those stated, in part, "That the church of Christ upon earth is essentially, intentionally and constitutionally one."

The *Declaration and Address* was based on the teaching of John Locke (1632-1704) in his significant *Letters Concerning Toleration*. The philosophy of the latter was originally presented in his *Essay on the Human Understanding*. Both of the Campbells were introduced to Locke's philosophy before coming to America. As the new religious reformation, which the father instituted and the son launched, began to develop and spread, both men studied Locke's philosophy diligently and applied its clear accents to religion. Some of Locke's writings were reprinted and discussed for years in the periodicals of the Disciples of Christ. The democratic heritage which the Campbells subsequently left to thousands of followers thus had the same philosophic roots as the American Declaration of Independence whose writer, Thomas Jefferson, espoused Lockian concepts.

As the *Declaration and Address* was issued in the autumn of 1809, Alexander Campbell (1788-1866), then 21 years old, and the rest of his father's family, arrived in America.[20] The preceding year Alexander had studied at the University of Glasgow and while there he, too, abandoned the Seceder Presbyterian Church. Already persuaded toward the ministry, he thus found himself happily in agreement with his father's new religious convictions. Alexander's seminary studies in Glasgow con-

---

[20]According to a persistent legend, Thomas Campbell read to his son, Alexander, from proof pages of the *Declaration and Address*. The proofs may still be in existence as they were in 1909 at the time of the Pittsburgh Centennial Convention of Disciples.

vinced him, among other things, of the validity of the weekly observance of the Lord's Supper, congregational independence, the priesthood of all believers and a reasonable scriptural interpretation for understanding the Christian Gospel. Alexander Campbell soon became the acknowledged leader of the new movement.

In 1811 the Christian Association constituted itself as the Brush Run Church to become the first congregation of the Campbellian source of the Disciples. Alexander Campbell was soon licensed to preach, and on Jan. 1, 1812, was ordained to the ministry by that congregation. A study of the Scriptures convinced both father and son of the validity of immersion as Christian baptism so they were immersed on June 12, 1812, by Matthias Luse, a Baptist preacher. The Brush Run Church, too, began to require immersion of converts.

The Brush Run Church became a member of the Redstone Baptist Association in 1815,[21] although the Campbells differed with the Baptists on several issues. That same Redstone Association, in 1816, heard Alexander Campbell's significant "Sermon on the Law." In it, he declared that the Christian dispensation was free of Old Testament law that was not reiterated in the New Testament. He later claimed that persecution for the supposed heresy of that sermon was the cause of his advocacy of another reformation.

In 1823, when a move was under way in the Redstone Association to expel Alexander Campbell for heresy, he and 31 others left the Brush Run Church to organize a congregation in nearby Wellsburg (now in W. Va.). That church was received into the new liberal Mahoning Baptist Association of Ohio in 1824.

Publication of the *Christian Baptist,* a monthly magazine, began in 1823. Alexander Campbell, editor and publisher, thus gained a wider dissemination of his religious ideas to restore the "ancient order of things." The teaching of Christian unity remained in the back-

---

[21]William Herbert Hanna, "The Campbells and the Redstone Association," *Shane Quarterly,* Oct. 1940, p. 347.

ground then. The restoration concept was not unique.
Nearly every Protestant group since Luther's Reformation assumed that it was restoring apostolic Christianity.
The little controversial periodical had a wide circulation
and a mighty influence among the disputatious Reformers, as the Campbell followers were designated, and
other Christians on the frontier. The publication of the
Christian Baptist was followed in 1830 by the monthly
Millennial Harbinger.

In 1826 Alexander Campbell published a scholarly
translation of the New Testament from his own press.
There were several editions and printings which won
friends and made many enemies.

The more orthodox opponents did not stop at simply
misrepresenting Mr. Campbell, his motives, and his
teachings. They hurled slander, invectives, and issued
libelous material. In a discussion of those accusations,
Editor Campbell, perhaps with a twinkle in his eye as
he took up his pen, said, " 'The church is in danger,'
and 'damnable heresy,' is the chorus of every verse in
these new Lamentations of these weeping prophets. They
are not *dumb* dogs; but they bark at something which
they cannot bite." [22]

The restoration of apostolic Christianity, advocated by
Mr. Campbell, was influenced by English and Scotch
movements of a similar nature. They were led by John
Glas (1695-1773) and his son-in-law, Robert Sandeman
(1723-1771), and two brothers, Robert Haldane (1764-
1842) and James Alexander Haldane (1768-1851). Their
representatives influenced Alexander Campbell during
his Glasgow studies. Earlier, Thomas Campbell, too,
received that significant liberalizing influence. The English and Scotch movements did not emphasize Christian
unity. They advocated, rather, an exact, detailed re-
production of the worship, ordinances, ministry, and organization of primitive Christianity. Strangely, however, they had no evangelistic urge. The influence of
those movements virtually forced Alexander Campbell

---

[22]*Christian Baptist*, Feb. 1, 1830, p. 155.

to leave the Seceder Presbyterian Church while he was
in Glasgow. (It seems likely that those dissenters, in
turn, were influenced by Archbishop William King [1650-
1728?] of Dublin and his *Discourse Concerning the Inventions of Men In the Worship of God*—a rare pamphlet
not yet studied by scholars investigating origins and
backgrounds of Disciples of Christ.)

Alexander Campbell finally advanced beyond the legalistic pattern of restoration. Both he and his father were
assiduous students. No wonder their ideas were so far
in advance of their time. Alexander Campbell's views
were never mandatory for those who accepted his general teachings. Many of his early followers, to their
credit, never accepted his views in all details. Diversity
and independence were chief characteristics of the Reformers from the beginning of the movement.

The teachings of Alexander Campbell permeated many
Baptist churches and caused dissension. His influence
spread through his periodicals, numerous powerful sermons, and his unusual power as a debater. He was, indeed, a salient figure, crying in the wilderness as he
threw off the shackles of a decadent religious past. He
engaged the attention of thousands of persons, far and
wide. Groups of Reformers developed in many Baptist
churches. That was especially true in Kentucky and
Ohio, and as the movement grew, elsewhere. A contemporary account of Campbell's travels and influence
was given by Bishop John B. Purcell of Cincinnati. A
debate between the two men was termed the "Battle of
the Giants," and made them friends for life. The Bishop
wrote:

It was his habit occasionally to pass through the southern portions of Ohio and Indiana and Illinois, and through the fine
bluegrass region of Kentucky and the rich farming sections of
the Missouri River, where the farmers are and always have been
exceedingly intelligent and hospitable. Perhaps there is not a
finer set of people on the face of the globe. These interesting
pilgrimages began somewhere about 1824, or perhaps a little
earlier than 1820—that era, and lasted perhaps a quarter of a
century with some intervals. His discourses attracted vast

crowds of people, who came from distant points and who listened
to every word that fell from his lips and felt in their heart of
hearts all the burning zeal of Peter and Hermit. At that time
the religious propensities of the people were very strong, and
there were but few churches in the country and no places of
amusement. People would ride fifty miles to attend a large
baptizing, a camp meeting or a religious debate. Mr. Campbell
was regarded as a kind of religious Goliath, and was met at
every cross road and every toll gate by well intentioned, half informed preachers of the different denominations and challenged
to produce his credentials, to enter into a discussion in defense
of his original and peculiar views. Our hero was nothing loth
to do so. Such opportunities were precisely what he desired.
A vast audience would gather together to hear what to them
was vastly more attractive than a great battle to the death between two celebrated gladiators.

These debates were brief and decisive. Campbell floored his
opponents in a few moments. Their arguments fell to pieces as
if they had no more strength than a potter's vessel. So quickly
was all this accomplished that they could hardly realize their
discomfiture. The people saw all of this and it made Campbell
thousands of proselytes; and their children and their children's
children have to this day stuck to his church like grim death,
and they will stick for generations to come.[23]

Walter Scott (1796-1861) was born in Scotland where
he was educated at the University of Edinburgh. He
met Alexander Campbell at Pittsburgh, Pa., during the
winter of 1821-22. Scott was teaching in an academy
and was a member of the small Haldanian or Scotch
Baptist Church there. The congregation had been led
by George Forrester (1782?-1820), native of Scotland,
and his library had provided Scott's introduction to the
thought of Glas, Sandeman, the Haldanes, Locke, and
perhaps King.

Like Alexander Campbell and Barton W. Stone, Scott
became an editor during his career. It was Scott who
supplied the missing evangelistic drive so essential for
the emerging movement.

In 1827 Scott was chosen evangelist of the Mahoning
Baptist Association on the Western Reserve of north-

[23]Quoted in John T. Christian, *A History of the Baptists of the United
States: From the First Settlement of the Country to the Year 1845*
(Nashville, Tennessee: Broadman Press, 1926), II, 423 f.

eastern Ohio. Using a dramatic "five-finger exercise," he told how salvation could be obtained through faith, repentance, baptism, remission of sins, and gift of the Holy Spirit. He was a persuasive speaker for the "Gospel restored," as he called it. By the end of Scott's first year of evangelistic preaching, 1,000 converts had been added to the churches.

Scott remained the Mahoning evangelist for three years. At his insistence and against Alexander Campbell's wishes, the Mahoning Association was dissolved in August, 1830, since it was "without scriptural sanction."[24] The 60-page *Millennial Harbinger* Extra of July 5, 1830, with its firm stand for the "Remission of Sins," was taken by Baptists as sufficient reason for separation from the Reformers. Previous to that time, a growing number of Reformer churches dropped from Baptist ranks.

The dissolution of the Mahoning Association, more than anything else, accounted for the fact that the Reformers, hereafter called Disciples of Christ, became a separate religious body.

It was almost inevitable as Alexander Campbell's reputation increased in Kentucky, following his debate with W. L. Maccalla, Presbyterian, in October, 1823, that he should meet Barton W. Stone. That historic occasion the next year was described by John Allen Gano, as follows:

In the year 1824, Elder A. Campbell paid a visit to this State [Kentucky]. While at Georgetown he and Elder Stone became acquainted. They conversed freely together, and were mutually led to love and highly esteem each other as brothers. . . . Union and liberty, was their motto. . . .[25]

That was it. Victor Hugo once said that "nothing is so powerful as an idea whose time has come." The idea whose time had come for the frontier Disciples and Christians was Christian unity with diversity of opinion.

---

[24]Dwight E. Stevenson, *Walter Scott: Voice of the Golden Oracle* (St. Louis: Christian Board of Publication, 1946), p. 116.

[25]Rogers, *op. cit.*, p. 140 f.

The growing longing had already found expression in England, Scotland, Ireland, and it was soon to be realized in America. Events were moving toward the merger of the Stone and Campbell movements.

Union of the Two Movements

While the movement under Alexander Campbell's leadership expanded, the followers of Stone were not idle. In 1826, Stone began the publication of the *Christian Messenger*, a monthly periodical, from Georgetown, Ky. The little paper, along with Stone's own liberal influence, helped to bring the Christians and Disciples together.

The two groups, by that time, agreed on the essentials of the Christian faith and affirmed that they should not contradict reason. These essentials included Christian unity, rejection of creeds, practice of immersion, use of biblical names, and the simple, public confession of "Jesus is the Christ, the Son of the living God" (which was the thesis of John Locke's volume, *The Reasonableness of Christianity*).

While the Christians practiced immersion generally as the form of baptism, they refused to make it a test of fellowship. The Christians observed open communion while the Disciples followed the Baptist custom of close communion. The Christians broke the bread at the Lord's Table less frequently than the Disciples who communed weekly.

The Christians brought broad freedom of opinion and a primary emphasis on Christian unity to the merger. The main attention of the Disciples was centered on the restoration of the "ancient order of things."

Walter Scott's common-sense, reasonable evangelism prevailed as the two groups came together. That avoided extreme emotionalism and stressed logic and the Scriptures in a constant challenge to the mind.

Disagreement over the name for the united religious movement began with the merger, or before, and has plagued the churches, their members, and the Christian forces at large ever since. There has never been any final agreement on a specific name for the fellowship.

Both Stone and Thomas Campbell preferred the name Christian. Alexander Campbell contended that Disciple and the numerical Disciples of Christ were preferable, not only because they were scripturally older, but because they were not being used. Walter Scott first chose Disciple, but later became an ardent supporter of Christian. These designations, and many others, both proper and nicknames, formed the nomenclature for this indigenous American religious movement. However, all of the early leaders, and their thousands of successors, have firmly repudiated human names.

The eponym "Campbellite," or some equivalent of it, was used often by the opponents. An indication of what this meant to Thomas Campbell, one of the founding fathers, was suggested in one of his letters in 1830, as follows:

The outrageous and malevolent opposition is ripening the harvest for the reformers. A Campbell, Campbellism, Campbellites, and heretics, are the chorus, the overword, the tocsin of alarm, in the mouths of the opponents, in almost every sentence, from the one end of Kentucky to the other; yea, in the opposition and in the papers from Georgia to Maine. You can not conceive what a terrible dust our humble name has kicked up. If it were not coupled with the pure cause of God—the ancient Gospel of the Savior, and the sacred order of things established by his holy apostles, I should tremble for the consequences! But, alas! the enemies have blasphemed the blessed Gospel by pasting our sinful names upon it, to bring it into disrepute.[26]

With most of the differences resolved, at least by the outstanding leaders and advocates of union, a uniting assembly became possible. It was held on Jan. 1, 1832, at Lexington, Ky., with representatives of both groups present. Stone was chief spokesman for the Christians with "Raccoon" John Smith (1784-1868) and John T.

---

[26]Alexander Campbell, *Memoirs of Elder Thomas Campbell,* Together With a Brief Memoir of Mrs. Jane Campbell (Cincinnati: H. S. Bosworth, 1861), pp. 151 f.

Johnson (1788-1856) for the Disciples. The democratic, but unofficial, union was unanimously approved as the natural consequence.

As a climax, Stone offered his hand as a token of fellowship. It was eagerly accepted by Smith and the union was thus symbolized. The Christians and Disciples at the meeting shook hands to begin the consummation of the union. Then, around the communion table, was realized a Christian fellowship which symbolized unity and the release of men's minds from religious shackles.

Only the Lexington congregations were involved in the merger. There was no overhead authority. Every other local church had to decide whether to accept the union proposals. There was opposition, stemming from differing points of view and prejudices. However, "Raccoon" John Smith and John T. Johnson for the Disciples and John Rogers (1800-1867) and Stone for the Christians proved to be effective evangelists in urging the churches to consummate the union.

The Christians who opposed union at that time remained apart, merging eventually with the O'Kelly group and the New England Christians to become "The Christian Convention in the United States," finally merging in 1931 with the Congregationalists to form the Congregational Christian Church.

The *Christian Messenger,* far more than Campbell's *Millennial Harbinger,* supported the union of 1832. Stone confirmed it by naming John T. Johnson, with whom he previously worked and worshipped at Georgetown, Ky., as co-editor of the periodical. First comment by the two editors on the union included a picturesque illustration that drove the meaning home. It appeared under the heading, "Advice," in part, as follows:

Several persons from different points in the West start separately to Philadelphia. They all meet together on the great highway—They learn each others destination, and agree to travel together; just so the Christians and the Reformers (formerly so called) met together in the great highway to Heaven, and agreed to walk together there, and assist each other in their journey. They walk together, because they agreed to walk together; without which agreement, no two can walk together: but with which all God's people can, irrespective of their different opinions.[27]

Statistics of the membership and number of churches of the Disciples and Christians for that period are few and likely based on mere approximations. Stone stated in 1829 that the Christians had "1500 congregations, with a membership of 150,000."[28] In 1835, three years after the merger, Campbell's paper said that the Disciples did "not much, if at all, fall short of one hundred and fifty thousand."[29] Contemporary historians estimate the membership of both the Disciples and the Christians, at the time of the 1832 union, to have been 22,000 to 30,000.[30]

Following the union, as before, proclaiming evangelists of the Disciples of Christ took advantage of the prevalent, if often inarticulate, longing for Christian unity and a reasonable, scriptural scheme of salvation. Like the Methodist circuit rider and the Baptist lay preacher, the usually rode long trails on a pack horse, their saddlebags carrying tracts and magazines that contained new, factual, and potent religious ideas. Campbell's biographer indicated what sacrifice was involved in the pioneer preaching tours, as follows:

. . . the individuals who felt impelled to use their efforts for the spread of truth were obliged to do this not only without the prospect of any present remuneration, but to the neglect of their own affairs and the expenditure of their own limited means. On one occasion one of them, having a series of appointments to meet, and being without a horse to ride, borrowed one from a neighbor, for the shoeing of which he was to pay two

[27]*Christian Messenger*, April, 1832, p. 111.

[28]*Ibid.*, June, 1829, p. 190. Stone's estimate apparently represented the total national membership of the Christians, rather than that in Kentucky, or the "West," alone.

[29]*Millennial Harbinger*, December, 1835, p. 595.

[30]Garrison and DeGroot, *op. cit.*, p. 325. Garrison, *op. cit.*, p. 200.

dollars. Having filled his engagements and received nothing
but compliments, he had, upon his return, to work four days
for the blacksmith in order to pay the debt he had incurred.[31]

In addition to their distinct sense of mission, Disciples
were given attention because they advocated the priesthood of all believers. They could democratically administer the ordinances—spread the Lord's Supper and
baptize—as well as perform weddings, bury the dead,
and preach a logical plan of apostolic life and work to
the scattered frontier settlers.

So from ocean to mountains in Georgia, where the
union of 1832 was only partially effected, those pioneers
went often yet always confidently and eagerly. Not only
their message, but their lives commanded attention.
True, they were not always consistent, for indeed, the
democratic pattern of their faith was not yet completely
clear. They were vigorous, though, God-fearing and sec-
tarian-fighting parsons, well read for their day, called
only of God.

The story of their struggles in Georgia, confronted
with much vehement opposition, to have the newly found
truth accepted, developed, and passed on will now be
described.

---

[31]Robert Richardson, *Memoirs of Alexander Campbell* (Philadelphia:
J. B. Lippincott & Co., 1870), II, p. 262.

CHAPTER III

The Beginnings Arouse Orthodox Opposition

Here will unfold on a state level the record of the attempt to establish a religious movement, based on factual knowledge and understanding of the Scriptures, consonant with Georgia's democratic freedom. Thus, following their honest convictions, the pioneers were labeled heretics and endured the furious opposition of more orthodox Christian neighbors. Yet, like Luther at Wittenburg, they exclaimed, "Here I stand, I cannot do otherwise; God help me!"

Reference was made on a previous page to Barton W. Stone's trip into Georgia, starting from Kentucky in the autumn of 1797. The journey was made before the Cane Ridge revival and preceded Stone's break with the Presbyterians. He later wrote in his autobiography that after he had settled some business matters and visited relatives, he "preached throughout the country for several weeks."[1]

The quotation suggests that Stone preached in a number of places. Changes of a definite character took place in his mind while he was absent from Georgia. He felt more certain of his religious convictions as a result. Yet how often he preached, in what places, and how many persons he converted are matters for speculation.

Any speculation concerning Stone's Georgia preaching in 1797 must take into account the religious situation of the frontier. Religion was not generally regarded with favor by the ungodly frontiersmen. Many churches were rent asunder with dissension. However, people frequently attended preaching services just to see and

[1]Rogers, *op. cit.*, p. 27.

talk with their farm neighbors if for no other reason. Some were open to conviction on religious issues and avidly studied their Bibles.

The historian of Wilkes County, Ga., where Stone taught and where a brother resided, stated that,

> . . . in the early history of the county the country churches were the active organizations, and the town people, when they were church members, belonged to country churches. I am afraid the gospel did not flourish much in Washington.[2]

Barton W. Stone, known as an educated man and a teacher, was undoubtedly influential wherever he preached. He created a favorable impression likely when he stood in the pulpit and in personal conversation. His influence may have increased during other trips into Georgia about which he left no record. Then, too, he exercised considerable prestige as knowledge of his teachings became more widespread.

GEORGIA'S FIRST CHURCH OF DISCIPLES

The first congregation of the Disciples of Christ to be established in Georgia, according to available information, was near Scull Shoals in the southern part of Clarke, now Oconee, County, about 16 miles from Athens. It was about 1807. The little group was composed of immigrants from North Carolina. The new Georgians transplanted their faith, being known as "O'Kellyites," that is, Republican Methodists who had abandoned nonscriptural divisive practices. Consequently, the congregation, now Antioch, was called Republican Church for some years.

Their original church building, constructed in 1807, was replaced in 1820 according to Mrs. Annie Charlotte (Jones) Miller (1850-1926), historian of the congregation.[3] She wrote, also, that by 1822 the members had reorganized and began to call themselves "Bible Chris-

---

[2] Eliza A. Bowen, *The Story of Wilkes County, Georgia.* Edited, Annotated, and Indexed with Introduction by Louise Frederick Hays (Marietta, Ga. Continental Book Co., 1950), p. 112.

[3] Miller, *op. cit.,* p. 18.

tians." Another writer on those origins implied that the little band was "aided directly or indirectly by the saintly Barton W. Stone."[4] The members were designated "Stoneites," too, in that period. The influence of Alexander Campbell did not penetrate Georgia until later.

Students of the Bible, their views of religion changed:

> They so truly desired to return to apostolic practices that they very earnestly studied the Bible and were led by their research to drop some of their former methods: For instance they abandoned the christening of infants. Mr. D. W. Elder said, "they threw away all human creeds and planed themselves on the Bible alone, but they did not go far enough to reach Jerusalem. It was a step in the right direction, which made it less difficult in later years to come into the Reformation as taught by Alexander Campbell.[5]

It does not seem strange that such a Christian group permitted the community's denominations to use Republican Church for worship. However, each band maintained its own "peculiar views and methods."

SOURCES OF SAVANNAH AND VALDOSTA CHURCHES

Two men, Shelton C. Dunning (1780-1858) and Christian Herman Dasher (1789?-1866), were responsible for congregations of Disciples at Savannah and near Valdosta during early years of the nineteenth century. The former, born in Connecticut, had been a Baptist. The latter was a Salzburger Lutheran. Both changed their religious views, after thoroughly studying the New Testament, about 1819, although it may have been earlier.

Dunning, first, became convinced that his baptism had failed to meet scriptural commands and customs. In that conclusion he may have been influenced in his native state by Elias Smith or Abner Jones of the New England "Christian" movement. Dunning found some

---

[4]J. S. Lamar, "Georgia," in John T. Brown, *Churches of Christ* (Louisville: John P. Morton & Co., 1904), p. 213.

[5]Miller, *op. cit.*, p. 9.

"competent" person to immerse him after a simple confession of faith in Christ. That act buoyed his spirits for a time. A businessman, he began to preach and teach wherever he went, always carrying a large New Testament on his daily rounds. His opponents claimed that he was likely to cram scriptural texts down the throat of nearly anybody.

Christian Dasher resided several miles north of Savannah at the Salzburger Lutheran settlement of Ebenezer in Effingham County. His father may have been either John Martin Dasher or another Martin Dasher. Both men were members of the Lutheran Church Council at Ebenezer in 1775. No Dashers were listed by Strobel, however, as being residents of Ebenezer in 1741.[6] So the father of Christian Herman Dasher (born in 1789?) sought refuge in Georgia from Roman Catholic persecution as an Austrian Salzburger after 1741, but before 1775.

While a soldier, Christian Dasher began to read and ponder the Bible. While searching the Scriptures, he chanced to learn, through Mrs. Sarah (?) Threadcraft of Savannah, about another eccentric Christian, namely, Shelton C. Dunning.[7] After trying unsuccessfully to get his Lutheran pastor to immerse him, Dasher went to see Dunning at Savannah. The two religious zealots learned that they shared similar ideas about baptism. When Dunning immersed Dasher, the two, with one Negro woman became the unorganized New Testament congregation of Savannah.

. . . As regularly as the Sunday came the table of the Lord was spread in Mr. Dunning's parlor or hall, and there, with any that were disposed to meet with them, would sit around it, with hymns and prayers and Scripture reading, expositions and exhortations, followed by the sacred supper. . .[8]

---

[6]Strobel, *op. cit.*, pp. 180, 181, 112.

[7]James A. Harding, "The Church of God at Valdosta, Georgia," *Gospel Advocate*, February 15, 1883, p. 102.

[8]Brown, *op. cit.*, p. 214.

The same writer suggested uncertainty in the minds of both Dunning and Dasher when he described their rebaptism of each other thus:

... Now and then these earnest men, feeling after the light, would reach a conclusion that their baptism had not been altogether up to the apostolic model; for instance had not been "for the remission of sins," and, not caring at all for what men might think or say, but caring everything for what Christ said, they would forthwith proceed to baptize each other again— Dunning immersing Dasher, and then Dasher immersing Dunning; or their consciences would be disturbed by the fact that Saul was told to be baptized and wash away his sins, *calling upon the name of the Lord*—resulting in another solemn march to the canal and another reciprocal immersion.[9]

An account, published in 1855, provided other information apparently about Dasher and his baptisms, as follows:

There is a singular incident with the history of this church at Goshen [Georgia], which it may be proper to insert here. The facts are given, but, out of respect to the feelings of their families, the names of the parties are suppressed.

Two gentlemen, Mr. D____ and Captain W____, labouring under a strange hallucination, imagined themselves called, by a special revelation from heaven, to preach the gospel. By dwelling too much upon this subject, they ultimately became somewhat monomaniac, and announced themselves respectively as John the Baptist and the Messiah. They made an appointment to preach at Goshen, but owing to their insane pretensions, the elders closed the church against them. Nevertheless, they attended at the church at the time appointed, and announced to the large congregation assembled, that, as an evidence of the divinity of their mission, the doors and windows would fly open miraculously, precisely at *twelve o'clock*. But their prediction was not verified, and they were compelled to leave the assemblage, being deeply mortified at their disappointment. Of course, the whole affair proved a miserable farce. Mr. W____ left his house the next day, under great mental excitement, and wandered about in the woods until he died from hunger and exhaustion. Apart from this strange delusion, he is represented as having been one of the best and most exemplary men of his day, and was even honoured with a seat in the Legislature. Mr. D____, who had once been sheriff of Effingham County, after

[9]*Loc. cit.*

being immersed some three or four times, connected himself with the "Bible Christians or Campbellites." He still lives and is a man of great integrity, and possesses many fine traits of character.[10]

Even as later as 1839, Christian H. Dasher was troubled about the validity of his baptism. In that year he addressed an inquiry to Editor Charles F. R. Shehane, as follows:

Bro. Shehane if a man was to say to you that he knew nothing about believing upon testimony, neither did he know any thing about immersion for the remission of sins when he was immersed, but now he believes the truth and would ask you if it was necessary for him to be immersed for the remission of his past sins as though he never was immersed what would be your answer?[11]

The editor's reply that followed was not one to quiet the disturbed Dasher's mind. It stated, in part: "I say that it is necessary for him to be immersed for the remission of his past sins as quick as possible."

When Dasher returned to Ebenezer from Savannah, he soon immersed his wife (formerly Elizabeth Waldhauer?), her sister and the sister's husband. He led many of his Salzburger neighbors to accept the new doctrine. That was about 1819. It was a time when many Salzburger descendants were forsaking the faith of their fathers; Methodist and Baptist congregations, with services conducted in English, were established among them about that time.

About 1825, Dasher and a group of 30 or more persons moved from Ebenezer some 150 miles west. Many Salzburgers were then emigrating to other Georgia counties. The Dasher group settled in the wire-grass area of Lowndes County when that frontier region beckoned them. Dasher later formed a church near Valdosta. He died on Feb. 26, 1866.

---

[10]Strobel, *op. cit.*, pp. 254 ff. In the Savannah newspapers of Jan. 1811, C. H. Dasher, as Sheriff of Effingham County, advertised sheriff's sales. Additional advertisements, until 1813, were signed by C. Dasher, presumably the same man.

[11]*Morning Watch*, May, 1839, pp. 154 f.

The new Disciples of Christ who remained at Ebenezer, eventually abandoned, formed the church at what
became Guyton. They were led in that effort in 1837 by
another Christian Dasher, a relative of Christian H.
Dasher. First services of the group of five persons were
held in 1834 or 1835. One of those was Christian Wisenbaker, reader of the *Millennial Harbinger* in 1830. The
first building was erected about 1837 in the woods about
seven miles from where Guyton is now located. After
Dasher's death the congregation built a frame structure
one mile from Guyton.

REPORTS OF OTHER PIONEER CHURCHES

William Guirey, born in the Georgia backwoods in
1773, had a checkered connection with the Episcopalians,
Methodists, "O'Kellyites," and Christian Baptists, between 1792 or 1793 and 1810. An immersionist, he seceded from the O'Kelly group in 1810 over the baptismal issue. "After he united with the Christian Church"
(the "O'Kellyites"), a historian of that group wrote,
"he traveled from Philadelphia to the southern frontier
of Georgia, preaching the Word."[12] The extent of his
influence in winning converts or establishing congregations that may later have joined with the Disciples in
Georgia is unknown.

Occasional references to other congregations, besides
those noted, appeared in the *Christian Messenger,*
monthly magazine edited and published by Barton W.
Stone at Georgetown, Kentucky, beginning in 1826. The
reports indicated beyond a doubt that a number of other
congregations existed in Georgia.

Two letters from James Buys, preaching elder of De
Kalb County, Georgia, contained much information. The
first one stated:

The work of the Lord is going on in this state, in spite of
all the opposition against it. I hear of a good work in many

12W. E. MacClenny, *The Life of Rev. James O'Kelly and the Early
History of the Christian Church in the South* (Raleigh, North Carolina:
Edwards & Broughton Printing Co., 1910), p. 130.

places in this state; but in DeKalb county the Lord is pouring out his spirit in a wonderful manner. Since my last letter I have immersed near twenty, and expect to-morrow week to immerse twenty more. There was a communion meeting at Bethel Meeting House, in the county above mentioned, which commenced on the 8th of this month, which was attended with good consequences. The number of Elders present was eleven, to which number was added three more. Their names are as follows: — Willis B. Nalls, Jacob Callahan, George L. Smith, Archibald Standifer, Theo. J. M'Gaughey, Arthur Dupree, James Buys, Zechariah Holloway, Wm. M'Gaughey, Adam Clements, Thos. Jones, Wm. L. Anderson, John Cook, Wm. A. Tattle. The three last were ordained at that meeting. The number of communicants is not known, but supposed to be two hundred. Nor is the number that professed faith in the Messiah [*sic*], exactly known; but we have a knowledge of fifty-two. Twenty-six joined the Church of Christ at this meeting. Help is greatly needed, and if any of our preaching brethren would visit us, we would be glad to see them. Adieu for the present.[13]

Several of the elders mentioned figured in subsequent history of Georgia Disciples. The next autumn Mr. Buys wrote another letter to Editor Stone. Excerpts from it follow:

In Dekalb county, our Camp-Meeting commenced on the 7th of October. The preachers and brethren came together in the spirit. . . About twenty professed faith in Christ, and fourteen joined the Church. At this meeting there was as much good done as at any former meeting in the State; yet we have had more than double the number of converts at one meeting.

On the 21st of Oct. I attended another Camp-Meeting in Jackson county . . . the result was, about fifteen professed faith in him; ten joined the Church, and about the same number were baptized. The meeting continued four days.

Also—there was one held at the same time in Pike county . . . about ten made an open profession of faith in Christ, while christians were much encouraged. . . .[14]

A communication published in the same issue of the *Christian Messenger* was from Arthur Dupree, another

[13]*Christian Messenger*, December, 1828, p. 43. The January, 1830 issue, p. 47, had an editorial correction that added the name of Joshua Parker to the elders listed above.

[14]*Ibid.*, Jan. 1830, pp. 46 f.

evangelist or preaching elder, whose post-office address was not given. The letter probably contained the most information, up to 1830 or thereabouts, of the early years of Georgia Disciples. Because of its significance, the full letter is quoted, as follows:

August 21st, 1829.

Brother Stone—The brethren and friends of the north western section of this State, having solicited me to inform you of the present situation of the Churches of Christ among us, I have, in compliance with their wishes, been induced to make the following statements:

In the bounds of my circuit there are 23 churches, or congregations. These churches, it is thought, will, upon an average, number 25 members of good standing.

If I am correct in these calculations, and I feel confident that in them I have fallen below the real number of communicants, you will discover our number to be at least 575 church members. With us there are 20 Elders and 6 licensed preachers and exhorters.

We have an annual Conference of the Elders and Preachers. Deacons, delegates, and private, or lay members, present, have the right of participating in all matters which come before the Conference. Our Conference assumes no authority to legislate —nor does it carry into effect its own resolutions by penal enactments; but by simple recommendations. The powers of the Conference are restricted to the bare regulation of the temporal concerns of the church—nor can it go one step beyond this, without manifest innovations, in which case the members are not bound by any natural or moral tie to submit. Our annual Conference takes place, or rather commences on Friday before the third Sabbath in December, annually.

Our Camp-Meetings commence the last of July, or first of August in every year, and are carried on till the first of the enusing November at various times and places. They are conducted in the main after the fashion of the Methodist Camp-Meetings.

With regard to doctrine, perhaps I ought not to say anything, for fear it might be said that I exhibit something too near a tie to a confession of faith. But an idea of this kind I as heartily discard as I do any and every confession of faith under the sun, the Bible excepted.

Of this sacred repository of the divine will I think I can say it is the first and the last with the Christians here. We know of no other road to heaven—consequently, we feel disposed to travel along the king's highway till we be passed the borders of all confessions of faith and authoritative creeds.

This book, the Bible, we love, because we do believe in the truth from God. We regard it as the only rule of christian faith, and consequently we defend it to the last point. Our only source of sorrow is, that we have not sufficient strength to proclaim it out to Christianized Infidels and to heathen lands. Yes, my brother, I feel, as regards myself, willing to spend and be spent in the glorious work of bring back a lost and ruined world to the purer fountain of life, whence flow the clear streams of eternal salvation. But with regard to the doctrine generally taught by our preachers here, and which is, with some slight shades of difference, received by the churches, I can say, they are such as are taught in other States by the Christian Preachers.

We believe in the first place, that Jesus Christ is truly and properly the Son of God. Secondly—That he existed with the Father before the world was created. Thirdly—We believe that Jesus Christ, our Saviour, is the CONSTITUTED LORD of all things. We believe in atonement as expressed in your letters, or address to the churches in Kentucky. [A reference to Stone's, *An Address to the Christian Churches in Kentucky, Tennessee, and Ohio, On Several Important Doctrines of Religion,* published first at Nashville, 1814; 2nd. ed., printed in 1821.] We believe in Baptism by Immersion, after conversion, &c. Our cause in this State is advancing in some neighborhoods rapidly, and in others but slowly. The 3d day of last July I baptized an old lady of 70 years. She had formerly been a Methodist. On the 4th Sabbath of the same month I baptized 4 of the following ages—sister Montgomery 80—sister Jones 63 —sister Truett 61, and brother Truett 73. It was almost a novel sight to see these persons, bending under accumulated years, submitting at the last stage of life to the great command of Christ. Surely the word of God is powerful. At our Camp-Meeting in Clark, near Scull-Shoals, we had a good time. The number of converts I know not, but I think comparatively few. With great respect I remain yours, in the bond of the gospel.[15]

To summarize, the letter reported twenty-three churches in Georgia with a minimum estimated membership of 575. The elders were the preachers of that period; licensed and ordained ones totaled about twenty-five. It was many years before more impressive figures

---

[15]*Ibid.,* Jan. 1830, pp. 44 ff.

depicted the situation in Georgia for Disciples of Christ. No record of the annual conference was located elsewhere. Like present-day conventions and assemblies of the Disciples, the conference had no legislative authority. The doctrinal statement indicated that immersion was the prevailing practice, at least with most of the congregations. The significant omission was lack of reference to the Lord's Supper. Arthur Dupree, who wrote the letter, preached at the Republican Church and other pioneer churches.

A Georgia publication of 1827 briefly stated that no account of the "Christians" was available, adding: "They have several churches in the state."[16] Likely, the Baptist editor of that publication did not read Stone's *Christian Messenger*. Otherwise, his statement might have been more accurate.

Mr. Dupree referred to camp meetings. A description of that phenomenon, as conducted from about 1837 to 1847, follows:

. . . In middle Georgia there were great lavishness and almost extravagance displayed at these meetings. For weeks before arrangements were made for tenting. The tent was a large sheathing house, with a dirt floor and a broad-covered roof. The floor was covered with wheat straw, and the beds placed either on scaffolding or on the straw. The great log fire behind the tent served for a cooking place. Pigs and lambs were barbecued, and chickens by the score were prepared for the hosts of guests who received free entertainment. Every one was welcomed, and for all an abundant feast was provided. The tabernacle was generally a large shed covered with boards. There was preaching four times every day, and the preacher had full swing. These open-air meetings were the field services of this century. The negroes had their place reserved and came in great numbers to the meetings. These meetings were of all grades, from the humblest in the mountains to the elegant encampments in Burke or Warren or Green. But the regular protracted meeting, or four days' meeting, as it was called, was becoming an institution among Methodists and Baptists. Each

---

[16]Adiel Sherwood, *A Gazetteer of the State of Georgia* (facsimile reprint of original 1827 ed.; Athens: University of Georgia Press, 1939), p. 131.

of these churches was energetically pressing its work as the tide rolled westward, and was winning large numbers of adherents, native Georgians.[17]

In addition to the annual encampments, other preaching services were held when a preacher was available. Traveling evangelists rather than located pastors were customary among Georgia churches during much of the nineteenth century. They traveled far and wide. Some went to other states. A letter from Covington County, Ala., mentioned "an interview with Elder William M'Gauhy from Georgia, the first man I ever saw of the Christian name."[18]

Those pioneer preachers had little formal education and no assured payment for their services. They often began to preach early in life. An "Elder M'Gaughy" (1804-1830) of Georgia became a Christian when sixteen and was preaching in 1821 at the age of seventeen.[19] Many were farmers or artisans. Prejudice against an educated, salaried minister was a matter of principle rather than of economics. Tolbert Fanning, noted editor and pioneer Tennessee Disciple, discussed the matter thus:

. . . for about a year the disciples met and attended to *their own* worship; but unfortunately, they finally employed preachers to worship for them a good portion of the time; since which, they have not done so well. The best preacher in the world, preaching three times on every Lord's day, to keep the saints alive, will kill them spiritually; and without great care, eternally. Preachers should plant churches and set them in order, but permit the churches to attend to their own worship. . . . Christians should be cautious that they lose not their reward, in listening to good sermons instead of studying the word and attending the worship for themselves.[20]

A minister from a pioneer Georgia congregation was Isham Hicks (1803-1888). He

[17]George Gilman Smith, *The Story of Georgia and the Georgia People,* 1732 to 1860 (Atlanta: Franklin Printing & Publishing Co., 1900), p. 477.

[18]*Christian Messenger,* July, 1829, p. 229.

[19]*Ibid.,* Nov. 1830, p. 262.

[20]*Christian Review,* Dec. 1844, pp. 266 ff.

. . . united with a body of worshippers known as Bible Christians (a name sometimes applied to Disciples now, which is misconstrued) in Georgia at the age of 18. He was baptized by Elder Callahan, of that order. He preached the gospel before he heard of Alexander Campbell.[21]

All of the preaching of Hicks was in Georgia except two years in Alabama. He established many churches and baptized about 500 persons.

The letters quoted from Stone's periodical remain indisputable evidence of the existence of forgotten Georgia congregations. Nathan W. Smith, pioneer Georgia preacher, wrote that a Tennessee evangelist, William R. Hooton, after preaching in Georgia for several months in 1836, stated "that the churches in their then present organization would die out, which has been literally fulfilled."[22]

The lack of records giving names of preachers and lay leaders, locations, exact dates, and accounting for some activities of the congregations has remained an unfortunate characteristic of Disciples of Christ.

Those pioneer churches could easily have faded away without much trace of their struggles. That was because (1) their membership was small numerically, (2) their organizations were not rigid ones, (3) their buildings were of a temporary character, and (4) preaching was irregular. Located in rural areas, some distance from other congregations of the same fellowship, association with their brethren was unusual rather than ordinary and always voluntary. As towns developed, the rural members gradually scattered as new churches were started in the towns. Only one tenth of Georgia's inhabitants were church members in 1831. Many such congregations might normally have vanished under the difficult circumstances of the wild, pioneer times.

By about 1830, then, churches of the movement that became known as the Disciples of Christ had been planted

---

[21]*Missionary Weekly*, Dec. 20, 1888, p. 8.

[22]Nathan W. Smith, "An Old Preacher's Experience," *Christian Standard*, May 10, 1879, p. 150.

apparently in at least the following sixteen counties of Georgia: Chatham, Clarke, Crawford, De Kalb, Effingham, Fayette, Gwinnett, Hall, Jackson, Lowndes, Monroe, Newton, Pike, Screven, Walton, and Wilkes. Others were soon added to the list.

A DISPUTE ABOUT ALEXANDER CAMPBELL

By 1830, periodicals edited and published by Barton W. Stone and Alexander Campbell were regularly and carefully read among their followers, and others, in Georgia. The printed word was an indispensable means of winning friends and arousing antagonists for their reform programs. However, the number of subscribers to those periodicals was probably not large in the state of Georgia.

M. T. Elder wrote from Pike County, Oct. 25, 1830, that he had been a "consistent reader of the Messenger for a long time." Annually, during the early 1830's several issues of Stone's periodical listed receipts from Georgians. Sometimes a person remitted for a number of subscribers, often for more than one annual volume. Subscribers were supposed to pay one dollar a year for 12 numbers, often through an agent. News reports, letters, and occasional essays appeared in the papers from Georgia readers. All were a testimony to the faithfulness with which the magazines were read. Mr. Elder's letter also stated:

. . . As it respects the Christian cause in this section, I hardly know whether I had best say I hope it is progressing, or to say *positively* it is gaining ground, . . . for there is greater enquiry at this time for the truth, than we have ever witnessed in Georgia. Great tumult, and in some places uproar among the people about reformation—the Baptists and Methodist are here splitting and dividing—many churches of the Baptist have reformed, and others are waiting an opportunity. . . .[23]

The *Millennial Harbinger* followed the *Christian Baptist* in 1830. Both were edited and published by Alex-

---

[23]*Christian Messenger,* Jan. 1831, p. 24.

ander Campbell at what is now Bethany, in the West
Virginia Panhandle, not far from the steel city of Pittsburgh. The first Georgia subscribers included S. C. Dunning, C. Dasher, A. Marshall, D. Hook, J. Shannon, Richard Tubman, and J. J. Trott. The *Millennial Harbinger*
Subscription Book for 1833-36 indicated 43 Georgia subscribers in 1833, including 29 who had received the periodical from its beginning in 1830.[24]

Dunning, Dasher, and Marshall, who resided at or
near Savannah, were mentioned previously. Dr. Daniel
Hook was responsible for organizing the Augusta Church
and a prominent churchman for years. James Shannon
was then a noted Baptist preacher at Athens. Richard
Tubman, an Episcopalian, was the husband of Mrs.
Emily H. Tubman. James J. Trott, Methodist missionary to the Cherokee Indians, read Campbell's writings
while imprisoned in Georgia for refusal to take an oath
of allegiance to the State. Reading the *Millennial Harbinger* led to his identification with the Disciples. He
later evangelized for many years in Georgia and Tennessee.

However, the reading of the *Harbinger* did not always
result in such a favorable outcome for the emerging Disciples. Shaler Granby Hillyer was one reader, baptized
by James Shannon about 1831, who remained a Baptist,
although disturbed for a time. He wrote that he had
been "grievously perplexed with the fascinations and
subtleties of Campbellism. I had read extensively the
pages of the *Millennial Harbinger,* and in my inexpe-
rience I was bewildered with its reasonings."[25]

---

[24]The subscriptions books for the *Millennial Harbinger* and Alexander
Campbell's *Ledger* of receipts are available in The Disciples of Christ
Historical Society, Nashville, Tenn. S. C. Dunning, Dr. Daniel Hook, and
J. J. Trott were early Georgia agents for the *Harbinger*. The 1833
Georgia subscribers resided in 13 different counties, in addition to the
Cherokee Nation.

[25]*History of the Baptist Denomination in Georgia* . . . , *op. cit.*, p. 190.
Sketch of Hillyer, pp. 264 ff.

"Opposition is great, but we are gaining ground"[26] was the triumphal note sounded by Jacob Callahan in the summer of 1832 in a letter from Walton County, Georgia. It became the constant theme of those pioneer Christians. It was part of the daily struggle to stand firm for one's convictions.

Reference was made in the first chapter to the Rev. Andrew Cox Marshall, Negro preacher of Savannah. He became minister of a large Baptist church there about 1815 and became noted as the town's ablest preacher of any color. In 1832 when Alexander Campbell was reputed to have visited Savannah (his *Millennial Harbinger* and Savannah newspapers failed to mention such a visit), the Negro congregation had about 3,000 members (actually 2,795 in 1831). Marshall's adherence to Campbell's religious views, after hearing them proclaimed, gave rise to a lively controversy that raged for five years. From the conflicting accounts of the dispute, it appeared that

Dr. Alexander Campbell (then called the great new-light preacher) visited Savannah, and was permitted by the Pastor, Rev. A. Marshall, to preach in the church his new doctrine. The orthodox Baptists of the city and vicinity, with the leading officers of this church and a large part of the members, disapproved of the pastor's course, and became highly displeased with him. The pastor also, in some remarks from his pulpit, seemed to give the impression that he was favorably inclined towards Dr. Campbell's doctrine. The effect was terrible. Disputes arose in the church to such an extent that even in the meetings for public worship, as well as in those for business, the disorder was so great that the city officers were called in to disperse them, and some of the most turbulent were caught and severely whipped on one Sunday evening by the city marshal. The church became hopelessly divided. . . .

Rev. A. Marshall withdrew from the building with one portion of the church, the other remaining, under the leadership of Deacon Adam Johnson, the most able and influential of the deacons. The great power of his preaching and the general popularity of Mr. Marshall drew a large majority of the members after him, and for a long time the disputes waged between the majority and the minority parties, without their seeming

[26]*Christian Messenger*, Aug. 1832, p. 245.

to know what was the issue. It was principally the Marshall
and Johnson parties, the latter accusing the pastor of preaching false doctrine, . . .[27]

Another account of the dispute, without such a pre-
tentious title, was published the same year by a representative of the congregation that developed from the minority faction. That author mentioned Campbell's

> . . . eloquent and profound sermons [which] had telling ef-
> fect upon the mind of Rev. Andrew C. Marshall, who partially,
> if not very largely, accepted the doctrine of Mr. Campbell and
> proclaimed his views. . . . This kindled a fire that was not soon
> nor easily put out, but which burned with a furious destruc-
> tion for five weary years.[28]

Simms stated that the controversy engaged approximately 1,100 of the Savannah members (about 1,800 resided on plantations) who took sides according to par-
tiality, with Marshall or Johnson, rather than "upon
any merits of the question at issue." Many were confident that Marshall was persecuted for his Christian
convictions and to prevent teaching of slaves. He had
been prosecuted a decade or so before for illegal transactions with slaves. However, in 1838, he exercised unusual influence, and was worth $20,000 at the age of 81,
Alexander Campbell reported.[29] After Marshall was 50
years old, be bought the freedom of his wife and children and then paid $600 to liberate himself.

The Sunbury Baptist Association met on Nov. 9-11,
1832, and voted, at the insistence of the white Savannah
Baptists, that Marshall be "silenced indefinitely" and
that his congregation "be considered as dissolved; and
that measures be adopted to constitute a new church as a
branch of the white Baptist church"[30] of Savannah.

---

[27]James M. Simms, *The First Colored Baptist Church in North America*
(Philadelphia: J. B. Lippincott Co., 1888), pp. 93 f.

[28]E. K. Love, *History of the First African Baptist Church* . . .
(Savannah: Morning News Print, 1888), p. 10.

[29]*Millennial Harbinger*, Apr. 1839, p. 188.

[30]1832 Minutes, Sunbury Baptist Association, p. 6, quoted in Simms,
op. cit., p. 95.

The minority faction obtained possession of the Negro church building by legal means and continued to use it. The white Baptist building had just been vacated, however, so Marshall purchased that more commodious structure. He had gained public support because he was condemned without a public hearing. Prominent white friends helped to purchase the edifice. "This bold effort on his part," Simms declared, "gave him a great advantage over his opponents, and drew the people to him in means and numbers."

While Marshall basked in the public favor, the Sunbury Baptist Association met, in 1833, and voted:

Resolved, That this Association, having undoubted testimony of Andrew Marshall holding the sentiments avowed by Alexander Campbell, now declares him and all his followers to have thrown themselves out of the fellowship of the churches of this Association, and it recommends all of its faith and order to separate from them, according to the advice of the Savannah Baptist Church.[31]

Large groups of slaves were prohibited at that time from assembling without the presence of a white person. Moreover, the courts would not grant Negro ministers required annual licenses to preach or permission to preside at church services without prior endorsement by at least two white preachers.

Thus the means, legal, if necessary, were readily at hand for Marshall's opposition to develop into hostility. Marshall recognized that his ministerial privileges could be withdrawn or withheld. He was thus restrained effectively because of deviation from orthodox Baptist doctrine. Cornered, he sought reconcilation. Prudently, Marshall and his followers issued the renunciation insisted upon by their white brethren for readmittance to the Sunbury Association. Obviously, under the circumstances of slavery, the urging of a white group was the same as a command.

[31]1833 Minutes, Sunbury Baptist Association, p. 6, quoted in Simms, *op. cit.,* p. 103.

However, the Marshall faction was not readmitted to the Sunbury Association upon application in 1835. Action was postponed while a committee investigated. When the committee later met at Savannah, the minority faction reiterated the claim that Marshall had proclaimed

> . . . from his pulpit the erroneous doctrines of Mr. Campbell, thereby creating a schism in the church and all the attending evils arising in the church and among the people since; that Mr. Marshall had denied that he had so preached from the pulpit, and that from said denial a question of veracity existed, which, as the representatives of this church, he and his brethren thought should be settled; that they had no malicious feeling against him, neither did they desire to hinder the good among his people that he was so capable of doing; that they appeared there simply in the defence of truth, and all they asked, on their part, was that Mr. Marshall would make confession that they had not misrepresented or wronged him.
>
> Mr. Marshall, being called upon by the council to answer, rose with grave submission and, with his native eloquence, *confessed*. He said that what Brother Adam [Johnson] and the other brethren had said about this matter was true, only with this difference—that he did not say from his pulpit that he agreed with Mr. Alexander Campbell's doctrine, but that being favorably impressed from hearing him expound them, when he had examined the doctrines for himself, if he found them true according to Mr. Campbell's views of them, then he should join him; but upon a more thorough examination of the Scriptures, he saw no reason to change his faith in the doctrines as now held by his Baptist brethren.[32]

The wrangle was settled in 1837 when the Sunbury Association met. The congregation had to deny "any adherence to the doctrine of Alexander Campbell" and Marshall disavowed "any belief in the doctrine of Mr. Campbell, which he had all along denied." The conditions having been met as required by the all-powerful white Baptists, "the church was restored to the association in 1837 with a membership of 1,810."[33]

The records do not show how much pressure was exerted on Marshall, favorably impressed when he heard Campbell, by the power of his obstinate, white opponents,

---

[32]Simms, *op. cit.*, pp. 119 f.

[33]Love, *op. cit.*, pp. 28 f.

either as *white* persons or as *Baptists*. If there had
been a congregation of influential white Disciples at
Savannah then, to aid and support Marshall, the results
of the controversy might have been different. Available
evidence failed to show that S. C. Dunning or any other
Disciple assisted Marshall.

During the 1830's in addition to differences over Campbell's doctrine, the ranks of Georgia Baptists were split
over other issues. There was sincere opposition to missions, societies, ministerial education, salaried preachers,
religious publications, and Sunday schools, as well as
human innovations devised for their promotion. All
were considered unscriptural.

By the end of the decade many Georgia Baptist
churches and associations were so divided that the "anti"
group—called Old Side, Primitive or Hard-shell Baptists,
with another faction eventually called Two-Seed-in-the-
Spirit Baptists—withdrew fellowship from the regular
or missionary Baptists. The missionary-minded members were expelled by many churches. One association
even decided not to *correspond* with a missionary society!

Some historians have connected Alexander Campbell
with the Baptist anti-missionary influence of the 1830's.
English Baptists who visited America in that decade
wrote: "Some of the churches have been affected with
the anti-effort spirit, and with the anti-missionary and
anti-union views of the Campbellite baptists, but the
denomination is advancing in intelligence and in exer-
tion."[34]

A Georgia Baptist historian discussed the matter
thus:

No sooner was the anti-mission and anti-temperance war over,
and perhaps before the din of arms had entirely ceased, than
there arose a new trouble. The prophet of Bethany, Alexander
Campbell, had been for some time scattering over the country

---

[34]F. A. Cox and J. Hoby, *The Baptists in America;* A Narrative of
the Deputation from the Baptist Union in England to the United States
and Canada (New York: Leavitt, Lord & Co., 1836), p. 457.

his peculiar notions. Mr. [J. H. T.] Kilpatrick's discerning
eye quickly pierced the dextrously-wrought disguise, and discovered the true features of the so-called "christian system."
And so vigorously and wisely did he combat the heresy, that,
. . . the vaunted reformation met a signal defeat. . . . Able and
faithful men everywhere stood up valiantly for the truth. And
as the result of the whole, under God, the Georgia [Baptist]
churches were almost entirely preserved from the inroads of
this plausible but dangerous delusion. When we behold what
sad consequences have ensued elsewhere, we bless God for raising up such men.[35]

Anti-missionary sentiment did not prevail on the
American frontier among Presbyterians or Methodists.
The condition characterized Baptists mainly. One of
the ablest contemporary church historians of the American scene, Dr. William Warren Sweet, asserted that
Alexander Campbell and his comrades were largely responsible for the harm rendered frontier interest in
missions, education, and benevolences. During the period
of the *Christian Baptist,* 1823 to 1830, Campbell did
attack, as Prof. Sweet declared:

. . . every denominational practice for which he found no
scriptural authority. Missionary societies, Bible societies, associations, synods, presbyteries, creeds, confessions, church constitutions, bishops, reverends, doctors of divinity and a multi-
tude of other innovations fell under his displeasure and were
mercilessly dealt with in the columns of the *Christian Baptist.*[36]

Campbell subsequently, however, endorsed missionary
societies, colleges, and conventions, and he became an
enthusiastic advocate of effective religious cooperation.
The effect of his anti-mission diatribes among Georgia
Baptists spent most of its force during the 1830's. What
occurred later was of lesser intensity. The "anti" seed
thus sown, however, plagued Campbell's own spiritual
descendants with strife and division across the years
with the last round in the struggle yet to be finally decided.

[35]J. H. Campbell, *Georgia Baptists:* Historical and Biographical
(Macon, Georgia: J. W. Burke & Co., 1874), p. 393.

[36]William Warren Sweet, *Religion on the American Frontier: The
Baptists,* 1782-1830 (New York: Henry Holt & Co., 1931), I, 70.

Common-Sense Preaching Develops

The religious interest of Georgia's frontier residents reached a high point of intensity at camp meetings. Pioneer Disciples were no exceptions for years. Such a revival was conducted in 1832 at Republican Church near Scull Shoals in Clarke County. Arthur Dupree immersed a "large number of converts." Nathan Williamson Smith (1813-1899) was one of the group. Probably 19 years old then, he soon assumed a place of responsible leadership, being set aside to the Christian ministry in 1836.

Pioneer camp meetings provided the means for Christian people to get acquainted. Charles F. R. Shehane, evangelist from Tennessee who became an editor, preached often in Georgia. He first met Willis B. Nall, another preacher, at such a meeting in Fayette County.[37]

As time went on, the disorderly emotional demonstrations that characterized pioneer revivals among the Disciples gradually faded away. That was due to the penetration into Georgia of Alexander Campbell's common-sense teachings and the fact that such phenomena were modified by the civilized growth of the frontier backwoods. S. C. Dunning was likely one of the first Georgia Disciples to view the meetings with disfavor. In 1838, he wrote, as follows:

. . . What would Paul say, if present, to such exhibitions, his language to the churches in Galatia may well be referred to. What would be his disgust on visiting a Camp Meeting or a modern Association? Would he not with all emphasis, pronounce the whole proceedings sublimated folly? The language of Jesus to the Jews "In vain ye worship me teaching for doctrines the commandments of Men," applies with full force, and the anathema of the Apostle to the Gentiles, is not inapplicable to such cases. Truly the world have fallen on evil times.[38]

Another manifestation of early Georgia preaching, by and among Disciples, as was to be expected, was "a good deal of talk and argument among preachers and mem-

---

[37]*Morning Watch*, July, 1839, p. 219.

[38]*Ibid.*, May, 1838, p. 221.

bers.'' That reference was to sermons in several counties of the state by Thacker V. Griffin, of Winchester, Tenn., visiting evangelist, in the winter of 1833. Smith wrote that Griffin ''was the first preacher I heard preach the principles of the Disciples.''[39] A letter from Griffin gave some impressions of that preaching tour:

> . . . Myself and brother C. F. R. Shehane, are at this time in the State of Georgia, many persons oppose the view we offer on ''the remission of sins,'' though we flatter ourselves that me [*sic*] are able in meekness to instruct those who oppose themselves, and to stop the mouths of gainsayers.—Brother Buys, has met a host of opposition in this country, when endeavoring to advance the gospel plan of a present salvation, but we hope, with him and old brother Dupree to give a strong impulse to the farther advancement of the reformation in this section, . . .[40]

Mrs. Miller qualified that trip of Griffin's, saying that he came ''to visit relatives living near'' the Republican Church. She added that ''during his extended visit he often preached at the little church.''[41] Although he encountered much opposition, she implied that one result of his preaching was the baptism, the next year, 1834, of William T. Lowe in Old Rose Creek, near the church, by William R. Pendleton. Lowe later preached for the congregation for many years. Mrs. Miller called Lowe's immersion ''the first record in Georgia, of a baptism for remission of sins, (except perhaps that of Shelton C. Dunning and Christian Dasher, who baptized each other.)''[42] No mention was made of the theological basis of Smith's immersion in 1832 by Dupree. Certainly the Griffin letter just quoted, dated Sept. 25, 1833, stated emphatically that he and Shehane were advocating the doctrine of ''remission of sins.''

William R. Shehane, also from Tennessee, made a preaching trip among the Georgia churches in April, 1835. ''In 1836 he returned to teach school and to

---

[39]Nathan W. Smith, *loc. cit.*

[40]*Christian Messenger*, Oct. 1833, p. 319.

[41]Miller, *op. cit.*, p. 10.

[42]*Ibid.*, p. 13.

preach."[43]   He was likely related to Charles F. R.
Shehane, previously mentioned. Yet another minister
from Tennessee, William R. Hooton, evangelized in
Georgia "in the winter and spring of 1836, . . . for several
months . . . and he . . . immersed twenty-six believers on
confession of faith."[44]

The obituary of Dr. D. W. Elder (1809-1901) stated
that he "was one of the first men in Georgia" to become
a Disciple. Born in Clarke County, he was, for years,
an elder of the Republican Church in his home county,
and a preacher. He was said to have read the Bible
through "hundreds of times."[45]

ORIGIN OF THE AUGUSTA CHURCH

The third thread in the skein of Georgia Discipledom
was the one at Augusta. Details of the origin of the
Christian churches in the state are so uncertain, however,
that the congregation may have been, rather, the *second*
Georgia church to survive pioneer days. The Augusta
beginning was due to the tireless labors of Dr. Daniel
Hook (1795-1870), an eminent medical pioneer.[46]

An Episcopalian, he settled at Louisville, Jefferson
County, Ga., about 1817. In 1823 at the age of 28, he
went to Augusta for confirmation. That started a careful study of the Bible that continued the rest of his life.
In 1828, through the kindness of a neighbor, he was
introduced to Alexander Campbell's writings. Consequently, he soon sought immersion from a Baptist
preacher. After many objections, the Rev. Jonathan
Huff (1789-1872) baptized him in Brushy Creek near
Ways Meetinghouse. The ordinance was performed
without the relation of a prior religious experience

---

[43]*Loc. cit.*

[44]Nathan W. Smith, *loc. cit.*

[45]*Southern Evangelist*, Apr. 12, 1901, pp. 7 f.

[46]Detailed biographical sketches of Dr. Hook and other able pioneers
appear in the next chapter.

ordinarily required by Baptists. Dr. Hook's wife objected to his becoming a Baptist and she remained a strict Presbyterian until 1842.

Dr. Hook attended services of the Ozzias Baptist Church near Louisville. That congregation even licensed him to preach. There he often read the Scripture, commented upon it, and offered prayer. That is, he did until the pastor, the Rev. J. H. T. Kilpatrick (1793-1869), became disturbed at the effects upon other members of the parish. Then, in a sermon, the pastor denounced Dr. Hook for being a wolf in sheep's clothing. Thus, the little church was closed to Dr. Hook's teaching and he was isolated from that fellowship.

In 1832 Dr. Hook moved to Augusta. Shortly afterwards he rejoiced upon learning that Capt. Edward Campfield, a Baptist, was attracted by the plea of the Disciples. The two, with Mrs. Campfield, were expelled from the Baptists for communing with the little group of Disciples at Savannah. Three years later, in 1835, Dr. Hook was joined by Captain Campfield and his wife, Margaret, in the organization of a church of the Disciples at Augusta. The three zealous Christians stimulated their new fellowship by meeting in their homes for prayer, the reading of the Bible, singing, and the observance of the Lord's Supper. Soon Dr. Hook began to discuss the Scriptures for their mutual instruction.

One year later, in 1836, the little group's morale was greatly lifted when they welcomed Mrs. Emily Harvey (Thomas) Tubman (1794-1885) into their fellowship. It was the same year in which she became the widow of the wealthy Richard Tubman. She had resided at Augusta since 1819, following her marriage. She had been immersed in the Kentucky River near Frankfort, Ky., her home town, in 1828. Soon afterwards she met Alexander Campbell and accepted his religious views. Her devotion, generosity, and widespread influence for good, not only at Augusta, but in many places throughout Georgia and the world brotherhood of the Disciples, make her memory precious to those who seek comparable spiritual insights.

However, the increasingly distinguished community service of Dr. Hook, along with Mrs. Tubman's social prominence, failed to overcome the intense prejudice and bitter animosity which the Augusta Disciples endured for years. Local resentment in other Christian bodies, of course, did not prevent the Augusta congregation from becoming one of the most influential groups within the state among the Disciples.

The Augusta Disciples suffered what all of their brethren in Georgia and elsewhere went through for many long years. They asked for it, in a sense, because they sought to reform entire congregations through proselyting individuals. It does not seem strange, therefore, that they constantly faced antagonistic opponents who denounced them with anathemas.

ANOTHER PIONEER RELIGIOUS JOURNAL?

Georgia may hold a unique distinction in the brotherhood of Disciples of Christ for having been the locale of a pioneer religious periodical—the first issued in the deep South. If the journal was actually published, it was issued as a contemporary of the *Christian Reformer* (Paris, Tenn., John R. Howard, editor) and *The Disciple* (Tuscaloosa, Ala., Alexander Graham and others, editors), both printed for the one calendar year of 1836. All that is presently known about the possible Georgia paper is found in the prospectus that was published in a copy of the *Christian Messenger*. If the paper was really published, no copies are known to be in existence.

The prospectus of September, 1835, indicated that C. F. R. Shehane expected to publish *The Religious Investigator*, "semi-monthly in newspaper form," from Jefferson, Jackson County, Ga. That is, if he was "sufficiently encouraged." Since copies of the *Christian Messenger* are scarce, the prospectus follows in its entirety:

PROSPECTUS
OF THE
RELIGIOUS INVESTIGATOR

Regardless of the smiles of flattery and the frowns of bigotry, or the sneers of ungodliness, it will be the Editor's constant aim to dispel the glooms of superstition, by spreading abroad the uncontaminating light of the *Holy fount*—The Bible, to the consolation of its friends who may chance to read the efforts of his humble pen. He wishes to sweep down the pillars that support the *Temple of pseudo-religionist,* and call the attention of his fellow mortals to "A KINGDOM WHICH CANNOT BE MOVED." In endeavoring to accomplish which, he will honestly contrast *sectarian dogmas* with the living word of God, and hold them up to public view.

Free investigation on all topics deemed important to the melioration of human society, shall be invited and encouraged; for, in the language of Milton, *"whoever knew truth put to the worse in a free and open encounter?"*

What earthly sagacity can say in truth, that the tracts, pamphlets, etc, of proud sectarianism, if unrepelled, shall not be ultimately the means of subjugating the sons of AMERICA to worse than African servitude?

Let the friends of republican and religious freedom stand on the watch-tower of blood-bought liberty; "cry aloud and spare not" the abominations of clerical tyrants. To your posts O sons of freedom.—*Veritas est omnipotens.* [Truth is omnipotent].

————

TERMS.—The Religious Investigator, if sufficiently encouraged, will be published semi-monthly in newspaper form, at $100 per annum, paid on the reception of the first number, of $125, at the end of five months, and if not paid then, $150 will be required. None will be permitted to discontinue, unless at the discretion of the editor, until arrearages be paid. Let each subscriber be particular in naming the office to which he wishes the paper sent. Any person obtaining five subscribers and becoming responsible for the same, shall have one copy for so doing.

Postage on this work will be one cent per number under 100 miles; one and a half over that distance.

All letters must be post-paid, addressed to

C.F.R. SHEHANE, *Jefferson, Jackson co. Ga.*[47]

September 5, 1835

————

[47]*Christian Messenger,* Sept. 1835, pp. 215 f.

It may be assumed that *The Religious Investigator* was issued, as announced, at least until proof is established to the contrary. Copies of it, like other rare materials so invaluable for thorough scholarly research, may yet be found in somebody's attic or private library.

Outside of the prospectus, only one other reference to the periodical was located in the literature of the Disciples. That was brief mention in the *Millennial Harbinger*, which stated: "I am not sure whether *C. F. R. Shehane* has commenced, or is about commencing a periodical in Georgia. A report to that effect has reached us."[48]

Whether or not *The Religious Investigator* did circulate, Shehane left evidence of editorial labor in the *Morning Watch*. It began publication two years later at Evergreen, S. C., with the November, 1837, number. The magazine appeared monthly thereafter, except for November and December, 1838, through the calendar year of 1839. A third volume may have been issued, for the December, 1839, number indicated that other issues would appear. The first year Shehane was "junior editor" to John M. Barnes (1805-1850), but the second year Shehane had complete editorial supervision.

Nearly every number of the *Morning Watch* contained much material about Georgia churches and persons. A series of short essays by Dr. Daniel Hook appeared under the pseudonym of "Luke." In the May, 1838, issue, he discussed his favorite theme of Christian union under his own name. Those expressions were in addition to occasional letters under his own name. Nathan W. Smith wrote several short discourses. Other letters, reports, or queries were from the following Georgians: A. Clements, C. H. Dasher, Arthur Dupree, Wyche M. J. Elder, Elijah M. Harris, Archibald Standifer, Barnabas Strickland, Ephraim Strickland, and Lee Strickland.

The pioneer Georgia evangelist, Nathan W. Smith, declared that the *Morning Watch* was his introduction to both S. C. Dunning and Dr. Hook. It may have been

---

[48]*Millennial Harbinger*, Dec. 1835, p. 618.

the means, too, of Smith's learning about Alexander Campbell and the larger brotherhood, for in 1837 he "began taking the *Millennial Harbinger,* and continued to do so until it was stopped"[49] by the Civil War.

When the *Morning Watch* was published, Dr. Hook wrote from Augusta, as follows:

> . . . I had not anticipated such prompt and energetic effort in the cause of the reformation at the south, where reformers have heretofore had so little encouragement; and consequently this first number has excited and interested me . . .[50]

Editor Barnes, who often preached in Georgia, urged Dr. Hook to "proclaim the *truth* to the citizens of Augusta, [though] you may lose both wealth and popularity on earth by doing it, ..." The editor probably did not realize how prophetic his utterance would prove to be.

The *Morning Watch* was referred to by Shehane as "perhaps the most liberal of any in all the south." That judgment was expressed because "if a man wish to oppose us," he said, "we will give him line for line and then let the people judge for themselves."[51] In an early issue of the paper, the editor said that it was "like the beacon light in the midst of the waves . . . surrounded on every side by enemies."[52]

The first number of the little periodical was circulated to less than 300 subscribers. The total soon reached 550. At the end of the first year, however, it was reported that 350 subscribers had not paid for the first volume. At the start of the 1839 volume, the circulation had increased to about 700. Editor Shehane then believed that the periodical had three readers for every subscription.

From May 18 until late November, 1838, Shehane was confined by illness to Meriwether County, Ga., except possibly for a debate. He had other Georgia associa-

---

49Nathan W. Smith, "An Old Preacher's Experience," *Christian Standard,* May 24, 1879, p. 166.

50*Morning Watch,* Dec. 1837, p. 55.

51*Ibid.,* Mar. 1839, p. 85.

52*Ibid.,* Feb. 1838, p. 128.

tions. Born in North Carolina, Charles F. R. Shehane resided in Tennessee from boyhood to manhood. He became a Disciple while residing at Columbia, Tenn. He was a schoolmate of Tolbert Fanning's. Fanning was an editor, later, at Nashville. The two men subsequently disagreed violently on religious matters and indulged in unchristian name-calling. About 1843, Shehane joined the Universalists and was ordained as one of their ministers. In 1844 he was co-editor of the *Messenger of Glad Tidings,* a Universalist paper at Wetumka, Ala. At that time, Fanning was president of Franklin College, near Nashville, which had a "devoted Universalist" as one of its teachers.[53] In the 1850s, Shehane was a corresponding editor of the weekly *Universalist Herald* of Notasulga, Ala. He was author of a published sermon, of a debate with Dr. Lovick Pierce, held at Americus, Ga., in March, 1850. Another volume[54] referred to "A Discourse on the Second Coming of Christ," written in 1832, which was about the time that he arrived in Georgia.

RELIGIOUS DEBATES PROVE EFFECTIVE DEMOCRACY

Public debates were widely used as a democratic medium to discuss vital religious questions in Georgia and elsewhere on the American frontier. Disciples of Christ were at home from the start in such controversies. They debated, as principal contenders, with little planning, if necessary. They seldom avoided such disputes, in fact, welcomed them. It was a time when the religious interest was exclusively theological.

A debate was held at Teman, Henry County, Ga., July 30 and 31, 1838, between Charles F. R. Shehane and Barnabas Strickland, a Baptist. Shehane, asked to speak on the first day of a three-day program that turned into a five-day affair, declined because of illness. Invited

---

[53]*Christian Review,* Aug. 1845, p. 176. For Fanning's difficulties with Shehane see same magazine, Dec. 1844, pp. 269 ff.; June, 1845, pp. 121 f.

[54]C. F. R. Shehane, *A Key to Universalism* (Griffin, Georgia: Published by the Author, 1854).

again, the next day, he spoke and reported that he
"succeeded in untying the knots to the satisfaction of
all unbiased minds that heard me."

On the third day, Sunday, July 29, Shehane preached
the eleven o'clock sermon. He referred to the scapegoat
mentioned in the sixteenth chapter of Leviticus in an
attempt to show how biblical people "might have ridiculed one of God's ancient institutions." Some listeners
misinterpreted his remarks and reported "that Shehane
had made a saviour of a goat!!"

After the sermon, Barnabas Strickland "pounced"
upon it with "vengeance." The challenge to debate
came when Strickland claimed that he thought Shehane
"held some unfounded and pernicious errors and that
he was willing on any day to point them out, &c. He too
affected to misunderstand the goat-business." Shehane
explained the matter satisfactorily, he thought, for
Strickland "immediately jumped on Peter's words Acts
2:38 and substituted *blood* for the *name* of Christ." Then
Shehane declared before everybody present "that there
was no backing out in me, and as Barny had expressed
a willingness to investigate the difference I was ready at
any time."

Subsequent "conversation among the leading men on
the ground" resulted in agreement for a debate beginning
on Monday morning, July 30, "with the understanding,
that B. Strickland take exceptions" to Shehane's published writings and oral addresses. That, of course,
made the evangelist-editor the defender.

The contenders met on Monday as arranged. Modera-
tors were chosen and speeches were limited to 25 minutes
at one time. As first speaker, Strickland "attempted to
prove that the Israelites under the Law understood that
the scape goat represented the *vicarious* sufferings of
Christ." Shehane denied, arguing that "the Bible said
nothing about vicarious suffering."

"Following a few rounds on this antiquated notion,"
Strickland took exception to a statement of Shehane's in
the *Morning Watch* that "the New Testament brings to
view at least four sorts of baptism, viz, *Spirit, fire,*

sorrow and water baptism. The last of which is for the remission of sins.'' When the disputing men had talked for ''about seven hours'' they stopped. It was decided, however, to resume their discussion the next morning on the question, ''Does the Spirit of God operate upon the heathens who are destitute of God's revealed word? Or is it confined to his word?''

On Tuesday morning, Strickland sought ''to sustain the proposition that God's spirit does, without the word, operate upon the heathens.'' Shehane anticipated the trend of his opponent's arguments and replied with a few remarks and many scriptural quotations. The use of Scripture was always certain to convince one's supporters that the opponent's argument was completely deflated. Several years later, Tolbert Fanning charged Shehane with ''great effort to recite Scriptures, without connection or common sense, to be eloquent, and to excel others in writing.''[55]

Shehane reported that he was prepared ''for a long heat,'' but Strickland ''got out of breath after running about five hours,'' and confessed that Shehane was ''perfectly intangible—out of his sight.'' Both men agreed to the publication of their remarks in the *Morning Watch,* but they did not appear apparently. Even publication of the correspondence describing the debates (from which this description was written) was delayed for six months, finally appearing in the January, 1839 (pp. 26 ff.), issue of the periodical.

Verbal debates were not enough for Shehane. He took up his pen and ''asserted the necessity of total immersion,'' time and again, in the *Morning Watch* and in correspondence. In Clarke County, Ga., about 1837, he used letters to defend immersion against J. J. Flournoy, a Presbyterian. That was recalled in an extended exchange in the *Morning Watch* for April and May, 1839. Mr. Flournoy made a pertinent observation which time continued to demonstrate authentically, as follows:

. . . I do not quote every text—since it is mainly a tedious course, which few readers will, however goodly disposed, follow

[55]*Christian Review,* Dec. 1844, p. 271.

and since they that so quote the words of the Bible are apt to mistake at times its express spirit, its essence, or its decision, and to lay together the word of God and the words and mere proverbs of men, as of equal authority!![56]

The following final selection, at this point, from the material on baptism in the state's pioneer times, indicated the absurdity to which constant thought on the subject may lead anybody. The discussion became prominent because different views on baptism engendered controversy as the followers of Stone and Campbell united their forces in Georgia. The basis of the fellowship of pioneer Georgia Disciples was broad enough to include those who had been sprinkled with those who were immersed. The fellowship became more restricted in succeeding years with a blighting legalism. Archibald Standifer, who raised the issue, had preached at the Republican Church. His letter in the *Morning Watch* took six pages of fine print that requires a reading glass. The editor's reply, in two installments, ran about eight such pages. Brief extracts follow:

> I now sit down to comply with my promise to offer my objections to the present doctrine of baptism by immersion for the remission of sins . . . I will try to take the subject up, in a calm, cool, and deliberate manner, and if I should misrepresent any thing, it will be an error of the head and not of the heart. It has been but a few years since I first heard the doctrine of immersion for the remission of sins promulgated. Since that time I have read the scriptures, Brethren Stone, and Campbell, with yourselves, and a host of minor writers on the subject both for, and against the doctrine. . . . But great men are not always wise; . . . The result of all my inquiries on the subject, and the settled conviction of my mind is, that those that support the doctrine, are wrong.
>
> . . . I professed religion in the time of the great revival in the western states, baptism by sprinkling was then taught to be the scriptural mode; I submitted to it in that way, and have been satisfied with it ever since (But for arguments sake) I will now say that I am convinced that it was not the right way that I was deceived, and that I have not performed the only act, by which my sins can be remitted. What am I to do? am I to walk or ride to some remote part of Georgia, South Carolina, Ten-

---

[56]*Morning Watch,* May, 1839, p. 136.

nessee, or Kentucky, several days journey; before I can get one that believes in the doctrine, or that will baptize me for the remission of my sins; I might die before I reached the place of destination, and if I got there safe the administrator might be dead, or from home, for we have no lease on our lives: and I assure you, those of that faith are very scarce in Georgia. Do you believe that my salvation stands on such precarious ground, that I must travel several days journey, or several hundred miles after I believe in the doctrine, before I can have my sins remitted. . . . When I preached, I told the people, Now is the acceptable time, and now is the day of salvation, that all things are now ready, . . . But agreeable to the doctrine of immersion for the remission of sins, now is not the acceptable time, now is not the day of salvation; this evening that I write it would be impossible, for me to comply with the ordinance of immersion for the remission of sins; there is no one in my reach to perform the ordinance, and of course (unless I do it myself) I must wait for a more convenient season, . . .

ARCHIBALD STANDIFER.[57]

REPLY

. . . there is a bluntness in written composition which does not appear in ordinary conversation. . . . if any thing in this reply, wears a rugged aspect, it is not my intention. . . . I look upon you as an honest but mistaken man. . . . You appear to make no distinction between the salvation from sin and the salvation from the grave. Did you not see my dear sir, that in striking this blow, you hit yourself upon your own head? For if no person can be saved without believing in Christ, all pagans, . . . perish: and all infants dying without faith . . . are in the same unhappy condition. I use your own logic, not because I think it good, but to show you its absurdity and some of its awful consequences. . . .[58]

You suppose a number of extreme cases, to all of which, I, in Bible language, make this short response, viz. *"It is required according to what a man hath, and not according* to what he hath not.". . . it is no part of the doctrine which I hold to condemn a man for not performing impossibilities. For the God whom I worship does not require of his children more than they can perform. Nor does he give commands to some of the earth's inhabitants, and punish others for disobedience to those commands who never heard them. . . .

[57]*Ibid.*, Oct. 1838, pp. 358 ff.
[58]*Loc. cit.*

Why is it that men will strain their eye-balls, heat their brains, and wither their nerves in pursuit of arguments, smart sayings and witticisms, to keep out of the water when it is so plain from the tenor of the N. Testament that not only Jesus himselfe, but the primitive disciples were buried in baptism?...

C. F. R. SHEHANE.[59]

ALEXANDER CAMPBELL'S VISIT, 1838-39

Late in 1838 and early in 1839, responding to frequent requests from Georgians and other southerners, Alexander Campbell made a prolonged visit south. He sought, in face-to-face relations with friend and stranger alike, to obtain and dispense knowledge on both religion and morals. He realized that whereas many persons were unable to read, others were unwilling, and, therefore, that the warmth and power of the living voice was a more persuasive force with such persons than the printed word.

So the Sage of Bethany, then 50 years old, accompanied by his daughter, Lavinia, and Joseph T. Henley (1828?-1870), recently of the Georgetown (Ky.) College, left the rambling Virginia mansion on Oct. 8, 1838. They went to Washington, D. C., then to Fredericksburg; from the latter place, in Virginia, they had the company of R. L. Coleman (1807-1880), then known across Virginia as the publisher of a periodical, the *Christian Publisher*. They stopped at Richmond and Charlottesville.

On that trip, Lavinia Campbell met her future husband, William Kimbrough Pendleton (1817-1899), who was a student at the University of Virginia. The two were married at Bethany in 1840. She was a beautiful young woman with dark chestnut hair worn in long ringlets. Intellectually charming, she had "brilliant conversational gifts" wrote Pendleton's biographer. She exercised "unusual skill in discussing Bible subjects and

---

[59]*Ibid.*, Jan. 1839, pp. 3 ff.

in defending the doctrinal position held by Mr. Campbell."[60]

They traveled from Virginia to Charleston, S. C. From there, by rail, at 15 miles per hour, they went to Augusta, Ga. Mrs. Emily Tubman, of Augusta, a friend of Campbell's for about a decade, was one of a party who hoped to meet Campbell at Charleston. They missed each other for some unknown reason.

The welcome extended to Campbell by his brethren at Augusta and vicinity was offset by the closing of Presbyterian and Baptist meetinghouses to him. That was the price of his spreading fame. Upon his arrival, the Savannah River Baptist Association was meeting in the Beach Island Church, Edgefield District, S. C. Upon learning of the reformer's presence in the area, that body approved, with one "solitary no," the following preamble and resolution:

> Whereas we are required by the word of God to mark them that cause divisions amongst us, and keep aloof from them; and whereas Alexander Campbell, of Virginia, is *notorious* for *producing strife, division,* and *confusion* among the regular Baptist Churches, wherever his doctrines have been countenanced; and whereas the said Alexander Campbell is now making a tour through our community for the purpose of propagating his peculiar views among our people.
>
> Be it therefore resolved that we caution the churches of this association to be guarded against the *vexatious* heresy, usually known as "Campellism"; and that we think it contrary to the best interest of divine truth to open their houses of worship to Mr. Campbell or his disciples, and advise them to act accordingly.[61]

The resolution, introduced by the Rev. Iveson L. Brookes, who had heard Campbell speak at Augusta, "gives you a fair glimpse of its author . . . and the kind of man he was,"[62] wrote a Baptist historian. Brookes

---

[60]Frederick D. Power, *Life of William Kimbrough Pendleton,* President of Bethany College (St. Louis: Christian Publishing Co., 1902), p. 68.

[61]1838 Minutes, Savannah River Baptist Association. Quoted in *Millennial Harbinger,* Mar. 1839, pp. 114 f.

[62]B. D. Ragsdale, *Story of Georgia Baptists* (Atlanta: Foote & Davies Co., 1932), I, 247.

was graduated from the University of North Carolina and went to Georgia from the Tar Heel State about 1820. So his prejudice against Campbell and his doctrine did not stem from lack of education as might have been true with some Baptists of that time.

The Disciples, too, were so suspicious of the Baptists that they kept an eagle eye on their pronouncements. For instance, in September before Campbell reached Georgia, the *Morning Watch* had issued an eight-page "extra" for circulation among Baptists. It was entitled, *"A WARNING VOICE or an Echo from the Prophetic and Gospel Trumpet, addressed to the people calling themselves Baptists."*

It is interesting, in this connection, to note how questions were raised about the mere formation of a Baptist ministerial association at Augusta. The group was formed early in 1838. An anonymous writer to the *Morning Watch* assumed that the association was formed to "oppose" and to "arrest the onward progress of the reformation" of Campbell and his followers "at all hazards." The anonymous Watchman regretted it if he had "done them injustice" in questioning the motives of the Baptists. However, he considered that it was wrong for the Baptists to form a new Christian society, whatever their reason; wrong to take an oath (the members "solemnly" pledged before God "to promote each other's interest"); and wrong to exclude other Christians from their organization.[63]

The actions of Campbell's more orthodox opponents actually increased interest in the man and his ideas. He reported that "it created a curiosity to know what the heresy was; and even the preachers . . . attended many"[64] of his lectures.

---

[63]*Christian Index*, June 7, 1838, p. 351, referred to in the *Morning Watch*, Sept. 1838, p. 346.

[64]*Millennial Harbinger*, Mar. 1839, p. 116.

Campbell delivered his messages at Augusta to large audiences in the Methodist church on Sunday and Monday, Nov. 25 and 26, and in the Unitarian church on Nov. 27-29. He went from Augusta to Erwinton, S. C.— in the large area now allegedly used exclusively by the United States Government to build hydrogen bombs— and preached there for several days. Proceeding to Savannah, his party included Ephraim Augustus Smith, traveling evangelist and book and tract salesman, among others.

The morning after reaching Savannah, Campbell left the hotel, where he had gone after arriving in the night, for the home of S. C. Dunning. As Savannah host, Dunning provided accommodations "as they were wont to do in ancient times." Only the Unitarian church was available for Campbell's lectures. "They permitted me," he reported, "both in Augusta and Savannah, boldly to avow my sentiments in opposition to their Unitarianism, and to proclaim my views without restraint. We delivered five discourses in Savannah [probably Dec. 7-10], and had a fair and attentive hearing."[65] As already noted, while at Savannah, Campbell conferred with the Rev. Andrew C. Marshall, the famous Negro Baptist, which was after Marshall's clash with the Baptist Association had been resolved.

Campbell found "a little church, of about twenty members," at Savannah, meeting weekly, "in a private house, after night, on the Lord's day, to break the loaf."[66] That suggested the Savannah congregation had taken permanent form before that.

Leaving Savannah, he crossed the river with Dunning from "whom we parted in primitive style." That is, they bade each other farewell with the holy kiss. Campbell and Smith rode in the Dunning carriage seventy-five miles to a friend's. The rest of the party ascended the river via steamboat.

[65]*Ibid.*, Apr. 1839, p. 188.
[66]*Loc. cit.*

The Baptist opposition to Campbell at Savannah was in his report of the journey, thus:

... a brother Harris, a Baptist minister of high commendation for moral worth, from a Georgia Association, who heard our discourses in Savannah, came and partook of the Lord's Supper with us, and is now about being cast out of the Baptist sect for this high offence. It is also, I learn, alleged against him, that he was seen walking in the street with brother Dunning![67]

The Baptists practiced close communion, that is, they partook of the Lord's Supper only among themselves. Non-Baptists were prohibited from participation. Many of the early Disciples, too, followed the same custom.

Details of that excommunication were published in the *Morning Watch*. The minister, Elijah M. Harris, worshiped with the Disciples and heard Campbell's lectures on four occasions. Shortly thereafter he was called before his Baptists brethren to explain why he forsook "stated worship" after an absence of only one Sunday. At the examination, he explained:

... we were to arrive at a correct knowledge, of the Scriptures, by the same rules of interpretation, that are applied to any other writings of the same antiquity. This is what they call forsaking "the faith and practice of the Baptist denomination," for which I was excommunicated from their fellowship.

The resolution of the congregation, voted Feb. 5, 1839, which severed fellowship with Mr. Harris, read thus:

... Voted that he be and hereby is forbidden any more to Preach the gospel as a baptist member that his licence to preach and commendatory letter from this body, be forthwith destroyed and that he be excluded from all connection and privilege with this Church.

The Baptists decided to publicize the matter in their state periodical, *The Christian Index*. Mr. Harris, however, was given an opportunity to prevent that by returning the third document, a commendation from the Hepzibah Baptist Association, within 24 hours of receipt of the request.

[67]*Loc. cit.*

Harris yielded, upon request, his license and the commendation from the Savannah Baptist Church. He refused, however, to return the Hepzibah document, reasoning, that it was not the Savannah group's property. The church clerk at Savannah wrote Harris, saying, "We deeply regret that such a cause has become necessary as you certainly can have no further use for a *baptist* recommendation being no longer of that body."[68]

Harris informed the Hepzibah Association, through a friend, that, upon its request, he would return the disputed document, if, he was given a certificate explaining why the document was demanded.

Savannah's leading Disciple then was S. C. Dunning. He referred to the excommunication as "one feature of Baptist Infallibility." Such an action proved to him that the word "Campbellism" had become a "panacea" for both Baptist editors and churches, "of equal import with Heresy." No Baptist dared to think for himself any longer, he contended, without crying out, "Great is the 'Baptist faith!'"[69] There were other instances of "thought control" among the Baptists as they attempted to root out the heresy of "Campbellism" from their midst.

On Tuesday, Dec. 18, 1838, Campbell was back at Augusta where Mrs. Emily Tubman was his hostess. Her mother, Ann Chiles (Mrs. Edmund Pendleton) Thomas, of Frankfort, Ky., was there, convalescing from a respiratory infection occasioned by attendance at the earlier Campbell lectures. The Sage of Bethany spared no words in describing the poor condition of meeting-houses in the South. He was unable to associate "a flourishing spiritual temple" with "an open, leaky, tottering, windowless, stoveless, wooden tabernacle as its residence."[70] Those were pioneer times and he found that many of the church buildings were

---

[68]*Morning Watch*, Mar. 1839, pp. 89 ff. Early records of the present First Baptist Church of Savannah contain several references to members being disciplined for adhering to doctrines of Alexander Campbell.

[69]*Ibid.*, Nov. 1839, pp. 340 f.

[70]*Millennial Harbinger*, Feb. 1839, p. 55.

. . . generally without stoves, and many of them without windows. This is one of the greatest *"crosses"* which Southern Christians have made for themselves. I have spoken in some Baptist meeting-houses on the present tour, in which there are members said to be worth from 100,000 to 500,000 dollars, living in splendid mansions, and *"worshipping"* in a house merely weather-boarded, without windows and without stoves, and almost without doors. They may be good summer-houses, but certainly they are not adapted to Southern or Northern constitutions in the winter months.[71]

Campbell lectured at the Augusta Methodist church the evening of Dec. 18 to a "very respectable and attentive audience." He departed the next day, with John M. Barnes and Tinsley W. Rucker, in the latter's carriage. They traveled to appointments in both South Carolina and Georgia. At Evergreen, S. C., Campbell met Charles F. R. Shehane, then the young editor and publisher of the *Morning Watch,* as previously indicated. The party then proceeded to Ruckersville and Elberton, Ga., where Campbell spoke to interested crowds. He enjoyed an evening with the family of Gen. Jeptha V. Harris at Farm Hill near Ruckersville. That was one of the most widely known and beautiful estates in Georgia prior to the Civil War.

Returning once more to Augusta, Campbell lectured at the Unitarian church on Friday through Sunday, Jan. 4-6, 1839. After the last lecture, he wrote, "a few of us having assembled at 9 o'clock P.M. at the house of sister Tubman, we broke the loaf of blessing, and commending one another to the Lord, we separated."[72] Early the next morning, Ephraim A. Smith saw Campbell and his daughter leave for Alabama. In 60 hours of travel by stage, plus 50 miles by rail, they covered the 320 miles from Augusta to Montgomery.

Campbell's parting observations about the Disciples in Augusta and vicinity were as follows:

Before leaving the brethren in Augusta, it was agreed by them, in conjunction with our other brethren in South Carolina,

---

[71]*Ibid.,* Apr. 1839, p. 189.
[72]*Ibid.,* Apr. 1839, p. 191.

that brother [John M.] Barnes should itinerate the current year
in the two states, spending half his time in Augusta. Our good
brother Dr. Hook, in connexion with the few that have agreed
to keep the commandments of the Master in that city, might be
more useful were it not that he is so deeply, and perhaps necessarily involved in the business transactions of this life.[73]

The summary of Campbell's addresses, while he was
yet in the deep South, was similar to that of a presidential
candidate. Writing from Alabama to Robert Richardson, he said that he had delivered 20 addresses in Georgia
and 23 in South Carolina. He gave 44 others in Virginia
and Alabama. In addition to those 87 long lectures, he
delivered "some hundred fireside sermons, almost as
laborious as those in public assemblies. I am a wonder
to myself in enduring fatigue; often almost done out,
yet as fresh in the morning as ever."[74]

Some of Campbell's recorded impressions of his
journey into the South were regarded as caustic. To
R. L. Coleman, he said, in part:

. . . Favorable impressions have been made in all places, and
a few converted. But our population in the South is much
more ignorant than in Virginia. We have a few educated intelligent men, as we have a few rich and powerful; but the
majority are poor, ignorant and uneducated. . . . Such persons
are not interested in clear, distinct perceptions; they are fond
of mystic doctrines, man-worship and enthusiastic feelings. The
brethren are of the best class of citizens and of very respectable
attainments. But it will require many sermons and labors, or
much reading, to achieve much in these regions. . . . Still, I
would not have you to think that little has been done, or that
little can be done, in this benighted region.[75]

As might have been expected, Editor Shehane of the
Morning Watch recorded lengthy objections to Campbell's immoderate criticisms. He stated, in part:

. . . Did they not go out to hear him, and who would not?
Who would not go ten miles to *see* him? Surely Mr. C ought

[73]*Ibid.*, Apr. 1839, p. 192.
[74]Robert Richardson, *op. cit.*, II, 451.
[75]*Ibid.*, II, 453, f.

to have curbed his temper . . . A *great Reformer* ought not, in our view, to be a great fighter simply, but great in practice, forbearance, kindness.[76]

A mere layman's judgment of Campbell's trip was given by Tinsley W. Rucker, a "gentleman of talents and education," in a letter from Montevideo, Elbert County, as follows:

. . . In all this country you have accomplished much, very much—removing the prejudices of some against, prepossessing others in favor of, the ancient gospel; and producing a good effect generally in favor of the cause you plead.

Whilst I was with you, you spoke of writing an article warning the brethren of the impropriety of wearing any other name than that of Christian or Disciples of Christ. [See *Millennial Harbinger*, August, 1839, pp. 337 ff.; September, 1839, pp. 401 ff.] Our brethren are now scattered through the whole length and breadth of the land, and wear different names in different sections. Many seem inclined to that of Reformers; and unless you write something on the subject, I fear that will ultimately become our distinctive appellation. I am aware that you wrote much on this subject in your Christian Baptist; but there are no doubt hundreds who read the Harbinger, who have never read those articles. The sectarians are greatly incensed against those of us who call ourselves Disciples or Christians. . . .

Can you not suggest to us some Evangelist, able eloquent, and prudent, who might be induced to visit the South? The prejudices of the community against the ancient gospel have been very much broken down by your visit; and all we need now, under the blessing of God, to reap an abundant harvest, is the labors of such an Evangelist. If you will suggest such a one, I think that, though we are poor, we can bear his expenses. Truly, the harvest is plenteous and the laborers are few.[77]

Campbell traveled over part of Georgia in the carriage of Tinsley White Rucker. He was the oldest son of Joseph and Margaret (Speer) Rucker and was born at Ruckersville in 1813. He was graduated from the University of Georgia in 1833 and shortly afterward married Sarah Elizabeth Harris, daughter of Gen. Jeptha V. Harris. Rucker represented Elbert County in the State Legislature in 1836. Early in 1838 he was im-

[76]*Morning Watch*, Aug. 1839, p. 251.
[77]*Millennial Harbinger*, May, 1839, pp. 236 f.

mersed near his home by John M. Barnes. His younger
sister, Mary Rucker, became the first wife of James S.
Lamar who played a prominent part in subsequent history of Georgia Disciples.

The recurring note of orthodox Baptist opposition to
the heretical Disciples was offset in part, in Georgia, by
the open-mindedness of Cyrus White, a Freewill Baptist,
to Campbell's teachings. John M. Barnes, while editor
of the *Morning Watch,* engaged White in discussion of
mutual experiences.[78]

The Freewill Baptists had their origins in the eighteenth century from independent congregations in North
Carolina and New Hampshire. Benjamin Randall, their
leader, was a convert of George Whitefield's. He believed that "freedom of the will" was available to any
person desiring to accept Christ and to follow him according to his own understanding and interpretation of the
Scriptures.

Several Georgia Freewill Baptist churches, perhaps
six or more, became identified with the Disciples without
any perceptible religious change. The transfer of their
fellowship began as early as 1835 and continued several
years. White assisted Disciples to receive a considerate
hearing in several places for which he suffered from misrepresentation, calumny, and defamation. In Georgia
the "Whiteites" were sometimes called "Soft Shell"
Baptists.[79]

White broke bread with the Disciples which "mere
difference of opinion" did not prevent, opposed the
adoption of human creeds, considering publishing a
paper with Barnes, possessed and read many of Alexander Campbell's writings. He claimed, however, that
those "writings become the creed of many, and his sect
will soon be as strong as any."[80]

---

[78]*Morning Watch,* Feb. 1838, pp. 108 ff., p. 128; Apr. 1838, pp. 179 ff.;
June, 1838, pp. 248 ff.

[79]*Primitive Baptist,* Mar. 24, 1838, pp. 85 f. National negotiations
for union of Disciples and Freewill Baptists began in 1904. In the meantime, Freewill Baptists and the Northern (now American) Baptist Convention effected a merger in 1909.

[80]*Morning Watch,* Apr. 1838, p. 181.

The Savannah River Baptist Association of 1839, with Alexander Campbell many safe miles distant, passed the following compassionate resolution about their "erring" brother:

While reading the letters from a few of the churches, which referred to discord produced among them by the introduction of sentiments generally attributable to Mr. Alexander Campbell, it was agreed, on motion of Brother Fuller, to unite in solemn prayer to God, that he would overrule those things for his glory; and bless his servant who once ministered among us in holy things, but has gone out from among us; and as he has generally erred, to convince him of his error, and restore him to the fellowship of his brethren. Prayer was accordingly offered by Brother H. D. Duncan.[81]

In view of such an expression of Christian concern, it was strange that the Association shortly afterward issued the following corresponding letter:

. . . We perceive that one or two of the churches have been, for a short time, annoyed by the doctrines of Mr. Campbell; but we bless God, that, as with individual Christians, so with churches, afflictions tend to purify and elevate. We should never forget, that as there is a gathering time, there will also be a season of winnowing and sifting. "There must needs be heresies, that they which are approved amongst you may be made manifest." With regard to this error, we earnestly entreat you to use mildness, with firmness. Many real Christians may at first be "carried away by the cunning craftiness of those who lie in wait to deceive," and many who are "God's own children" may be "children tossed to and fro by every wind of doctrine." We advise, you, then, to be gentle, and never to precipitate measures—pray for such—weep over them—and endeavor to restore them in the spirit of meekness. We know there is a point where discipline must begin, and "them that trouble you be cut off;" but we recommend that this be viewed as a last resort.

The writings of Mr. Campbell authorize us to say, that he teaches many things contrary to the word of God, and fatal to the salvation of men. He degrades the exercises of the heart, and ascribes to externals an undue importance; he expressly

---

[81] 1839 Minutes, Savannah River Baptist Association, quoted in James Harkness Barfield, Sr., "A History of the Disciples of Christ in Georgia, 1819-1914" (Unpublished B. D. Thesis, School of Religion, Vanderbilt University, 1938), pp. 58 f.

denies that the term "sanctification" is "expressive of any
quality of mind, or any personal attribute of body, soul, or
spirit"—and declares it to signify only "a state or condition"—
by which he means a *relative* change as opposed to an *actual*
and *personal* change; he makes this change to be the result of an
external bodily act, and this act to be baptism: he declares that
regeneration, or the new birth, and baptism, are the same thing.
With regard to the operations of the Holy Ghost, his writings
are full of studied ambiguity, but yet enough can be detected of
his meaning to warrant the assertion that he admits the influence
of the Spirit of God in convincing men only as contained or
embodied in the Bible, just as the spirit of any author is
breathed in his writings, and denies thus the actual personal
operations of the Holy Ghost. We might enumerate errors of
this kind, but these are enough. The *Millennial Harbinger
Extra* contains these pernicious docrtines. Now we cannot
believe that any truly converted soul, will long adhere to such
doctrines. He may for a season be ensnared; but as soon as
the novelty has passed, he will see that they are opposed to
the truth of God, or feel that they contradict his own experience.
We view this heresy, therefore, without any alarm, and class it
among those evils out of which God will bring good.[82]

Campbell used little space in his magazine to comment
on that Baptist expression of his ideas. To him, the
letter was "wilful and perverse" misrepresentation, and,
he added, there was "no excuse for these slanders."

DISCORD, SOME CONVERTS, MORE DISCORD

The Augusta Disciples welcomed M. R. Campfield into
the fellowship soon after their organization. James F.
Atkinson and James Calvin were received from the
Baptists early in 1839. In 1840, Dr. Hook was elected
mayor of Augusta. Thus, many of his friends began to
attend Sunday services of the congregation. Accommodations of the Campfield home became inadequate for
services, so the group began to meet in a rented "upper
room" on the northwest corner of McIntosh and Reynolds Streets. The church met there for two years.
Much encouragement was given in 1842 when Mrs. Tub-

---

[82]*Millennial Harbinger*, May, 1840, p. 236.

man liberally contributed funds for erection of a substantial and commodious church building on Reynolds Street.

Ephraim Augustus Smith, of Danville, Ky., preached and sold religious tracts in several Georgia counties, beginning in the winter of 1838. He accompanied Alexander Campbell on part of his travels at that time. Smith returned to the South for several winters thereafter, but seldom remained long at one place. He wrote from Augusta in 1842 to exclaim:

I seize my pen in haste to inform you that we still have good news here. Last week I informed you that Mr. Hibber and his wife were immersed. On last Lord's day a Mrs. Cocke, sister of sister Thomas, was to be immersed—when, lo! Mrs. Hook presented herself. I had the pleasure of going down *into* the water with them. She has been a staunch Presbyterian of long standing, was sprinkled at the age of 14, when she joined. She made a bold confession, declaring with her own lips the faith in all points.[83]

Thus, the same year that the Augusta congregation had a new meetinghouse, Dr. Hook was able to welcome his wife into the fellowship with his brethren. That same year, too, his son, James, united with the church; the daughter, Mary, joined in 1845. So the membership increased to a total of 13 souls.

According to a letter from Tinsley W. Rucker, a church was established near Montevideo, Elbert County, on Sunday, Jan. 5, 1840. The dedicated layman probably had much to do with formation of the little congregation. He wrote, in part, as follows:

. . . On the first Lord's day in this month [Jan. 5], at a meeting of the Disciples near this place . . . twelve of the brethren, who had been recently immersed upon a profession of their faith, gave each other the right hand of fellowship as a pledge of Christian union in a congregational character. . . . so that we now have a church of Christ, at this place, which, in all matters of faith and practice, discards every book except the inspired volume, and every name except those which are sanctioned by the Book.[84]

---

[83]*Ibid.*, June, 1842, p. 274.

[84]*Ibid.*, Jan. 1840, p. 38.

The conflicts of those years were not all with the Baptists and other evangelical Christians. As noted, the merger of the Stone and Campbell forces, declared on Jan. 1, 1832, at Lexington, Ky., resulted in discord in Georgia, as elsewhere. William R. Pendleton wrote from Clarke County, in 1836, that "a majority of the people called 'Christians' have become advocates of the ancient order of things."[85] Those who did not accept the program of restoration of New Testament life and work may have been a minority, but they were adamant. The differences in belief over immersion and other doctrinal issues had to be resolved within each congregation. What happened at Republican Church was similar, no doubt, to other dissension elsewhere.

By 1842 a division had developed in the Republican Church. Under the leadership of Jacob Callahan, who had "continued to preach, in his turn," the dissident minority tried to exclude those who advocated principles enunciated by Alexander Campbell. In her historical statement, Mrs. Miller mentioned a difficulty between Callahan and another preacher. Both were forced to undergo a trial at Republican Church with the congregation deciding against Callahan.[86] Nathan W. Smith, then pastor, stated that only about seven persons left the congregation of 40 or more members. Eventually four of the number returned.[87] Callahan, George L. Smith, and Wytch M. J. Elder were the three preaching elders who were separated from the fellowship.[88]

Nathan W. Smith, the Republican minister at the time of the division, had moved to Clarke County from his native North Carolina in 1831. He was baptized by Arthur Dupree in 1832 and united with the little congregation. At first, he "opposed the teachings of the

---

[85]Ibid., Apr. 1836, p. 184 [182].

[86]Miller, op. cit., p. 14.

[87]Nathan W. Smith, "An Old Preacher's Experience," *Christian Standard*, May 10, 1879, p. 150.

[88]Barfield, op. cit., p. 25.

Disciples,'' but later accepting them, he was set aside to the ministry in 1836. Early in 1838, he wrote of his work thus:

> I am travelling and trying to preach the word of God, the only travelling preacher in the reformation in the whole state of Georgia that I know of, and I have left my family to spend the year in the good cause, and have not the promise of one cent as a reward for my time, from any man or set of men.[89]

Following the division, Nathan W. Smith led in the reorganization of the Republican Church. He induced the group to change the name to Antioch since "the disciples were called Christians first in Antioch." (Acts 11:26.) The name seemed appropriate since that congregation was considered the first Christian church to be established in Georgia. The group began to meet weekly in 1844. Smith wrote of the activities, after the separation, thus:

> The brethren in 1844, then numbering near one hundred, concluded to send me out as evangelist, saying, they would support my family. They kept me in the field for three years. During these three years I traveled extensively in Georgia, Alabama and South Carolina, and I immersed a great many persons and organized small congregations, that were built up from very small beginnings to large and respectable churches. Those were days of trial, labor and sacrifice. Part of the time I was in feeble health, but preached many a sermon from one to two and a half hours long, with only a biscuit and a glass of water for my breakfast; . . .[90]

The County Line Church, the first to be formed in the Griffin district, was established by Smith in 1843. The group consisted of Disciples from adjoining corners of four counties, hence the name chosen. The first edifice, constructed on two acres of land given by Robert Westmoreland, had a center aisle separating the men from the women.

However, County Line Church was neither the first nor only congregation planted from Smith's labors and

[89]*Millennial Harbinger*, June, 1838, p. 183.

[90]Nathan W. Smith, "An Old Preacher's Experience," *Christian Standard*, May 17, 1879, p. 158.

the concern of the Antioch Church. Others were the Mount Vernon Church, Walton County, organized in 1842; Union Church, Oconee County, formed in 1845, and Bogart Church, Oconee County (formerly Bethany, Jackson County), begun in 1863, and perhaps others.

Antioch Church, known and honored for many years as the Republican Church, thus earned the "distinction of being called the 'Mother Church' of the Disciples in Georgia," and Mrs. Miller so designated it in her history of the congregation.

The Savannah church, of about 20 members, was meeting in 1838, probably in the home of S. C. Dunning, when Alexander Campbell was the honored guest. Services usually consisted of singing, prayers, reading from the *Living Oracles* (Campbell's translation of the New Testament), book by book and chapter by chapter, consecutively, and comment on the Scripture by Dunning. In 1841, John Mallery and Stephen B. Williams were baptized in the canal. Those men and their families provided inspiration and encouragement to the group of five families. The church began, after six or seven years, conducting services in the Fireman's Hall on Oglethorpe (South Broad) and Abercorn Streets, opposite the old Colonial Cemetery. The first Sunday school of any church of the Disciples in Georgia was conducted by this congregation.

Through the efforts of Christian H. Dasher, after his removal to Lowndes County, as previously noted, a group of Disciples began to meet in his home. Among those who joined with Dasher for worship were Joseph Hevelstein, James Wisenbaker, and James Bergsteiner. Hevelstein and Wisenbaker were probably settlers who had moved from the eastern part of the state. They were soon joined by their families and neighbors. All but Bergsteiner and a Mr. Sego were related. When homes proved inadequate to accommodate the crowd for services, a school was used. The school building was erected on Dasher's land, out from Valdosta, by his son,

James A. Dasher, who became quite influential with the brethren in that area. The building stood until the end of the Civil War.

As indicated, the Mount Vernon Church, Walton County, grew out of the evangelistic interest of the Antioch Church. The minutes were written with ink made from oak tree balls and remained legible after a century. The first minutes had the following preamble: "Georgia, Walton County, August 24, 1843. We the Church of Christ at Mt. Vernon do agree to take the Scriptures for our only rule of Faith and Practice through life. Done by order of the Church."[91]

The Mount Vernon Church was named after the home of George Washington. The first building, near a generous spring, was constructed of hewn logs with mortised corners secured by wooden pegs. It could not be heated. The seats, uncomfortable without backs, were puncheons with holes bored in the ends for logs. Since no lights were provided, preaching was on Saturday as well as Sunday mornings. Business transactions usually followed the Saturday services. The building also served as a school. The original log church was replaced with a frame structure in 1844. William McGaughey helped to form the congregation. Robert Mayfield, James P. Elder, and Nathan W. Smith were early ministers.

A revival was conducted at the Antioch Church in August, 1843, by Nathan W. Smith with the help of Dr. Daniel Hook of Augusta, John Moore of the Anderson District, S. C., and President James Shannon (1799-1859) of Bacon College, Harrodsburg, Ky. The visitors preached and baptized alternately.

Shannon was widely and favorably known in Georgia where he had resided from about 1821 to 1836. He married an Athens woman and the death of her father

---

[91]Mary Wright Burson, Arlevia Burson, and Belle Wright Phillips, *One Hundred Years at Mt. Vernon Christian Church* (Near Monroe, Ga.) 1842-1942 (n. p., 1942?), p. 5.

there brought Shannon to Georgia that summer. He
reported the meeting at some length. His letter, quoted
in part, follows:

In Clark Co. Ga. at Republican, near Scull Shoals, during
the progress of our meeting 13 were added, eleven by confession and baptism, one from the baptists, and one reclaimed; and
since the close of the meeting six others, including a Baptist
and a Methodist, have been added to the Church—making in all
nineteen in that neighborhood, who, within the space of a few
weeks, have practically evinced their wise and noble resolution
to esteem the reproach of Christ as greater riches than the treasurers of Egypt. I shall never forget the heavenly joy—unspeak-
able and full of glory—that inspired the saints at Republican,
who for many years had been patiently suffering reproach *for
the cause of Christ*, when they saw the triumphs of the cross and
witnessed the willing subjection of so many of their beloved
friends and neighbours to the Saviour's most delightful yoke.
Oh! that *all the world* could know what fulness of joy may be
found under the reign of Messiah in believing what God says,
and doing what he commands.

In Augusta also, and at Indian Springs, and in Athens,
Georgia, I delivered several discourses. And, though none
obeyed the gospel at these points, nevertheless, I had good reason to believe, that the truth was not spoken in vain. So far
as I could learn, the general sentiment every where was, that as
a people we had been grossly slandered, and misrepresented.
At various points the Methodists, Presbyterians, and Baptists
with comendable liberality, tendered me the use of their meeting-houses, seemed well pleased with our exhibition of divine
truth, and, so far as we have been able to ascertain, considered
their hospitality as neither misplaced, nor unrewarded. . . .

Republican was the only point, at which our labors were continued long enough to afford a reasonable hope of making proselytes. . . .

. . . In the present state of the public mind, it would be un-
reasonable to expect, that much could be accomplished by occasional discourses at intervals of months or even weeks apart. . . .[92]

That last sentence of Shannon's letter was more prophetic than he realized perhaps. A discerning, educated
leader, he was persuaded that a settled pastorate was
necessary for the struggling churches of Georgia. A
recent history of Ohio Disciples repeated an earlier

[92]*Christian Journal*, Oct. 7, 1843, pp. 97 ff.

author's claim that Isaac Errett, in 1844, received the
first call to a located pastorate among the Disciples of
Christ from the congregation at New Lisbon, Ohio.[93]

In the same journal, a week later, Nathan W. Smith
made some observations about the revival's results which,
compared with Shannon's letter, revealed the varied reac-
tion to the message proclaimed by the pioneer Disciples.
Smith stated:

> Since our protracted meeting last month there has been a
> tornado hurling its fury against the truth of the living God
> (wickedly called by the sects, 'Campbellism'). During its con-
> tinuance I would say, that, perhaps the most furious blast was
> blown the first Lord's day of this month, at a Methodist Camp-
> meeting, at the 11 o'clock service, in the presence of not less than
> three thousand persons, blown, too, by the (self-styled *Rev.*)
> William J. Parks, a Presiding Elder, who is thought by his
> church to be one of the best theologians in the State. As he
> does not at this time preside in this Circuit, there is some strong
> circumstantial evidence that he was sent for, for the express
> purpose of making this mighty effort to save his tottering fabric,
> which had been so recently shaken by the force of truth. . . .[94]

Interestingly enough, the *Christian Journal,* published
at Harrodsburg, Ky., with R. French Ferguson as editor,
had Georgia agents. An issue in 1843 listed four: A
Moore, Athens; Dr. D. Hook, Augusta; A. S. Smith, Walton, and Dr. J. Shannon, "Gullettsv'e."[95]

The evangelist, James J. Trott, mentioned earlier in
this chapter, conducted some revivals in Georgia late in
1844. Reporting on them, he wrote that there was one
congregation of about 20 members in Dade County; another with an unknown number of members in Walker
County, and

> . . . in Cass there are 7 disciples in one neighborhood in the
> Oogegeloge valley. The brethren in Cass are very anxious the

93Henry K. Shaw, *Buckeye Disciples,* A History of the Disciples of
Christ in Ohio (St. Louis: Christian Board of Publication, 1952), p. 32.
Alanson Wilcox, *A History of the Disciples of Christ in Ohio* (Cincinnati:
Standard Publishing Co., 1918), p. 43.

94*Christian Journal,* Oct. 14, 1843, p. 123.

95*Ibid.,* Sept. 30, 1843, p. 96.

preachers should visit them, and I am authorized to invite the brethren in passing from Tennessee to Georgia and South Carolina to call and preach to them.[96]

Time and again, a communication from those pioneer Georgia evangelists appealed for aid from their brethren. The steady and intense opposition was developing a closely knit Christian fellowship, within Georgia, and beyond. They assumed mighty responsibilities and were sustained in them because they had an enduring faith in an omnipotent God. Shut out from meetinghouses, they resorted to the use of court houses and shady groves for their services.

Above everything else the pioneers became marked Christians because they were always courageous enough, cost what it might, to move in new directions. How adaptable some proved to be and the legacy of their stouthearted adventures will be described in detail in the next chapter.

---

[96]*Christian Review*, Jan. 1845, p. 23.

CHAPTER IV

Intrepid Pioneers Set the Pace

A distinct sense of mission drove the pioneer Disciples of Christ in Georgia. They met physical, geographical, and spiritual frontiers with vision, devotion, courage, and inadequate resources. Cantankerous on occasion, they were never dull. Many of their orthodox opponents doubtless thought they had more courage than intelligence, but they learned that they possessed both in unlimited quantity.

A fitting tribute was paid to them years ago by one of their grandsons, who said:

. . . The way of the pioneer is one of trial and sacrifice, whether it be across unknown seas, through trackless forests, or into new realms of thought, across the boundaries set by long cherished opinions. In no field have pioneers met more forbidding obstacles or more chilling discouragements than did those courageous spirits who . . . saw a new light, and dared to follow it, even across the threshold of an intolerant church, or an unsympathetic family circle.[1]

Without the pace-setting endeavors of those crusading pioneers, there would be little of the priceless legacy now claimed by their spiritual descendants. The adventurous lives of six such pioneers crisscrossed often. Their names remain imperishable in the annals of Georgia Discipledom, yet basic facts of their lives are almost inaccessible. They were determined persons of flesh and blood, wit and enthusiasm, frustration and achievement. They were: Shelton C. Dunning, Dr. Daniel Hook, James J. Trott, Nathan W. Smith, Mrs. Emily H. Tubman, and James

---

[1]Edward B. Hook, ''Dr. Daniel Hook'' (Unpublished MS., Memorial Address, 1878?), p. 1.

Shannon. All were introduced in the preceding chapter.
Additional brief sketches attempting to rescue each one
from undeserved oblivion follow.

SHELTON C. DUNNING (1780-1858)

A singular man, utterly devoted to the New Testament,
Shelton C. Dunning was considered fanatical, perhaps
naive. Yet no one ever questioned the sincerity of his
convictions.

He was of medium height, stood quite erect. He usually
carried a walking cane. He wore no beard and had a
healthy, reddish complexion with abundant, light hair.
A charming smile, combined with a sense of humor, made
him a delightful conversationalist.

Born in Welton Township, Fairfield County, Conn.,
in 1780, his parents were Episcopalians. It is not known
when he moved to Georgia and located at Savannah. He
became a Baptist minister, but seceded from the Baptist
church. As related, his study of the New Testament led
him to immersion about 1819.

Dunning was a charter member of the Savannah Steam-
ship Co., incorporated by the Georgia Legislature on
Dec. 19, 1818. When the stockholders met, Feb. 25, 1819,
he was chosen one of five directors for the firm. "There
was a ready sale for shares of the company, due to the
well-known character and high standing of the incorporators."[2] Those businessmen were responsible for the
construction of the "City of Savannah," the first steam-
ship to sail the Atlantic, which was in 1819. Dunning
earned much money from his maritime interests, but lost
heavily and left the business. With a reasonable com-
petency, he later turned to writing life insurance.

His first marriage was to a Miss Richards. They had
four children: a daughter, Sarah, who became Mrs.
Henry Davis Weed, mother of Episcopal Bishop Edwin
Gardner Weed (1837-1924) of Florida; and Gertrude,
William, and Shelton Dunning. A Mrs. Osborne became

---

[2]Knight, *op. cit.*, II, 229.

the second wife. The family resided in a frame, duplex house, old and unusual, on Broughton Street, Savannah. The husband and father did the marketing and liked to work in the garden.

Dunning was one of the founders of the Savannah City Hospital, but his life centered in his strict religious interests. The casual observer was apt to regard him as stern. Well educated, he was a zealous student of the Bible. He searched the Scriptures at his office, as well as at home, and conversed in biblical language. Nathan W. Smith called him "the most constant reader of the scriptures of any man I ever saw."[3]

Dunning's eccentricities likely increased the difficulties of establishing a congregation of Disciples at the seaport. Friends would smile tolerantly and go their separate ways. When James J. Trott, Cherokee missionary and evangelist, was once Dunning's guest, he preached in the home, as was customary. Later, he referred to "some of the brethren" being "too zealous for the letter."[4] Such literalism was responsible, no doubt, for the failure of the Disciples to grow at Savannah in those years.

In August, 1844, Dunning joined Dr. Daniel Hook in conducting a protracted meeting at the Antioch Church in Clarke County. It was credited by Nathan W. Smith with arousing the evangelistic passion of the struggling congregation: "The church had been so edified and strenthened in numbers . . . that a missionary spirit pervaded it, and so wonderful was this influence that they started me out as their evangelist to preach at different points."[5]

Dunning sought to follow the New Testament practice of every Christian being an evangelist. Smith and Dunning joined in the summer of 1846 for preaching in

---

[3]Nathan W. Smith, *op. cit.*, May 17, 1879, p. 156.

[4]*Gospel Advocate*, Apr. 1857, quoted in Barfield, *op. cit.*, p. 34.

[5]Mary D. Howell, "The Life of Dr. Daniel Hook" (Unpublished MS., 1875), p. 53. Typed copy in possession of The Disciples of Christ Historical Society, Nashville, Tenn.

Georgia and Alabama. Thereafter, until Dunning's death, every summer and into the autumn, the two preached together at many places.

Like Alexander Campbell in 1838, and other brethren, Dr. and Mrs. Hook were among those who enjoyed the Christian hospitality of the Dunning home. Dr. Hook and Dunning traveled and preached together often. Early in 1856, the Hooks were in Savannah and South Carolina. Dr. Hook preached in the Dunning home "and in the houses of other members."[6]

Dunning died of apoplexy at Savannah, Apr. 2, 1858, at the age of 78.[7] He was buried in Laurel Grove Cemetery there. When his estate was settled, it was found that a corner lot in Savannah, owned by Dunning, was kept vacant for years. It seemed that he intended to use it for a church building. However, there was no provision for disposition to the church, so the property went to his heirs. After his passing, the Dunning family moved to Augusta and no more was heard of the members in the annals of Georgia Disciples.

DR. DANIEL HOOK (1795-1870)

Largely responsible for organizing the Augusta, Griffin, Acworth, Sandersville, and other congregations, Dr. Daniel Hook was Georgia's first state evangelist among the Disciples. He was one of the first persons to proclaim their plea in the Deep South. His frank, cordial manner and commanding appearance made him an attractive person.

Youngest of four children, he was born Apr. 6, 1795, at Point of Rocks, Frederick County, Md., the son of John and Sarah (Burgess) Hook. He was christened an Episcopalian. While an infant, his mother died. His father married again and moved to Kentucky. Daniel and his sister, Mary D., were adopted by a wealthy

---

[6]*Ibid.*, p. 60.

[7]*Millennial Harbinger,* May, 1858, p. 293.

bachelor uncle, James S. Hook. The boy's childhood was spent at the uncle's Potomac Hills estate, Daniel's birthplace.

After attending school near home, Daniel enrolled at Carlyle College in Pennsylvania. His uncle urged him to take up law, but the young man preferred medical study. He was graduated from the University of Maryland School of Medicine at Baltimore with the M.D. degree in 1820. He had received a B.M. degree in 1819. The uncle lost his slaves and land, making Daniel dependent upon his own resources.

Twenty-two and single, Dr. Hook began practicing medicine at Louisville, former state capital in Jefferson County, Ga., in 1817. Medical licensure was not strict then. In the spring of 1818 he was married to Miss Catherine Schley. She was the daughter of John Jacob Schley and the sister of William Schley, Georgia Congressman, elected twice, and eighteenth Governor of Georgia (1835-37), and several other distinguished brothers. The couple lived together more than 50 years before death separated them. They had two sons and four daughters; one, Mary, became, in 1853, the wife of Clark Howell, a judge. A son, James Schley Hook, became a judge and married the sister of T. M. Harris, preacher for years in Georgia churches.

Already a Disciple, as noted previously, Dr. Hook moved to Augusta in 1832. He built his home, Richmond Hill, six miles south of the town. In 1834 or 1835, every member of the family was stricken with scarlet fever. The two youngest children, Emily and America, died. The home was sold eventually to Dr. Hook's brother-in-law, Judge John Schley, and the Hook family established residence at Augusta. When William Schley was elected Governor of Georgia in November, 1835, Dr. Hook became president of the Richmond Factory, for cotton and woolen manufacture, which the two owned.

In the summer of 1839 a yellow fever epidemic scourged Augusta. Dr. Hook discovered it and remained in town

with the stricken.   After successfully treating more than
200 patients, and losing only two, he became ill.

. . . When he found the fever coming on him, he sat down on
the steps he was ascending to see a patient, and wrote out his
own treatment, and directed his driver when he returned to
his carriage, to give it to Dr. Johnson (who had adopted his
treatment) and tell him to pursue it strictly.   He was ill for
several weeks, but finally recovered.[8]

As a result of his sacrificial service, the citizens of
Augusta expressed their gratitude by electing Dr. Hook
mayor, first in 1840 for a one-year term, and then re-
electing him in 1842.   His name was first proposed for
the honor by a local newspaperman.

He received additional recognition, too.   He was elected
a trustee of the University of Georgia by the State Legislature.   He was a member of the first Board of Trustees
of the Atlanta Medical College and served on the 1853
Board of Health there.   He was the first physician in the
state to use quinine in medical practice.   As a Mason,
he was the first grand secretary in Georgia of the Masonic
Grand Lodge and had an address on Masonry printed
and circulated widely by that fraternity.

Those things, however, did not cause him to neglect
his religious interests and his fervent desire for the union
of all Christians.   Seldom did anything interfere with
Dr. Hook's preaching.   His daughter narrated one time
when something did, however, in the following words:

. . . Such was his zeal that he could preach to a few with as
much fervor as though the house had been filled with an enthusiastic audience.   One night just for a little pleasantry, the
seven persons who composed the congregation, seated themselves
in seven pews in front of the other in a straight row.   Dr. Hook
saw a straight streak of faces looking at him merrily, and while
his face showne for one moment with an amused expression, he
at once proceeded with his duties and with all the solemnity
and order of the occasion.[9]

---

[8]Mary D. Howell, *op. cit.,* p. 17.   Most of the material for this sketch
came from Mrs. Howell's unpublished biography of her father.

[9]*Ibid.,* pp. 25 f.

After Alexander Campbell's popular visit to Augusta in the spring of 1845, the orthodox residents concocted a scheme to discredit Dr. Hook and the congregation of Disciples. Even a professional boycott was resorted to, apparently, for, financially embarrassed, Dr. Hook, 50 years old, moved from Augusta.

The Augusta brethren aided him in the crisis. They sent him out as a general evangelist in May, 1845, supporting his family. In March, 1849, he organized the Griffin church with seven members. He was welcomed in both Georgia and South Carolina, but the small compensation temporarily crushed him.

He moved back to Jefferson County in August, 1847, and resumed medical practice with his son, Dr. Edward D. Hook. He preached whenever doors were opened to him, which was seldom. Meanwhile, he continued as presiding elder of the Augusta church and attended services there "pretty regularly in winter, and by consent, irregularly in summer."[10] Samuel J. Pinkerton of Kentucky became the Augusta pastor in 1847 after Dr. Hook's departure.

In 1849 Dr. Hook's Georgia brethren really honored him. He was their representative at the first national convention of the brotherhood at Cincinnati, Ohio, in October. There he was elected vice-president of the assembly and helped to organize the American Christian Missionary Society that had elected Alexander Campbell as its first president. The spirit of cooperation was lifting the spirits of the brethren from Georgia to Ohio and beyond!

In 1849 Dr. Hook was unanimously elected as the first Georgia state evangelist. In August, 1851, he moved to Atlanta and soon established a congregation which became the First Christian Church. As previously stated, he helped to organize other churches. The number included Berea of Henry County which sent more youth into the ministry than any other Christian church in Georgia.

---

[10]*Ibid.*, p. 36.

About 1857 he had a debate with a Methodist minister of Sandersville. Dr. Hook answered the pamphlet attack on him, called *Campbellism Exposed,* with another entitled, *A Tract in Reply to An Attack of Rev. Mr. Mysic.*[11] Dr. Hook's last days were "financially easy." His biographer stated:

. . . He was in very comfortable circumstances in life. His home, bought in Atlanta, on Decatur Street, proved a good investment, and other sales of property, both in Atlanta and Alabama, had realized fair profits on the cost, and his services as minister were highly appreciated, and paid for accordingly, so that his last days are best in every way—financially easy—and his whole heart and life consecrated to the work of God.[12]

His death occurred on July 27, 1870, at the home of his daughter, Mrs. Howell, near Atlanta. He was 75 years old. "He did not die rich, but he died with all the honors that became a man and a Christian."[13]

JAMES JENKINS TROTT (1800-1868)

One of the most dramatic personalities among Georgia's pioneer Disciples is hardly known to his spiritual descendants. He was James Jenkins Trott, fearless missionary to the Cherokee Indians and traveling evangelist who almost became a martyr.

Born in North Carolina, Nov. 4, 1800, he moved with his parents about 1815 to Middle Tennessee. His parents were Methodists. In 1823 James joined the Methodist "travelling connexion" and soon showed missionary qualifications. In 1825 or 1826 he was commissioned by the Tennessee Methodist Conference to preach and teach among the Cherokees in Georgia. In 1828 he married a part-Cherokee girl, Sallie Adair, and later baptized her in the Oothealoga River. They were parents of two children, Benjamin Walter and Mary Thompson Trott. The wife and mother died in 1831.

---

[11]*Ibid.,* pp. 23, 64, 65. Claude E. Spencer (Compiler), *An Author Catalog of Disciples of Christ and Related Religious Groups* (Canton, Missouri: Disciples of Christ Historical Society, 1946), p. 154.

[12]Mary D. Howell, *op. cit.,* p. 68.

[13]*Ibid.,* p. ii. *Christian Standard,* Aug. 27, 1870, p. 276.

The Methodist Mission to the Cherokees began in 1822. It supplemented the work of Presbyterians and Moravians. The missions were a significant civilizing influence for the Indians. By 1831 the Methodist Mission, with which Trott was affiliated, had "seventeen missionaries, including interpreters."[14] There were six schools, about 120 pupils, and 930 Indian Christians.[15]

Agitation to remove the Indians to territory west of the Mississippi River increased across several years. President Thomas Jefferson advocated such a policy in 1803. A large number remaining in Georgia decided not to leave. A long legal struggle ensued before the last Cherokees left Georgia in 1838. The conflict grew in intensity because the Georgians regarded presence of the Indians as intolerable. Georgia charged the Federal Government with sectional favoritism.

The Georgia Legislature, determined to resist the Indians to the limit, on Dec. 20, 1828, extended the state's jurisdiction over the Cherokee country. Gold, discovered in Georgia in 1829, brought lawless people into the area. In 1830, the Legislature required all white people, including missionaries, to obtain a license for residence in the disputed area. Such persons were also to take an oath solemnly swearing to "support and defend the constitution and laws of the state of Georgia, and uprightly demean"[16] themselves as citizens thereof. The missionaries' contempt for the state's authority was shown in their refusal to request the permits, thus inviting arrest. That took place on Mar. 12, 1831.

After arrest of the missionaries, and others, they appeared before Judge Augustin S. Clayton in Gwinnett

---

[14]J. M. Reid, *Missions and Missionary Society of the Methodist Episcopal Church* (New York: Hunt & Eaton; Cincinnati: Cranston & Curts, 1879), p. 113.

[15]Enoch Mudge, *History of American Missions to the Heathen,* From Their Commencement to the Present Time (Worcester: Spooner & Howland, 1840), p. 539.

[16]Quoted in C. D. Mallary, *Memoirs of Elder Jesse Mercer* (New York: John Gray, 1844), p. 219.

County Superior Court. The missionaries were released on their plea that they were Federal government agents educating and Christianizing the Indians. Subsequently, the Governor advised the missionaries to take the oath, or abandon their labors and leave the state within ten days or be arrested again.

The missionaries ignored the Governor's urgent plea and remained indignant at repeated intimidations. Consequently, there were additional arrests on July 7. The missionaries were then brutally manhandled by the Georgia militia who chained them and compelled them to walk 22 miles to Camp Gilmer where they were placed in custody. Three of the eleven arrested were missionaries, including Trott. He was under bond for residing in the Cherokee area without the required license, refusal to take the oath of allegiance, and for returning to his family while the case was pending. He could die at his post, if necessary, but he would not desert it.

The trial took place at Lawrenceville in September. The prisoners were defended by several attorneys, including General Harden of Athens, who volunteered in their behalf and worked without compensation. The jury found all guilty and they were sentenced to four years in the State Penitentiary. Executive clemency was recommended if the convicted men would take the oath of allegiance or leave the Cherokee territory.

Upon arrival of the convicts at the penitentiary at Milledgeville, they learned that Governor George R. Gilmer (1790-1859) had directed the penitentiary inspectors to learn from each prisoner if he would promise to leave Georgia and accept a pardon. A formal report of the conversations was made to the Governor the same day.

. . . It briefly states the conversations with each of the convicts, the promises of all but the missionaries of the Board [Samuel A. Worcester and Elizur Butler], to leave the State if pardoned, and the testimony of Mr. Worcester and Dr. Butler to the general good character of their fellow convicts. Those who promised, were all pardoned and discharged.[17]

Most historians of the exciting episode stated that Trott was released because he took the oath of allegiance to Georgia. However, he wrote under the pseudonym of "Cherokee" just a few weeks after the incident that "I have been arrested, chained, imprisoned, condemned, reprieved, and banished the territory of the state, because I refused to take, what I believe to be, an unconstitutional and impious oath!"[18]

Trott's detailed account of his insubordination varied with others, contemporary and otherwise. It was written in answer to the remarks of "Tsawna" in the Nashville *Christian Advocate* of May 14, 1831, regarding Trott's "wearing a chain for the Lord's sake." The Trott account is not readily available in Georgia so it is inserted here, complete except for three introductory paragraphs and two incidental concluding sentences from the *Christian Review,* as follows:

1. The God of Nature and of Nations, in the exercise of a wise Providence, placed the Cherokees on the territory which they then occupied.

2. The Kings of Great Britain, the Collonial governments and the United States solemnly guaranteed to them, in numerous instances, the perpetual occupancy of the same.

3. The Congress of the United States had passed many "intercourse laws," making it the sworn duty of the Executive department of our great Nation to employ the military force of the United States to protect them in the peaceable occupancy of their territory against all the powers of earth.

4. In the winter of 1830, the Legislature of Georgia made a law extending the criminal jurisdiction of the State over a large portion of the Cherokee territory, making it a high misdemeanor, punishable by four years' confinement in the Penitentiary, at

---

17Joseph Tracy (Compiler), *History of the American Board of Commissioners for Foreign Missions,* p. 218, included in Mudge, *op. cit.* Gilmer, twice Governor of Georgia, had a brother, John Gilmer (1792-1860), who was an elder of the Disciples of Christ at Columbus, Miss. (*Gospel Advocate,* Feb. 1860, pp. 62 f.).

18*Millennial Harbinger,* Feb. 1832, p. 85.

hard labor, for any white man to reside in that part of the Nation, after June 1st, 1831, without first having taken an oath to "support the Constitution and laws of the State, and uprightly to demean himself, as a citizen of the same;" and a military force called the "Georgia Guards," was sent into the country to enforce the law.

5. In the fall of 1830, I was reappointed as a Missionary to the Cherokee Nation, by the Tennessee Conference of which I was then a member, being the fifth year of my missionary labors among the Cherokees. At the time of my appointment, the Conference knew nothing of the law above named, for it was not then passed, and consequently I had no instruction from the Conference in regard to it.

6. *Believing* that the law was *unconstitutional,* and *knowing* that it was passed for the purpose of stripping the Cherokees of religious and educational privileges, by driving the Missionaries from the field of their labors, in order to force the Nation into a treaty with the United States, I could not conscientiously take such oath. I was compelled to do this, leave my field of labor, without any instructions to that effect, or continue at my post of honor in the Lord, and leave the event with Him; and, in the name of the Lord, I prefered the latter alternative.

7. Shortly after the law was enforced, I was arrested by the Georgia Military Guard, compelled to walk over one hundred miles, chained and imprisoned several days, transfered to the civil authorities, committed, and gave bond and security for my appearance at the ensuing Superior Court for trial. I then returned to my field of labor, supposing the inhuman treatment I had received would suffice.

8. But this "civil power" of Mr. "Tsawna" was not content with one act of _____ _____. Having traveled once around my circuit I was torn a second time from the fond embrace of an affectionate family and put in chains. Two Missionaries of the American Board—Messrs. Worcester and Butler,—were also arrested at this time. On our way to headquarters Mr. Mc-Leode,—the Superintendent of the Methodist Missionaries among the Cherokees,—who came as a kind of brother to "minister to my necessities," was also arrested, and became one of our fellow prisoners, "for the Lord's sake." This is not all: Mr. Wells, his fellow traveler, who followed after, at a respectful distance, leading McLeode's horse, was severely beaten with a club, by the commanding officer of this "civil power." Mr. Butler was compelled to ride some distance, after night, with one end of a chain fastened around his neck and the other around the neck of the horse. We now had four preachers in chains, and a fifth cruelly beaten with a club. On, we were

driven afoot, exhausted, cursed, slandered, ridiculed at the point of the bayonet, some 80 miles to Head Quarters, and then cast into a filthy prison. The last command we received from the Captain of the band was:— ''D____ you, go in there! and from there to hell.'' Mr. McLeode was released after some three days' imprisonment. After twelve days' resistance in this military purgatory we were handed over to the civil authority, committed, gave bond and returned home.

9. We appeared at Circuit Court in September for trial. The ablest counsel in the State were employed on both sides. The case was argued some four days; and what do you suppose was the result? We were found guilty! Guilty of what? Of living on the face of the earth without swearing allegiance to the State of Georgia! Citizens—free born citizens of the United States, whose fathers purchased and sealed to them, with their heart's blood, the heaven born privilege of breathing the air of every clime and every State in this great Republic, without being molested in their civil or religious rights,—found guilty of a *high misdemeanor,* and sentenced to four years' imprisonment!

10. We were carried in bonds to the capital of the State. Mr. St. Clair, the stationed preacher of the Methodist church at that place, on our arrival had an interview with us, and kindly sought our release. We were urged to take the oath, or petition the Governor for a reprieve. We refused. Messrs. Worcester and Butler had specific instructions. I had none. They were ordered to *prison,* and I was *banished!*

Now, in view of the above facts, who, but some cold hearted political or religious partisan, would seek to slander those who suffered such indignities for the Lord's sake, by publishing them to the world as rebels against ''the civil power?''

But, this is not all: he says, ''I took the oath! This is a slander, and has not the shadow of truth in it, whether written or oral, and is utterly false in every shape and form. I was not only willing to be imprisoned four years, but by the help of my Lord and Master, to suffer death even, rather than take such an oath as I understood that to be. . . .[19]

By 1834 white people were occupying Cherokee land in Georgia. As the unhappy impasse dragged on, the Indians were given two years to leave. By 1838, after additional legal maneuvers and President Andrew Jackson's continued refusal to enforce a Supreme Court

[19]*Christian Review,* Aug. 1847, pp. 257 ff. *Gospel Advocate,* Apr. 29, 1869, pp. 399 f.

decision, Federal troops under General Winfield Scott forced the departure of the Cherokees for the West over the unfortunate "trail of tears." Those able to avoid the ruthless roundup finally obtained a legal foothold on a North Carolina reservation where their descendants reside to this day. Thus, the economic interests of Georgia, rather than the Constitution of the United States, won the long struggle with the missionaries claiming a moral victory.

In 1831, while Trott was in prison, he read Alexander Campbell's writings. Trott was immersed in Overall's Creek near Murfreesboro, Tenn., on Oct. 31, 1831, by Peyton Smith, popular Baptist minister who had become a Disciple. Trott regarded his immersion as a "withdrawal from the Methodist connexion."[20] The 1832 Tennessee Methodist Conference, therefore, left him without an appointment.[21]

Although Trott was dedicated to service to the Cherokees, he did not follow them immediately into the new territory. He engaged in evangelistic work in Georgia, some of which was noted previously, and Tennessee with white Disciples and won many converts. It is not certain how he was able to travel, let alone evangelize, in Georgia following his abrupt banishment. Yet the records indicate that he did visit and preach in Georgia often.

In 1843 Trott resided at Woodbury in Cannon County, Tenn. Apparently he lived there for several years. During the spring of 1847, he preached at Augusta, Ga., and in South Carolina. He reported subsequently, as follows:

> The brethren in Augusta have an excellent meeting house, . . . The congregation is small; but the brethren and sisters are intelligent and pious, and, if they continue faithful, will, no doubt, be as a light shineth in a dark place, to the citizens of Augusta.
>
> Dr. Daniel Hook is the Bishop of this congregation. Brother Hook was among the first to plead the cause of reformation in

---

[20]*Millennial Harbinger*, Aug. 6, 1832, p. 389.

[21]*Ibid.*, Sept. 1833, p. 472.

the South. His labors have not been in vain. His venerable appearance, intelligence and ardent devotion, give him considerable influence, and qualify him to be very useful, especially in his evangelizing tours. . . . I preached three times on Lord's day, and once each night till Wednesday night, . . . The brethren evinced joy and gladness, and appeared to take fresh courage.

Friday, the 12th, we took our leave of brother Hook and his interesting family, and, in a short time, crossed the Savannah, and found ourselves in the "Palmetto State.". . .

Wednesday, March the 4th, . . . in company with brother [Ephraim A.] Smith, we directed our course to the Savannah river, where we awaited till Thursday morning about day light, for the arrival of a Boat. Then we parted, in the old fashioned way—"The Lord be with my dear brother!"

About day break, Friday morning, we landed at Augusta, and I remained with the brethren till after Lord's day, . . . [22]

Many of Trott's evangelistic travels, "trusting in the Lord for food and rainment," were in Tennessee, Georgia, and South Carolina. He was chairman of the Tennessee Cooperation Meeting in 1848 and was the first state evangelist for the Volunteer State.

According to the *Gospel Advocate* of April, 1856 (pp. 110 ff.), Trott surveyed the Cherokee situation. During four months he traveled 3,000 miles into Arkansas and Missouri by boat, rail, stage, horseback, and foot. He collected $166 for Indian work from Missouri friends and churches with the sanction of the American Christian Missionary Society. By late 1859 he had resumed his Cherokee Mission in what is now Oklahoma. He married Rachel Pounds Adair, also part Indian, years before; they had five sons and three daughters. Just before the Civil War began, a report from Trott stated:

We already have about 75 disciples in the Cherokee Nation. . . . Some of these are the result of our humble efforts in the old nation more than twenty years ago. . . . Having volunteered our humble efforts in this missionary field, free of charges to church or state, and having a large family to care for, we have not been able to devote as much time to preaching the word as we desired, and as the cause demands.[23]

[22]*Christian Review,* Apr. 1847, pp. 134 ff.
[23]*Millennial Harbinger,* Sept. 1860, p. 506.

The armies entered Cherokee territory in 1862 and Trott's provisions were confiscated, one son, Timothy, was killed, and the family driven away to Arkansas, then Missouri. As the family finally fled to Kansas, a daughter, Elizabeth, died of exposure on Christmas, 1862. In 1864, Kansas Disciples, convened at Tecumseh, chose Trott a state evangelist with some aid from the ACMS. Undaunted, in June, 1866, the unconventional Trott left Bellmont, Kan., to return to his mission work with the Cherokees.

Finally, broken in health, he realized that privations of the war years had taken their toll. Returning to Tennessee, James J. Trott died of pneumonia near Nashville on Dec. 10, 1868. He was 68. He was buried near Gallatin, Tenn. His wife, Rachel, five sons and three daughters survived.[24]

NATHAN WILLIAMSON SMITH (1813-1899)

Many congregations in Georgia, rendering an effective Christian witness, are living tributes to the long, sacrificial labors of Nathan Williamson Smith. As a pioneer evangelist, he preached in 40 counties of the state, was an organizer of several churches, and served 14 as pastor. He was the last of the six pioneers sketched in this chapter to be born and the last of them to die.

He was born about 40 miles from Greensboro in Rockingham County, N. C., on Sept. 4, 1813. "He had little education," he stated, attending "old field schools," where he learned to read, write, and do simple arithmetic. "He had access to about six books, but no newspapers."[25] Nevertheless, he taught school some and farmed to earn a livelihood.

Smith's acceptance of the plea of the Disciples was related in the preceding chapter. He was influenced by

[24]*Gospel Advocate*, Oct. 24, 1867, pp. 853 ff.; Jan. 7, 1869, p. 15; Mar. 25, 1869, pp. 271 ff. Emmet Starr, *History of the Cherokee Indians and Their Legends and Folk Lore* (Oklahoma City: Warden Co., 1921), pp. 406, 407, 605, 670.

[25]Nathan W. Smith, *op. cit.*, May 3, 1879, p. 142.

the Methodists. In 1832, about four months after his immersion by Arthur Dupree, Smith attended a revival, also held by Dupree, in Wilkes County. There Smith was fortunate to meet Miss Martha White. "After a few good horseback rides to and from campmeeting," —some 20 or more miles—he succeeded in "cutting out another young fellow who insisted upon a prior claim."[26] The two were married on Jan. 21, 1834, and lived together more than fifty-eight years before she died on Feb. 2, 1892. They had three sons and three daughters.

The Antioch Church sustained Smith as a general evangelist in Georgia for three years. He preached in schools, houses, brush arbors, and on the banks of streams. Seldom was a church building available. Often, when he preached, "great scalding tears [would] suffuse his face,"[27] a friend declared. He sang gospel songs during his younger years. His preaching was more often in Georgia, South Carolina, and Alabama, but occasionally it was in Tennessee, Kentucky, and Mississippi.

When Alexander Campbell preached at Augusta in 1845, Smith was present to hear the great reformer and to become acquainted. Both Dr. Hook and Mrs. Tubman had seen to that. Mrs. Tubman later supported Smith as state evangelist. Smith was so impressed with Campbell that he named one of his sons in honor of the religious editor and reformer.

Smith mentioned an act of Campbell's, following the 1845 trip, that throws light on Campbell's methods of distributing his publications, as follows:

. . . . After I saw Bro. Campbell in Augusta, in 1845, he sent me a lot of books to sell, of which I knew nothing until I received the invoice. I subsequently ordered from him books, and also Bro. James Challen while in Philadelphia, and then from Bro. H. S. Bosworth, of Cincinnati. But selling books at that time was rather a slow and not a very profitable business.

26A. G. Thomas, "Nathan W. Smith," *Christian Standard*, Apr. 9, 1892, pp. 310 f.

27*Loc. cit.*

My main object was to have them circulated and read by the
brethren and friends. I also sent and bought some tracts to
circulate among the people who would read them. . . .[28]

After Campbell's visit, Dr. Hook and Smith evangelized together in South Carolina and eastern Georgia,
forming several congregations. The difficulties of pioneer evangelism, even to physical exhaustion, were put
into the record by Smith in the following sentences:

The two Bros. Fears, A. B. and Wm. S., came to the knowledge of the scripture truths as taught by the Disciples, by reading our publications, and they have been great workers. I received them into a small congregation I had gathered in Fayette
county. They rode 25 miles from their homes to have and
enjoy church privileges. I used to preach in a school-house
in their vicinity in passing, but so great was the prejudice and
opposition, could not get more than a half-dozen hearers. And
in 1845, while Bro. Hook was with me, Bro. Wm. S. Fears made
an appointment for us to preach at his house, and gave the
appointment publicity through the neighborhood. The time
came and we were on hand. Now for our hearers. Two neighbor young men and Bro. Fears' family of whites and blacks, all
told.

Bro. Hook, always ready to do all he could, preached doubtless, a good sermon. I was tired and sleepy, and I confess I
took a short nap.[29]

The year 1849 was significant for Georgia Disciples
and Nathan W. Smith. He traveled across the state, at
his own expense, promoting the first state-wide cooperation meeting of his brethren at Griffin. Always, he remained a staunch advocate of Christian cooperation.
Then, he moved to the new Cass County (now Bartow),
near Acworth, where he resided for several years,
preaching at Griffin, County Line and Berea (at Hampton) churches. He built a home, called Enon since
"there was much water." He later resided at several
other places.

Smith usually preached for a freewill offering. In
1838, after six months of evangelizing, he received a

[28]Nathan W. Smith, *op. cit.*, May 24, 1879, p. 166.
[29]*Loc. cit.*

"salary" of four dollars.[30]   One year he made $700, but that was the exception.   Otherwise, the most he earned in one year was $400.   "While some of them paid a very small salary and some paid nothing, I do not think I exaggerate by saying nearly one-half my labors have been given to the good cause gratuitously; . . ."[31]   He was tried most severely during the war years, as will be noted later.

Death came to Smith at the home of his daughter, Mrs. R. M. Mitchell, at Acworth, on Aug. 10, 1899, when he was 85.   He gave more than 60 years of consecrated service to establishing the cause of the Disciples in Georgia.

Mrs. Emily H. Tubman (1794-1885)

Probably the most generous, philanthropic, pioneer woman of the Disciples in Georgia, or elsewhere, was Mrs. Emily H. Tubman of Augusta.   She was a notable example of Christian stewardship in that she prayed and paid.

Emily Harvey Thomas was born at Ashland, Hanover County, Va., about twenty-five miles north of Richmond, Mar. 21, 1794.   Her father, Edmund Pendleton Thomas, moved his family to Lexington, Ky., in 1796, and from there to Frankfort.   He was appointed registrar in the land office, but died about 1802.   As pioneers, Thomas and his wife, Ann (Chiles), named their first son, Western.   They had two other children: Louise A. and Landon A.

After her father's death, Henry Clay (1777-1852), American orator and statesman, became Emily's legal guardian.   In 1818, she accompanied her mother's cousins, Mr. and Mrs. Nicholas Ware, to Augusta, Ga., when they returned from Frankfort.   The young lady rode horseback, taking her wardrobe in saddlebags.   During

---

[30]*Loc. cit.*

[31]*Ibid.*, May 31, 1879, p. 174.

a season of gay social festivities in the Ware home at
Telfair and Center Streets, Emily met Richard C. Tub-
man, wealthy Marylander. They were married in 1818.
After a honeymoon in Kentucky, they returned to
Augusta in 1819 to make their winter home, going to
Frankfort for the summers.

The Tubmans entertained many prominent Americans
like Henry Clay and Alexander H. Stephens (1812-1883),
later vice-president of the Confederacy. She directed
the women who planned the banquet at Planters Hotel,
Augusta, in 1825, honoring Marquis de LaFayette (1757-
1834). Mrs. Tubman led the graceful minuet with the
illustrious French general.

Every summer the Tubmans journeyed to Frankfort
in their carriage[32] and from there, often, to health re-
sorts like White Sulphur Springs, Va. He was in poor
health for several years prior to his death in 1836. He
died in his wife's arm at Lincolnton, Wilkes County, Ga.,
enroute to Kentucky. He was buried there, but the remains were later removed, according to his request, and
interred in a crypt beneath historic St. Paul's Episcopal
Church, Augusta. A vestryman of the congregation, he
gave generously for erection of the building. Mrs. Tubman attended Episcopal services with her husband, but
never joined that church.

The Tubmans had no children. So after his death, Mrs.
Tubman's sister, Mrs. Louise A. Keiningham, resided
with her.

As previously noted, Mrs. Tubman was baptized near
Frankfort, Ky., in 1828, four years before organization
of the Christian church there. She met Alexander Campbell soon afterward and advocated his religious teach-

---

[32]After Mr. Tubman's death in 1836, she drove in her carriage, until
railroads operated, every June, via Nashville, to Frankfort, to visit her
brother, Landon A. Thomas, in his palatial home, a landscaped mansion
still standing at 312 Washington Street, three blocks from the Frankfort
church. She returned to Augusta every November.

ings after a thorough study of them.[33] In 1836, the year of her husband's death, Mrs. Tubman joined the little group of Augusta Disciples.

Mrs. Tubman's gifts to Disciples and their work were most generous, time and again, for many purposes.

At Augusta, she provided the first building of her brethren. It was a brick edifice on Reynolds Street, in 1842. It cost about $8,000. It was replaced years later on centrally located lots which Mrs. Tubman bought at Greene and McIntosh Streets. Her gift of more than $100,000 erected and furnished the structure, with organ. An adjoining manse was provided and the pastor's salary endowed! Dedication was on Jan. 2, 1876. The old church building, given to the city, became Tubman High School.

When Chapman S. Lucas (1849-1896) was Augusta minister, he formed a new church. It was provided, in 1882, by Mrs. Tubman, with a building and the minister's salary was endowed. The congregation is now known as the Central Christian Church.

The Savannah church, in 1886, had a revival with Mr. Lucas preaching. Services were in the new building even though the walls had no plaster. It was in January and cold weather forced early closing of the meeting. Mrs. Tubman learned of the situation when Mr. Lucas returned, and sent the Savannah brethren $1,000 to complete their edifice.

Mrs. Tubman also gave funds for rebuilding of Hunter Street Church (now First Christian) in Atlanta, after

---

[33]Many religious books, pamphlets, and periodicals from Mrs. Tubman's personal library are preserved, in 1954, in the Philip Fall Memorial Library of the First Christian Church of Frankfort, Ky. Nearly all are rare items of Discipliana, the more so because they have her autograph. The most interesting, perhaps, is Isaac Errett's *Talks to Bereans* (Cincinnati, 1872) inscribed on the fly leaf thus: "To Mrs. E. H. Tubman with Christian regards of Isaac Errett, Cinti. Oct. 21, 1872." He dedicated the new Frankfort church, in August, 1872. Another item is *A Discourse on the Three Salvations* by B. F. Hall, printed in 1838 by J. C. Noble, Cheapside. The proceeds, if any, after paper and printing charges were paid, went to Bacon College, the brotherhood's first educational institution that began in 1836 at Georgetown, Ky.

the Civil War, and the Athens church. She aided, too, in financing the publication of the *Christian Union,* a periodical that began in 1856.

As might be expected, Mrs. Tubman contributed generously to public and private charities of Augusta, totaling perhaps as much as $25,000 a year. She gave to many church building projects of Augusta. A tract, *The Name Christian,* by E. R. Clarkson, provided an interesting account of how carefully Mrs. Tubman distributed her funds. The incident was described thus:

. . . On one occasion a certain minister of that city solicited Mrs. Tubman for a donation to rebuild his church, which had recently been destroyed by fire. This ardent advocate of "Bible names for Bible things," replied that she would gladly contribute toward the rebuilding of the house of worship on the condition that it would honor only Christ in the name it should bear. Whereupon the Reverend gentleman endeavored to convince the good woman that there is really nothing in a name. When he had concluded his rather lengthy and learned argument, Mrs. Tubman, without a word, turned to her desk and wrote him a check for a handsome sum, signing it with the name of one of her Negro servants. Flushed with pride over his supposed victory, the minister hastened to the bank to deposit the check, and without having examined it, presented it to the bank clerk for deposit. But to his great amazement the clerk refused to accept the check, saying that "this name is not known by the bank." Incredulous, the minister seized the check and for the first time discovered what he believed to be an error on the part of the donor, and rushed back to her home to apprise her of the mistake. But Mrs. Tubman calmly replied: "No, I have made no error. Did you not argue with me long and learnedly that there is nothing in a name. I only wished to convince you of the fallacy of your argument. This woman's name would not answer at the bank because it is unknown to the authorities. These human, distinguishing names are not known in the Bible, and will not be known in Heaven where we will all be one."[34]

Many young men obtained their education through Mrs. Tubman's generous assistance. Such gifts indicated a concern for a trained ministry. Those assisted included James S. Lamar and W. T. Moore (1832-1926), both, later, prominent Disciples. A gift from her helped

---

[34]Quoted in Barfield, *op. cit.,* p. 70.

to erect a Henry Clay monument at Lexington, Ky. During a cholera scourge in Kentucky, Mrs. Tubman sent funds to relieve the distress. When Alexander Campbell went to Europe in 1847, Mrs. Tubman sent $300 by him for the poor of Britain and Ireland.[35]

The Frankfort church always had a fond place in Mrs. Tubman's considerate heart. In 1872 a Romanesque building was dedicated by Isaac Errett, editor of the *Christian Standard,* on downtown Ann Street where the congregation still worships. She bought additional property for the structure, erected to replace one destroyed by fire in 1870. Her gift, including the cost of furnishings, totaled about $30,000. A simple inscription on the bell named Mrs. Tubman as the building's donor.[36] Her brother, Landon, was a trustee of the church at that time.[37] The stained window in the chancel of the present building is in memory of Mrs. Tubman.[38]

Christian educational institutions, too, received a share of Mrs. Tubman's funds. Bethany College was given $16,000 in 1857 and 1858 to endow the Tubman Chair of Modern Languages. Mrs. Tubman was entitled to keep five students at Bethany, tuition-free, as long as she lived.[39] She gave $1,000 to the college in 1844-45.[40] On behalf of her Kentucky brethren, she paid one-fifteenth of the endowment for Bethany's Chair of Sacred History. Her original gift to the college was $100.

---

[35]*Millennial Harbinger,* Apr. 1848, p. 214.

[36]Mrs. Robert Richardson Gum and Mrs. M. C. Darnell, ''History of the First Christian Church, Frankfort, Kentucky.'' Dedicated to the Memory of Mrs. Emily H. Tubman (Unpublished MS., 1947), p. 6.

[37]*Centennial Frankfort Christian Church,* Frankfort, Kentucky, 1832-1932 (No publisher, no date, no pagination).

[38]Mrs. Tubman, accompanied by her sister-in-law, Mrs. Landon Thomas, purchased a communion service for the new Frankfort church, in Cincinnati. The plates were used until July, 1938, and are now in the Philip Fall Memorial Library of the church.

[39]W. K. Woolery, *Bethany Years,* The Story of Old Bethany From Her Founding Years Through a Century (Huntington, West Virginia: Standard Printing & Publishing Co., 1941), p. 45.

[40]*Millennial Harbinger,* July, 1845, p. 332.

Her educational investments also included a gift of
$20,000 for the endowment of the Kentucky Female Or-
phan School, Midway, Ky. She also contributed, too,
various amounts to Hiram (Ohio) College, Butler University of Indianapolis, and Transylvania College of
Lexington, Ky.

At her death, Mrs. Tubman's will provided "about
$200,000 to charitable purposes,"[41] it was reported. The
amount included a bequest of $30,000 for the Foreign
Christian Missionary Society. It was the largest single
gift that board had received. She was a life director
of that society. George Darsie (1846-1904) was the
Frankfort minister from 1876 until his death in 1904.
He claimed credit for Mrs. Tubman's significant support
of foreign missions, as follows:

> If I were asked what was the most important sermon I ever
> preached in this pulpit as regard financial results, I should say
> a sermon on foreign missions, preached on Sunday night, Oc-
> tober 21, 1883, which was heard by a noble Christian woman who
> said to me at the close of it, "I believe you have converted me
> to your view of the subject," and who, passing to her reward
> shortly after, left a bequest of $30,000 to our foreign missionary
> society, the largest it ever received.[42]

Mrs. Tubman shunned publicity about her gifts and
permitted no record to be kept of them. It was "a mod-
est characteristic of the Thomas family."[43] She received many pleading letters seeking aid, read them
with tears in her eyes often, frequently responding with
gifts of $50.00 to $200.00. She personally considered
every appeal. Her Frankfort pastor of her last years
said that, "One could approach her as easily as a child
its mother." On the other hand, her Augusta pastor
for many years, James S. Lamar, remarked at her funeral, in a sermon, that her giving was "never the result
of weakness and superficial sentiment."

41*Christian Companion*, Aug. 1885, p. 278.

42George Darsie, *Twenty-Five Years at Kentucky's Capital*. A Sermon
Preached at Frankfort, Ky., December 7th, 1902 (St. Louis: Christian
Publishing Co., 1902?), pp. 13 f.

43Gum and Darnell, *op. cit.*, p. 7.

After a short illness, Mrs. Tubman died at her Augusta
home on Tuesday morning, June 9, 1885. The funeral
was held at the First Christian Church on June 11, with
Mr. Lamar preaching. Chapman S. Lucas, Augusta pastor then, offered prayer and read the Scripture. The
remains were taken to Frankfort, Ky., for burial. The
diary of George Darsie, Frankfort minister, briefly described his participation in the final rites:

Friday, June 12, 1885

I arrived [at Frankfort, from Ohio] at 2:30 P.M.
Draping the church in memory of Mrs. Tubman.
Preparing for a memorial service Sunday.
The service tomorrow on arrival of remains will be very brief.

Saturday, June 13, 1885

Mrs. Tubman's body came on the 8 a.m. train. Procession
moved directly from depot to the cemetery. Bro. [Philip S.]
Fall prayed and I gave the benediction. Quite a long concourse.
I worked all forenoon and afternoon on the memorial address
and got it done by supper.

Sunday, June 14, 1885

Large cong. in morning to hear the memorial address on Mrs.
Tubman. My text—Prov. 31:31—Read it. About half hour
long.
Sent it off to the [Louisville] Courier-Journal at 5 p.m.
Bill Newhall says it will appear tomorrow.[44]

The body of Mrs. Tubman was laid to rest in the old
Frankfort Cemetery, where it remains, in an unpreten-
tious hill spot, overlooking the winding, enchanting Kentucky River, almost within sight of the grave of another
famous pioneer—Daniel Boone. Her brother and sister
survived Mrs. Tubman.

On the Sunday after her passing the Augusta congregation voted to have the "church and the pew which she

[44]Unpublished Diary of George Darsie for 1885, one of more than 30
of his annual journals in the Philip Fall Memorial Library of the First
Christian Church, Frankfort, Ky.

occupied" to "remain clad in mourning," the former
for sixty days and the latter for the remainder of the
year.[45]

Soon after Mrs. Tubman's death a memorial booklet
of twenty-seven pages was issued. It was entitled: *In
Memoriam. Mrs. Emily H. Tubman, born March 21st,
1794. Died June 9th, 1885.* It contained the funeral and
memorial messages of Lamar and Darsie.[46]

Born when George Washington was president of the
United States, Mrs. Tubman lived under all of the 22
American Presidents who had served up to the time of
her death. She died when Grover Cleveland was in his
first presidential term. Her most significant tribute,
perhaps, was expressed by George Darsie thus: "What
a glorious example she has left to our great brotherhood, and to Christian people everywhere, of the supreme
blessedness of giving!"

JAMES SHANNON (1799-1859)

Many Georgians of pre-Civil War days were fortunate
to have known and heard James Shannon, brilliant
thinker and an illustrious educator. One of the best educated pioneers of Georgia, he resided in the state fifteen
years or more, was married to a Georgian, and may have
become a Disciple while in the state.

James P. Shannon was born in Monaghan County, Ireland, Apr. 22, 1799. The son of farmers, he was educated for the Presbyterian ministry at the University of
Belfast. He won prizes in Latin, Greek, mathematics,
and philosophy. He was graduated when nineteen. Two
years later he received the Master of Arts degree when
he completed his seminary course. Then, for eighteen
months, he assisted James Carley in his academy.[47]

---

[45]*Augusta Evening News,* June 23, 1885, reprinted in the *Christian
Standard,* July 4, 1885, p. 215.

[46]The only copy known to be preserved in 1954 is in the Philip Fall
Memorial Library of the First Christian Church at Frankfort, Ky.

[47]Charles Hunter Hamlin, ''The Militant James Shannon,'' *Discipliana,*
July, 1944, p. 15.

In 1821, Shannon became president of the Presbyterian's Sunbury (Ga.) Academy, considered one of the best schools in the state, "at the unheard of salary of $2,000."[48] He sought ordination to the ministry with the Presbyterians, but after a study of infant baptism, he refused to be ordained. About 1822 or 1823 he was immersed by Charles O. Screven, Baptist minister. In 1826, Shannon succeeded W. T. Brantly, Sr., as pastor of the Augusta Baptist Church.[49]

Shannon took an active part in Georgia Baptist affairs. He delivered the significant educational address at the 1827 Georgia Baptist Convention and vigorously defended the right to promote education. The address was published in the convention minutes. He subscribed $100 to the Baptist educational fund started at the 1829 convention. A Baptist historian nominated Shannon near the bottom of a list of twelve pioneer "apostles of Baptist education in Georgia."[50]

About 1830 Shannon left Augusta to teach ancient languages in the University of Georgia at Athens. While there he established the Athens Baptist Church and was its pastor until 1835. He baptized his pulpit successor there.

Shannon left Athens in 1835 to become president of the College of Louisiana, a state school at Jackson. While there he first met Alexander Campbell who was his guest and lectured eight times. Shannon also organized a new congregation of Disciples at Jackson. The desire, if nothing more, for the fellowship of the Disciples was stimulated while he lived and worked in Georgia. He received the *Millennial Harbinger* as early as 1830. One writer indicated, however, that he did not

[48]George L. Peters, *Dreams Come True*, A History of Culver-Stockton College (Canton, Missouri: Culver-Stockton College, 1941), p. 49.

[49]Ragsdale, *op. cit.*, I, 43.

[50]*Ibid.*, I, 34.

become a Disciple until after his removal to Jackson.[51]
His ties with Georgia Disciples were never broken completely after he left the state.

After Shannon left Georgia, he wrote a series of essays for *The Christian Index,* Georgia Baptist periodical. His eighth article to the editor was submitted for publication, but it was returned. The refused essay appeared in the *Morning Watch* of the Disciples.[52]

The continued influence of Shannon in Georgia was shown by the reprinting in the *Morning Watch* of his sermon, "How to Be Saved," in four monthly issues, beginning in December, 1837, and running through March, 1838. It was taken from the *Christian Preacher* of Cincinnati, where it ran in the July and August, 1837, numbers. A lengthy appendix, which the *Morning Watch* did not publish, indicated Shannon's religious trials. In "flagrant injustice" to his views, he was represented as a "furious, pugilistic sectarian." In his refutation, he said:

. . . Heaven is not farther from hell than this representation is from the truth. So far from pursuing a sectarian course, I have repeatedly, during the last fourteen years, put all my earthly prospects in jeopardy, because *I would not be a sectarian,*—prospects, too, I may safely say, without the least imputation of vanity, as bright as were enjoyed by but few of my age in the Union. During that period, for no other cause than that I would not be a sectarian, I have suffered all but martyrdom, in feeling, perhaps fifty times. So far from crying "water," all the time, as if "folks were going to be saved by water, and nothing else," it is almost the only point in religion about which I have been silent. In the last ten years, or thereabouts, I have spoken but once on the mode of baptism and that, too, in reply to a direct attack that was made upon me in the state of Georgia.[53]

---

[51]M. C. Tiers, *The Christian Portrait Gallery:* Consisting of Historical and Biographical Sketches and Photographic Portraits of Christian Preachers and Others (Cincinnati: Published by Author, 1864), p. 130.

[52]*Morning Watch,* Apr., 1839, pp. 101 ff. The June, 1839, issue had Shannon's, "An Inquiry Into the Terms of Christian Union," pp. 161 ff.

[53]*Christian Preacher,* Aug., 1837, pp. 179 f.

From the College of Louisiana, in 1840, Shannon went to the presidency of Bacon College, Harrodsburg, Ky., at great sacrifice and pecuniary loss. He was also minister of the Harrodsburg Christian Church. The school had moved there from Georgetown, Ky., where it began in 1836 as the first collegiate institution of the brotherhood with Walter Scott as the first president, at least in name.

In November, 1843, while at Bacon, Shannon was one of four persons to assist Alexander Campbell in his debate with the Rev. N. L. Rice, Presbyterian, at Lexington, Ky. It was just a few weeks after the stirring revival meeting which Shannon assisted his brethren in conducting at Antioch Church, noted in the last chapter.

Campbell heard Shannon preach in April, 1857, at Augusta, Ga., from Acts 11:26. The Sage of Bethany was stimulated and subsequently investigated Shannon's position thoroughly, but failed to change his own original attitude. Campbell, was, however, impressed by Shannon. One observer who knew them both stated:

. . . Mr. Campbell regarded James Shannon not only as a Christian gentleman, but as a scholar of rare culture. I heard him remark that the address delivered, or read, before the Bible Union Convention at Memphis, 1852, by President Shannon, was composed of the purest English he had been permitted to hear in the United States.[54]

That was extravagant praise, indeed, the more especially so, considering its source.

Shannon left Bacon College in 1850 to become the second president of the University of Missouri at Columbia, where he served, also, as pastor of the Disciples. That state university was not opened to women students until the 1870's. As a result of that restriction, Shannon was instrumental in the establishment of Christian College in 1851 at Columbia. It was the first college for

[54]W. C. Rogers, *Recollections of Men of Faith* (St. Louis: Christian Publishing Co., 1889), pp. 17 f.

women west of the Mississippi River. He had eight
daughters and went "to Columbia with the distinct understanding that a college would be established to teach
his girls, and the daughters of other parents who sought
these advantages for them."[55]

He delivered the oration for the cornerstone of Christian University (now Culver-Stockton College) at Canton, Mo., which was placed in 1853. In 1855, Shannon
was removed as president of the University of Missouri.
He held strong pro-slavery views which may have been
the reason. By 1856 he had left Columbia to become
president of the new Christian University at Canton.
He did not serve there long, however, since death took
him after a short illness on Feb. 25, 1859. He was buried
at Columbia.

Another tie which Shannon had with Georgia was with
his daughter, Virginia. She became the wife of John
Faulk and they resided on a plantation in Houston
County. A Christian church, organized there in November, 1885, was named Virginia Hall Church in Mrs.
Faulk's honor. Her brother, Lenoir, was baptized at
that time, thus making all of Shannon's eight daughters
and three sons members of the Disciples of Christ.

Thus, the records show after a century, that the six
outstanding pioneers of the Disciples in Georgia were
quite varied personalities. They were associated with
other noble spirits, critics of tradition, too, and all
stormed the citadels of orthodoxy and firmly established
their faith in the state. Their voices and bodies often
grew weary, but seldom their spirits. They realized that
they, with the help of God, could change the pattern of
orthodoxy and answer men's deep longings. Laboring
sacrificially, they were concerned with immediate results,
of course, but they built stronger foundations for the
future than they realized. Their pace was forward, even

---

[55]St. Louis (Mo.) *Globe-Democrat*, Jan. 14, 1951, quoted in *The Culver-
Stockton College Bulletin*, Nov., 1952, p. 3.

though slow. Their moment of time on the stage was relatively brief, but they died firm in the faith. Understanding their steadfast Christian purpose and spirit, the unfolding drama assumed more meaning. The next chapter again picks up the thread of the chronological narrative.

CHAPTER V

The Struggle for State Cooperation Begins

It took much preaching, more praying, and some paying for Georgia Disciples of Christ to increase their numerical strength and influence in the pre-Civil War years, 1845-1861. The drama slowly developed as new characters joined in the struggles. Congregations were established in spite of steady opposition. While the scenes were enacted during those years, another appearance of the star performer, Alexander Campbell, attracted hundreds of interested persons in April, 1845.

Campbell and R. L. Coleman, traveling via Baltimore, Richmond, and Charleston arrived at Augusta, Ga., on Apr. 3. They were domiciled at the home of Mrs. Emily H. Tubman. Again, Campbell found the churches shut against him. In 1845, it was the Baptist, Methodist, Presbyterian, and Episcopal churches that had closed their doors to the eminent reformer. That was a matter of little concern, however, since Augusta Disciples had occupied a building of their own since 1842. It "had never been filled since its erection till our arrival," Campbell reported.

During the 10-day meeting, Campbell delivered 13 messages. Coleman spoke six times. Campbell's report, in part, was as follows:

. . . Brother Coleman's pungent remarks on some interrogations propounded to the audience, somewhat excited the attention of those present, and very probably those absent. . . . How far his pithy and spirited and convincing address may have convicted them of their apathy and indifference, I presume not to say; but so it was, I addressed on the next day, both in the forenoon and at night, a very fine congregation, even a full

147

house of the most erudite, intellectual, and inquisitive citizens of the town and neighborhood. From this time to the end of the meeting, as far as circumstances, business avocation, marriages, and social parties (not at all rival meetings!) together with new and strange preachers introduced, or fortunately happening by chance to visit Augusta during the next week, we had respectable attention and sometimes very large audiences, so that the house became indeed much too small for the accommodation of those who desired to hear the word of the Lord. Even the Jews themselves became an example to the Gentiles, not only in their public attendance, but in their private calls and attentions to our communications.[1]

Another account of Campbell's sermons, each of which was two hours and 10 minutes long, was given by Judge James Schley Hook (1824-1907), who stated:

This would seem to be a long time to preach, but he held the close, strict, and deeply interested attention of his audiences all the time and they seemed sorry when he quit. The capacity of the church would seat seven hundred persons comfortably, but it did not begin to accommodate the crowds that attended to hear his sermons. Hundreds went away each time after the pews, the aisles, the seats about the pulpit and the window sills were all jammed. Distinguished men from all over this state and some from South Carolina came to hear him.[2]

Campbell became acquainted at that time with former Governors James Henry Hammond (1807-1864) of South Carolina and William Schley of Georgia. They and Alexander H. Stephens, future Confederate Vice-President, with other distinguished men, "were all in constant attendance" at Campbell's lectures.

Hammond invited Campbell and Dr. Hook to his spacious South Carolina home, 16 miles from Augusta.

---

[1]*Millennial Harbinger,* July, 1845, pp. 278 f.

[2]Quoted in Mrs. B. O. Miller, "The First Christian Church of Augusta" (Unpublished MS., 1904?), now in possession of The Disciples of Christ Historical Society, Nashville, Tenn. Son of Dr. Daniel Hook, Judge Hook was Commissioner of Education for Georgia, 1887-1891; Judge of the Superior Court, 1863-1867; member of the 1865 Georgia Constitutional Convention; trustee of the Washington County Female Institute when it was chartered in 1851, and an elder of the Augusta First Christian Church (Dorothy Orr, *A History of Education in Georgia* [Chapel Hill: University of North Carolina Press, 1950], p. 394).

They viewed an art collection and discussed religion. Former Governor Schley, as noted earlier, was Dr. Hook's brother-in-law. Campbell wrote that Schley

> . . . had not yet decided the greatest of all questions for himself,—whether he ought, and with what community he ought, to make the Christian profession. At the close of our last interview I had the pleasure to learn from him that all his doubts and objections were removed; and I trust, if he have not already, he soon will take a decided stand on the side of the faith formerly delivered to the saints.[3]

While it is not known whether Schley ever became identified with the Disciples, his interest in the movement continued apparently. He later paid one dollar for the first volume of the *Christian Union,* Georgia periodical of the Disciples.[4]

Campbell left for Virginia on Monday, Apr. 14. He considered the visit to Augusta "very agreeable" except for the oppressive climate and "excessive labors by day and night."[5]

Ephraim Augustus Smith was a traveling evangelist who made his winter home in Georgia for several years. A zealous book and tract salesman, he traveled in a buggy or spring wagon and "sold to those who could buy, but freely distributed among the poor."[6] He was an agent for Barton W. Stone's *Christian Messenger* and other periodicals.

Smith was named a vice-president of the American Christian Bible Society that was formed by a group of Disciples at Cincinnati on Jan. 27, 1845.[7] In the same year, he became a trustee of Bethany College. Even though an officer of the Bible Society, he was also an agent, in 1848, for the American and Foreign Bible

---

[3]*Millennial Harbinger,* July, 1845, p. 281.

[4]*Christian Union,* May, 1856, p. 160.

[5]*Millennial Harbinger,* July, 1845, p. 280.

[6]John Augustus Williams, *Reminiscences* (Cincinnati: F. L. Rowe, 1898), p. 114.

[7]*Bible Advocate,* May, 1845, p. 114. *Christian Review,* Jan., 1845, pp. 80 f.

Society and served without salary.[8] During 1848, while
Smith was traveling in Georgia, scattered Disciples generously contributed nearly $150 for the American and
Foreign Bible Society.[9] That was one of the first tan-
gible expressions of a missionary concern, beyond the
borders of Georgia, on the part of the brethren.

It was mentioned in the preceding chapter that Dr.
Daniel Hook and Nathan W. Smith undertook joint
evangelistic labors in South Carolina and Georgia after
Alexander Campbell's 1845 messages at Augusta.

One of the Georgia revivals was in the County Line
meetinghouse, Fayette County. On Aug. 27, Smith reported 11 additions in the four-day meeting, *"two* from
the Baptists and nine from the world."[10] Dr. Hook reported, on July 16, six additions, one of whom was from
Pike County. That member, Dr. Hook stated, was an
"immersed Protestant Methodist," but "we were entirely satisfied with his obedience to the Lord, although
done among and through others."[11]

The acceptance of other Christians into the fellowship
of the Georgia Christian churches was the continuation
of an earlier practice which stemmed from the strong
influence of Barton W. Stone. He did not make immersion a condition of membership, but considered it a
matter of opinion in which there should be liberty. However, different theological views led to varied practices.
Some congregations required the re-baptism of immersed
believers from other churches. There was a difference,
Smith contended, between immersion "in the name of
the Lord" and immersion "into the name of the Lord."
He sought more uniformity "in our practice for the
future."[12] The contrary to such legalistic, hairsplitting

---

[8]*Christian Review,* Dec. 1844, pp. 279 f. The American and Foreign
Bible Society was formed in 1837 by Baptists after the American Bible
Society refused to permit the use of *baptizo* in a New Testament translation
for distribution abroad.

[9]*Christian Magazine,* June, 1848, p. 192; Apr., 1848, p. 124.

[10]*Bible Advocate,* Oct., 1845, p. 236. The editor, John R. Howard,
urged proselyting among the "numerous and intelligent" Baptists.

[11]*Millennial Harbinger,* Sept., 1845, p. 430.

[12]*Gospel Advocate,* Mar. 14, 1867, p. 218.

was expressed by Jacob Creath. He wrote that the issue
had to be decided by each congregation for itself.[13]
Georgia Disciples gradually and without coercion from
any source adopted such a valid polity. It thus became
common practice among their churches to receive immersed Christians without re-baptism.

Augustus Buck Fears and his brother, William S.
Fears, were two Henry County pioneers. Augustus was
a Protestant Methodist preacher before becoming a Disciple in the spring of 1844. He wrote frequently to
church papers. In 1845, Augustus reported that there
were then only two other Disciples in his area, both aged
women and 10 miles distant. One, Susannah West, held
membership with the Fears brothers at a Fayette County
church, 30 miles away, but usually attended the monthly
meetings. Augustus had p r e a c h i n g appointments
"among those who oppose the truth, calling us by the
most opprobious epithets, and using their utmost endeavors to keep the people from hearing" the message of
the Disciples. He was hopeful of success because some
people were "beginning to read and investigate."[14]

The baptismal issue concerned Augustus B. Fears.
He wrote about it in January, 1846, stating that the
"worthy and talented brethren who have written upon
the subject, have not been so full and clear as" he "could
have wished."[15] The letter and the reply of Editor John
R. Howard occupied several pages. The issue was discussed at length in an open letter addressed by Mr. Fears
to the Rev. Isaiah Wallace, Methodist, the same summer
of 1846.[16]

Nathan W. Smith sent newsy reports frequently to the
Bible Advocate. He and Shelton C. Dunning evangelized
together, the summer of 1846, in Georgia and Alabama.
"When we were with the Disciples," Smith wrote, "our
principal efforts were . . . trying to get them to keep the

[13]*Ibid.*, Apr. 18, 1867, pp. 308 ff.
[14]*Bible Advocate*, Jan., 1846, pp. 21 f.
[15]*Ibid.*, Feb., 1846, pp. 36 ff.
[16]*Ibid.*, Sept., 1846, pp. 203 ff.

ordinances as delivered by the apostles.''[17] They included "the fellowship, or contribution for the poor saints," the Lord's Supper, prayers, and exhortations.[18] At the end of this evangelistic work, Smith's letter told of his dire circumstances, thus:

> I have just closed my evangelizing labors for the present year—having traveled nearly 3000 miles, and labored most incessantly. This makes the third year I have been in the field.— But such are my circumstances that I must desist. I should rejoice we had some one to take my place. We have some noble hearted brethren here, but they are few. One congregation in Fayette county, contributed to the amount of one hundred dollars this year. If we had many such congregations we could have Evangelists.—I love the truth and the cause, and wish to see our periodicals prosper, but I have sacrificed till I can sacrifice no more at the present.[19]

An outstanding rural congregation was established in Coweta County in 1847 by John Smith. It was named Liberty since the members had separated themselves from sectarianism. The first building for this church was constructed in 1854.

By 1848, Augustus B. Fears wrote that "there are twenty now advocating the cause of Reformation where there was one four years ago." A "spirit of enquiry" had "emboldened" him to proclaim amid the "opposition of thousands."[20]

It was in 1848 that John R. McCall, a Tennessee traveling evangelist, reported that a Georgia Freewill Baptist Church, "near the Alabama line," renounced the Baptist name and decided to practice only the New Testament

---

[17]*Ibid.*, Dec., 1846, p. 282.

[18]*Millennial Harbinger*, Nov., 1846, p. 671. A vital discussion of the "Fellowship" by S. C. Dunning was in the *Christian Magazine*, Aug., 1848, p. 252; Sept., 1848, pp. 286 f.; with Editor J. B. Ferguson's reply in Oct., 1848, p. 310 f. Alexander Campbell advocated calling the collection or offering "The Fellowship," which had New Testament sanction.

[19]*Bible Advocate*, Dec., 1846, pp. 282 f.

[20]*Christian Magazine*, Feb., 1848, p. 62.

ordinances. The church had about 120 members, who took the changed position unanimously, after hearing several messages by a Disciple.[21]

A letter from H. S. Campbell, layman of Gainesville, explained some difficulties encountered in advancing the new religious movement in Georgia. He wrote, as follows:

. . . I stand alone in this community, surrounded by the different parties in religion, none of whom seem willing to examine the things advocated by the Disciples of Christ.

I became obedient to the faith some sixteen months since by reading the word of God, aided therein by bro. A. Campbell's writings. I seldom see a Disciple and but two or three proclaimers of the ancient gospel have ever visited this place. Bro. E. A. Smith stopped with me a day or two in 1844, and I have been anxiously wishing his return, hoping he would bring some of the proclaiming brethren. I hope some of the brethren who proclaim the ancient order of things will find it convenient to pass through this country and call on me. My eldest daughter would become obedient now, but there is no one under sixty miles to immerse her.[22]

James J. Trott and John Eichbaum, Tennessee evangelists, preached at the Augusta and Antioch (with others, they called the latter, Republican) churches in late 1848. They enjoyed association with S. J. Pinkerton, Dr. Daniel Hook, and Nathan W. Smith. Trott referred to being "borne away swiftly by the harnessed steam" and riding the "fire-car" of the railroad.[23] In February, 1851, Trott held a meeting in the Griffin church.

The Antioch brethren "had just completed a neat and comfortable house" at the time of their annual camp meeting in the summer of 1849. Sixteen members were received then, according to J. S. Havener, South Carolina elder.[24] However, another report by John Moore, also a South Carolina preacher, stated that there were 14 additions to the membership, including 11 by immersion.

21*Ibid.*, June, 1848, pp. 189 f.; July, 1848, p. 221.

22*Ibid.*, June, 1848, p. 190.

23*Ibid.*, Feb., 1849, pp. 77 f.

24*Millennial Harbinger*, May, 1850, p. 298.

Such conflicting reports often appeared. Mr. Moore stated also that "at the same time a church was organized at Princeton, 2 miles from Athens, with good prospects."[25]

Perhaps the first honorary degree conferred on any of the brethren was received by I. N. Loomis of Milledgeville. The award was an honorary Master of Arts degree from Franklin College of Tennessee at commencement, Oct. 17, 1849.[26] John M. Barnes, preacher in Georgia a decade or so before, received a similar honorary citation at the same time.[27] M. A. Smith of Georgia was graduated from Franklin College in 1850.[28]

THE REALITY OF FELLOWSHIP IN COOPERATION

An exaggerated fear of ecclesiasticism was the basis of controversies that began to entangle Disciples of Christ, even in pre-Civil War days. Many, perhaps most, of the pioneer leaders had bitter experiences with presbyteries and associations. Thus, they became suspicious of all ecclesiastical authority and forms of organization extending beyond congregations. It took years for the progressive-minded Disciples to learn the inherent values of genuine Christian cooperation.

The possibilities of a general missionary organization were argued, pro and con, for several years before 1849. A national convention was finally called for Cincinnati, Oct. 22-27. There were 156 representatives from 100 congregations in 11 states. The convention organized and then formed the American Christian Missionary Society for work at home and abroad. Alexander Campbell was unanimously elected president of both the con-

---

25*Christian Magazine*, Dec., 1849, p. 467.

26*Ibid.*, Nov., 1849, p. 430.

27Barnes had been in Alabama and Tennessee since 1843 and had recently moved to Hopkinsville, Ky., "because a large family demand more extended means of support," he wrote in the *Christian Magazine*, Jan., 1849, p. 31. He died at Hopkinsville, Feb. 4, 1850, at the age of 44 years.

28James E. Scobey (Editor), *Franklin College and Its Influences* (Nashville: McQuiddy Printing Co., 1906), p. 327.

vention and the society. Dr. Daniel Hook of Georgia
was named tenth of 20 vice-presidents of the new assembly. Samuel J. Pinkerton, Augusta pastor, was a member, with Walter Scott, of the committee on order of
business and the nominating committee.[29] He was made
a life member of the American Society when the Midway,
Ky., church paid the fee of $20.00 in his behalf.[30] Pinker-
ton was also named a member of the corresponding committee.[31]

Such an assembly provided a needed organization that
strengthened the brotherhood's unity and gave a sense
of direction to the struggling churches. It stimulated
fellowship and furthered the acquaintance of the brethren. More important, there was discussion of controversial matters through a free exchange of ideas and
viewpoints.

The year 1849 also found Georgia Disciples expressing
religious maturity in state cooperation. Nathan W.
Smith traveled through the state at his own expense to
promote the first state assembly of the brethren. Dr.
Daniel Hook also encouraged such a cooperative venture,
being "one of the first to urge upon the brethren of
Georgia and South Carolina, the necessity of a thorough
and systematic State cooperation."[32] The meeting provided the brethren with a blueprint upon which to build
a substantial state brotherhood. Assumption of such
responsibility, of course, met with indifference and opposition that caused tensions to develop. Nevertheless,
it was an important epoch for Georgia Disciples, marking
the start of an enlarging state fellowship and conscious-
ness.

The first Georgia cooperation meeting of the state's
few and scattered Disciples convened at a school, since

29Charles Louis Loos, *Our First General Convention,* Held at Cincinnati,
Ohio, October 22 to 27, 1849 (Louisville: Guide Printing & Publishing
Co., 1891), p. 29.

30*Ibid.,* p. 60.

31*Millennial Harbinger,* Dec., 1849, p. 693.

32Dr. J. D. Erwin [Jr.], quoted in Mary D. Howell, *op. cit.,* p. 45.

the use of church buildings was denied the brethren, at
Griffin on Saturday, Sept. 15, 1849. The Griffin church
was organized in a private home by Dr. Daniel Hook and
Augustus B. Fears, Mar. 11, 1849, with seven members.[33]
The congregation met monthly and had 13 members when
the state meeting convened. Five or six additions were
received during the convention.

The state convention had delegates, called "messengers" according to Baptist custom, from four congregations. Dr. Hook could not attend because of an "afflic-
tion" in his family. A letter from him declared the
Augusta church favored cooperation. H. S. Campbell,
Gainesville layman, also sent a letter.

"The kindliest feelings prevailed during our deliberations," wrote Augustus B. Fears.[34] N. B. Johnson reported that the

. . . meeting was exceedingly pleasant and harmonious, all
seeming to be renewed in their spiritual strength and energy.
. . . The Co-operation constituted our Church its agent to
employ an Evangelist to labor in Georgia, and I am exceedingly happy in being enabled to inform you that we have procured the services of our beloved Bro. Dr. Daniel Hook, who
is in the field . . .[35]

Another indication that Dr. Hook was called and actually at work as state evangelist, shortly after the 1849
convention closed, was a letter from Ephraim Augustus
Smith, who, on Apr. 12, 1850, referred to "Dr. Hook,
Evangelist for Georgia."[36]

The only other known record of the first Georgia convention of Disciples of Christ was a list of eight churches
and their numerical strength, along with the names of

[33]*Christian Magazine*, Mar., 1850, p. 94. *Millennial Harbinger*, Nov.,
1849, pp. 651 f.

[34]*Millennial Harbinger*, Nov., 1849, p. 651.

[35]*Christian Magazine*, Mar., 1850, p. 94.

[36]*Ibid.*, June, 1850, p. 189. In issue of Oct., 1850, p. 318, Dr. Hook,
writing from Gamble P.O., Jefferson County, reported "large and attentive congregations" heard him preach during a "long and laborious tour
of duty," adding: "The principal points of labor were Chattanooga in
Tennessee; Stilesborough, Cass Co., Ga., Atlanta in Dekalb co., Griffin and
Zebulon, in Pike county; Monroe and Mt. Vernon in Walton county;
and a schoolhouse and Antioch in Clark county."

four congregations not represented. Contributions from churches and individuals, presumably for support of a state evangelist, were noted. The original report was in the handwriting of Nathan W. Smith. The data from that report follows:

Churches	Counties	No. Members	Contributions
Bethel	Clarke	8	$10.00
P. Factory . . .	"	8	10.00
Antioch	"	50	42.00
County Line . . .	Fayette	50	25.00
Mt. Vernon . . .	Walton	24	31.00
Griffin	Pike	20	30.00
Augusta . . .	Richmond . . .	25	
Etowah River . .	Cass	21	

NOT REPRESENTED

Savannah	Chatham		
Hydes	Coweta	9	
Jones	Walker		
Atlanta . . .	DeKalb		

INDIVIDUAL CONTRIBUTIONS

Dr. Daniel Hook	Jefferson Co. . . .	20.00
H. S. Campbell .	Gainesville	10.00
Daniel Swobe . .	Cass Co.	5.00
		$183.00[37]

Another state convention was scheduled for the next year. So, the 1850 Georgia Cooperation Meeting met at Griffin, Sept. 13 and 14. "Many brethren were expected to attend," wrote E. A. Smith.[38] With the financial aid of the community, a brick church building was completed at Griffin in March, 1850.[39] The convention was more definitely organized. A set of "State Co-operation Rules" was submitted by Pendleton Cheek of Snow Hill, Catoosa County, as follows:

Whereas no body or organization of men can act officially unless it be a permanent, responsible body

---

[37]*Year Book of the Churches of Christ in Georgia. For 1903* (Atlanta: Mutual Publishing Co., 1903?), p. 2.

[38]*Christian Magazine*, June, 1850, p. 189.

[39]*Millennial Harbinger*, Sept., 1845, p. 430.

1st. Be it resolved, therefore, that we now organize the members present as the co-operate of the State of Georgia.

2nd. Resolved, that we adopt some constitutional organic form of government. The following is a copy of the rules of organization for the State Co-operation meeting at Griffin:

GEORGIA CHRISTIAN COOPERATION.

Whereas, the importance of evangelical labors in the State of Georgia has been presented to the churches of Christ in the state and whereas under the influence of strong desire to sound out the truth in every section of the broad land—they have determined to co-operate in this good work and have in consequence sent forward messengers or delegates to carry their purposes into execution. Therefore, we the messengers and representatives of said churches having assembled in Griffin according to the adjournment of the last year's meeting, do now the better to execute the duty entrusted to us, resolve as follows:

1st. That this body shall be called "The Georgia Christian Co-operation" composed of messengers from the churches and shall meet annually.

2nd. That the officers of this meeting shall consist of a president and vice-president; and a secretary to keep a record of its proceedings.

3rd. That it shall have an agency for collecting contributions, distributing funds, appointing evangelist and selecting fields of labor.

4th. The customary rules of order and decorum which regulate all deliberate assemblies shall regulate this body and as these give to the president full power to preserve order his decisions will in all cases be final, unless reversed by a majority of the members present. This to be ascertained by an appeal to the meeting.

5th. Where no objection is made the majority present shall determine every question, but when so requested each church shall have an equal number of votes.[40]

A more complete report on the 1851 Georgia Christian Cooperation was published, in part, as follows:

The Messengers from the churches composing the Georgia Christian Co-operation, assembled at Griffin on Friday [Oct. 10] preceding the 2d Lord's day in October. Only five churches were represented. Several others who had formerly co-operated were not represented, from having misapprehended the pur-

---

[40]*Christian Magazine*, June, 1850, p. 189.

poses of our association. The increase of members to the five
congregations has been 80 for the last year.

The deliberations of the assembled brethren were had with
a calmness, earnestness and fervor becoming the momentous
crisis of the cause in our State; and what was best of all, notwithstanding the difficulties of our affairs, all was conducted
with Christian harmony and love.

It was resolved to send out two Evangelists for 1852, viz:
the dearly beloved bros. Dr. D. Hook and A. B. Fears. The
zeal, devotion and ability of these men is gladly spoken of by
the whole Georgia brotherhood. The liberality of the little band
(five congregations composed of less than 250 members) is, it is
believed, unparalleled in the annals of the Reformation.—The
brethren have agreed to raise $1300 for the support of our Evan-
gelists. Three-fourths of the amount is already secured. . . .

The brethren, after four days of cordial, endearing converse,
and many godly admonitions, separated. While together we
had the ineffable gratification of baptizing and receiving 13
worthy persons. This was effected mostly by the efficient labors
of Bros. Hook and S. J. Pinkerton of our State. Thus were we
refreshed by precious spiritual enjoyments for which we praise
the gracious Giver of all good.

By order of the brethren.

D. SWOBE, *Sec'y.*

P.S. The Evangelists were directed to labor among the co-
operating congregations and among such other churches and
places as should receive them.[41]

That report indicated increasing opposition to such
cooperation. Already differences among the brethren
had caused certain local churches to be designated "co-
operating congregations."

Reports of the 1852 and 1853 conventions, if held, are
missing. It is likely that they were held, even in the face
of growing opposition, but not reported in the church
press. A reference by Dr. Daniel Hook indicated that
the 1854 convention met at Griffin on Oct. 6.[42] In 1855,
the "Georgia State Cooperation Meeting" was announced by Philip F. Lamar of Griffin for "Clark county,

---

41*Ibid.*, Dec., 1851, pp. 375 f.

42Mary D. Howell, *op. cit.*, p. 59.

Ga., commencing on Thursday [Oct. 11] before the 2nd
Lord's Day [Oct. 14] in October, 1855."[43]

The 1856 convention met at Atlanta. It was reported by A. G. Thomas, corresponding secretary, as
follows:

The annual Co-operation Meeting of the Churches of Christ in
the State of Georgia was held in Atlanta, commencing Friday
[Oct. 10] before the Second Lord's Day in October last. Messengers from most of the churches were present. The meeting
was called to order by the President of the last annual meeting,
Dr. D. Hook. After prayer, the messengers registered their
names and presented letters showing the condition of the congregations which they represented. The congregations all appear to be in the spirit of earnestness and zeal which always
characterizes the true disciples of Christ.

Dr. D. Hook was unanimously re-elected Evangelist for the
State at large. The body cordially approved of the manage-
ment and editing of the Christian Union, during the period of
its publication until that time. J. S. Lamar tendered his resig-
nation as editor of the Christian Union, which was received
with regret by the brethren. The body then appointed A-G.
Thomas Editor and D. Hook Associate Editor of the Christian
Union, for the ensuing year. It was further resolved that
J. S. Lamar be requested to continue his connection with the
Christian Union as one of its editors. Also passed resolutions
providing for the increase of the subscription list of the Christian Union, and for the securing of its permanency as the advocate of Christianity in the State.

The gospel was preached to congregations assembled at the
Meeting House at 11 o'clock, A.M., 3 and 7 o'clock, P.M., each
day of the meeting.

The next annual meeting was appointed to be held with the
Congregation at Liberty, Coweta county, on Friday [Oct. 16]
before the Third Lord's Day in October, 1857.[44]

In October, 1857, the convention met with the Atlanta
church. Messengers attended from most of the congregations. Dr. Daniel Hook was again chosen state evangelist.[45] A primary source, the journal of Dr. Hook, re-

---

[43]*Gospel Advocate*, Sept., 1855, p. 92.

[44]*Christian Union*, Nov., 1856, pp. 350 f.

[45]Mattie Mitchell, "The First Cooperation Meeting Held in Georgia,"
Christian Messenger, Mar., 1936, p. 1.

ferred to his evangelistic work "at and after Cooperation meeting, in 1857."[46] Insofar as the records indicate,
the 1857 convention was the last one of Georgia Disciples
of Christ until after the Civil War, when, in 1870, the
Georgia Christian Missionary Society was organized.

Thus did the Georgia brethren grope their way toward
an effective state-wide, cooperative fellowship that would
give their movement identity and stability. It was a
rough road. They contended with each other, but were
resolved to do all things scripturally. The debates came
in deciding what was the scripturally approved way.
They were learning that negative scorn heaped upon
sectarian heads did not suffice to establish a state brotherhood.

Alexander Campbell's observations on cooperation,
about which he wrote persuasively and often, were pertinent to the situation in Georgia, as elsewhere. He
stated:

We want co-operation. Some of our brethren are afraid of
its power; others complain of its inefficiency. Still we go for
co-operation; but it is the co-operation of Christians; . . . We
go for the co-operation of all the members of that one church in
whatever communities they may happen to be dispersed, and
for their co-operation in heart and soul, in prayers, in contributions, in efforts, in toils, in struggles for the salvation of their
fellow-men at home and abroad. . . .

We must find a way of doing Christ's work together, and
doing it more effectively than we have been doing it.

At the risk of making mistakes, we must work closely enough
together to do what in Christ's name must be done.[47]

Fortunately for the cause of the Disciples in Georgia,
those words and similar expressions carried weight with
the majority of the brethren, contentious or not. They
began to realize, not only that they ought to survive as
a religious body, but that growth was necessary to sur-
vival.

The 1849 Georgia Cooperation meeting provided what
was likely the most accurate and complete statistical

---

[46]Mary D. Howell, *op. cit.*, p. 67.

[47]*Millennial Harbinger*, June, 1838, p. 269.

survey of pioneer Georgia Disciples. A few other records may be compared with those figures, just recently cited.[48]

The Christian Register of 1848, the brotherhood's first statistical compilation, listed only five Georgia churches, with membership, and three preachers, as follows: "Liberty Grove 25, Eld [Elderly] ones, Rockey Ridge 35, R Jones, Pr., [Preacher] Augusta 40, D Hook. pr. Savannah, 50, S C Denning, scull Shoals, 60, N Smith."[49]

A publication of 1849 was slightly more accurate in listing the counties of Georgia with Christian churches. The volume stated: "Disciples of Christ, or Christians. —There are numerous congregations in Georgia, particularly in Chatham, Cass, Richmond, Walton, Fayette, Merriwether, and Walker" counties.[50]

Yet another comparison is possible from Table XIV, published as an Appendix in an 1855 Georgia volume, as follows:

Christian (counties)	No. of Churches	Aggregate Accommodations	Total Value of Church Property
Baldwin	1	150	400
Campbell	1	200	100
Dade	1	60	50
Pike	1	500	1,500
Richmond	1	800	10,000
	5	1,710	$12,050[51]

All of which show, if nothing more, the difficulties then, as now, of obtaining correct religious statistics of the Disciples of Christ!

DEVELOPING CHURCHES AT ATLANTA AND ELSEWHERE

From 1845 to the beginning of the Civil War in 1861, perhaps 25 or more congregations were established

---

[48]*Cf. ante.*, p. 157.

[49]Alexander Hall (Compiler), *The Christian Register*. (Loydsville, Belmont County, Ohio: Alexander Hall, 1848), p. [2].

[50]George White, *Statistics of the State of Georgia* (Savannah: W. Thorne Williams, 1849), p. 102.

[51]George White, *Historical Collections of Georgia* (3rd ed.; New York: Pudney & Russell, 1855), pp. 34 f.

among Georgia Disciples. Several were welcomed from
the Baptists. Only incidental references to some of the
congregations occurred in pioneer Disciple periodicals.
Names of several such churches were unknown and other
data were incomplete. The list which follows is as
accurate as available sources make possible:

Year Organized	Church Name	County
1845-46	Union	Clarke (now Oconee)
1847	Liberty	Coweta
1849	Griffin	Pike (now Spalding)
1849?	Fairburn	Campbell
1849?	?	Campbell
1849	Princeton	Clarke
1850?	?	Heard
1850?	Cane Creek	Walton
1850	Bethel	Jasper
1850?	Bethel	Pickens
1850	Enon	Cass
1851	Atlanta	DeKalb (now Fulton)
1852	Pleasant Hill	Cherokee
1853	West Point	Troup
1854	Berea, Hampton	Henry
1855?	Bennett Mills	Henry
1856	Antioch	Washington
1857	Sandersville	Washington
1857	Bethesda, Tennille	Washington
1857?	Bethesda (Negro)	Washington
1857?	? (Negro)	Johnson
1857	Toomsboro	Wilkinson
1858	Acworth	Cobb
1850s?	Corinth	Lowndes
1860	?	Jackson
1860	Christian Chapel	Barrow
1860	Ludville	Pickens

The anti-missionary sentiment that prevailed among
some pioneer Disciples was reflected by a letter from
Pendleton Cheek of Campbell County, as follows:

. . . If our good and wealthy brethren of the west knew of
such a place as *Georgia*, and what a vast missionary field is
here open to their zeal, their wealth, and their religious enterprise, surely they would quit their worse than useless squabbles
about how they are to help the Baptist *cause* in Burmah, and

assist us in building up their own cause—the cause of God, and his holy word—in their own happy land and our dear sunny South. So may it be![52]

There were supporters of benevolence, too. One such was James Rahn of Springfield, Effingham County. There were only eight of the brethren in the entire county, he wrote, and from two to four met fortnightly. He said:

> . . . I think, if a brother will come and labor among us we can give him a support; of course he would have to travel about among us. If you think proper, send or get one to come as a missionary. . . . Something can be collected here, in my opinion, not only for himself, but also for other benevolent purposes, as now engaged in by the Disciples.[53]

As mentioned several times, letters in pioneer magazines contained desperate appeals for evangelistic help. On occasion, the editors echoed the pleas. J. B. Ferguson, editor of the *Christian Magazine* of Nashville, responded in person during early January, 1851. Accompanied by James J. Trott, he was "jolted over frozen roads and mountain pass-ways, in closely packed stage coaches" part of the way. They barely escaped accidents enroute. Ferguson delivered eight sermons at Augusta during one week. Beginning with small attendance, he concluded with overflow crowds, the "largest hearing" the Disciples ever had there, or so he reported.[54]

Atlanta, originally called Terminus and Marthasville, by 1850 was a busy, dusty town, even then well on its way to becoming a mountain metropolis. When the Civil War began, the town's population totaled 10,000.

Nathan W. Smith and Dr. Daniel Hook preached to the few Disciples they found at Atlanta, as early as 1848 and 1849. A letter of Dr. Hook's in July, 1850, mentioned that Atlanta was one of the main places for his evangelistic labors earlier in the year.[55]

---

[52]*Millennial Harbinger*, Jan., 1850, p. 54.

[53]*Ibid.*, May, 1850, p. 300.

[54]*Christian Magazine*, Apr., 1851, p. 115.

[55]*Ibid.*, Oct., 1850, pp. 318 f.

In August, 1851, Dr. Hook removed to Atlanta and soon established the congregation that became the First Christian Church. The organization occurred in the home of Mr. and Mrs. Elzy Baker Reynolds on Walton Street. They and the Hooks were four of the eight charter members. Two others were Mr. and Mrs. F. Plion Perdue. Dr. Hook and Mr. Perdue preached without compensation for the Atlanta church from 1851 until 1855.

On present-day Capital Place, the first building site, "particularly desirable," was given by Samuel Mitchell. He gave all Atlanta churches a building lot. However, "one of the trustees or elders traded it away for a very inferior one," Dr. Hook's biographer stated. Dr. Hook "viewed it as a fraudulent transaction, and labored unceasingly for some time to recover it, but without success."[56] The first building was erected in 1853 at Pryor and Mitchell Streets, location of the exchanged lot. The next year the structure was exchanged for a building on Decatur Street near Ivy. Decatur was the location of Dr. Hook's home, which he had bought.

Dr. Alvinzi Gano Thomas (1833-1903) became the first salaried minister of the Atlanta church in January, 1855. He served until the Civil War when he became a Confederate chaplain. Born at Tarversville, Twiggs County, Ga., June 10, 1833, his father was a Baptist minister and teacher. A. G. Thomas studied under his father and attended Mercer University for one session. He then enrolled at Bethany College in Virginia and came under the influence of Alexander Campbell. He was Georgia's first student at Bethany, receiving the A.B. degree on July 4, 1851. He then taught school at Griffin and Hampton, Ga., while studying law and became a Disciple at Griffin in 1853. Both his father and Dr. Hook influenced him to enter the Christian ministry.

Graduate studies followed at Bethany College for the brilliant A. G. Thomas. He was there nearly two years

---

[56]Mary D. Howell, *op., cit.*, p. 58.

and had the A.M. degree conferred upon him in 1856.[57]
He read 10 languages and spoke four. He often accompanied Campbell on his preaching visits to the churches.
He was ordained to the ministry at Bethany with Campbell, Isaac Errett (1820-1888), and D. S. Burnet (1808-1867) officiating. After taking the Atlanta pastorate,
he also studied at the Atlanta Medical College, beginning
about 1859, and received the M.D. degree. In 1857 he
was married to Miss Susan Adelaide Reynolds, daughter
of Mr. and Mrs. E. B. Reynolds of the Atlanta church.

The Bethel Church of Jasper County abondoned its
Baptist associations in 1850. Its action read thus:

> After much deliberation, it was unanimously resolved, that
> all human confessions of faith, or creeds, so called are wrong
> in theory and tendency, and are contrary to the word of God;
> and therefore that we, as a church, will no longer be governed
> by them, but with one voice, solemnly agree to take the Old
> and the New Testaments as our only rule of faith and practice.
> Done in conference, by order of the Church, Nov. 23d, 1850.
>
> Joel Lane, Moderator.[58]
>
> Wm. D. Lane, Clerk

Referring to the Bethel Church's coming into the
fellowship of the Disciples of Christ, G. W. Cornwell, of
Jasper County, said that the "Flint River [Baptist]
Association is greatly alarmed. Many of the churches
are about passing the same resolutions."[59] One of two
other congregations "organized . . . on primitive principles" in 1849 by Pendleton Cheek, probably in Campbell County, included a former "Missionary Baptist
Church in good standing."[60]

It was in 1850, too, that a congregation of Disciples
was established in Heard County. The report of this
group was from J. J. Reynolds of Coweta County, as
follows:

> . . . Although surrounded by strong opposition, we have
> succeeded in planting a small church in Heard county, Ga.

---

[57]*Millennial Harbinger*, Aug., 1856, p. 462.
[58]*Christian Magazine*, Mar., 1851, p. 90.
[59]*Millennial Harbinger*, Apr., 1851, p. 240.
[60]*Ibid.*, Jan., 1850, p. 54.

It was organized with only 9 members; still, they have erected a house of worship, and feel encouraged and hope for better days. We have had but two meetings since the house was finished. The first of these lasted three days, and was favored by the labors of Bros. D. W. Borden and W. A. Davis, of Alabama.[61]

While the Disciples proselyted without hesitation then, occasionally one of their number departed for another religious association. Samuel J. Pinkerton was such a preacher. After serving the Augusta church for about six years, he resigned in December, 1853, and joined the Episcopal Church.

The Union Christian Church of Clarke (now Oconee) County stems from two sources. The older was established in the winter of 1845-46. Nathan W. Smith was assisted in that effort by Wm. J. Elder and Charles I. Winn. A building was erected about two miles west of Watkinsville. In the summer of 1852, Dr. Daniel Hook and S. J. Pinkerton conducted a revival in a brush arbor about four miles northwest of Watkinsville with ten confessions. The group worshiped in Chisolm's School until a building was constructed. Land for the church was donated by Josiah A. Browning, Baptist, in a deed dated June 1, 1852.[62] By the spring of 1853, the structure was completed. The older building, constructed by Smith and others, was moved and incorporated in the later structure.

The "Christian Union" Begins Publication, 1856

The first pre-Civil War periodical definitely known to have been published by Georgia Disciples of Christ was the *Christian Union*.[63] The first issue of the monthly, containing 32 pages, published at Augusta, was dated January, 1856. "God Is Love" was the subtitle. Pub-

---

[61]*Ibid.*, Oct., 1850, pp. 597 f.

[62]Jack Mathews Daniell, "The Disciples of Christ in Northeast Georgia," (Unpublished B. D. Thesis, The College of the Bible, Lexington, Ky., 1950), p. 33.

[63]*Cf. ante.*, p. 87 ff., for reference to possible publication of the *Religious Investigator* in 1836 from Jefferson, Jackson County, Ga., by Charles F. R. Shehane.

lication began with James S. Lamar and A. G. Thomas
as editors, Dr. Daniel Hook and Philip F. Lamar as
associate editors.

The *Christian Union* was a courageous, short-lived
attempt to fill the void in Georgia's Disciple journalism.
"Our labors are thrown in. We receive nothing, we ask
nothing for them," wrote James S. Lamar.[64] One writer
mentioned that Mrs. Emily H. Tubman provided funds
to help assure publication.[65] A prospectus for 1857 appeared in the December issue.[66]

The *Christian Union* spoke frankly for the Disciples
in a phase of the controversies they had during those
years with the Baptists. *The Christian Index,* Georgia
Baptist journal of which T. D. Martin, Penfield, was
editor, reflected upon the Disciples when it published an
item about Drewry Hutchins of Forsyth County. Hutchins, Baptist preacher for 25 years, was accused of
"Campbellism" by the Baptist periodical. The charge
was not published, however, until after publication of
accounts of alleged misconduct by Hutchins. The *Index*
stated:

> . . . We know of but one preacher of this name in that part
> of the State, who, although he was called a Baptist, was,
> nevertheless, accused of a strong tendency to Campbellism.
> Brethren who knew him best, did not hesitate to locate him
> in the ranks of A. Campbell. He baptized many, but upon
> insufficient grounds, as many Baptists have again and again
> testified.[67]

[64]*Christian Union,* June, 1856, p. 190.

[65]Barfield, *op. cit.,* p. 80.

[66]The *Millennial Harbinger,* Feb., 1857 (p. 113), mentioned actual receipt of the January, 1857 number of the *Christian Union* in "enlarged
form." It is not known how many numbers of the 1857 volume of the
latter were issued. Copies of the rare 1856 volume of the *Christian Union*
are in the Carolina Discipliana Library, Atlantic Christian College, Wilson,
N. C., and the Library of George Pepperdine College, Los Angeles 44,
Calif. The Pepperdine copy was once owned by Judge Jas. S. Hook of
Sandersville, Ga., whose name is inscribed therein; the notary seal of
T. M. Harris, impressed on its pages, also suggests that the latter owned
it.

[67]Quoted in the *Christian Union,* June, 1856, p. 187.

The reply of Editor James S. Lamar in the *Christian Union* did not mince any words. His barbed sarcasm, defending the Disciples, was, in part, as follows:

. . . Although it is well known that we have repudiated the name Campbellite, and shown its inappropriateness to us a thousand times, we cannot be ignorant of the fact that the Disciples of Christ are those referred to by our opponents under this *sobriquet*. Hence the propriety of our noticing the above unlooked for and uncalled for innuendoes.

Why take pains to say this man was tinctured with something called Campbellism? So long as he was preaching for the Baptists, and baptizing men and women by scores into their church, we hear nothing about his Campbellism. The Index is as silent as the grave. Surely if his doctrine was unsound, the people should have been warned of it at the time he was successfully proclaiming it. But not so—he was then "an able Baptist clergyman"—he was swelling the ranks of the party—and no matter if he did preach Campbellism, it must not be breathed outside of the circle, because he was an influential and successful preacher, baptizing more people than any body else. They could not spare him to the "Campbellites" then; but the moment he turns out . . . [otherwise], the Index could . . . insinuate that it was the holding of our principles that caused him to act as he did.

. . . if he preached the views that we hold, he did not more than Baptists generally are doing, while they traduce us for holding them.

We desire to notice this matter, that they may see to what means even the best of sectarians resort, to forestall our influence. Here is a man very distinguished as a Baptist preacher, receives a letter of dismission and *recommendation* from the Baptist church, . . . and is then for the first time published to the world as having a leaning towards Campbellism!![68]

Apparently, the preacher, Mr. Hutchins, was one who earlier wrote to the *Gospel Proclamation,* an Ohio journal of the Disciples. He was quoted as saying "that *scores* of sinners are bowing to the authority of Zion's King, and that there never was, since that county [Forsyth] was settled, a greater interest exhibited upon

---

[68]*Loc. cit.*

the subject of christianity.''[69]   The Disciples, guilty of proselyting, asked for much of the criticism and persecution which they endured.

Dr. Daniel Hook, like James Shannon[70] before him, had a letter declined by *The Christian Index* for publication. When it was printed in the *Christian Magazine,* Disciple periodical of Nashville, Tenn., a note stated: ''It is the last of a series of friendly letters written to the Editor [of *The Christian Index*], and the only one he has refused to publish.''[71]   Such refusal to publish submissions did not necessarily mean, however, that the Baptist editor was acting from partisan bias.

The *Christian Union* added its voice to the discussion that became perennial on ''The Support of the Ministry.''   James S. Lamar wrote about the matter, in part, as follows:

> . . . so soon as the churches in Georgia become *willing* to give as much for the support of the ministers as the ministers now sacrifice in order to serve them, there will be no lack of means, no stinted support, no drudgery all the week as a preparation for preaching on Sunday, and no anxious fears lest their families shall come to want. . . .
> . . . There is not a country preacher, in the whole state who receives any thing approximating $600. [Yet] . . . our preachers give *one fourth* of their income to support the gospel. Some give one half, some two thirds . . .
> We will now repeat that if the brethren in Georgia, . . . will give but half as much as the ministers, give, they will not only be supplied with able pastors and teachers themselves, but will have the means to employ an efficient corps of Evangelists for the state, and missionaries to go abroad.[72]

This plea for a ''living wage'' was echoed a short time later by the evangelist, Nathan W. Smith. He wrote that the ''want of preachers, and the means of sustaining them, was never more felt than at present.''[73]   Lack of

---

[69]*Gospel Proclamation,* Dec., 1847, p. 238.

[70]*Cf. ante.,* p. 143.

[71]*Christian Magazine,* Aug., 1850, p. 234.

[72]*Christian Union,* Oct., 1856, pp. 316 ff.

[73]*Millennial Harbinger,* Oct., 1858, p. 596.

funds made Mr. Smith return to farming and teaching in order to support his family. This lack of stewardship, so apparent before the Civil War, continued to characterize Georgia Disciples.

James Sanford Lamar was the younger of two brothers on the editorial staff of the *Christian Union* at its beginning. He was born, the son of Philip and Margaret Anthony Lamar, in Gwinnett County, Ga., May 18, 1829. His parents had stopped there temporarily while prospecting for a permanent place to reside in western Georgia. The next November, the family moved to Muscogee County, about 10 miles from the town of Columbus, where they were near Mrs. Lamar's parents and other relatives.[74]

James had his early education at an old field school.[75] Later studies followed under a college graduate, Charles H. LaHatt, in an academy. Due to poverty, James would teach school one year in order to earn sufficient funds to study another year at LaHatt's academy. That course was followed even after the teacher had moved to another district. After completing his studies at the academy, James Lamar bought the two volumes of Blackstone and began to read law. He was admitted to the bar in 1850 at Columbus.[76]

Through conversations with a friend, John Tillery, the plea of the Disciples became familiar to James Lamar. Tillery had studied at Franklin College, near Nashville, Tenn., under Tolbert Fanning. Later, James Lamar was immersed by John Reeves, Freewill Baptist minister. The usual requirement of the narration of a religious experience was overlooked. Subsequently, Reeves was tried by his church for that breach of Baptist custom, but was acquitted. His scriptural defense was too convincing.

---

[74]James S. Lamar, *Recollections of Pioneer Days in Georgia* (n. p., 1906?), pp. 3 f.

[75]A detailed account of James S. Lamar's experiences at the "Old Field School" is recorded in Lucian Lamar Knight, *Georgia's Landmarks, Memorials and Legends* (Atlanta: Byrd Printing Co., 1913), II, 252-262.

[76]Lamar, *op. cit.*, pp. 55 f.

The older brother, Philip F. Lamar, was a Methodist like his mother. A few months later, he was immersed too. Their farmer-father was a Baptist. The brothers read a published communication from Dr. Daniel Hook in a newspaper. Impressed, they invited Dr. Hook to preach at Columbus which then had a population of 6,000 persons. They had "no place of worship—no brethren —and all of the *orthodox* to contend against."[77]   Dr. Hook responded to the invitation, preaching in a hall the young men rented for the purpose. It resulted in a decision by the Lamar brothers to become Christian ministers.[78]

Dr. Hook asked Mrs. Emily H. Tubman to help defray James S. Lamar's expenses as a student at Bethany College. She did so and James enrolled at Alexander Campbell's school in January, 1853. Enroute, he met Mrs. Tubman at Augusta for the first time.[79]   At Bethany, when the venerable Thomas Campbell died, Jan. 4, 1854, James S. Lamar was one of the pallbearers.[80] James was graduated with the A.B. degree on July 4, 1854, as the valedictorian of a class of 17. His address was published in Campbell's periodical.[81]   He was set aside to the Christian ministry in rites at Bethany, Va., (now West ¡Virginia) by Campbell, Isaac Errett, D. S. Burnet, W. K. Pendleton, and Robert Richardson (1806-1876), all to become prominent Disciples of Christ. Lamar received the M.A. degree from Bethany College in 1859 and the same year was chosen a trustee of his alma mater.[82]

The *Christian Union* published James S. Lamar's persional impressions of Alexander Campbell, including his devotional and home life.[83]   Lamar, upon Campbell's rec-

[77]*Christian Magazine*, July, 1852, p. 222.

[78]Edward Hook, *op. cit.*, p. 6.   Mary D. Howell, *op. cit.*, p. 22.

[79]Lamar, *op. cit.*, p. 60.

[80]*The Evangelist*, Nov. 20, 1897, p. 1.

[81]*Millennial Harbinger*, Sept., 1854, pp. 524 ff.

[82]*Ibid.*, Sept., 1859, p. 530.

[83]*Christian Union*, Sept., 1856, pp. 257 ff.

ommendation, began a pastorate with the Augusta church on Nov. 15, 1854. His brother, Philip, was then preaching in the Griffin, Ga., Church.[84] After laboring with the Augusta congregation for six months, James Lamar reported, as follows:

> . . . I am happy to say, that the truth is succeeding here beyond our most sanguine expectations. Some one makes the good confession and is immersed almost every Lord's day. We have had 14 accessions within the past two or three months, which, considering the circumstances that surround us, is highly encouraging. We now have large and intelligent audiences, who seem to be much interested in our simple reasonings out of the Scriptures. Prejudice is giving way; our position is beginning to be understood, and the prospect altogether is as promising as we could desire.[85]

James S. Lamar early began the literary work that was to cause him to become known, later, all across the nation. His first book was published in 1859. It was entitled, *The Organon of Scripture,* or, the inductive method of biblical interpretation. Alexander Campbell called it a "volume of much value."[86] Lamar mentioned the notices the 324-page book had received when he wrote to D. Pat Henderson (1810-1897), then pastor of the church at Louisville, Ky. In a letter from Augusta, dated Mar. 16, 1860, Lamar indicated that he was planning a trip to Louisville "expressly to hear" Henderson preach, adding, "Sister Tubman says she cannot give her consent for me to go on any other condition. She is anxious for me to learn how to preach from you."[87]

During 1859, Lamar was elected one of 21 vice-presidents of the American Christian Missionary Society at its annual meeting at Cincinnati.[88] Earlier, in 1857, he

---

[84]Lamar, *op. cit.,* p. 64.

[85]*Millennial Harbinger,* June, 1855, p. 360.

[86]*Ibid.,* Feb., 1860, p. 101. Note also pp. 84-88, the same issue, for a review by W. K. Pendleton.

[87]Original letter owned by Mrs. Cornelia Bowlin, granddaughter of D. Pat Henderson. Typed copy in possession of The Disciples of Christ Historical Society, Nashville, Tenn.

[88]*Millennial Harbinger,* Dec., 1859, p. 695.

was president of the Middle District Cooperation of South Alabama that met at Selma.[89] That was essentially an honorary position, customarily tendered visiting speakers at such conventions of the brethren.

On June 19, 1856, James S. Lamar was married to Miss Mary Rucker (1833-1864) of Cedar Grove plantation, Ruckersville, Elbert County, Ga.[90] Three children were born to that union; a son and a daughter suffered tuberculosis and died. The oldest child, Joseph Rucker Lamar (1857-1916) became an associate justice of the United States Supreme Court in 1910. Mary Rucker Lamar died in 1864. The next year, after the Civil War was ended, James S. Lamar took Miss Sarah May Ford of Augusta as his wife.

Philip F., oldest of the two preaching Lamar brothers, was also a native of Georgia. He was born on Nov. 14, 1826. He was influenced by his mother, who was a Methodist and her preaching Methodist brother, Samuel Anthony. Philip became a Methodist as a lad. His ministry, minus the educational advantages of his brother James, began with the Griffin Christian Church. His contemporaries called him the "Great Evangelist." He preached throughout Georgia as state evangelist (1870-71) and helped to organize churches in the northeastern part of the state. He made his home near Watkinsville.

Congregations which Philip Lamar led in establishing included Christian Chapel (1860), Barrow County; Corinth (1861), Walton County; Bethany, now Bogart (1863), Oconee County; and Galilee (1868), near Jefferson, Jackson County. He baptized more than 2,000 persons during a ministry of more than 25 years.

Philip Lamar was the author of *A Practical Grammar*, published in Philadelphia by Howard Challen. The book began its greatest usefulness at the outbreak of the Civil War.

---

[89]*Ibid.*, Mar., 1857, pp. 177 f.

[90]*Cf. ante.*, p. 105. An account of James S. Lamar's first meeting with his first wife's father, Joseph Rucker, who owned a dozen cotton plantations then, is in Clarinda Pendleton Lamar, *The Life of Joseph Rucker Lamar, 1857-1916*, pp. 20-23.

Documentary materials that record the life and work of Philip Lamar are scarce. Perhaps he was satisfied to bask in the limelight of his younger brother's renown. Philip Lamar died on Sept. 3, 1878, and was buried in the cemetery of the Galilee church, overlooking the Oconee River.

ALEXANDER CAMPBELL'S LAST VISIT TO GEORGIA

The last visit of Alexander Campbell to Georgia was made in the spring of 1857 when he was 68 years old, nine years before his death in 1866. That trip through the South was made in behalf of Bethany College, the school he began in 1840 in the Panhandle of what is now West Virginia.

He arrived at Atlanta from Montgomery. His friend, Dr. Daniel Hook, met him and they proceeded to Augusta on Friday, Apr. 24. Again, Campbell was a guest in the mansion of Mrs. Emily H. Tubman. Before he left Augusta, she gave $16,000 to endow the Tubman Chair of Modern Languages at Bethany College.[91]

The evening of Campbell's arrival at Augusta, he heard with pleasure a "learned lecture," by President James Shannon, a brother minister who was then president of Christian University at Canton, Mo.[92] Dr. Hook "remained over ten days there, helping Brothers Campbell, Shannon, Lamar and [Nathan W. ?] Smith. Preached several times. Additions, thirteen," he wrote in his journal.[93]

Few details are now known of Mr. Campbell's messages or the hearing which they received. Some Baptist ministers, meeting in convention at Augusta then, favored Campbell "with their presence." He departed for Bethany, via Richmond, Washington, and Wheeling, on Wednesday morning, Apr. 29, after less than a week in Georgia.[94]

[91] Woolery, *op. cit.*, p. 45.
[92] *Cf. ante.*, p. 144.
[93] Mary D. Howell, *op. cit.*, p. 64.
[94] *Millennial Harbinger*, Sept., 1857, pp. 507 f.

Upon leaving Augusta, Dr. Hook continued evangelizing. In June, he was at Sandersville. His journal stated that he

. . . preached twice there, and on Saturday [June 20] went to neighborhood of Zion Hope, baptized Brother [T. M.] Harris and three others—organized a Church of seven members, took many confessions of persons, not ready to be baptized until 1st Lord's Day in July [July 5], when Brother Harris appointed Elder of the Christian Church, as he had been before of the Methodist Church, is to baptize them. Preached twice to very attentive congregation; then returned to Sandersville; preached twice through the week, by request of the Methodist preachers and people; and once on the 4th Lord's Day [June 28] in reply to a rude, ignorant and sophistical attack, from one of the Methodist preachers. I think he will be more cautious how he attacks us in the future.[95]

The decision of Thomas Mercer Harris (1829-1893) to line up with the Disciples was so impressive that it was termed "like a revolution" in a letter of the time.[96] He was born near Davisboro, Washington County, Ga., on July 6, 1829, and had been preaching as a Protestant Methodist for a decade in 1857. His parents, Daniel and Vashti Harris, were members of the Methodist Episcopal Church. His mother was a lineal descendant of Jesse Mercer, Georgia Baptist preacher, editor, and educator.[97] As early as 1851, T. M. Harris began to hear about Alexander Campbell and the Disciples through his sister, Miss Emily Jane Harris, who had married Judge James Schley Hook, son of Dr. Daniel Hook. That source also provided T. M. Harris with Campbell's writings to read and study.

When T. M. Harris decided to become a Disciple, he invited his Methodist parishioners to accept the faith of the new movement. About 40 Methodists from the three churches served by Mr. Harris took their stand with him. He was then 28 years old.

95Mary D. Howell, op. cit., pp. 64 f.

96Millennial Harbinger, Sept., 1857, p. 535.

97A. C. Bruce, "T. M. Harris," Christian Standard, June 13, 1891, pp. 494 f.

T. M. Harris was married in 1852 to Miss Mary Smith, member of a wealthy family in that section of Georgia. He, too, had inherited wealth. That gave them economic independence, social prestige, and favorable influence, unusual for a preacher to enjoy, then or now. Consequently, he gave his pastoral and evangelistic services without cost. "He said he did not need the money, but the people did need the gospel."[98] At his own expense, he had erected a building on a lot which was donated to the congregation.

Thus, 1857 marked the beginning of many years of preaching and evangelizing, particularly in the central part of Georgia, by T. M. Harris. He worked with many of the newly established churches. His brethren called him "our Georgia orator."[99] He organized 20 churches, perhaps, including 13 in South Georgia. Those included both the Athens and Macon congregations.

He wrote from Davisboro, Oct. 12, 1858, to report the organization of five congregations within the year, at the beginning of which there were only four members at Davisboro.[100] The next year he wrote to the *Millennial Harbinger* and offered $425.00 to any preacher recommended by Alexander Campbell. He stated:

. . . We are rapidly growing in numbers, and in ability to pay a preacher, and we hope, by another year, if we have the services of the right sort of a man, to be well able to pay for preaching. Whoever comes will have but five preaching places to attend to, they are close together, and easy of access. We have excellent good houses to preach in.[101]

When the Civil War interrupted his work, Mr. Harris enlisted in the Confederate Army in 1862. He became a captain, receiving an honorable discharge after suffering a serious attack of typhoid fever.

---

[98]Ella Mitchell, *History of Washington County* (Atlanta: Byrd Printing Co., 1924), p. 152.

[99]Nathan W. Smith, *op. cit.*, May 31, 1879, p. 174.

[100]*Millennial Harbinger*, Nov., 1858, p. 657.

[101]*Ibid.*, Jan., 1859, p. 56.

Dr. Daniel Hook's evangelistic work took him into South Carolina for nearly a year about that time. He helped to ordain Dr. J. D. Erwin to the Christian ministry in 1859. The rites were conducted at Halcyondale, Barnwell County, S. C., with fasting, prayer, and the laying-on-of-hands ceremony. The Erwinton congregation concurred in the service. Elder J. S. Havener of Boiling Springs, S. C., participated in the ceremony.[102]

It was in 1859 that Nathan W. Smith began another three years' labor of evangelism throughout Georgia. He was sustained for this period through the generosity of Mrs. Emily H. Tubman of Augusta. He reported over 200 additions during 1859 to 25 churches with "one thousand or more members."[103]

The population of Georgia in 1860 was 1,057,286. There were 2,393 churches of all faiths in the state. The United States Census of that year revealed that 1,100 Disciples of Christ in Georgia composed 15 congregations. However, one writer of Georgia Disciple history stated that "in 1860, . . . the Disciples had in Georgia more than sixty churches."[104] No authority for the statement was cited.

A decade before, the Disciples, nationally, with a membership of 118,000, had ranked sixth among the nation's Protestant bodies. The Civil War years and the subsequent, difficult reconstruction era made significant growth among Disciples in Georgia a constant struggle. Yet the younger leaders of those years, the Lamars, A. G. Thomas, and T. M. Harris, became increasingly influen-

---

[102]*Southern Evangelist*, June 2, 1901, p. 9. The Erwin family was prominent for years in Georgia and South Carolina. The Erwin plantation was across the Savannah River from Augusta. Dr. J. D. Erwin's second wife was Mrs. Anna B. Miller of Screven County, Ga. He was the son of Dr. Wm. R. and Julia C. Erwin. Two brothers and two sisters of Dr. J. D. Erwin resided in Georgia.

According to Mary D. Howell, *op. cit.*, p. 25, while Dr. Hook was then preaching in South Carolina, a nearby Methodist church had a pastor named Dr. Crook. A neighborhood jester remarked that the sinners better watch out or the churches would get them "by Hook or Crook."

[103]*Millennial Harbinger*, Feb., 1860, p. 113.

[104]Barfield, *op. cit.*, p. 95.

tial. They were a source of inspiration to their brethren, so small in numbers. However, no one likely realized more than they did that *what* leads a religious movement is far more significant than *who* leads it.

SLAVERY BECOMES THE ISSUE

The narration of the pre-Civil War history of Georgia Disciples of Christ cannot be concluded without mention of the significant events which transpired with reference to the Negro brethren.

By 1860 slavery was not viewed dispassionately in the North or the South. The distrust of stubborn and fanatical persons on both sides was manifested by division in the major Protestant denominations.

The Methodists split in 1844 over slaves owned by Georgia's Bishop James O. Andrew. Division among the Baptists came when the missionary board would not appoint slaveholders as missionaries. Messengers from eight slave states organized a separate convention at Augusta, Ga., in May, 1845. The southern Episcopal churches withdrew into a separate fellowship on July 3, 1861, as a result of the war. The Presbyterian schism occurred at Augusta on Dec. 4, 1861, from war-caused issues.

The slavery controversy became a live issue among the Disciples about 1845. Before that, Barton W. Stone liberated his own slaves.[105] Alexander Campbell did likewise.[106] In 1835, Stone wrote:

. . . I have in principle and practice been a conscientious opposer of slavery for near 40 years; but how to remedy the evil I knew not. I am persuaded it will be done, but I am ignorant of the means by which it shall be accomplished.[107]

Walter Scott maintained that the requirements of an inclusive Christian fellowship were set forth explicitly

---

[105]John Rogers, *op. cit.*, p. 44.

[106]Selina Huntington Campbell, *Home Life and Reminiscences of Alexander Campbell* (St. Louis: John Burns, 1882), p. 454.

[107]*Christian Messenger*, Nov., 1835, p. 263.

in the New Testament. No church, he insisted, had any authority to change those conditions.[108]

"I can assure the disciples of the south," the Nashville editor, Tolbert Fanning, wrote in 1845, "that those of the north are generally neither *northern* or *southern* men, but prudent *Christians,* who have the cause of God more at heart than the abstract question of slavery."[109] However, it was not to remain an "abstract" issue much longer.

Alexander Campbell emphatically declared his position in a series of articles in the *Millennial Harbinger* of 1845. "We are the only religious community in the civilized world whose principles (unless we abandon them) can preserve us from such an unfortunate predicament," he stated early that year when separation was impending in other religious bodies.[110] Until then, there was little discussion of slavery in the *Harbinger,* Mr. Campbell stating that "we have more important matters on hand."[111]

Campbell held a mediating position in regard to slavery. "I neither assume to be an apologist for American slavery," he wrote, "a reformer, nor an abolitionist of American slavery."[112] He considered slavery to be an economic danger, not a religious issue. The Scriptures, he contended, do not forbid or sanction slavery. On the other hand, he maintained that the relations of slave and master were regulated by biblical teaching. Since that conduct was not condemned in the New Testament, he insisted that it should not be made a matter of discipline or become a test of fellowship by any group of Christians. He understood church membership to include slave-holder, abolitionist, and slave.

Abolitionists denounced Campbell for being pro-slavery. In addition, he was attacked for anti-slavery views.

[108]*The Evangelist,* Sept., 1834.

[109]*Christian Review,* Oct., 1845, p. 234.

[110]*Millennial Harbinger,* Feb., 1845, p. 51.

[111]*Ibid.,* Aug., 1842, p. 375.

[112]*Ibid.,* Mar., 1845, p. 108.

The Baptist, Iveson L. Brookes, who had opposed Campbell on other counts published a pamphlet defending slavery against Campbell's hostile criticism.[113] A large property owner himself, Campbell's sympathies were actually closer to those of the slave-holders than the slaves. He wrote two of his 1845 articles on slavery while he was at Augusta. In one, he stated:

> . . . As a political economist, and as a philanthropist, I have many reasons for preferring the prospects and conditions of the Free to the Slave States; but especially as a Christian, I sympathize much more with the owners of slaves, their heirs, and successors, than with the slaves which they possess and bequeathe.—These opinions I express as freely in Georgia as in Ohio and Pennsylvania, . . .[114]

In fact, Campbell held views on slavery not much different from those of Abraham Lincoln. Campbell proposed formally to Virginia in 1829 and again to Kentucky in 1849, a plan for the gradual, governmental emancipation of slaves. In this respect, too, Campbell and Walter Scott agreed. They wanted a reasonable emancipation with justice for the slaveholder and freedom for the slave.

An unpublished letter of that turbulent era discussed the issues that arose from slavery. It was written by D. Pat Henderson, pastor at Louisville, Kentucky, and sent to James S. Lamar of Augusta, Nov. 26, 1860, just after Lincoln's election as President. Mr. Henderson stated, in part:

> I am personally acquainted with Mr. Lincoln—have been for a quarter of a Century. He was an old line Clay Whig. Like Mr. Clay, he has always been, what thousands of Southerners are this day, an Emancipationist. He looks upon

---

[113]Cf. ante., p. 97. The rare pamphlet was entitled: *A Defence of Southern Slavery. Against the Attacks of Henry Clay and Alex'r. Campbell* (Hamburg, S. C.: Robinson and Carlisle, 1851). The second edition did not carry the name of the author, Iveson L. Brookes, as did the first, but stated that it was "By a Southern Clergyman." A copy of the 2nd ed. is in possession of The Disciples of Christ Historical Society, Nashville, Tenn.

[114]*Millennial Harbinger*, May, 1845, p. 234.

Slavery as an evil to the white population, but a blessing to the black race. He is for remuneration to the masters, and a country in which to colonize the African race. He is for gradual Emancipation. These I am sure are his sentiments. He is no more of a modern Abolitionist than either you or I. He thinks slavery retards the progress of this nation, and engineers strife among our citizens. This is the "irrepressible conflict" of which he speaks. . . . Mr. Lincoln is not an extremist. . . . I differ with him on many points. I voted against him with all my heart. But I do not fear his administration. . . .

He and I commenced our public lives in Illinois. He practiced law in my Court. I was on the bench four years and to some extent mingled in politics. He and I were of the same school, and next to Mr. Douglass, he was the strongest political speaker in the state. What I say of him, therefore, is from personal knowledge. . . . I am for the Union as it was, as it is, and I hope as it now will be, till Messiah shall come. God gave us this great heritage, and we must not sell it for either supposed or real injuries. We must seek a redress for wrongs *in the Union,* not out of it. If we have bad men in the Church, we must not secede from it, but execute the laws, and put out the offenders. . . .

. . . Kentucky cannot be driven out of the Union. . . . Will Georgia leave her? You tell me not this year, perhaps never. God grant it.[115]

There were heated arguments, pro and con over slavery and secession, among the brethren. Southerners regarded slavery as an institution sanctioned by divine authority. Campbell sought to "preserve unity of spirit among Christians of the South and of the North."[116] The sin of division in the Body of Christ was regarded by him as greater than any other.

Disciples of Christ escaped division over slavery by always regarding it as a matter of opinion. Since there was no specific scriptural instruction, the churches, as such, could not take a stand on the matter. Slavery, of course, did cast its shadow across the brotherhood. However, the distinction between faith and opinion, which

---

[115]Original letter owned by Mrs. Cornelia Bowlin, granddaughter of D. Pat Henderson. Typed copy in possession of The Disciples of Christ Historical Society, Nashville, Tenn.

[116]*Millennial Harbinger,* May, 1845, p. 195.

the brethren cherished, avoided any division. In 1860, the Disciples had 1,241 congregations in the North and 829 in the South. They were most numerous in the border states.

James Shannon, prominent figure among Georgia Disciples, held views that were prevalent among many, if not most, of the brethren in the state. One writer declared:

> . . . President Shannon also held the view that if American slavery was not ordained in God, it could be maintained by the teaching of Christ and his apostles, and ought to be perpetuated. No man that I have ever been permitted to hear on this subject could array as many and as strong, plausible arguments from the Scriptures, in favor of this position, as could he.[117]

The attitude of the benevolent Mrs. Emily H. Tubman differed greatly, however. She owned slaves and favored their gradual freedom, in this respect like both Campbell and Henry Clay, her former guardian. Soon after the death of her husband in 1836, Mrs. Tubman liberated a number of their slaves. She permitted all to choose freedom or to remain her slaves. About 75 remained with Mrs. Tubman. Sixty-nine chose their freedom and asked to be sent to Liberia.

Mrs. Tubman contributed generously to a colonization fund for endowment of a home for former slaves in Liberia. She paid the transportation of any of her own former slaves who wished to join that colony. Therefore, she sent the 69 manumitted Negroes to Liberia. They were colonized at Harper, the leading city of Cape Palmas, Maryland County, Liberia. A Tubmantown in the same county was named for the Tubman family.

John Augustus Williams wrote about one of those Negroes, as follows:

> I remember affectionately a young negro man who was my faithful attendant when I was a child. He was a favorite servant in my father's house, but he was transferred to the

---

[117]W. C. Rogers, *op. cit.*, p. 17.

estate of Sister Tubman, a wealthy, Christian lady of Georgia. She sent him, in company with others, to establish a colony in Liberia. They prospered there, as I afterward learned.[118]

The writer, Mr. Williams, did not live long enough to learn how well the descendants of that colony fared. The far-reaching significance of Mrs. Tubman's attitude and generosity was never shown more magnanimously, however, than in the fact that today's eighteenth President of Africa's Republic of Liberia is William Vaccanarat Shadrach Tubman. Elected in 1944, he was re-elected in 1952. He was born in Maryland County on the southeastern coast of Liberia in 1895. He is the son of Alexander and Elizabeth Tubman and the grandson of William Shadrach and Sylvia Ann Elizabeth Tubman. The latter were two of those 69 Negroes manumitted and sent to Liberia by Mrs. Emily H. Tubman more than a century ago.[119]

In this connection, it is of interest that Dr. James Turner Barclay (1807-1874), the first missionary of the Disciples, who began a mission in Jerusalem in 1851, was a slaveholder when he was called for foreign service. He inherited four slaves. When he offered them their freedom, provided they left Virginia as required by state law then, they refused to go. A Disciple friend of Dr. Barclay's finally bought the four Negroes.

Ephraim Augustus Smith's peregrinations among his Disciple brethren, in and out of Georgia, have been mentioned several times.[120] His part in the sending of Alexander Cross (1811?-1854), former slave, to Liberia as the second missionary of the Disciples is little known. The following excerpts from a published letter set forth the fascinating account:

Four years ago, a beloved brother in Kentucky and myself resolved to have the land of Ham examined as to its suitableness for a home for the free people of color of the United

---

118Williams, *op. cit.*, p. 149.

119Reid Wiles, Second Secretary of the Embassy of Liberia in Washington, D. C. Letter to J. Edward Moseley. Dated Mar. 3, 1953.

120*Cf. ante.*, p. 149.

States. It fell to my lot to attempt the voyage. We sought out a colored brother [Alexander Cross] to engage as our Missionary in Liberia. Such a one was found, and purchased by a few brethren in Southern Kentucky, and sent out with his family.

I arranged my affairs, gathered my funds, and set out for the voyage. In the eastern cities I procured a fine supply of books, tracts &c., for gratuitous distribution. Also upwards of $100 cash to aid our Missionary.

It was my purpose to go out in an emigrant vessel, which I had been informed, usually remained on the coast of Africa six or eight weeks, giving one much time for visiting the towns, and settlements along the coast. I had been assured that, in order to escape the African fever which so often proves fatal to the white man, I must sleep on board the vessel.

I had made all my arrangements to remain with the vessel which might take me out, visit the land during the day, and return to the ship for the night. Hoping thus to be able to see and do as much as the object of my mission might require; and then return on the same vessel, or go to England if I should find a suitable vessel, and chose to do so. On reaching New York, in October, I learned that three vessels would sail in the course of two months. But finding that these vessels could not afford me the facilities for exploring Liberia, I declined taking passage on them. Our Missionary came on, and he too agreed with me, and my friends in Baltimore, that it would be best for me to remain and labor to sustain the mission; and stir up friends to aid in building a suitable vessel for the transportation of emigrants and their goods. A good sailing vessel, which would comfortably accommodate three hundred emigrants and all they would take out, could be built, and fitted out, for about $50,000 or $60,000. I have pledged $100, and a friend in Baltimore another $100. Cannot friends north and south, east and west, be found to push this work to completion? The good Lord help us! I consented to remain, but accompanied them as far as Norfolk. I had opportunity for doing much for them.—Many books and tracts were distributed amongst them; and what good counsel I was capable of giving them. I am satisfied, and so is the Secretary of the Am. Colonization Society, that I have done what was best. I do not regret that I came on east. I have learned much of importance connected with African Colonization.—Have procured, and sent out many valuable books &c. My presence was also needed by our good Missionary and his family. I hope good will result from my humble labors.

Our people are waking up to a consideration of the importance of African Colonization. Our State meetings in Kentucky and Virginia have both passed resolutions recommending the brethren to aid this cause. The Am. Christian Missionary Society will labor to sustain the missionaries sent there. Our good brother, Alex. Cross, will make regular reports from Liberia. The Lord go with, and bless him, is the prayer of many. May it be even so, amen.[121]

The former slave, Alexander Cross, arrived at Monrovia, Liberia, in January, 1854. His untimely death occurred the following month. His was the first foreign missionary grave of the Disciples of Christ anywhere.

The comprehensive fellowship of the pre-Civil War Disciples was further evidenced by an unusual fact. An abolitionist, J. O. Beardslee (1814-1879), was the third missionary to be sent to a foreign field by the Disciples through their American Christian Missionary Society. He went to Jamaica in 1858.

A slaveholder was the first missionary of the Disciples of Christ. A slave, purchased, liberated, and educated, was the second. An abolitionist was the third. Georgia Disciples generally shared in the sending of all through every way in which they shared with the American Christian Missionary Society and its program.

Negroes were, indeed, members of the early Christian churches at Cane Ridge in Kentucky and Brush Run in Pennsylvania. The slave members of the Georgia Christian churches met with the white slaveholders on a segregated basis, generally, with the slaves in a balcony or in a corner of the sanctuary.

Separation of Negro and white Disciples began to occur in Georgia several years before the Civil War. Dr. Daniel Hook's journal described the nature of the liberty permitted the Negro brethren in their separate services, as follows:

. . . At night on the Lord's Days he generally preached to the colored people, then in a state of slavery, a comfortable house

121Ephraim Augustus Smith in a letter dated Nov. 28, 1853, from Richmond, Va., to the *New York Chronicle*, quoted in the *Christian Friend*, Jan., 1854, pp. 115 f.

having been prepared for their special accommodation. Many of them were members of the church of Christ. They sang with a zest and enjoyed these opportunities greatly. On one of these occasions, William Hall, a colored brother, having been requested to lead in prayer, began vociferously, yet fervently to hold forth, and warming up he went on. He concluded with what he thought was a touching reference or tribute to his Bro. Hook in these words, "O, Lord, bless the old Deacon who come from afar, with his head like a white blossom, standing with one foot in the grave, and no one to tell what business he had with the other one out." Several of the white brethren, as usual, had accompanied the Doctor to this meeting, and on their way home suggested, as a piece of pleasantry, that an explanation should be called for as to this personal reflection, the "business of the other foot." The Doctor laughed heartily, then remarked, "I am very thankful to my Brother Bill for his earnest prayer in my behalf. ..."[122]

T. M. Harris and his wife with their independent means rendered significant service to Negro Disciples in Georgia prior to the Civil War. Mr. Harris, one writer said,

... preached to them, baptized them, ordained their ministers, organized their churches and taught their ministers. Mrs. Harris, likewise, showed an interest in the Negroes, donating to each of the two congregations, which her husband had organized ... a tract of land large enough for a church, parsonage, schoolhouse and cemetery, and had erected at her own expense a church house for each.[123]

When Bethesda, the first Christian church established in Washington County, Ga., erected a building, accommodations were provided also for the Negro brethren. A partition separated the two groups at worship. The old church building reverted to Mrs. Harris when a new one was constructed. She then gave the old one to the Negro brethren. A congregation of the Negroes was organized by T. M. Harris with the same name of Bethesda, about 1857. This Bethesda Church is still in existence and is considered the oldest congregation of Negro Disciples in Georgia. After the end of the Civil War and the emancipation of the slaves, the church al-

---

[122]Mary D. Howell, *op. cit.*, pp. 41 f.

[123]Barfield, *op. cit.*, p. 93.

most died. However, it was revived by Thomas N. Johnson, a Negro who learned the Scriptures from Mr. Harris. Also, about 1857, Mr. Harris organized a church of Negro Disciples in Johnson County. It does not now exist.

Disciples of Christ never separated along racial lines nationally. A few of the congregations in various parts of the brotherhood have always welcomed members of any minority group. This is the more remarkable in view of the fact that Disciples owned 101,000 slaves in 1851 according to the annual report of the American and Foreign Anti-Slavery Society. If the report was accurate, then historians have pointed out that "Disciples on a per capita basis were the leading slaveholding religious body in the United States."[124]

So slavery embroiled the nation in unfortunate controversy and resulted in deathly conflict, pitting physical and religious brothers against their own brethren. It was a tragic experience for all concerned. The scene of much bloody fighting, Georgia and the Disciples there suffered heavily. The account of those years will be set forth, as fully as extant records permit, in the next chapter.

---

[124]Garrison and DeGroot, *op. cit.*, p. 468.

CHAPTER VI

The Ravages of War and Reconstruction, 1861-1870

The Civil War was imminent when Abraham Lincoln was inaugurated President of the United States in March, 1861. On Jan. 19, Georgia had become the fifth state to withdraw from the Union. The shocking American tragedy began on Apr. 12 with the attack on Fort Sumter in Charleston Harbor by the Confederate forces.

The Confederate States of America was organized at Montgomery, Ala., on Feb. 4, 1861. Jefferson Davis (1808-1889), West Point graduate and former Secretary of War, was chosen President. Alexander H. Stephens (1812-1883), militant anti-secessionist of Georgia, became Vice-President.

Alexander Campbell called the war "the climax of all human inconsistencies."[1] As noted previously, the Disciples of Christ did not divide over the issues of the war like the major Protestant bodies, even though membership of the Christian churches was concentrated in the border states. The annual national conventions were held in Cincinnati during the war, as they had been since 1849. However, Disciples of Georgia were unable to attend the sessions. The fellowship was disrupted, too, by the failure of Campbell's *Millennial Harbinger* to reach Southern subscribers. The *Gospel Advocate,* of Nashville, Tenn., suspended publication from 1862 to 1866. It had several subscribers in Georgia and was started because Southern Disciples had no periodical to read "without having their feelings wounded by political

---

[1]*Millennial Harbinger,* June, 1861, p. 348.

insinuations and slurs." That fact, more "than all other circumstances combined" caused publication of the *Advocate*.[2] It soon became the main opponent, at least in the South, of missionary societies and instrumental music in the churches.

Religion in the South sanctioned secession as it did slavery. The churches generally supported the Confederate cause with complete abandon. The war years demonstrated unselfish devotion and personal sacrifice by most patriotic citizens. They included many of the several hundred Disciples who resided in Georgia where the fighting became bitter and the hardships acute. Georgians learned tragically that every day of stirring heroism had to be paid for with weeks of terrorized suffering. Before the conflict ended, Georgia's scattered Disciples, some against their will, joined in the struggle. The fighting damaged several church buildings and disrupted congregations, driving members penniless from their homes.

Southern preachers were often more loyal to the Confederacy than many of the politicians. One such in Georgia was Dr. A. G. Thomas. Tolbert Fanning, then editor of the *Gospel Advocate,* was in Georgia shortly before the war began. Arriving at Atlanta on Dec. 21, 1860, he was a guest in the home of Dr. Thomas who was pastor of the Christian church there. Fanning wrote:

> Dr. A. G. Thomas is a brother of fine address, superior talents and learning, but we saw him with a feather in his hat and a glittering sword in his right hand, and doubted if he would be able to hold the sword of Georgia in one hand and the sword of the Spirit in the other.[3]

Yielding to intense patriotism at the start of the conflict, many Southern preachers became chaplains. Dr.

---

[2]*Gospel Advocate,* May 1, 1866, p. 273.

[3]*Ibid.,* Feb., 1861, p. 39. When the "Atlanta Rifles" were organized in May, 1861, Dr. Thomas became an orderly-sergeant (Wallace P. Reed, *History of Atlanta, Georgia* [Syracuse, N. Y.: D. Mason & Co., 1889], p. 116).

Thomas was one such minister. He was commissioned and assigned to the 7th Georgia Volunteer Infantry Regiment. He served throughout the war.

Other Georgia preachers of the Disciples served in various ways with the military forces. T. M. Harris enlisted as a private, but not until 1862. He was honorably discharged because of typhoid fever when he had advanced to a captaincy. In 1864, he was named a major in Washington County's militia which was called for emergency duty when necessary. The Georgia militia aided in the defense of Atlanta that year.

William Harrison Jones, later a minister, enlisted in March, 1861, although not 18 years old. The last year of the war, he was a clerk in the office of the provost marshal at Newnan, Ga.[4]

Dr. E. B. Hook, son of Dr. Daniel Hook, went to war as captain of the Sandersville Volunteers; his brother, Judge James S. Hook, was rejected for Confederate service because of physical disability. Evan Park Howell (1839-1905), son of Clark Howell, Sr., enlisted in the 1st Georgia Regiment as an orderly-sergeant and went to fight under "Stonewall" Jackson in Virginia. Evan had been educated at the Georgia Military Institute. He became an artillery captain and commanded a battery in Claiborne's Division in the defense of Atlanta. His brother, Albert Howell, enlisted as a second lieutenant with the Davis Infantry in February, 1861.[5]

A Kentucky Christian minister, Dr. Winthrop Hartly Hopson (1823-1889), was a chaplain with his friend, General John Hunt Morgan (1826-1864), Confederate guerrilla raid leader. Hopson was given a commission "with pay as colonel" and was ordered "to do whatever seemed good in his sight." In January, 1863, Hopson traveled to Atlanta on leave "to supply himself with

4*Southern Evangelist,* Mar. 2, 1901, p. 7.

5Mary D. Howell, *op. cit.,* p. 80. Raymond B. Nixon, *Henry W. Grady, Spokesman of the New South* (New York: Alfred A. Knopf, 1943), p. 128. Reed, *op. cit.,* pp. 71, 111. *Georgia Historical Quarterly,* Mar. 1917, pp. 52 f.

clothing and a proper outfit.'' The daring Morgan raiders were then on the defensive and quartered at Mc-Minnville, Tenn. Dr. and Mrs. Hopson were reunited, after a forced separation, at Augusta that January. She described those days thus:

> Dr. H. met me at the depot. We were very glad and grateful to our heavenly Father that we had been preserved through many dangers to meet again in health. After a day or two of rest in Augusta, we left for Atlanta, where the Doctor resumed his meeting and remained over Lord's day. He thought it best to return to his command the following week, and we started for McMinnville . . .[6]

Apparently, Dr. Hopson took time during his leave to hold a revival for the Atlanta Christian Church on Decatur Street.[7] When Morgan launched offensive tactics within a few months, Dr. Hopson resigned as chaplain. The Hopsons then went to Virginia. While residing with Mrs. Pichegru Woolfolk at Bowling Green, 40 miles from Richmond, young Charlie P. Williamson, later pastor of Atlanta's First Christian Church, was a 14-year-old member of the household.[8]

Growing up together during the war years at Augusta were Joseph Rucker Lamar and Thomas Woodrow Wilson. The boyhood schoolmates resided in adjoining parsonages at Telfair and Seventh (McIntosh) Streets. Dr. Joseph Ruggles Wilson, father of Woodrow, was pastor of the First Presbyterian Church while James S.

---

[6]Ella Lord Hopson (Editor), *Memoirs of Dr. Winthrop Hartly Hopson* (Cincinnati: Standard Publishing Co., 1887), p. 125.

[7]The Atlanta congregation had nine members when Mr. and Mrs. Samuel Alexander Orr joined in 1862. Elected an elder, Mr. Orr held the position faithfully until his death in 1915. They were the parents of Maggie Orr (Mrs. Lane) Mitchell. Services were conducted during the war at Antioch Church, Clarke County, with preaching once or twice a month by P. F. Lamar or W. T. Lowe (Miller, *op. cit.*, p. 16). Miss Martha A. Fears was baptized in 1864 by W. S. Fears after traveling 30 miles to make her confession and receive immersion (*Gospel Advocate*, Mar. 25, 1869, p. 284). She had learned about the Disciples through periodicals and tracts, not through emotional preaching. On July 3, 1861, L. Pyron of Georgia received the M.A. degree from Bethany College (*Millennial Harbinger*, Aug., 1861, p. 473).

[8]Hopson, *op. cit.*, pp. 131 f.

Lamar was minister of the First Christian Church. The boys were pupils at Professor Derry's School, played on the Lightfoot baseball team, and debated in the attics of their homes. By 1870, when the Wilson family moved to Columbia, S. C., Joseph R. Lamar and his brother Philip were enrolled in the Martin Institute at Jefferson, Jackson County, Ga. Going their separate ways across the years, Woodrow Wilson and Joseph R. Lamar did not meet again until 1913, the day after the former had been inaugurated President of the United States and the other was an Associate Justice of the nation's Supreme Court.[9]

Mary Rucker Lamar, wife of James S. Lamar, died at Augusta on Jan. 27, 1864, at the age of 30. The bereaved family was alarmed by the advance of Sherman's Army in Georgia. General William Tecumseh Sherman (1820-1891) was a West Point man. The South, however, had placed an indelible stamp upon Sherman, who approved slavery, for 25 years. His superior forces of nearly 100,000 men were on the offensive against General Joseph Eggleston Johnston (1807-1891) and his retreating, outnumbered Confederate Army of Tennessee with 45,000 men.

The Lamar family feared Sherman's objective might be Augusta where gunpowder was manufactured. The main Confederate plant for making gunpowder and explosives was there. It was decided, therefore, that the family would leave the city. Mary, the daughter and sister, went to a relative's. James Lamar took his two sons to Burch Place, a plantation that was part of his wife's estate.

As war refugees, father and sons remained at Burch Place until the war's end. Joseph R. Lamar later recalled how his father provided makeshift toys for the boys at Christmas while they were blockaded. A ball was made from an unraveled yarn sock. He claimed, too, to recall his father reading and explaining Lincoln's

---

[9]Clarinda Pendleton Lamar, *The Life of Joseph Rucker Lamar*, 1857-1916 (New York: G. P. Putnam's Sons, 1926), pp. 32, 233 ff.

Emancipation Proclamation to the assembled slaves at the plantation. The Proclamation declared that on Jan. 1, 1863, more than three million slaves in Georgia and other southern states would be forever free. Joseph Lamar did not remember that any of the freed people left then, which was many months before the war ended.[10]

Other Disciples who fled before Sherman's Army were members of the Acworth Christian Church. Nathan W. Smith, the minister, sold his possessions and moved to Jonesboro, southeast of Atlanta. He took the church bell and pew cushions with him. He "fell into the lines of both armies, and by them" lost nearly everything that he owned.[11] While the Confederate soldiers were camped at Jonesboro, under command of General John Bell Hood (1831-1879), who replaced Johnston in July, they took the bell and rang it day and night. Two officers, Cols. McIntyre and McAlpin, maintained headquarters at the Smith home. Unable to endure the constant bell ringing, Mrs. Mary Henderson and Mrs. White Smith, daughter and daughter-in-law of Nathan W. Smith, begged the officers to return the bell to them. It was done. The Smiths later moved 200 miles to Mitchell County where they remained until the spring of 1865.[12]

The Federal troops camped for some time at Acworth and left the thriving railroad village in ruins. They tore the Christian church building down, Mr. Smith reported, and moved it to Allatoona "to build shanties."[13]

Sherman fought slowly down to Atlanta, strategic railroad center, in a campaign termed by General Grant (1822-1885) "one of the most memorable in history." The city fell to Sherman's Army on Sept. 2, 1864. Sherman arrived at Atlanta shortly afterward. He later wrote, "I took up my headquarters in the home of Judge Lyons, which stood opposite one corner of the Court-

---

[10]*Ibid.*, p. 28.

[11]*Gospel Advocate*, Feb. 6, 1866, p. 88. *Christian Standard*, Aug. 25, 1866, p. 165.

[12]*Gospel Advocate*, Mar. 27, 1866, p. 204.

[13]*Ibid.*, Feb. 6, 1866, p. 88.

House Square.''[14]   The Sherman headquarters escaped
the Atlanta conflagration and from 1919 to 1928 housed
the Southern Christian Home, the house having grown
from four to 14 rooms.   The rock garden on the present
landscaped grounds of the brotherhood home for children
at 1011 Cleburne Avenue, North East, Atlanta, was made
from foundation stones of the historic Civil War house.

General Sherman ''was resolved to make Atlanta a
pure military garrison or depot'' requiring no troops
''to guard and protect the interests of a hostile population.''   Therefore, the city's evacuation after Federal
occupation meant the forced expulsion of about 12,000
civilians.   It followed a sharp, wordy exchange of letters
between Sherman and Hood.   The city was destroyed
by fire after much of it had been torn down or blown up.
The mass of ruins included the central business district
and the Christian church building.   The frame church
structure that burned was on the south side of Decatur
Street, between Collins and Lloyd Streets, near the
depot.   At least three-fourths of the city's buildings—
all but 400 of 4,500 houses and commercial structures—
were leveled.   Sherman was a ''kind of careless man
about fire,'' Henry W. Grady (1851-1889), Atlanta editor,
remarked later in his famous address on ''The New
South.''[15]

Sherman's Army included the 4th Kentucky Regiment.
John Beverly Vawter (1838-1897), later a noted Iowa
preacher of the Disciples, was a member of the regiment.
He was one of 2,000 soldiers sent around Atlanta by
Sherman to stop Confederate supplies by cutting rail
and telegraph lines.   The regiment was attacked and
nearly all of its members were captured or killed.   Vaw-

[14]William Tecumseh Sherman, *Memoirs of Gen. W. T. Sherman* (4th ed.
revised, corrected, and complete; New York: Charles L. Webster & Co.,
1891), II, 111.

[15]The complete text of ''The New South'' is in the Appendix (pp. 340-
350) of Nixon, *op. cit.*

ter went to the Andersonville Prison in Sumter County,
60 miles southwest of Macon, Ga.[16]

During the Atlanta campaign, General George Stone-
man (1822-1894) and about 700 of his Federal raiders
were captured by Confederate Cavalrymen and forced
to surrender. One of the raiders was Pvt. Archie Campbell, nephew of Alexander Campbell. He was imprisoned
at Andersonville with other members of his 14th Illinois
Cavalry. He had expected to become a preacher like
his famous uncle, but in June, 1854, he left Bethany, Va.
(now W. Va.), where he was born, with John Robinson's
Circus. A famous clown, he received many privileges
while at Andersonville from the Rebel officers with whom
he was a favorite. He was released from Andersonville
in an exchange of prisoners.[17]

Before the fall of Atlanta the Confederates were en-
camped along the Chattahoochee River near Walnut
Grove, plantation home of Judge Clark Howell, Sr., just
outside of the city's West End. A Disciple layman, the
Judge was the son-in-law of Dr. and Mrs. Daniel Hook
who then made their home with the Howells. The Judge
and Mary D. Hook were married in 1853. The Howell
estate had a chapel named Mount Hope (also New
Hope?) where the family and slaves worshiped with
Dr. Hook preaching when he could. When the Confederates were camped nearby, the chapel services were
crowded with the men in gray. Often there were confessions of faith in Christ with baptism following in the
river. J. William Jones, a Civil War preacher-historian,
claimed that as many as 150,000 Confederate soldiers
professed their Christian faith during the hostilities.[18]

[16]Sergeant Oats [John Beverly Vawter], *Prison Life in Dixie* (Chicago:
Central Book Concern, 1880), pp. 1 ff. On pp. 61 f. there is an account of
religious services in prison.

[17]Gil Robinson, *Old Wagon Show Days* (Cincinnati: Brockwell Co.,
1925), pp. 173 f.

[18]John William Jones, *Christ in the Camp; or, Religion in Lee's Army.*
Supplemented by a Sketch of the Work in the Other Confederate Armies
(Richmond: B. F. Johnson & Co., 1887), p. 390.

The Sherman troops, camped on the north bank of the Chattahoochee, prepared to take Atlanta. So the Howell and Hook families were moved to Sandersville to live with James S. Hook, oldest son of Dr. and Mrs. Hook. The servants subsequently followed and some household goods were moved. Finally, Dr. Hook and Judge Howell went to Sandersville by rail.

Sherman's Army was quartered at Walnut Grove for six months. When the soldiers left, the buildings on the estate were burned except the mill and miller's cottage. Even the sanctuary in the woods was destroyed. A series of skirmishes followed the capture of Atlanta. Sherman's march to the sea began anew, Nov. 15, 1864, and ended with the capture of Savannah just before Christmas.

The Hook and Howell families were overtaken by the Federal forces at Sandersville. Judge Howell and his family had, in the meantime, moved outside of town a few miles and he and Dr. J. D. Erwin, Sr., were in business together. On Nov. 26, when General Sherman arrived at Sandersville, there were 62,000 Yanks concentrated there for the drive to Savannah. "Fighting Joe" Wheeler's Rebel Cavalry gradually yielded Sandersville in a skirmish with Sherman's massive Army.

Many of the possessions of the Hooks were looted. A graphic account was left by Dr. Hook of the sacking of their Sandersville residence and the terrifying experiences which members of the household went through. His account follows:

When the infantry made their appearance they were exceedingly numerous, and were halted in every direction about us. Very soon they came into the yard to get water, as they said, but in a few minutes every part of the premises were robbed, outside of the dwelling, the storeroom pantry, smoke-house, corncrib, hen-house, cellar, and dairy. Up to this time two officers had kept them out of the dwelling. Now they suddenly left, and the roughs entered the house in all directions, and stole everything that they wanted, upstairs and downstairs, and as fast as one gang left, another entered and the work of pillage [continued]. Bedclothes, ladies' clothes, men's clothes—everything they fancied disappeared. Drawers, trunks, valises, and closets were opened, and contents scattered over the floors, in their rapid search for things they chose to appropriate. If I could persuade one of them to leave the articles he had, they would be taken by another. I finally let them alone, and looked on with as much apathy as possible. Plates, knives, spoons, teacups, saucers, etc., nearly all disappeared. One man met me with a handful of saucers, and being ashamed, said he would return them after dinner, but the promise was not kept.

One of the officers who protected the house for the first hour, had told the women and children to go into a room, and lock the door. For this kindness [we] were greatly indebted. It was not broken open, but the door had to be opened occasionally to let them see that I was telling the truth. One who had committed other depredations, now went to the door, and putting his foot against it, was ready to burst it open when I appealed to an officer in the parlor, to protect us from this violence. His answer was a fearful oath, threatening to blow my brains out if I did not clear out. Whether my appeal had roused another officer's attention to the ruffian, I know not, but when I turned around, one was interfering for our safety. He commanded the fellow to desist and leave the house, but this he refused to obey, he then walked off, and it was strange to notice the officer that had threatened my life for asking for protection. He jumped up, ran to the door, crying, "Yes, shoot him." I now returned to my room, where drawers, trunks, papers, etc. were scattered over the floor, and there found at the window, a negro putting on the only fine pair of cloth pants I had, threw it over his arm, and without looking at me walked off.

In the evening, or afternoon, after they had pillaged the house until they were tired, two surgeons, a chaplain, and an officer, whose rank I did not hear, came in, and conversed with me some time. They seemed to feel a sympathy for me, and I told them the men had left us nothing to eat, and yet they sent us nothing. I appealed to the Chaplain as he left to procure me protection. He promised, but nothing came of it, that I was sensible of. Another surgeon came in and talked to me very fairly. I remember he said that he never stole anything, but afterwards I met him coming downstairs with a table cloth in his hands. When he saw me he said he would like to have it for dressing wounds.

Towards night two men came downstairs, each with a mattress. I said, "Are you going to leave us nothing to sleep on?" One of them answered, "We will bring them back tomorrow." But nothing of the kind was done. On the contrary, when our servants went out to the camp for something to eat, they found the mattresses and brought them home, after women telling them that the soldiers had given the mattresses to them.

After a most horrible trial, night came on, and I fastened the doors, but soon a knock compelled me to open, for fear it would be forced. This crowd wanted whiskey. I told them that there was none, and they left. In a little while they returned, and said that they would search the house for it, and one took a candle and commenced rummaging a closet, where there was cotton thread, and I feared every moment that the house would take fire. This exhausted my patience and I said that I would not submit to it—that he or I should die first. Instantly he drew a long bowie knife and threatened my life, but seeing that I was entirely without arms, to which I called his attention, by saying if he chose he could strike as I was without arms. He said he would kill me, and burn my house over my head, if he or I must die, but the noise brought out the women and children, and their cries I think affected him. He said he would spare me on account of my gray hairs. He then went upstairs, promising not to burn the house. He soon came down, and he and his men left, and we were troubled no more that night.

The next day I kept the house locked, and only opened it when compelled to do so. The house was so completely rifled the day before, that they found but little now to take, but still, in small crowds, they continued to search every place. The negroes were robbed as well as the whites, and their clothes taken. They not only robbed them and us of everything that they could find, but took nearly everything we had to cook them. Fortunately for us our servants proved very faithful, and what with having some lard and flour that they failed to find, begging some potatoes, and picking up some meat at the Camps, we had something to eat, even before the army left. One of the male servants we have not heard of since they left. I presume he was so frightened that he is afraid to attempt his escape. The other was forced to go over thirty miles with them, when finding a hiding place, he concealed himself until they were gone, and then came home.

Late in the afternoon of this second day's stay among us, a very gentlemanly dressed man walked into the yard, and said, seeing some of the men in the houses, "I came in to inquire how they came here." I told him that some of the men were here nearly all the time, and that there were two upstairs. He went to the stairs and called the men down and scolded them very severely. He told them they were disgracing the army, and making him ashamed of it. They seemed very much scared, and while apologizing, called him, General. By this time another officer came in and the General said to him, "Major, I think we had best string these fellows up." The Major made no reply, and after a while the General said to the men, "Go to your posts, and let me hear of no more such conduct." I thanked the officer, who protected the ladies' room from violence, and requested him to continue his protection. His answer was that he cared for neither me nor my property, but acted alone for discipline. On the third day, which was Monday, they did not disturb as much, and the last incident that occurred in our sight was their rapid flight before our door, from the Confederate Cavalry.[19]

Sherman's Army reached the coast and captured Savannah just before Christmas, 1864. Within a few more months, after additional losses for the Confederacy, the South had to admit in the face of the grim reality that its cause was lost in defeat. The surrender at Appomatox was followed by Lincoln's assassination and death. The remnant of the Confederate cabinet held its last meeting at Washington, Ga. President Jefferson Davis was captured at Irwinsville, Ga., in May, 1865, and imprisoned for two years. Vice-President Alexander Stephens was arrested at his Crawfordville home, "Liberty Hall," May 11, 1865, and confined at Fort Warren, Boston Harbor, until Oct. 12, 1865, when he was released on parole.

THE DIFFICULTIES OF RECONSTRUCTION

The agonizing struggle of Civil War in Georgia, as elsewhere in the devastated areas of the Confederacy, led to the bitter era of social, economic, and political reconstruction. Andrew Johnson (1808-1875) of Tennessee was Lincoln's successor in the White House. It was a difficult time for the Disciples of Christ and their fellow-Georgians.

The long war that saved the American Union left Georgia prostrate. Prejudice and rancor were slow to die in the hearts of many destitute citizens. Most words

---

[19]Mary D. Howell, *op. cit.*, pp. 82-87.

and actions were "construed into something sectional."
After fighting bravely against terrific odds, there was
gloom and sorrow for all Southerners before any sem-
blance of real brotherhood emerged. Editor Tolbert Fanning doubted the "propriety of a hasty religious *reconstruction* with the friends of Christ North or South."[20]
The nation of 31,000,000 people had suffered a war death
loss of 600,000, including approximately 258,000 Southerners.

Georgia's economy was sadly disrupted. Confederate
money and investments were worthless. Political freedom for the Negroes meant an economic loss of $272,000,-
000 to their former owners. The ragged, footsore, and
half-starved Confederate soldier returned home to be
greeted by ruined homes, farms, and towns. The hero
of the gray jacket and cap was eloquently described by
Henry W. Grady, Atlanta editor and florid orator, in his
classic address of 1886 on "The New South." The stock
was gone, former slaves free and hungry in many cases,
barns empty, and trade disrupted. The cultural life that
had prevailed with a feudal magnificence in Georgia had
become only a memory of antebellum days. On every
hand there were reminders of the revolution that had
taken place throughout the South.

Destitution was common throughout Georgia. The per-
plexing problems called for the courage of a wounded
soldier, as urged in one of Grady's moving perorations.
Yet it was no secret that Atlanta recovered rapidly with
fortunes for those who quickly seized their opportunities.

The difficulties of reconstruction were increased by the
temporary disfranchisement of the former Confederates.
Then, Georgia was forced to endure military rule twice
within a few years.[21] During many months the Federal
and State offices were in the hands of Negroes, Northern

---

[20]*Gospel Advocate*, Apr. 17, 1866, p. 243.

[21]Two prominent Disciples, James S. Lamar and James S. Hook, were
delegates to the 1865 Georgia Constitutional Convention. On Apr. 10,
1867, when the State began proceedings in the U. S. Supreme Court to
test the constitutionality of Congressional reconstruction legislation, a
Pennsylvania Disciple, Jeremiah Sullivan Black (1810-1883), was one of
three counsel representing Georgia (Clark Howell, *op. cit.*, I, 583, 586).

adventurers or carpetbaggers, and Southern whites, sympathetic to Negroes, called scalawags. The state had one Negro Congressman in 1869-1871. When Georgia, in 1870, ratified the fifteenth amendment to the Constitution of the United States, it was readmitted to the Union. That amendment gave the franchise to Negroes.

The Civil War actually delayed enlightened emancipation of southern Negroes. The war's aftermath included the residue of a continuing racial problem. While nearly all Negroes readily accepted their legal freedom, yet they little understood its full significance or their responsibilities. Many white Georgians were concerned about the welfare of Negroes. The concerned white citizens sought to help the freed people, in cooperation with their brothers of the North "if permitted to retain their self-respect and freedom from constant insult" by those Northerners.[22] Thus slowly, Southerners began to realize that the Negro must not become a permanent liability to the South.

Numerous Negro churches and Sunday schools were formed in the South as Negroes emerged from slavery. The *Cincinnati Review* stated that, "The number of Disciples among the colored people is much greater in the South than is generally known."[23] There was some indication recorded of the attitude manifested toward Negroes by white Georgia Disciples during reconstruction days. One of the evangelists, Nathan W. Smith, wrote that

. . . the freedmen are working much better this year than last, and I think both classes are learning how to appreciate their new relationship, and consequently acting more in harmony with each other. I shall, myself, rejoice to see schools for the blacks all through this country. They should now be

---

[22]*Gospel Advocate*, Sept. 5, 1867, p. 709.

[23]Quoted in *Gospel Advocate*, Feb. 27, 1868, p. 199. At the 1869 Louisville National Convention of Disciples of Christ, Dr. Marshall of Atlanta "expressed his determination to preach the Gospel to both the colored and white people" (*Report of Proceedings* of the Twenty-first Anniversary Meeting of the American Christian Missionary Society, Held at Louisville, Oct. 19, 20 and 21, 1869 [Cincinnati: H. S. Bosworth, 1869], p. 24).

educated and elevated in their morals, and taught to read the Word of the Lord, that they may learn the true religion instead of so much superstition.[24]

That generous Disciple of Augusta, Mrs. Emily H. Tubman, provided for her former slaves who continued to farm. She gave them an acreage and furnished clothing and provisions regularly. Apparently she did not lose all of her property or investments during the period of war and reconstruction.

Philip F. Lamar, evangelizing in Northeast Georgia in 1867, reported to the American Christian Missionary Society that he considered it desirable that a "prudent and faithful colored man" should be sent by the Society to "labor among the freedmen in Georgia." He reported that "E. L. Whatley, a very able man who has recently joined us from the Baptists, is laboring with much promise, among the freedmen in Augusta, Georgia. He is mainly sustained in the field by Sister Tubman."[25]

By the end of the hostilities, the family of Judge Clark Howell, Sr., had resumed life at Walnut Grove near Atlanta. The miller's cottage was enlarged and the family resided there for five years. Capt. Evan P. Howell, who in 1876 became owner and editor of the *Atlanta Constitution,* had five dollars after his discharge. He cut the logs with his own hands to build himself and family a house. He cut timber and sold lumber from Walnut Grove for two years, along with farming routine.

Dr. and Mrs. Daniel Hook returned to Walnut Grove, too, as soon as possible. A school was constructed and Dr. Hook preached to neighborhood groups and assisted in conducting Sunday schools. Sunday morning services were held for white people and evening meetings for Negroes. He gave the Negroes a Bible and 165 copies of the New Version of the New Testament.[26]

---

[24]*Gospel Advocate,* Apr. 11, 1867, p. 293. Smith never owned a slave (*Christian Standard,* Aug. 25, 1866, p. 165).

[25]*Christian Standard,* Nov. 2, 1867, cover p. 343. The *Gospel Advocate* approved that "old preacher from our Baptist brethren" preaching in the Church of Christ at Augusta, adding that, "We need association, the wearing down of prejudice" (July 10, 1866, p. 443; July 24, 1866, p. 480).

[26]Mary D. Howell, *op. cit.,* p. 88.

There were large responsibilities in Georgia then to be assumed by the Disciples and other religious leaders, but they did not shirk them. The churches with their faithful supporters overcame much indifference and accomplished some things because of a heroic determination. They buckled down to their difficult tasks in spite of overwhelming destitution everywhere among whites and Negroes alike. The desire to earn a living was the absorbing thought with everyone, Dr. Hook's biographer stated.

CONCERNED BRETHREN AID THE DESTITUTE

A few months after the war's end, James Atkins, formerly of Akron, Ohio, the Federal revenue collector at Atlanta and an evangelist of the Disciples, urged that James S. Lamar be supported by the American Christian Missionary Society as a missionary at Atlanta. The Georgia Disciples, he stated, were unable to do much for themselves even though Atlanta had prospects of rapid growth.[27] Editor W. K. Pendleton endorsed the proposal and suggested that the missionary society consider it. Prompt action followed. The *American Christian Review* soon reported that the board had "appointed our very talented J. S. Lamar to labor as an evangelist in Georgia, at a salary of $1,000 per annum,"[28]

In 1860 a committee of the A.C.M.S., listed Georgia as one of eight areas that would produce evangelistic results if assistance was provided. The war intervened, however, and no progress in that direction was made until 1866. In spite of much opposition to the missionary society in Georgia, the brethren advocating the principle of cooperation received aid that year. The report

[27]*Millennial Harbinger*, Jan., 1866, p. 44. James Atkins received an honorary M.A. degree from Bethany College in 1870 (*Millennial Harbinger*, June, 1870, p. 358).

[28]Quoted in the *Gospel Advocate*, Apr. 17, 1866, p. 242. The mention of J. S. Lamar may have been an error as other reports mentioned his brother Philip F. Lamar as the A.C.M.S. missionary in Georgia.

of the Society's Board of Managers to the 1866 National
Convention in Cincinnati stated:

New York, Pennsylvania, Ohio, Indiana, Michigan, Tennessee, Kansas, Nebraska, California, with the addition of
Georgia, during the present year, comprise our home fields.
All of these have been faithfully cultivated by our missionaries so far as they have been enabled to extend their labors,
yielding with but few exceptions a rich harvest. . . . Our
mission in Georgia has been quite successful. Our Missionary
there has been actively at work since last March, and his labors
have resulted in great good.[29]

The convention action regarding mission work continuing in Georgia was, as follows:

With respect to the necessity of the Southern field, your Committee have been able to obtain no satisfactory information except in regard to Georgia. We find that portions of that State
are greatly in want of men; that other portions lack men and
money. We therefore recommend that Rev. P. F. Lamar be
continued as a Missionary, and that one more be employed, if
practicable, for that State.[30]

At the 1867 convention, a report from P. F. Lamar said
that he no longer needed outside help since the churches
for which he preached in Clarke, Jackson, and Walton
Counties were able to support him. He endorsed both
the idea of cooperation and the society as an organization
thus:

I feel that I owe the Society a debt of gratitude which I can
never pay. When it was impossible for me to be sustained in the
field by the brethren at home the Society sustained me for
them. . . . God bless you and all connected with the Society.[31]

Other Georgia Disciples kept busy evangelizing during the 1860's. They overcame many difficulties in their

---

[29]*Report of Proceedings* of the Eighteenth Anniversary Meeting of the
American Christian Missionary Society. Held at Cincinnati, Oct. 23, 24,
25, 1866. (Cincinnati: H. S. Bosworth, 1866), p. 10.

[30]*Ibid.*, pp. 14 f.

[31]*Report of Proceedings* of the Nineteenth Anniversary Meeting of
the American Christian Missionary Society. Held at Cincinnati, Oct. 22,
23, and 24, 1867 (Cincinnati: H. S. Bosworth, 1867), p. 10. *Christian
Standard*, Nov. 2, 1867, cover p. 343.

travel and preaching, thus making the record even more significant. Nathan W. Smith, at Jonesboro, was located 10 miles from the nearest Christian church, yet in 1865 he welcomed about 100 new members at preaching services.[32]

A. C. Borden was baptized at Cedartown, Ga., in July, 1859, after he heard Nathan W. Smith preach. Borden then read the Scriptures so much that he lost the sight of one eye. In the latter part of 1862, a surgeon stopped him from reading with the other eye. However, Borden did not stop preaching. In April, 1866, he wrote that he had preached 1,700 discourses during the last four years. He was often away from his home near Carrollton, Carroll County, four to six weeks at a time. During those years he received 325 additions to the several congregations he served and organized four new churches. He "once read over a hundred hymns without a book" and like many preachers of those years often repeated whole chapters of Scripture from memory.[33]

There were frequent moving letters from Georgia Disciples in the brotherhood periodicals concerning their sad plight amidst the destitution so prevalent after the war. The *Gospel Advocate* resumed publication at Nashville, Tenn., in January, 1866, and issued the first general appeal in the brotherhood for money, provisions, and clothing to relieve destitute brethren in the South. The *Christian Standard, Millennial Harbinger* and other periodicals soon joined in the relief appeal.

The 1866 National Convention in Cincinnati gave extended consideration to providing aid for Southerners. However, the gathering apparently decided (the minutes recorded no vote of adoption of the committee report) that the matter was "beyond the range of the constitutional limitations of this Society, and one therefore to which we can as a Society render no pecuniary aid."[34]

---

[32]*Gospel Advocate*, Feb. 6, 1866, p. 88.

[33]*Ibid.*, Feb. 27, 1866, p. 141; May 8, 1866, p. 303. During 1866 Borden received 200 members into churches in Carroll, Coweta, Fayette, and Spalding Counties, Ga., and four Alabama counties (*Gospel Advocate*, Jan. 3, 1867, p. 16).

[34]*Report of Proceedings, op. cit.*, 1866, pp. 5, 12 f.

Of course, in providing some missionary support for isolated Southerners, white and Negro, the agency made a minor contribution to the problem.

In 1866, Joseph Wheeler wrote from Chattooga County, as follows:

> . . . I have traveled and preached all the time of the war when able, but not only I, but almost all the country have been stripped and left without anything; yea, brethren, I, with many others, cannot get a sufficient amount of food and raiment, . . .
> . . . There is no money in this section, and nothing to sell to bring it till crops are made.[35]

Letters from Washington Bacon of Trenton and A. C. Borden, Carroll County, also described needs in their areas. By the autumn of 1866, with drought causing failure of crops in much of Georgia and elsewhere, a Nashville committee published its cooperative appeal for the destitute. The committee consisted of V. M. Metcalfe, P. S. Fall, and David Lipscomb. It was promised that gifts would be "scrupulously and sacredly forwarded, and equitably distributed." When considered necessary a "trustworthy agent" accompanied and distributed supplies.[36]

"The most needy congregation in the South" was Bethany Church of Jackson County, according to its minister, P. F. Lamar, who reported conditions thus on one occasion:

> . . . There are members there who are actually suffering for the necessaries of life. They are without meat, bread, or provisions of any kind, and not a single individual in the whole community able to assist them. The committee distributed the 120 bushels of corn you sent them last December amongst the widows and orphans—only one male received any of it—a poor maimed soldier. . . . J. M. Crow, their deacon, . . . gave me the names of no less than eight widows—having in all twenty-five children—who were without anything to eat.[37]

35*Gospel Advocate*, June 5, 1866, p. 359.

36*Ibid.*, Nov. 6, 1866, p. 719.

37*Ibid.*, Feb. 28, 1867, p. 176. A 10-dollar gift was acknowledged by the paper, June 27, 1867, p. 504, for the Bethany Church from "a brother at McKinney, Texas."

Later that spring Nathan W. Smith wrote: "The cry for bread comes up on every hand. I have given away out of that sent to me for my family, near fifty bushels of corn and a hundred pounds of meat. I cannot deny poor suffering women and children."[38]

In addition to Smith, other Georgia preachers who had help from the Nashville committee included Joseph Wheeler, A. C. Borden, Philip F. Lamar, and Washington Bacon. They also assisted in the distribution as overseers. One allotment of provisions and clothing sent to Georgia in the summer of 1866 was valued at nearly $2,000.[39] Generally, distribution was made to the "poor, needy widows and orphan children of the brotherhood."[40]

However, denominational or racial lines were seldom drawn in the distribution. Acknowledging a check, N. W. Smith said, "I shall not discriminate in favor of the 'whites,' as some are doing."[41] P. F. Lamar referred to the problem thus:

... We have had to feed Methodists, Baptists, and some who belong to no church. The calls were so very pressing that it was impossible to resist them. I have, however, instructed Bro. [W. Y.] Elder not to supply others while so many of our own brethren were suffering. Members of other denominations walk from six to ten miles beseeching him to give them only a small pittance to save them from starvation.[42]

In regard to the distribution of relief aid, David Lipscomb, a member of the Nashville committee, said, "Our

---

[38]*Ibid.*, May 23, 1867, p. 417. Acknowledging a check for aid sent by the Editor of the *Millennial Harbinger*, Smith said that he had distributed relief money and food "far and wide in our State for hundreds of miles ... I could once, in a small way, do something with my own means. But that day is past, and by a cruel war, which I had no hand in bringing on, I am reduced to poverty and want—myself and family" (*Millennial Harbinger*, Sept., 1867, p. 501).

[39]*Gospel Advocate*, July 31, 1866, p. 495.

[40]*Ibid.*, Oct. 2, 1866, p. 638.

[41]*Millennial Harbinger*, Feb., 1867, p. 86. See, also, *Christian Standard*, Sept. 29, 1866, pp. 204 f.; Dec. 9, 1871, p. 388.

[42]*Gospel Advocate*, Apr. 25, 1867, p. 330. A similar expression was made by Mr. Lamar in the periodical of June 6, 1867, p. 457. Hiram Travis of Spalding County also stated a similar viewpoint regarding distribution of provisions, according to a letter in the *Advocate*, Aug. 22, 1867, p. 676.

object is to relieve, first the destitute Saints [that is, Disciples]; second our suffering fellow mortal."[43]

The effect of distribution among others besides the brethren was not without beneficial effects to the Disciples. "Your contribution of provisions is having a most happy influence on the community," wrote Philip F. Lamar. He continued, "never were my congregations so large and attentive at this season of the year . . . all see we are practically exemplifying the great principles we teach."[44]

The generous gifts made for the destitute South were prompted by genuine Christian fellowship and were not to be construed from any political or sectional viewpoint. George W. Longan (1819-1891) wrote from Missouri that "gray-haired union men, whose sons followed the fortunes of the old flag on the tented field, were among the first and most liberal contributors."[45]

Some Georgia neighborhoods had persons able to feed and clothe themselves. The *Gospel Advocate* reported as follows:

> . . . One church in Georgia, for whose poor relief was proposed, replied with the tone of Christian spirit, "We have poor, but showers have been more abundant with us than in most neighborhoods, so we will be able to supply the wants of our own poor," and so transferred the proposed offering to a more destitute sister congregation.[46]

"Had I better send Bibles or Bread?" inquired Joseph Kirtley Rogers (1828-1882), principal of Christian Col-

---

[43]*Ibid.*, Nov. 6, 1866, p. 720.

[44]*Ibid.*, Apr. 25, 1867, p. 330. In the issue of June 6, 1867, p. 457, concerning food distribution, Mr. Lamar said: "all are pleased, and the whole community most favorably impressed. Had an overwhelming congregation . . ."

[45]*Ibid.*, Nov. 13, 1866, p. 736. The issue of July 10, 1866, p. 443, acknowledged a gift from a Kentucky "Christian and Baptist brother."

[46]*Ibid.*, Nov. 27, 1866, p. 757. That church *may* have been the one at Augusta which in 1867 or 1868 gave $27, and $32 the next year, to the A.C.M.S. (*Report of Proceedings* of the Twentieth Anniversary Meeting of the American Christian Missionary Society. Held at Cincinnati, Oct. 20, 21 and 22, 1868. [Cincinnati: H. S. Bosworth, 1868], p. 29. *Report of Proceedings, op. cit.* 1869, p. 29.)

lege, Columbia, Mo.   Editor Lipscomb adroitly replied, "Send bread now, brethren, and afterwards the Bibles and preachers."[47]

Letters expressing gratitude for the money and food appeared frequently from Georgia brethren in both the *Gospel Advocate* and *Millennial Harbinger*.   Gifts were often accepted with "tears streaming down the cheeks of the beneficiaries," it was reported.[48]   The Northeast Georgia Cooperation meeting of 1867, convened at Christian Chapel, Jackson County, Oct. 4, unanimously adopted resolutions expressing thanks for the substantial assistance provided.[49]

Gifts were received by the *Gospel Advocate* for the destitute of the South from some Southerners.   In addition, contributions came from the North, Middle and Far West.   The *Pacific Gospel Herald,* Santa Clara, Calif., sent more than $1,000 in gold in two installments.[50]   Some provisions and clothing were shipped free of charge by the railroads.   Some were designated for specific persons, particularly preachers.

More than $50,000 in provisions, clothing, and cash were collected and distributed to destitute Disciples and others in the South during the post-war years, it was reported by the *Gospel Advocate* in the autumn of 1869.[51]

By the summer of 1867, the Nashville committee was able to help meet the needs of destitute preachers, thus making it possible for them to devote more time to preaching.   One was W. T. Lowe, High Shoals, Morgan County.   Expressing thanks for $25.00, he said that a gift was never more "in season, as I have not one pound of meat of any description for my family to eat, and with-

---

[47]*Gospel Advocate,* June 13, 1867, p. 476.

[48]*Ibid.,* July 31, 1866, p. 496.

[49]*Ibid.,* Oct. 17, 1867, p. 833. *Millennial Harbinger,* Nov., 1867, p. 631.

[50]*Gospel Advocate,* Aug. 8, 1867, p. 626. Disciples in Southern Georgia sent $50 (*Gospel Advocate,* Apr. 18, 1867, p. 303). The Georgetown, Ky., Church sent $56.40 for Corinth Church, Walton County (*Gospel Advocate,* May 16, 1867, p. 387).

[51]*Ibid.,* Sept. 30, 1869, p. 890. Editor David Lipscomb later put the total at "over $100,000" (*Gospel Advocate,* Aug. 24, 1899, p. 537).

out a dollar upon earth. I have been almost ready, at times, to give up, but the Lord has always come to my relief."[52]   Another such preacher was Washington Bacon of Trenton. He walked most of the time to preaching appointments, though nearly 68 years old. One church was 23 miles from his home across Sand Mountain and the Tennessee River. He claimed that no other Disciple "has taken it on foot and done the amount of preaching that I have."[53]   Nathan W. Smith was another, who, late in 1867, had traveled 2,300 to 2,400 miles that year in evangelistic labors.[54]

The cry of too few preachers for the need was heard time and again from Georgians for many years. It was most unusual, therefore, when the Sandersville church advertised in the *Gospel Advocate* for a pastor "who can come well recommended."[55]

Appeals for funds with which to build or repair church buildings were conspicuous in the *Millennial Harbinger*. The Atlanta congregation was the outstanding Georgia church that received such assistance.[56]   James S. Lamar and F. P. Perdue both appealed for it. While the new Atlanta building was going up, the congregation met at Walton and Forsyth Streets in an upper room. It was occupied during the week as an office and furnished gratuitously for Sunday worship.[57]   Weekly meetings were the vogue for the congregation by 1869 or before. Mr. Perdue wrote early in 1868 that the new edifice was being erected on Hunter Street, but due to poverty of the members, the building was incomplete. Funds were sought to provide a roof for the exposed structure.[58]

[52]*Ibid.*, Oct. 10, 1867, p. 815.

[53]*Ibid.*, Oct. 3, 1867, p. 800.

[54]*Ibid.*, Nov. 7, 1867, pp. 896 f.

[55]*Ibid.*, Nov. 18, 1869, p. 1067; Dec. 16, 1869, p. 1144.

[56]A draft for $50 was acknowledged by J. S. Lamar in the *Millennial Harbinger*, Feb., 1867, p. 85. Material about aid to churches also appeared in the *Harbinger* for July, 1866, pp. 325 f.; Jan., 1867, p. 44; May, 1867, p. 271; Aug., 1867, p. 449.

[57]*Gospel Advocate*, June 4, 1868, p. 538.

[58]*Millennial Harbinger*, Apr., 1868, p. 225.

A year later there was $5,000 cash on hand, but $2,000 or $3,000 more was needed.[59]   The building cost $15,000 when completed.   Mrs. Emily H. Tubman of Augusta was one of the contributors. The structure, minus carpeting, was dedicated on Jan. 16, 1870, by J. S. Lamar.

F. Plion Perdue, Atlanta minister for several years, beginning in 1867, was a charter member of the congregation.   He had been immersed by Nathan W. Smith in Fayette County.   When Editor David Lipscomb stopped at Atlanta in 1868 and visited with Mr. Perdue "in his leather apron with his hammer and his anvil," the Georgia preacher was working "at his smith's forge in the machine shop of the State road of Georgia.   He is foreman of those shops."[60]

T. M. Harris became the Atlanta pastor late in 1869, apparently with a contract, the first indication that Georgia preachers were entering into such formal contractual relations with the churches.[61]   The congregation numbered about 80 members in June, 1870.[62]   The first Ladies' Aid Society was organized in 1870 with Mrs. S. C. Perdue as president.[63]   In July, 1870, James S. Lamar held a meeting for the Atlanta church; one of six additions was a prominent legislator, E. T. Higbee, Senator in the Georgia Legislature.[64]

RUEFUL CRIES OF UNSCRIPTURAL INNOVATIONS

The Christian Almanac, statistical report of the Disciples of Christ, was published in 1867.   It was compiled by Levi H. Dowling (1844-1911) of Indianapolis.   Much

---

[59]*Gospel Advocate,* Apr. 1, 1869, p. 305.   The pre-war Decatur Street lot was sold for $3,025; the central and larger Hunter Street site cost $2,000 (*Christian Standard,* Aug. 25, 1866, p. 165).

[60]*Ibid.,* Nov. 19 [26], 1868, p. 2029.

[61]*Christian Standard,* Dec. 10, 1870, p. 394.

[62]*Gospel Advocate,* June 9, 1870, p. 540.

[63]Mr. and Mrs. H. D. Bolles, "A History of the First Christian Church, Atlanta, Georgia, 1851-1951," in *One Hundred Years of the First Christian Church, Atlanta, Georgia, Centennial Celebration, 1851-1951* (Atlanta: Cullom & Ghertner Co., 1951), p. [16].

[64]*Christian Standard,* Aug. 13, 1870, p. 262; Sept. 3, 1870, p. 286.

of the material concerning southern churches, "except, perhaps Georgia," was reported unreliable by the *Gospel Advocate* which opposed publication of the survey.[65] The statistical table (p. 42) showed 5,600 Disciples in Georgia with 30 preachers.[66] However, the list of ministers included names of only 24.[67]

Religious books, including Bibles were scarce in Georgia since many were destroyed during the war by the ravages of the hostilities. The *Gospel Advocate* pages in 1869 and 1870 listed 21 persons from Georgia who received books, hymnals, and/or tracts. Those orders indicated an improving economical situation and suggested that the brethren knew the value of the printed word in promoting the cause in Georgia.

The brethren in Georgia began to get more attention in the *Christian Standard* when James S. Lamar became associate editor in 1869. The periodical began weekly publication in 1866 under the editorship of Isaac Errett.[68] Mr. Lamar was author of an instruction booklet for freedmen and others on biblical questions, published in 1867. It was entitled, *The Second Reader and Question Book for Sunday Schools.*[69] He was also a contributor of a sermon, "The History of Redemption Reproduced in the Redeemed," in *The Living Pulpit of the Christian*

---

[65]*Gospel Advocate*, Mar. 21, 1867, p. 239; Nov. 27, 1866, pp. 765 f.; Dec. 11, 1866, p. 800.

[66]At the 1870 Georgia Convention of Disciples, it was reported that there were "some 50 churches" in the state.

[67]Levi H. Dowling (Compiler), *The Christian Almanac* (Indianapolis: L. H. Dowling, 1867), p. 32. The incomplete Georgia list follows: James Atkins, Atlanta; A. C. Borden, Carrollton; W. Bacon, Trenton; J. O. Baker, Chattanooga; M. B. Doster, Athens; D. W. Elder, Watkinsville; W. S. Fears, Bear Creek; T. M. Harris, Davisboro; W. H. Hooker, Bainbridge; F. M. D. Hopkins, Colquit; Daniel Hook, Sandersville; Dr. Francis Jackson, High Shoals; Robert Mayfield, Monroe; H. Marshall, Atlanta; Eld. Mallory, Savannah; Eld. Norris, Colquit; F. P. Perdue, Atlanta; Jas. Rahn, Guyton; N. W. Smith, Jonesboro; E. L. Whatley, Augusta; and Joseph Wheeler, Tyron's Factory.

[68]Lamar's name as associate editor of the *Christian Standard* first appeared on the masthead, Aug. 14, 1869; his salutatory editorial was in the issue of Sept. 4, 1869.

[69]*Christian Standard*, Aug. 31, 1867, p. 275.

Church. The 1868 book contained biographical sketches
and portraits of Mr. Lamar and the other 27 contributors.
The popular volume was reprinted several times for
a generation.[70]

Philip F. Lamar, then of Jefferson, Ga., made one of
his rare appearances in print, other than with news reports and letters, in the *Gospel Advocate* of 1868. A
lengthy sermon was entitled, "Obedience to the Lord
the Only Safe Ground."[71]

A number of Georgia Disciples, mostly preachers, had
contributions in periodicals, especially the *Gospel Advocate,* during those years. That paper was then showing obvious signs of its later "anti"-organ stand. The
writers usually discussed biblical issues. One preacher
said, "Oh, that Christians would fight for Christ, talk
for Christ, and let Presidents and Presidential elections
alone."[72] Little did he realize, apparently, that there
was much for Christians to do in election campaigns.

Inquiring readers sought help from editors on many
matters. Such inquiries began, "Will you please give us
your views . . . ?" Controversial questions raised included missionary societies, weekly observance of the
Lord's Supper, foot-washing, etc. Interpretations of
the editors tended to become more significant as they increased their prestige with the passing of the years. The
legalism consistently proclaimed by the *Advocate,* which
had loyal supporters in Georgia, thus became firmly en-
trenched in the state and became an important factor in
resultant divisions that plagued the Georgia brethren.

The first National Convention of the Disciples in 1849
recommended to the churches "the duty and importance
of organizing and establishing Sunday schools in every
congregation."[73] However, the Georgia Christian
churches did not quickly establish such schools. Sunday

[70]W. T. Moore (Editor), *The Living Pulpit of the Christian Church*
(Cincinnati: R. W. Carroll & Co., 1868), pp. 401-410.

[71]*Gospel Advocate,* May 21, 1868, pp. 491-499.

[72]W. T. Lowe, *Gospel Advocate,* Aug. 13, 1868, p. 786.

[73]*Report of the Proceedings, op. cit.,* 1849, p. 36.

schools were sometimes introduced into southern communities or congregations for instruction of Negroes or illiterate whites. They gradually gained popular acceptance.

Exactly which congregation of Georgia Disciples conducted the first Sunday school, and when, is a moot question. Perhaps Savannah did so before the Civil War; Acworth, too, deserves consideration. Sandersville organized a school in 1865. By 1868 or 1869, Augusta doubtless had a school.[74] The several congregations served by A. C. Borden had Sunday schools in 1868.[75] The Corinth Church, in 1868, had a school of about 75 pupils, probably established by Lewis Allen and W. C. Nowell.[76]

The Georgia brethren thrived on their controversies of those years. They became the means, whether purposely or not, of gaining new adherents for the Disciples. Religious debates were popular and attracted crowds. Most of the preaching Disciples were fanatical in advocating legalistic views then commonly held.

No wonder, then, that most Georgia Disciples adhered rather rigidly in the reconstruction years to traditional beliefs and practices. Gradually musical instruments began to be introduced into church worship. However, the sentinels of the faith, led in the South by the *Gospel Advocate,* opposed the trend. All human expediencies and innovations were opposed without a "Thus saith the Lord" to prove their necessity in the church worship and organization. There seemed to have been no consideration at all of the alternative principle, "This is what the Lord expects us to be doing." The opposition was not only against missionary societies, musical instruments, and, often, Sunday schools; they protested also against colleges, conventions, printed lesson helps, and other things that came into use with increasing cul-

[74]*Ibid.,* 1869, p. 29.

[75]*Gospel Advocate,* June 25, 1868, p. 739.

[76]*Ibid.,* Sept. 17, 1868, p. 902.

tural progress. Were the Disciples to accept or shun those innovations? The lines were being drawn for a decisive battle.

A. C. Borden, a Georgia evangelist, joined with J. M. Barnes of Alabama in a lengthy statement concerning "missionary societies, evangelizing societies and co-operation meetings." It was argued that they had the same origin, that is, "the want of money to support ministers." The two preachers withdrew, in 1866, from their cooperation meeting, but contended that they were not "anti-missionary or anti-cooperation" in principle.[77]

However, in spite of opposition to missionary organizations, other Georgia Disciples supported them. James S. Lamar, an associate editor of the *Christian Standard* beginning in 1869, was among the group of adherents. Isaac Errett, editor of the *Standard,* later was one of the organizers and president until his death of the Foreign Christian Missionary Society.

The struggle in Georgia for freedom from exclusive tests of fellowship was only a reflection of the crucial one that was taking place in churches throughout the brotherhood. Like their brethren elsewhere, they approached their problems unhesitatingly, but more often with open mouths than with open minds. The opponents of missionary organizations completely overlooked the fact that Thomas Campbell's "Christian Association of Washington," Pa., was really only a missionary society formed to spread the gospel.[78]

A friend of the cause, Orrin Gates, disgusted with the prolonged controversy, put the issue in memorable words when he declared pointedly: "This despicable twaddle against Missionary Societies is a disgrace to our brotherhood, and is doing more to retard the onward progress of the truth, as it is in Jesus, than any other obstacle."[79]

It was possible for two Georgians, James S. Lamar and Mrs. Helen Atkins, to attend the 1866 annual meeting

[77]*Ibid.*, July 31, 1866, pp. 485 ff.

[78]W. K. Pendleton, *Report of Proceedings, op. cit.*, 1866, pp. 30 f.

[79]*Christian Standard*, Nov. 30, 1867, p. 379.

of the American Christian Missionary Society at Cincinnati. Lamar addressed the assembly and was a member of the committee that drafted a memorial resolution honoring Alexander Campbell. The last of the four "founding fathers" of the movement to die, Campbell passed on at his Bethany, W. Va., home, Mar. 4, 1866. Lamar was a vice-president of the A.C.M.S., from 1856 through 1860; in 1858 he became a life director when Mrs. Emily H. Tubman generously paid the $100 fee for him.[80]

Nathan W. Smith also attended a fellowship meeting in 1866. It was a "consultation" meeting of the brethren that met at Murfreesboro, Tenn. How Smith secured his expense funds is not known. Perhaps some more affluent brother assisted him. Or, it may be that Smith took advantage of the offer of the Nashville and Chattanooga Railroad to provide free return tickets to those paying one-way fares.[81]

At the Murfreesboro conference, Smith served on a committee and delivered "an excellent discourse" on the "value of Christian suffering."[82] He rejoiced, after his return to Georgia, at being permitted to attend for once in his life such a fellowship gathering.[83]

Joseph Wheeler of Trion Factory in Chattooga County represented Georgia at a similar consultation meeting in October, 1866, at Franklin, near Nashville, Tenn. He, too, urged aid for the destitute South.[84]

Cooperation meetings for both fellowship and business were conducted in Georgia during the 1860's. Apparently,

---

[80]*Report of Proceedings* of the Anniversary Meeting of the American Christian Missionary Society. Held in Cincinnati, Oct. 19, 20, 21, 1858 (Cincinnati: G. B. Bentley & Co., Printers, 1858), p. 24. *Report of Proceedings, op. cit.*, 1866, pp. 4, 11, 15.

[81]*Gospel Advocate*, May 22, 1866, p. 325. Smith knew Thomas Fears of Spalding County, Ga., who died at 85 on Oct. 17, 1868. Smith wrote that Fears was "remarkably benevolent . . . and gave liberally to the cause of Christianity. He gave away his means by the thousands" (*Gospel Advocate*, Nov. 12, 1868, p. 2003).

[82]*Ibid.*, June 26, 1866, p. 405.

[83]*Ibid.*, July 3, 1866, p. 419.

[84]*Ibid.*, Nov. 6, 1866, p. 720.

an effort was made in 1862 to form an evangelizing association. Nathan W. Smith referred to such an organization thus: "In 1862 a few met in Atlanta and formed an Evangelizing Society with its officers, this soon died."[85] That is all that is known about such a society.

The Northeast Georgia group of churches held a meeting for fellowship at Christian Chapel, Jackson County, Oct. 4-6, 1867. There were 23 "messengers" (delegates) from seven churches having 600 members with 74 additions reported by the churches for the year. A significant action for that time was approval of a recommendation for what became known as the "Lord's Acre" plan of stewardship. The report that was adopted stated:

> The committee are thoroughly impressed, that if each "tiller of the soil" will lay off one acre, more or less, of his best land, and *cultivate it for the Lord,* that the treasuries of the churches of Christ in Northeast Georgia will never be empty, while the families of our evangelists will never be in want. We desire to see the sisters engage heartily in this work, and earnestly recommend them to devote a portion of the proceeds of their dairies and poultry yards.[86]

It was estimated that 200 acres should be cultivated for God by Northeast Georgia Disciples if they followed the plan. No record tells the results of the far-reaching proposal. The plan, however, was an indication of the stewardship struggle beginning among the Disciples to give systematically according to the way they had prospered.

David Lipscomb, editor of the *Gospel Advocate,* attended the 1868 Northeast Georia Cooperation meeting in October at the Corinth Church near Walnutgrove, Walton County. He was there for 10 days, Oct. 24-Nov. 2. The Corinth congregation was a new one with a commodious meetinghouse. "Alas," Mr. Lipscomb said, "the congregations in Georgia that we visited do not meet weekly for worship."[87]

85*Ibid.,* Jan. 12, 1871, p. 30.

86Ibid., Oct. 17, 1867, pp. 833 f. *Millennial Harbinger,* Nov. 1867, pp. 631 f.

87*Gospel Advocate,* Nov. 19 [26], 1868, pp. 2029 ff.

The 1869 Northeast Georgia Cooperation meeting was at Antioch Church, Clarke County, Sept. 17-19, with W. T. Lowe as moderator. It was decided that churches within the district should raise $300 to pay for an evangelist's labors for the four months of July-October, 1870. The new Martin Springs congregation of Jackson County was represented in the fellowship for the first time.[88] Philip F. Lamar was chosen evangelist although no salary was promised for his services.[89]

On occasion, apparently, some of the brethren would be disfellowshipped. Nathan W. Smith wrote about such happening at County Line Church in 1867, as follows: "the Church had to withdraw fellowship from two erring brethren in disorder."[90] There was no suggestion of what was involved in the charge of walking disorderly.

In 1866, F. M. D. Hopkins, an evangelist of Colquitt, Miller County, reported that some of the Baptists in Southwest Georgia, "calling themselves 'United Baptists,' had expressed themselves to him as favorably disposed on the subject of Christian Union." Those Freewill Baptists proposed that an association meeting be held near Columbus, to consider Christian union "on the Bible alone as the all-sufficient creed." In addition to Mr. Hopkins, F. P. Perdue of Atlanta was the other Georgia resident who was appointed as a delegate to the union conference. No report of the conference was published in the *Gospel Advocate*.[91]

A less favorable reception to the Baptist attitude was expressed by James S. Lamar after he attended the Georgia Baptist Convention at Augusta in 1868. Prof. J. P. Boyce of Greenville, S. C., called the Disciples "rank heretics" in an address. In discussing the matter, Mr. Lamar said that in his "candid judgment, any union

---

88Ibid., Oct. 14, 1869, pp. 946 f.
89*Ibid.*, Jan. 13, 1870, p. 44.
90*Ibid.*, Apr. 25, 1867, p. 336.
91*Ibid.*, Nov. 20, 1866, p. 751.

between the two bodies, organically considered, is at this time wholly impracticable, and furthermore, wholly undesirable."[92]

When Georgia's other preaching Lamar was aroused, he took his pen in hand and wrote at length to uphold his convictions. An entire issue of 24 pages of the *Gospel Advocate,* early in 1870, was devoted to Philip F. Lamar's spirited defense of charges of "obnoxious doctrine." He addressed "A True Statement of the Case" to the Rev. H. Newton, Presbyterian, and the Rev. A. J. Kelly, Baptist, both pastors at Jefferson, Ga., where Mr. Lamar resided.[93]

With such unwavering adherence to convictions, it is not strange that those Disciples were usually engaged in controversies and confronted with "violent opposition."

SEVERAL NEW CONGREGATIONS ORGANIZED

On the basis of incomplete records, there were apparently about a dozen congregations of Disciples of Christ established in Georgia during the decade covered by this chapter. The churches and dates of organization were as follows:

1861—Corinth, Walnutgrove, Walton County
1863—Bethany, Jackson County (now Bogart, Oconee County)
1867—Antioch, Heard County
1867—Bethany, near Dallas, Paulding County
1867—West Point (reorganized), Troup County
1868—Poplar Springs, Deepstep, Washington County
1868—Valdosta First, Lowndes County
1869—Berea, Campbell (?), now part of Fulton County
1869—Galilee, Jackson County
1869—Martin Springs, Jackson County
1870—Smyrna Academy, later Red Oak, Fulton County

---

[92]*Millennial Harbinger,* May, 1868, pp. 267 ff.

[93]*Gospel Advocate,* Feb. 17, 1870, pp. 145-168. The issue of June 9, 1870, p. 546, announced the availability of "a few hundred copies" of the Lamar defense.

Some of the churches apparently existed only a brief period, for little is known about them now. The Corinth Church, one of several congregations formed by Philip F. Lamar during the decade, had 35 or so charter members. They included Mr. and Mrs. William L. Shelnutt, parents of Erastus Lamar Shelnutt (1865-1941). Mrs. Shelnutt (1838-1896), a Methodist, was the first person to take her stand with the Disciples at the family workshop in the summer of 1864. "Services at Corinth were discontinued during Sherman's invasion," that fateful year of 1864, "but the church was reorganized in 1866," one writer stated.[94]

Three congregations were formed apparently in 1867. A. C. Borden, Carroll County, started one or more. He recorded that "since June, 1861, I have preached twenty-five hundred discourses, organized seven new congregations, and had six hundred ninety-five additions."[95] The origin of the Bethany Church, near Dallas, was set forth by W. W. Busby thus: "We have here, a . . . congregation of disciples, organized by Bro. A. C. Borden, a little more than twelve months ago. We now have near fifty members."[96]

Two churches were formed in 1868. One was Poplar Springs, originally a Missionary Baptist Church, at Deepstep, Washington County. The other was the First Christian Church of Valdosta, Lowndes County.

T. M. Harris established the Poplar Springs Church on Oct. 12, 1868. It soon had a membership of more than 100, many of whom were well educated. There was a "working, zealous, and intelligent sisterhood." A number of the members must have had means, for they offered a "liberal salary" to a preacher. R. B. Strange and E. W. Jordan were the "bishops" or "overseers" as they were called by some, elders, by others.[97]

---

[94] A. Goff Bedford, "The Emergence and Growth of the Christian Church (Disciples of Christ) in Georgia" (Unpublished M. A. Thesis, University of West Virginia, Morgantown, 1953), p. 81.

[95] *Gospel Advocate*, Jan. 30, 1868, p. 111.

[96] *Ibid.*, Feb. 11, 1869, p. 135.

[97] *Ibid.*, Mar. 30, 1871, p. 290; Apr. 27, 1871, p. 394.

The Valdosta congregation resulted from the withdrawal of 20 members from the Dasher (Corinth) Church located seven miles south of the town when the railroad was completed. Corinth, as it was long known, was established in the 1850's, or before, by Christian H. Dasher and others. In 1871 a traveling evangelist of the Disciples wrote of "passing on the way the Corinth meeting-house, situated near a beautiful little lake on the shore of which the brethren have erected a baptistry, very conveniently arranged with dressing-rooms, pier and steps descending into the water."[98] Such consideration of baptismal candidates, the beauty of the rite and its setting were most unusual.

The Galilee Church, Jackson County, was organized by P. F. Lamar in 1869. It was perhaps the last church that the effective evangelist formed. John Lewis Elder donated land for a building and cemetery about three miles southwest of Jefferson alongside the Oconee River. Late in 1869, Mr. Lamar appealed for funds to complete construction of the Galilee building. The small congregation had given $250; double that amount was needed. The appeal was commended by the editor of the *Gospel Advocate*.[99] One of the first gifts acknowledged was $25.00 "from a 'Disciple of Georgia.' "[100] Mr. Lamar was the first pastor. After retiring from the ministry, he continued to reside in the community and was buried in the Galilee Cemetery.[101]

---

[98]*Ibid.*, Apr. 6, 1871, p. 310.

[99]*Ibid.*, Dec. 30, 1869, p. 1189.

[100]*Ibid.*, Mar. 17, 1870, p. 259.

[101]Philip F. Lamar lost his house and all its contents by fire one night in September, 1870. He and his family just escaped. W. C. Howell, Walnutgrove, Walton County, and T. M. Harris, Atlanta, appealed in the *Gospel Advocate* for funds to relieve Lamar's distress. David Lipscomb, the editor, suggested that the assistance "should be such as to make Bro. Lamar feel that it was a blessing to have his possessions burned."! He heartily approved the brethren sharing and having fellowship with Lamar in his loss. By March, 1871, the *Advocate* reported $36.50 received by it for Lamar (*Gospel Advocate*, Oct. 13, 1870, pp. 958 ff.; Oct. 20, 1870, p. 977; Nov. 3, 1870, p. 1039; Jan. 12, 1871, p. 34; Jan. 19, 1871, p. 64; Feb. 9, 1871, p. 140; Mar. 2, 1871, p. 205).

In August, 1869, P. F. Lamar held a meeting at a "new point in Jackson county, known as Martin Springs."[102] That congregation was represented in the Northeast Georgia Cooperation meeting of 1869, the next month.[103]

A. C. Borden and Isham Hicks of Carroll County formed the Berea congregation in Campbell (?)—now part of Fulton—County on May 30, 1869, with nine charter members. By the end of the year there were 53 members.[104]

Several preachers from Tennessee were refugees in Georgia during the war years. Those who settled in Southwest Georgia included Dr. W. H. Hooker, Madison Love, and James S. Havron.[105] They helped to establish congregations in Brooks, Decatur, Echols, Fulton, Miller, and Thomas Counties. One of Mr. Havron's reports stated:

The misfortunes of the late war forced me, with many others, to flee from our homes in Tennessee, and cast our lots with a strange people. A number of us, with two preachers, settled in Miller County, Southwestern Georgia, some forty miles from this point (Mt. Pleasant, Fla.), where Brother Woodless and myself, with our families, are living. Since coming to this country, we have established a number of congregations. One at Colquet, of sixty members, another at Pawtown, of one hundred members. Both of these are in Miller County, Georgia. The latter is not in as good condition as it should be. Besides these, we have planted one at Concord [Fla.], which numbers eighty-five members, and is a fine congregation, in healthy condition. I look for bright future for this church. There are also others, lately planted at More's Lake, Plank Road, Oil Still, Pleasant Grove, and Jackson's Bluff.

[102]*Gospel Advocate*, Sept. 30, 1869, p. 907.

[103]*Ibid.*, Oct. 14, 1869, pp. 446 f.

[104]*Ibid.*, Dec. 15, 1870, p. 1170.

[105]Mr. Havron died on July 25, 1867. A former member of the Tennessee Legislature, he joined Dr. W. H. Hooker, then of Attapulgus, Ga., in preaching to the 200 or 300 Disciples in Southwest Georgia (*Gospel Advocate*, Aug. 15, 1867, p. 657). Several Georgia pioneers died that decade in Texas, including David E. and Sarah Blakely, who left Clarke County in 1853 (*Gospel Advocate*, Jan. 10, 1867, p. 40; Nov. 12, 1868, p. 1091), and James Elder, Clarke County native (*Gospel Advocate*, Jan. 27, 1870, p. 91). All were doubtless members of the Antioch Church group that went to Texas from Clarke County, Ga., before the Civil War (Miller, *op. cit.*, p. 16).

Brother Hooker, who established the churches in Georgia, has also built up one at Bainbridge, Decatur County.   Brethren [Madison] Love and [F.M.D.] Hopkins, from the Baptists, and Neely, from the Methodists, have been our preachers in Florida. Brother Love is laboring at the last four points mentioned. . . . The sects, as usual are waging an unrelenting war against us.[106]

Little is now known about most of those congregations. Philip F. Lamar visited them early in 1871 and stated that the supporting brethren of the Miller County churches included John Pierce, P. M. Inlow, and Calvin Lowe.[107]

There were churches, too, in southern Georgia at Quitman, Brooks County; Thomasville, Thomas County; Cairo and Whigham, Grady County, and one in Echols County.   Another was at West Point, Troup County, in western Georgia.   Perhaps there was one at Irwinton, Twiggs County, where Dr. A. G. Thomas preached some after the war.[108]   Then, Liberty Church was two miles from Trenton in Dade County, below Chattanooga in the Lookout Valley.   Mt. Pisgah Church was near Stone Mountain; Mr. and Mrs. Elzy B. Reynolds, charter members of the Atlanta Church, were former members of Mt. Pisgah.   Doubtless there were other such congregations whose name and location are now forgotten.

While preaching for the Atlanta congregation, F. Plion Perdue reported, in 1870: "I am now preaching at different points in the country. . . . I organized a congregation 10 or 12 miles South of Atlanta, with good prospects for the future.   I go to-day to Stone Mountain to see what can be done there, in relation to building up a congregation."[109]   The church that he established at his regular preaching point south of Atlanta was doubt-

---

[106]*Gospel Advocate*, Nov. 20, 1866, pp. 746 f.

[107]*Ibid.*, Apr. 27, 1871, p. 395.

[108]After the war, Dr. A. G. Thomas was school principal at Irwinton, Twiggs County, Ga.   He preached there and at Toomsboro, Sandersville, and at other neighboring churches.   In the spring of 1869, he went to a pastorate at Greenfield, Ind.   A year or so later he became professor of Latin at what is now Butler University, Indianapolis.

[109]*Gospel Advocate*, June 9, 1870, p. 540.

less at Smyrna Academy, one mile northwest of Red
Oak. About 1875 the congregation moved to Red Oak
and erected a building.

Several of the Georgia churches of the Disciples suspended or disbanded during the Civil War. Many members were scattered as war refugees. Some of the suspended churches were not reorganized until the 1870s or
even later.

The Savannah church was one of those disrupted by
the war. By 1864 services had been discontinued at the
Fireman's Hall and resumed at the home of Mr. and
Mrs. Alexander Calloway. Sherman's Army captured
Savannah in December, 1864. The services may have
been temporarily suspended at that time. T. M. Harris
was recorded in the minutes of the 1870 Georgia Convention of Disciples at Atlanta as a delegate representing the Savannah Church and several others. Early in
1871, when Philip F. Lamar visited Savannah, he found
the cause there represented by the W. W. Carter family,
Dr. F. Y. Clark, Mr. Calloway, Mrs. Cooper, and Mrs.
A. C. Ulmer. Dr. Clark proposed to donate a well-
located lot, valued at several thousand dollars, for a
church building.[110]

THE LOUISVILLE PLAN AND 1870 CONVENTION

The Louisville Plan was a compromise attempt at cooperation by Disciples of Christ who sought to accommodate changing needs of the brotherhood through the
American Christian Missionary Society in an altered
form. The temporary truce plan received its name from
the 1869 Louisville Convention when the society's name
was changed to the General Christian Missionary Convention.

There had been criticism of the society because of its
"money basis" and alleged failure to represent local

---

[110]*Ibid.*, Apr. 27, 1871, pp. 394 f. W. W. Carter moved to Savannah
from Sandersville, Ga., after the Civil War, mainly to market Washington
County cotton. He was the father of Mrs. A. C. Bythewood.

congregations. Consequently, the high-principled, elaborate plan dissolved the individual membership in the organization and provided instead an unwieldy organization of churches, a set-up strange to Disciples, with delegate conventions on a district, state, and national basis.

The plan was drawn up by a representative committee of 20 outstanding Disciples that included James S. Lamar of Augusta.[111] The authorization for the committee's work was taken at the semi-annual meeting of the society's board which met in St. Louis on May 18, 1869. The text of that action stated:

Resolved, That a committee of twenty be appointed to take into consideration the whole question of evangelization and report, if possible, a scriptural and practical plan for raising money and spreading the Gospel, said committee to report at the Louisville meeting in October next.[112]

According to Grant K. Lewis, many years later a secretary of the A.C.M.S., the plan, briefly, was to function as follows:

. . . The churches were to send delegates to district meetings, the districts to state conventions, and the states to the national organizations. The churches were to send all missionary funds to the district treasury, fifty per cent to be forwarded to the state treasury, which in turn would send fifty per cent to the general work. Thus the latter, representing national and world missions, was to receive twenty-five per cent of the total funds raised.[113]

The committee of pro- and anti-society men met several days preceding the convention sessions at Louisville. Concessions were made to placate the "anti" brethren and every item was finally adopted unanimously. However, since some committeemen were ab-

[111]*Report of Proceedings, op. cit.,* 1869, p. 13. According to the minutes, p. 22 f., Lamar was elected a member of the Board of Managers of the organization.

[112]*Ibid.,* p. 11.

[113]Grant K. Lewis, *The American Christian Missionary Society and The Disciples of Christ* (St. Louis: Christian Board of Publication, 1937), p. 152.

sent, the report contained the signatures of only 11 of the group of 20.[114]   James S. Lamar did not sign the report.   There were 600 persons at the Louisville meeting and they approved the plan with only one dissenting vote.

In Georgia, nearly a year later, the comprehensive plan led to the calling of a convention.   Thomas M. Harris, F. P. Perdue, and James S. Lamar joined in calling for the attendance "of every Christian preacher in the State."   The call stated, in part:

> That our Churches are scattered over a large extent of territory, and some of them isolated and without the moral and material support of the others; that many of our preachers are strangers to each other, and are laboring mainly without concert or co-operation; that we are without system in the development and direction of our strength and resources,—all this is well known as it is earnestly deplored.[115]

The convention met at the Atlanta Church of Christ, Friday through Sunday, Nov. 4-6, 1870.   James S. Lamar was chosen chairman.   Edwin A. Lodge, Detroit, Mich., was elected secretary.   Both men had been at the Louisville Convention of 1869.   There were 18 delegates representing that many churches, plus a few visitors, from many sections of Georgia.

The entire Louisville Plan was read to the delegates. It was discussed vigorously.   Advocates of the scheme for organization and raising missionary funds were James S. Lamar; Dr. H. Marshall, Atlanta, who moved its adoption; James Atkins, Atlanta; N. Brum Clark, Augusta layman, and Mr. Lodge.   The two outspoken opponents were William S. Fears of the Berea Church, Henry County, and John Tillery, delegate of the New Bethany Church, Whitewater.

Two sessions were used for discussion of the plan with an intervening night for private consideration of it.   The plan was read to the assembled group twice. The motion for adoption carried with 14 affirmative

---

[114]*Report of Proceedings, op. cit.,* 1869, p. 21.

[115]*Gospel Advocate,* Oct. 13, 1870, p. 955.

votes and four negative ones, thus demonstrating that
the majority did not fear the establishment of any ecclesiasticism but were more concerned with a practical
plan for missionary cooperation.

The convention then created four districts in Georgia
for the Disciples. A constitution for the Georgia State
Board was adopted unanimously. James S. Lamar was
elected president and his brother, Philip F. Lamar, was
chosen corresponding secretary and evangelist. George
Linder was named state evangelist for work among Negroes. The officers with T. M. Harris, E. W. Jordan,
and W. S. Barrett were selected as the State Board to
conduct the Georgia missionary work for the brethren
according to the Louisville Plan.

In the election of officers, T. M. Harris was first chosen
corresponding secretary. But he had a contract as pastor with the Atlanta Church and the congregation was
not willing to dispense with his services. Consequently,
P. F. Lamar was elected to the office. However, the General Conventions of the Disciples for several years thereafter listed T. M. Harris as the Georgia state secretary
in the published minutes or *Report of Proceedings*. Actually, Philip F. Lamar apparently served as the state
evangelist only. In a brief report of the convention, the
Gospel Advocate stated that length precluded publication of the minutes. Reference was made to the Louisville Plan being the only "matter introduced. . . . Notwithstanding the meeting purported to be called for an
entirely different purpose."[116] That provided a basis
for criticism by others.

The *Christian Standard* printed the complete convention minutes in the issues of Dec. 3 and 10, 1870. It had
not been long since Isaac Errett, editor of that periodical, declared emphatically for cooperation thus: "We
have lifted up the cause to a good degree of strength

---

[116]*Ibid.*, Dec. 15 [22?], 1870, p. 1183. The convention ordered 500
copies of the Proceedings printed in pamphlet form; no copy was located
anywhere in 1954.

and enterprise through God's blessing on *organized effort*. Let the brethren go steadily on in the cooperative movements, and every year will add to their efficiency, and enlarge their sphere of influence."[117] After the death of Alexander Campbell in 1866, it was stated by Henry K. Shaw in *Buckeye Disciples* that "it was largely through Errett that the movement was saved from being torn apart by independent factions."[118]

Within a few weeks of adjournment of the Atlanta convention, the first district meeting was held by the Northeast Georgia churches at Union Church, Clarke County, on Dec. 31. A resolution, wholeheartedly endorsing the Louisville Plan, was adopted unanimously. Without the preamble, it stated:

Resolved, That we heartily accept the general plan of operation adopted and recommended to the churches for adoption by our brethren in the recent State meeting in Atlanta, and pledge ourselves to do all in our power to make it a success.[119]

Nathan W. Smith, who did not attend the Atlanta meeting for some reason not recorded, was unhappy about the results. He expressed himself at length in the *Gospel Advocate,* in part, as follows:

. . . This meeting has given me a great deal of sorrow and grief. . . .

Nor do I believe that there are three churches in the State besides the Augusta and Atlanta churches would now if the said Plan was read to them vote for it. . . . Now I am sorry for this movement for it is the third attempt in Georgia to organize and set on foot a human plan to do the Lord's work.

In 1850 some of the brethren met in Griffin, formed an organization and were going to accomplish great things, but it soon all fell through and in 1862 a few met in Atlanta and formed an Evangelizing Society with its officers, this soon died.

What will be the result of this movement time will show. It has brought division and sorrow with pain of heart to some of our best brethren already. I am sorry, . . . I dearly love those

117*Christian Standard,* June 1, 1867, p. 172.

118Shaw, *op. cit.,* p. 277.

119*Christian Standard,* Jan. 28, 1871, p. 26.

good brethren but must say I think that they have done a great deal of harm. They will doubtless call me an old fogy and say that I am opposed to co-operation. I am not opposed to brethren meeting and co-operating, but let us do it in the name of the Lord Jesus, and not in some other name. May we all exercise much patience and have an abundance of charity in our hearts.[120]

A. J. McGaughey of the Mt. Vernon Church soon had a letter in print, expressing his opposition to the Louisville Plan thus:

Bro. P. F. Lamar preached for us yesterday at Mount Vernon and gave us the Louisville Plan, and urged us to adopt it, but I would have prefered that he would have given us the Jerusalem Plan as it has a thus saith the Lord to it, while Louisville has not the thus saith the Lord.[121]

On a preaching tour into various sections of Georgia early in 1871, Philip F. Lamar, state evangelist, traveled over 1,800 miles, preached 51 times at 21 places and organized or helped to form two congregations. He "returned home more than ever in favor of the Atlanta meeting, its objects, aims, purposes and principles," he reported.[122] About the time he started on that three-month trek, Mr. Lamar ordered 100 copies of circulars on "Women's Work in Missions" and mentioned "one church that gives $250 for the missionary cause in Georgia."[123]

Little else was discovered about the operation of the Louisville Plan of cooperation in Georgia. Generally, all across the brotherhood, the plan languished only to fail rather dismally. The receipts for missions grew less and less because after the funds for districts and states were retained for *their recurring needs,* little was left for apportionment to the national agency for the regions

---

[120]*Gospel Advocate,* Jan. 12, 1871, pp. 30 f. In the letter, Mr. Smith reported that he traveled over 3,700 miles and delivered 143 messages with 54 additions to the churches during 1870.

[121]*Ibid.,* Jan. 12, 1871, p. 34.

[122]*Ibid.,* Apr. 27, 1871, p. 396.

[123]*Christian Standard,* Jan. 21, 1871, p. 19.

beyond.[124] Thus the controversial spirit among the Disciples began to wield its unfortunate influence.

By the 1870s then, Georgia Disciples of Christ began to make difficult advance. However, they were not ready organizationally to take advantage of the growth that came as railroads spread across the state with stations and subsequent settlements every few miles. There was, in fact, much opposition among the brethren to any human planning. Most of them, however, participated lackadaisically in cooperative Christian effort. They were learning through harsh realities the truth of the scriptural admonition: "We are members one of another." The years leading to the twentieth century were to demonstrate, in Georgia as elsewhere, whether the minority of "anti" brethren would go a separate, literalistic way or coalesce into a significant body with the majority of the Disciples of Christ. That phase of the chronicle will be treated in the following chapter.

---

[124]In 1881 the Louisville Plan ceased. Financial memberships were restored and the organization again became the American Christian Missionary Society (Lewis, *op. cit.*, p. 153).

CHAPTER VII

Division Follows Increasing Conflict, 1871-1899

The prolonged controversy among Georgia Disciples of Christ over missionary societies and instrumental music, among other issues, was not settled for years. The differences of opinion were widespread and apparent on many occasions. Georgia, the 1871 General Convention was informed, met more opposition to the Louisville Plan of missionary cooperation than any other state.[1]

The 1871 Georgia Convention met at Atlanta, Sept. 20-21. A. C. Borden maintained that the Louisville Plan "was a good one, and not anti-scriptural." P. F. Lamar claimed that "the churches in Georgia with few exceptions favored" the state organization. The convention voted unanimously to continue the state society.

T. M. Harris, re-elected corresponding secretary, introduced a resolution requesting that a synopsis of the minutes be published in the *Christian Standard* and that its publishers "send copies . . . to such names and addresses as may be forwarded to them by our Secretary."[2] Learning of the action, David Lipscomb, *Gospel Advocate* editor, charged the Georgians with acting indirectly

---

[1]*Report of Proceedings* of the Twenty-third Anniversary Meeting of the General Missionary Convention. Held in Cincinnati, Oct. 19, 20, 21 and 23, 1871 (Cincinnati: Bosworth, Chase & Hall, 1871), p. 13. The annual Georgia report showed (p. 11) $410 collected for missions, 165 new church members.

[2]*Christian Standard,* Oct. 21, 1871, p. 331. *Gospel Advocate,* Nov. 16, 1871, pp. 1066 ff.

and said that the Louisville Plan was "being manifested in the interests of a few men of one paper."[3] James S. Lamar replied in the *Standard,* as one of its editors, saying:

. . . [In Georgia] those who favor missionary work, do not, as a general thing, and will not, take his paper. He fights us to the bitter end; he clogs and fetters our movement in every possible way; . . . circulation in Georgia . . . of the *Standard* is very general and is constantly increasing.[4]

In a rebuttal, Lipscomb objected to a few "representative" brethren recommending "what paper shall, or shall not be taken."[5]

At the 1873 General Convention, Georgians reported $209 given for missions and 136 additions, "the highest ratio reported by any State." Statistics of the Federal Bureau of Education reported Georgia Disciples had 25 Sunday schools with 125 officers and teachers and 2,875 pupils.[6]

During the early 1870s, Thomas Mason Foster (1844-1910) succeeded P. F. Lamar as state evangelist. Foster was graduated from the Bible College of Kentucky University, Lexington, in 1872.[7] Born at Hopkinsville, Ky., Mar. 17, 1844, he was one of the first Lexington-educated ministers to serve in Georgia. He was prominent as Northeast District evangelist.[8]

[3]*Gospel Advocate,* Nov. 23, 1871, p. 1084.

[4]*Christian Standard,* Dec. 9, 1871, p. 388.

[5]*Gospel Advocate,* Dec. 21, 1871, p. 1188.

[6]*Report of Proceedings* of the Twenty-fifth Anniversary Meeting of the General Christian Missionary Convention. Held in Indianapolis, Ind., Oct. 21, 22 and 23, 1873 (Cincinnati: Bosworth, Chase & Hall, 1873), pp. 11, 24. T. M. Harris was listed as Georgia "state secretary" in the *Report of Proceedings* for 1871 (p. 70), 1873 (p. 2), and 1874 (p. 2).

[7]The College of the Bible, a graduate seminary, and Transylvania College, brotherhood educational institutions, continue that program now in Lexington, Ky.

[8]*Southern Evangelist,* Feb. 1, 1901, p. 7. In 1874, Foster married Miss Janie Paxon of Walton Co.; they had nine children before her death, Aug. 4, 1894. He married Miss Popia Thompson of Oconee Co., Feb. 2, 1895. He died Feb. 25, 1910 in Atlanta (*Christian Standard,* Mar. 12, 1910, p. 40).

A. Jud Cumbie, Decatur County, was chairman of the "Christian Convention of Florida and southern Georgia" at Concord, Fla., Oct. 22-23, 1875. Fifteen churches were represented; their membership of 642 included about 150 from South Georgia. Cumbie and J. C. Gibson were chosen to evangelize in Florida and adjacent territory, presumably South Georgia. The next convention was scheduled for a Decatur County church, Oct. 27, 1876.[9] They organized Mars Hill (originally Rock Pond) Church of Decatur County in 1878.

The Foreign Christian Missionary Society was organized at Louisville, Ky., Oct. 21, 1875. J. S. Lamar, then pastor there, was present. Writing about the need for the society, he said:

. . . The brethren everywhere began to ask if they were to be forever thwarted and obstructed in . . . fruitless controversy over "plans" . . . many were beginning to feel sure that some . . . opposition had . . . reference to the almighty dollar. . .[10]

Isaac Errett was elected president and served until his death in 1888. Lamar was elected second vice-president and soon afterward was appointed missionary to Italy. However, he declined the mission.[11] Concluding his Louisville ministry, he returned to his native Georgia and remained a staunch advocate of missionary cooperation through societies.

The Mt. Vernon Church was host to the Northeast Cooperation meeting, Oct. 18, 1878. Earlier district sessions were in the late 1860s.[12] Seven churches sent delegates. J. A. Perdue belittled barbecued meals, apparently being introduced, saying, "I do not think they are

---

[9]*Christian Standard*, Mar. 11, 1876, p. 82.

[10]Archibald McLean, *The History of the Foreign Christian Missionary Society* (New York: Fleming H. Revell Co., 1919), p. 33.

[11]*Report of Proceedings* of the First Annual Meeting of the Foreign Christian Misionary Society. Held in Richmond, Virginia, Oct. 18, 1876 (Cincinnati: Chase & Hall, 1876), pp. 32 f. Those minutes recorded that Lamar was re-elected vice-president of the Foreign Society, but McLean's *History* of the organization listed Lamar as serving only one year.

[12]*Cf. ante.*, pp. 218 f.

adapted to such an occasion. This one was entirely orderly, but not at all enjoyable.'' P. F. Lamar was scheduled to speak, but death intervened, Sept. 3 at the age of 51. A memorial service was held and a relief fund authorized for the widow and daughter.[13] His brother, J. S. Lamar, was in Europe. Since P. F. Lamar's work was ''so kindred to the purposes'' of the General Convention, his name appeared in its 1878 obituary report.[14]

The Washington District churches also had cooperation meetings. The 1878 session was at Antioch Church, Oct. 19-21. T. M. Harris, president, was reelected. It was voted to change the term ''cooperation meeting'' to ''Annual Christian Re-union,'' but the revision was probably never popularly accepted.[15]

Six contributions totaling $24.05 were the Georgia mission receipts reported at the 1879 General Convention. Sensing the need in Georgia, the national board had appropriated a small sum to enable J. A. Perdue to give one-fourth time to a ''destitute point'' in the state. James L. Adams, Dr. J. M. Ammons, Jr., and Perdue were mentioned as ''brave men'' who were ''doing their best to encourage the churches to co-operate in preaching the gospel in 'regions beyond.' ''[16]

The 1879 Georgia Convention was at Atlanta, Nov. 20-21. Thirteen preachers, one-third of those in the state, attended, including Brother Jones, an Atlanta Negro.

---

[13]*Christian Standard,* Nov. 9, 1878, p. 358. Albert G. Lamar, son of P. F. Lamar, died Sept. 27, 1940 after editing the Winder, Ga., *News* 40 years (*Christian Messenger,* Nov., 1940, p. 8).

[14]*Proceedings* of the General Christian Missionary Convention and The Foreign Christian Missionary Society. Held in Cincinnati, Oct. 23-26, 1878 (Cincinnati: Standard Publishing Co., 1878), p. 11.

[15]*Christian Standard,* Nov. 23, 1878, p. 374. The eight Washington District churches, with total membership of 359, were: Antioch, Bethesda, Buckeye, Davisboro, Jordan's Mills, Poplar Springs, Sandersville, and Toomsboro.

[16]*Proceedings* of the General Christian Missionary Convention. Held in Bloomington, Ill., Oct. 23-26, 1879 (Cincinnati: Central Book Concern, 1879), pp. 7, 8.

The meeting voted to become a delegated convention. T. M. Harris was elected state evangelist.[17]

Dr. J. M. Ammons, Jr., was elected Washington District evangelist at Sandersville, Oct. 26, 1879. He was to serve one-half time for $300 annually. He asked the national board for supplementary support.[18]

At the 1880 General Convention, it was reported Georgians gave $713.85 that year for national missionary work; collections for state work totaled $3,594.71, an amazing record. T. M. Harris, state evangelist and corresponding secretary, was assisted by six others during the year. A summary of state work showed 342 additions.[19]

Early in 1880, Nathan W. Smith, state convention chairman, urged the churches to send representatives to the annual meeting. He concluded with a significant question, "If two or more churches can cooperate, why not all?"[20]

Delegates attended the 1880 Georgia Convention at Atlanta, Nov. 10-12, from 25 churches, listed in the minutes, including three delegates from two Negro congregations. James S. Lamar was elected president. T. M. Harris, re-elected state evangelist, reported accomplishments in spite of opposition.[21]

The 1880 Northeast District, meeting at Corinth Church, Sept. 23, appointed T. M. Foster district evangelist and raised $500 for his support.[22]

---

[17]*Christian Standard*, Dec. 20, 1879, p. 402. J. A. Perdue was listed as the Georgia state evangelist in the *Proceedings, op. cit.,* 1879 [p. 2].

[18]*Christian Standard*, Nov. 29, 1879, p. 378. *Proceedings, op. cit.,* 1879, p. 8.

[19]*Proceedings* of the Thirty-first Anniversary of the General Christian Missionary Convention. Held at Louisville, Ky., Oct. 21-24, 1880 (Cincinnati: Central Book Concern, 1880), pp. 7, 9, 11.

[20]*Christian Standard*, Feb. 7, 1880, p. 42.

[21]*Ibid.,* Dec. 11, 1880, p. 394. The minutes, called "sensible and harmonious proceedings," were published as *Proceedings* of the Convention of the Churches of Christ in Georgia. Held at Atlanta, Nov. 10-12, 1880 (*Christian Standard,* Jan. 15, 1881, p. 23).

[22]*Christian Standard*, Oct. 23, 1880, p. 338.

While state evangelist in 1880, T. M. Harris organized eight district meetings after proposing nine. Announcing them, "undismayed by past failures," he said: "If there are any in the State opposed to this forward movement, it would be the utmost stretch of courtesy to say that they interpreted or in any way reflected the sentiment of our people."[23]

The assemblies seemed to discuss the same matters, reaching varied conclusions on some, however. The discussions concerned weekly church services and communion observance (generally agreed), regular fellowship offerings, foot-washing (not a religious ordinance and not to be practiced as such at church), Sunday schools, fairs and festivals for raising funds (should not be tolerated). Some brethren expressed opposite views on several issues.[24]

Harris was not state evangelist in 1881 since he "did not feel justified in engaging in the work without some more definite pledge." J. S. Lamar reported on the work in the State Convention at Augusta, Nov. 9-11. Several new churches were formed. Georgians that year gave $304.50 to the Washington National Church Fund, raised by the brotherhood after the death of President James A. Garfield (1831-1881), the only Disciple to serve the United States in the White House.[25]

Delegates attended the 1881 Georgia Convention from 23 churches, including two Negro ones, with a total membership of 1,839. J. S. Lamar claimed "at least sixty churches" were not represented. Dr. A. G. Thomas was

---

[23]*Ibid.*, Jan. 17, 1880, p. 18.

[24]*Ibid.*, Jan. 17, 1880, p. 18; Apr. 10, 1880, p. 114; May 15, 1880, p. 154; June 12, 1880, p. 186; Oct. 23, 1880, p. 338. Mary G. Jones and Lilly Reynolds (Editors and Compilers), *Coweta County Chronicles* . . . (Atlanta: Stein Printing Co., 1928), pp. 236 f.

[25]*Proceedings* of the General Christian Missionary Convention At Its Thirty-second Anniversary Held at Indianapolis, Indiana, Oct. 20-23, 1881 (Cincinnati: Standard Publishing Co., 1881), pp. 4, 5. Georgia delegates named to the 1881 General Convention by the 1880 Georgia Convention were: T. M. Foster, T. M. Harris, J. S. Hook, J. S. Lamar, J. A. Perdue, and Z. T. Sweeney (*Christian Standard*, Dec. 11, 1880, p. 394).

elected president. F. P. Perdue was chosen corresponding secretary. An extensive report did not record the election of a state evangelist.[26]

Georgia delegates at the 1882 General Convention were Dr. A. G. Thomas, T. M. Foster, and J. S. Lamar. Receipts included $20.00 from Georgia. Dr. Thomas was chairman of the tract committee. Lamar introduced the convention president, B. B. Tyler (1840-1922), for the annual address; served on the obituary committee, and addressed the closing session.[27]

Forty-five churches were represented in the 1882 Georgia Convention at Atlanta, Nov. 1-3, by about 75 delegates and visitors. The Chattanooga, Tenn., Church was represented and "cordially invited to enter the Georgia cooperation." Dr. A. G. Thomas presided without discord, according to an editorial report by Isaac Errett, *Christian Standard* editor. One result was the "highly encouraging" pledging of $1,060 for district work. J. S. Lamar was elected state evangelist.[28]

Lamar, while state evangelist, reported it was difficult for South Georgia brethren to cooperate because they were so scattered. That isolation was also a cause of their strict literalism, which in turn accounted for much opposition to missionary societies. In consideration of their customary practices, no district cooperation was formed.[29] However, Lamar did organize an East Georgia District Cooperation of churches in counties contiguous to the Savannah River and D. W. Oliver was chosen evangelist.[30]

---

[26]*Christian Standard* Supplement, Feb. 25, 1882, pp. 15 f.; Feb. 25, 1882, p. 61. Nine churches reported over 100 members each, as follows: Augusta, 250; Antioch (Oconee Co.), 195; Atlanta, Berea, and Corinth (Walton Co.), 150 each; Red Oak, 128; Union (Fulton Co.), 124; Bethany and Christian Chapel, 100 each.

[27]*Proceedings* of the General Christian Missionary Convention At Its Thirty-third Anniversary, Held at Lexington, Kentucky, Oct. 19-21, 1882 (Cincinnati: Standard Publishing Co., 1882), pp. 4, 18, 25, 26, 27, 30, 32.

[28]*Christian Standard,* Nov. 11, 1882, pp. 356 f.

[29]*Ibid.,* Mar. 17, 1883, p. 124.

[30]*Ibid.,* Jan. 13, 1883, p. 19.

During the 1882-83 missionary year, Georgia reported $2,700 raised for missions. At the 1883 General Convention, Dr. A. G. Thomas was elected president, thus honoring Georgia Disciples. No other Georgian, before or since, received such recognition from the national brotherhood.[31]

The 1884 General Convention met in the First Christian Church of St. Louis, Mo. Dr. Thomas delivered his presidential message on "Our Missions," Thursday night, Oct. 23, saying, "The ghosts of doubt and fears of plans, Louisville and non-Louisville, and even the spook of current opposition to the work of Christian missions at home and abroad, shall not disturb us more."[32] The address was a positive declaration for cooperative missionary endeavor. An editorial note in *The Christian-Evangelist* stated that "junior members of the Convention, accustomed to a simpler speech, looked askance when he spoke of 'an oligarchy of esoteric culture.' "[33]

The year's missionary report for Georgia showed 330 additions, six churches organized, $1,000 raised for state work, $10.15 for out-of-state work, and an estimated $750 for buildings and settling pastors. Georgia sent $86.50 to the national board which had employed Nathan W. Smith for $75.00 part of the year in Western Georgia. The state was recommended as a "field of special importance." C. S. Lucas (1849-1897), Augusta pastor, was chosen a vice-president of the General Convention in St. Louis.[34]

---

[31]*Proceedings* of the General Christian Missionary Convention At Its Thirty-fourth Anniversary Held at Cincinnati, Ohio, Oct. 25-27, 1883 (Cincinnati: General Christian Missionary Convention, 1883?), pp. 12, 13, 19, 23, 25.

[32]*Christian Standard*, Dec. 20, 1884, cover (p. 401).

[33]*The Christian-Evangelist*, Oct. 30, 1884, p. 697.

[34]*Proceedings* of the General Christian Missionary Convention, At Its Thirty-fifth Anniversary Held at St. Louis, Mo., Oct. 23-24, 1884 (Cincinnati: General Christian Missionary Convention, 1884?), pp. 5, 9, 11, 15, 18, 19, 23, 25, 27, 28, 33.

The 1884 Georgia Convention met at Atlanta, Oct. 7-
10. The summary of the work of T. M. Foster, state
evangelist, listed five churches organized and $960.50
pledged for state work. Dr. A. G. Thomas was re-elected
president. Richard Van Dyke Omer (1853-1916) was
chosen state evangelist.[35]

Augusta entertained the 1885 State Convention, Nov.
4-5 J. W. Mountjoy (1844-1886), minister of Columbia,
Mo., was the guest speaker.[36] He enjoyed the hospitality
of Henry Clay Foster, who had formed a law partnership
with Joseph Rucker Lamar in September, 1880, when the
son of J. S. Lamar returned to Georgia.[37]

During 1884-88, the Church Extension Fund of the
General Convention (which became the Board of Church
Extension in 1888) aided three Georgia churches with
loans. Athens and Eastman received $500 each and
Macon, $260.[38]

Atlanta's Hunter Street congregation was host to the
1893 Georgia Convention, Oct. 24-26, when "more than
one hundred delegates" attended. T. H. Blenus, Savannah pastor, was president. Thomas A. Munnell was state
evangelist. Nearly $700 was given and pledged for
church extension, a similar amount for foreign missions,
and over $200 for Georgia work, all in a year of financial
panic! Charles Pichegrue Williamson (1848-1903), Atlanta minister, was elected president. Memorial services for T. M. Harris were conducted.[39] While preaching his last sermon at West Point, the popular pulpit
orator was stricken with paralysis and died at Sandersville, Oct. 20, 1893.[40]

[35]*Christian Standard*, Nov. 1, 1884, p. 348. Born in Union County, Ky.,
Mar. 31, 1853, Omer died at Madisonville, Ky., July 8, 1916. While in
Georgia, he was pastor at Savannah, Athens, and other places.

[36]*Ibid.*, Nov. 28, 1885, p. 379.

[37]Clarinda Pendleton Lamar, *op. cit.*, p. 49.

[38]*Proceedings* of the General Christian Missionary Convention At Its
Fortieth Anniversary Held in Louisville, Kentucky, Oct. 23, 24, 25, 1889
(Cincinnati: General Christian Missionary Convention, 1889), p. 41.

[39]Atlanta (Ga.) *Constitution*, Oct. 24-27, 1893. *The Christian-Evangelist*,
Nov. 23, 1893, pp. 740, 745.

[40]*Christian Standard*, Oct. 28, 1893, p. 856.

The 1895 Georgia Convention elected Erastus Lamar Shelnutt (1866-1941) state evangelist. He served South Carolina, also, at $50.00 a month, plus railroad expenses. Born at Walnutgrove, Walton County, he was graduated from the Bible College, Kentucky University, in 1891. His first pastorate was at Sylvania, Screven County. He was an organizer for the American Christian Missionary Society in 1895. Later, he was Northeast Georgia evangelist, and for short periods, state organizer for the Christian Woman's Board of Missions and the Woman's Society for Georgia Missions. He established 28 Georgia churches before his death, Mar. 28, 1941.[41]

During the missionary year that ended Oct. 10, 1896, Georgia contributed $749.45 to foreign missions and $97.92 to home missions through national agencies.[42] Slowly, the Georgia brethren learned the cost of missionary support and cooperation with agencies from which they had benefited for years. The Macon Church, for instance, received partial ministerial support from the General Convention, beginning Jan. 1, 1889, for some years.[43] William Allen Chastain was president of the Georgia Christian Missionary Society at the turn of the century.

Periodicals and Other Materials Published

During 1871-1899, Georgia Disciples issued six papers, as follows: the *Southern Evangelist, Christian Telescope, Missionary Tidings, Southern Christian, The Evangelist,* and *Young Southron.*

The first issue of the *Southern Evangelist* was dated January, 1873. It was edited and published monthly at

41*Ibid.,* Apr. 19, 1941, p. 416. When Shelnutt's home burned, Dec. 10, 1896, his mother died in the flames (*Christian Standard,* Dec. 26, 1896, p. 1658. *The Evangelist,* Mar. 13, 1897, p. 3).

42*The Evangelist,* Apr. 17, 1897, p. 2. *American Home Missionary,* Dec. 1896, pp. 56, 57, 69, 70; the same paper (p. 7) stated that in 1895 the General Christian Missionary Convention, at Dallas, Tex., voted to change its name back to the American Christian Missionary Society; that was accomplished in Ohio Courts, July 28, 1896.

43*Proceedings, op. cit.,* 1889, p. 26. *Christian Standard,* Nov. 21, 1896, p. 1483.

Atlanta by T. M. Harris; Ed. W. Holland was manager. "The Missionary work will be a specialty," it was stated.[44] The first number was a 24-page pamphlet with three columns. It was "handsomely printed, and well filled, . . . a credit to the brotherhood in a literary point of view."[45] Apparently, no copy was preserved.

The next periodical to appear was the *Christian Telescope*. It began publication about June, 1881, at Watkinsville with a "variety of matter." J. M. Ratcliffe was editor and publisher. Early in 1883, J. A. Perdue joined the editorial control of the larger monthly.[46] A short time later it was moved to 55 Broad St., Atlanta, when Alexander Campbell Smith, son of Nathan W. Smith, became editor and publisher and Ratcliffe associate editor.[47]

A letter to A. C. Smith from R. N. Moody in the *Atlantic Missionary* mentioned its merger with the weekly *Telescope*, about April, 1886, thus: "I was very sorry for the Telescope to go down, . . . you did the best thing you could have done in consolidating it with the MISSIONARY." The *Atlantic Missionary* was edited by Isaac Jesse Spencer (1851-1922) at Cuckoo, Va.[48] Smith wrote Georgia news for it.[49]

J. S. Lamar wrote Spencer concerning the "failure" of the *Telescope,* saying:

. . . Between ourselves, I wanted the *Telescope* to fail,— simply because it was impossible in the nature of things for it ever to be made such a success as would be creditable to us. I

[44]*Gospel Advocate*, Dec. 12, 1872, p. 1186. *Religious Historian,* Dec. 1872, p. 383.

[45]*Christian Standard*, Jan. 11, 1873, p. 12. *Gospel Advocate*, Feb. 6, 1873, p. 140.

[46]*Christian Standard,* June 18, 1881, p. 197; Feb. 17, 1883, p. 79.

[47]*Ibid.,* July 14, 1883, p. 293. Smith was educated at Bethany College and named for its founder, Alexander Campbell.

[48]*Atlantic Missionary,* May 26, 1886, p. 5.

[49]*Christian Standard,* Apr. 24, 1886, p. 132.

did not wish our cause to be represented in the State by such a feeble and picayunish affair. . . . I did not wish to sustain that little representative.[50]

The failure of such religious papers, often due to financial difficulties, were also caused by too little circulation, competition, jealousies, and personality conflicts.

The merger of the two papers had hardly occurred when another periodical appeared in Georgia. Named the *Missionary Tidings,* it was issued monthly at Buchanan by A. B. Fitts. It sought to "encourage a missionary spirit among the Disciples of Christ." Calling the first number "very good," the *Christian Standard* questioned the paper's right to use the title *Missionary Tidings.*[51] The title duplicated that of the magazine published by the Christian Woman's Board of Missions in Indianapolis. T. M. Foster criticized the Georgia paper thus:

. . . I have received two copies and they were filled with good things. I think the location unfortunate in being so remote from the brethren in Ga. A paper to succeed well ought to be published at some of our great centers of influence. The time of its birth was also unfortunate.[52]

In 1892, C. P. Williamson, Atlanta pastor and former Kentucky editor, formed a stock company, and assisted by some prominent brethren, launched the weekly *Southern Christian,* Apr. 1, 1892. "We fire a salute of seven guns, and *speak* her *bon voyage!*" said the greeting of *The Christian-Evangelist.* The new paper became a weekly with the fourth issue, June 4. It appeared until

---

[50]James Sanford Lamar letter to Isaac Jesse Spencer, written at Atlanta, Ga. Undated; probably May or June, 1886. Autographed Letter Signed (A.L.S.). Original in I. J. Spencer Collection of The Disciples of Christ Historical Society, Nashville, Tenn.

[51]*Christian Standard,* May 15, 1886, p. 157. No copies of the Georgia *Missionary Tidings* are known to exist.

[52]*Atlantic Missionary,* June 23, 1886, p. 5. Some copies of the periodical are in the Carolina Discipliana Library, Atlantic Christian College, Wilson, N. C. Others are in the Library of the University of Virginia, Charlottesville.

1897 when E. L. Shelnutt purchased it from the stricken Williamson.[53]

The Evangelist began as a four-page, semi-monthly, Mar. 13, 1897, at Atlanta with the state evangelist, E. L. Shelnutt, editor. He had the assistance of Alfred E. Seddon (1846-1939) as business manager and later as office editor.[54] They issued the paper through Dec. 3, 1898, when it was leased to Marion Franklin Harmon (1861-1940), an Atlanta pastor who subsequently bought it, changed the name to the *Southern Evangelist,* and published it weekly with Seddon's help.

Another Georgia publication in 1897 was the *Young Southron.* It was supposedly issued monthly at Atlanta for youth with Miss Bunnie Love as editor and Miss Sara Alexander as manager.[55]

James S. Lamar continued to be the most prolific writer of published materials among Georgia Disciples. He concluded his editorial connection as associate editor of the *Christian Standard* on July 31, 1875. His farewell editorial urged his brethren to cooperate and put aside prejudices.[56]

In 1886, Lamar wrote I. J. Spencer that J. H. Garrison (1842-1931), then co-editor of *The Christian-Evangelist* of St. Louis, Mo., had urged Lamar ''with much entreaty to write for his paper. Like yourself he offered me liberal pay, but I felt obliged to say No.'' That letter explained Lamar's retirement from the staff of the *Standard,* as follows:

[53]*The Christian-Evangelist,* Apr. 7, 1892, p. 216; Apr. 14, 1892, p. 232; May 19, 1892, p. 312; May 26, 1892, p. 328. *Christian Oracle,* June 23, 1892, p. 387. *Southern Christian,* June 22, 1894; that issue, numbered Vol. III, No. 7, and the issues of June 29, 1894 and Feb. 28, 1895, are in the Carolina Discipliana Library, Atlantic Christian College, Wilson, N. C.

[54]*The Evangelist,* Mar. 13, 1897. Seddon promoted a cooperative, wealth-sharing colony, near Atlanta (*Christian Standard,* Oct. 9, 1897, pp. 1291 f. *The Evangelist,* Oct. 16, 1897, p. 2. *Christian Guide,* Oct. 22, 1897, p. 688).

[55]*The Evangelist,* Mar. 13, 1897, p. 4. No copy of the *Young Southron* is known to exist.

[56]*Christian Standard,* July 24, 1875, p. 236.

Another thing, since I am in the confessional mood, you know our brethren will not tolerate anything except faith, repentance and baptism! Well, I have got nothing more to say on these subjects—certainly nothing new—and I am not needed either to advocate or defend them. I essayed, near the close of my connection with the *Standard,* to go a little further and discuss some matters which I deemed of interest and importance, and to my amazement I brought upon myself a perfect avalanche of opposition, accompanied with some indignity. This induced me quietly to retire.[57]

Lamar was a contributor to a New Testament Commentary, issued in 1878, and wrote several tracts, among other things. One tract was *What Is the Christian Church? or, Who Are the Disciples of Christ?* It was reprinted in 1883 from *Frank Leslie's Sunday Magazine* for October. The 12-page leaflet, issued by the General Christian Missionary Convention, circulated 24,383 copies the first year after publication.[58] Lamar's editorial correspondence during his 1878 trip to Europe appeared in the *Christian Standard.*[59]

Memoirs of Isaac Errett was Lamar's most significant publication. The two-volume biography of the editor of the *Christian Standard* appeared in 1893. Lamar delivered the memorial addres for Errett at the 1889 General Convention of Disciples at Louisville, Ky.[60]

During 1886, Chapman S. Lucas, then pastor of First Church, Augusta, issued a tract entitled, *Is the Christian Church Orthodox?* An editorial note called it "a capital one," adding, "It is especially adapted to the SOUTH where we are *Simon-pure-heretics.*"[61] Disciples, then, as always, enjoyed freedom to proclaim heresies and, therefore, to be denounced as heretics.

---

[57]James Sanford Lamar Letter to Isaac Jesse Spencer, written at Atlanta, Ga. Dated Dec. 14, 1886. A.L.S. Original in I. J. Spencer Collection of The Disciples of Christ Historical Society, Nashville, Tenn.

[58]*Christian Standard,* Sept. 22, 1883, p. 372; Nov. 24, 1883, p. 445. *Proceedings, op. cit.,* 1883, p. 15; 1884, p. 15.

[59]*Christian Standard,* Sept. 14, 1878, p. 296; Sept. 21, 1878, p. 304; Oct. 26, 1878, p. 344; Nov. 9, 1878, p. 360.

[60]*Proceedings, op. cit.,* 1889, p. 10.

[61]*Atlantic Missionary,* Apr. 21, 1886, p. 4.

Gospel Light, a songbook edited by Harvey R. Christie of Oxford, Ga., was published in 1895 under a double imprint that included the R. M. McIntosh Co. of Atlanta. Christie and McIntosh helped to edit another hymnal in 1892. Christie later edited other songbooks. The McIntosh firm was in Atlanta's Equitable Building, Pryor St. and Edgewood Ave. McIntosh was president and a director. The vice-president and a director was Russell Errett, general manager of the Standard Publishing Co. of Cincinnati. Christie was also a director of the firm, incorporated in 1894.[62]

The Pattern of Segregation Takes Shape

After the Civil War, the concern of white Georgia Disciples for the welfare of freed Negroes was reflected in several ways. At the 1871 General Convention, T. M. Harris, a Georgia delegate, served with the committee on Negro evangelization. He said Georgia "was promising in respect to both white and colored." The minutes recorded that

They had three separate organizations of colored churches in that State, and in a number of cases colored people worshiped in white congregations. He strongly urged the appointment, as missionary, of a colored man whom he could indorse. It might be no recommendation to say that he was a member of the State Legislature and of the State Convention, but he would vouch for his worth and his genuine Christianity. He happened to know that, though he was a member of the Legislature, he returned from its sittings poor.[63]

At the 1872 General Convention, Harris was a member of the committee on Negro ministerial education.[64]

---

[62]Harvey R. Christie letters to Isaac Jesse Spencer, written at Oxford, Ga. Dated Feb. 16, 1893 and May 1, 1895. A.L.S. Originals in I. J. Spencer Collection of The Disciples of Christ Historical Society, Nashville, Tenn.

[63]*Report of Proceedings, op. cit.,* 1871, p. 34. The name of the proposed missionary is unknown.

[64]*Report of Proceedings* of the Twenty-fourth Anniversary Meeting of the General Christian Missionary Convention. Held in Louisville, Ky., Oct. 24, 25 and 26, 1872 (Cincinnati: Bosworth, Chase & Hall, 1872), pp. 20, 34, 35.

In 1874, James S. Lamar discussed the "Religious Future of the Negro." He insisted that Disciples lacked the means of converting Negroes, although he considered the brethren "peculiarly fitted for the work." Education of Negro preachers, he thought, was the best way to reach Negroes.[65]

Mrs. Emily H. Tubman, wealthy Augusta Disciple, expressed her view in action. When she died in 1885, provision was made for her Negro servants. She left a two-story house and lot on Green St., Augusta, to Gus and Rebekah Dorsey. He was Mrs. Tubman's butler and drove the carriage; she was the cook.

According to scarce records of Negro Disciples in Georgia before 1900, there were 19 or more churches formed. Few founding dates are now known. Seven of those congregations remained in existence in 1949.

A number of Negroes confessed their faith during a revival at Hickory Grove, near Lake Park, in 1870 when R. F. Lanier was evangelist. Among the number were Joe Corbett, Shep Corbett, Miles McLeod, and Eli Strickland, with their wives and families. In 1878, the Negroes formed their own congregation, called Antioch, located near Lake Park. There were 15 charter members. Joe Corbett was the first minister. There were 75 members by 1900. The work was strengthened by J. H. Rogers, graduate of Hiram (Ohio) College and Eli Strickland gave liberally of his time and means.

Joe Corbett organized the Salem Church, about six miles east of Valdosta, in 1878. Dave Shanks was a leader of the group that numbered 40 by 1900.

The first congregation of Negro Disciples at Atlanta was established by Dr. A. G. Thomas in 1879. In February, Mrs. Mary D. Howell informed Dr. Thomas that "a number of these colored friends, who had enlisted her interest and advice, were anxious to become members of the Church of Christ, and to be organized into a congregation."

Subsequently, seven Negro candidates for membership attended a meeting of the Atlanta church, with a num-

---

[65]*Christian Quarterly*, Apr., 1874, pp. 218 ff.

ber of members present, and were "duly received into the fellowship of the church, and instructed in their duties and privileges." One of the number, Brother Jones, was authorized to preach, as he had been doing while a Baptist; ordination was promised when he proved his worth. The Negroes met thereafter in a room on Marietta St. in Northwest Atlanta. There was a Sunday school and regular prayer meetings. A building was proposed on a donated site.[66] However, by 1900, there was no permanent home for the congregation that apparently became known as the Rocky Mount Church.

There was a Negro church at Augusta before 1900 with W. H. Williams preaching for it. The group had a building, but lost it because it was located on leased ground. The church used rented quarters at Turpenhill about 1900 when Nathan Freeman was the minister.

Impetus was given to the work in Washington County in 1881 by T. N. Johnson, who received scriptural instruction from T. M. Harris. Johnson was followed by W. H. Smith, also persuaded to preach by Harris. Late in 1881, Harris ordained Smith and the latter became pastor in 1884 of the Negro Bethesda Church near Oconee. The membership grew from eight to about 125 by 1900. The membership of most Negro churches was less than 100. C. E. Edwards ministered to Bethesda in 1896-98. Smith returned to that pastorate in 1899 and was minister of Bethesda when he died, Mar. 6, 1929.[67]

Both Johnson and Smith preached for the Toomsboro Church, Wilkinson County; it was organized by T. M. Harris. The Hopewell and Mt. Pisgah Churches, Thomasville, were organized by Harris and W. H. Goodloe. In Brooks County, two churches formed were Mt. Olive and Pine Hill. There was a congregation at Mitchell, Glascock County, by 1900. Good Hope Church near Milltown, Lowndes County, was established in 1896

---

[66]*Christian Standard,* Oct. 4, 1879, p. 314.

[67]*Minutes* of the Forty-first Annual Christian Convention of the Churches of Christ of the State of Georgia Held at Valdosta, Ga., Oct. 24 to 27, 1929 (Valdosta, Ga.: Chambers Printing Co., 1930), p. 11.

by Dave Shanks. Evergreen Church, Valdosta, was formed in 1897 with Dave Bell, William Black, Steve Dasher, and George Smith among the charter members. There was a Sunday school and Charlie Peterson was minister about 1900.

The church near Quitman, Brooks County, was organized by Aaron Wade. Congregations at Homerville, Clinch County; Berea, Dodge County, and Bethel, Eastman, were strengthened by E. L. Shelnutt, evangelist for the Woman's Society for Georgia Missions, about 1899. C. H. Hall was the Homerville pastor in 1897.[68]

Shelnutt preached for the Berea Church, which he reorganized, several nights in June, 1899. His report stated:

. . . This was a departure from my usual work and was done without permission from W.S.G.M. head quarters. If the W.S.G.M. likes it and if this convention likes it, I would like for you to tell me so; but if you don't like it, I would like to see you help yourselves. I never could read the commission of my Saviour so it would say, "Go into all the world and preach the gospel to the white man only." It says "every creature" and that means the colored man as fast as it does the white man.[69]

The 1879 and 1880 Georgia Convention had delegates present from Negro congregations. In 1879, Brother Jones represented the Atlanta church. R. Pickens, a preacher, and R. Murray, were two delegates enrolled from Atlanta's Rocky Mt. Church at the 1880 Convention while John Maynard, preacher, was delegate from Turknett Springs Church.[70] Two Negro churches also had delegates at the 1881 Convention. William Thomas represented Rocky Mt. Church's 20 members and Alexander Owen the Magdalen Church's 10 members.[71]

---

[68]*The Evangelist*, June 5, 1897, p. 2.

[69]*Second Annual Convention* of the Woman's Society for Georgia Missions Held at Atlanta, Ga., Nov. 15, 1899, in the First Christian Church (Atlanta: Evangelist Publishing Co., 1899?), p. 16.

[70]*Christian Standard*, Dec. 20, 1879, p. 402; Dec. 11, 1880, p. 394.

[71]*Christian Standard* Supplement, Feb. 25, 1882, p. 15.

A state convention of Georgia Negro Disciples was formed about 1889 by T. M. Harris.[72] The 1898 sessions were scheduled for Oct. 26 at the Augusta Negro First Christian Church, according to W. H. Williams, traveling evangelist. "All the preachers of the Christian churches" were cordially invited to meet with the Negro brethren.[73] During 1896-98, W. H. Smith was state evangelist.

Small numbers and inadequate support of Georgia's Negro Disciples prevented extensive work among Negroes. The pattern of segregation that developed after the Civil War arose from a fundamental desire of Negroes for recognition. The struggle over segregation was waged relentlessly in politics with the status quo finally victorious. Thus, the pattern became rigidly established among Georgia Christians by 1900.

Revivals Create New Congregations

Protracted evangelistic meetings continued to be a popular manifestation of religion in Georgia until well after the end of the nineteenth century. New congregations often developed from them. Seldom, however, did a preacher receive $1,000 for his preaching in a revival with no additions reported as Isaac Errett did at Augusta in 1871. Doubtless Mrs. Emily H. Tubman contributed a generous share of Errett's compensation for the 16 sermons.[74]

An evangelistic meeting, held on a plantation in 1885, resulted in a new congregation. John W. Mountjoy (1844-1886) of Columbia, Mo., went from the Augusta State Convention to Macon and then 25 miles to "Buzzard Roost." Crossing the Ocmulgee River, he went from Twiggs to Houston County and soon reached the

---

[72]Barfield, *op. cit.*, pp. 94, 107.

[73]*The Evangelist*, Feb. 5, 1898, p. 2.

[74]*Christian Standard*, Dec. 16, 1871, pp. 396 f. James S. Lamar, *Memoirs of Isaac Errett With Selections from His Writings* (2 vol.; Cincinnati: Standard Publishing Co., 1893), II, 61. People *knelt* for prayer, Errett reported, a custom not generally practiced among Disciples.

home of John Faulk, a relative, whose wife, Virginia, was the daughter of James Shannon.[75] Mountjoy's report follows:

For a number of years she sought and prayed for some one to come to preach the gospel in her community. She has been all alone as a Disciple. She has at times gone to Atlanta, one hundred miles distant, to meet and worship with the brethren.

. . . .

. . . The neighbors were notified, and gathered in, and the negroes on the plantation attended, so that we had a good and increasing audience from the beginning [November 8, 1885, in the Faulk house].

The hall in which I preached is wide and spacious and at each end are a piazza and large double doors. The colored people sat at the opening on the back piazza opposite from where I stood. We had one hymn book and I *"lined out"* the hymns. We sang familiar songs, and with great fervency. We all know with what Spirit and power the negro can sing his religious songs, and it is with peculiar zest these southern negros [sic] engage in such service. . . . I am satisfied, many a "hallelujah" was suppressed, . . . I was told that they did not know it was their privilege to obey the gospel under my preaching. I removed all fears and doubts on that subject. One night uncle Archie Wilson, a faithful and an intelligent old colored man walked forward and gave me his hand. I pointed him to a seat near by, and he knelt down with his face in his hands, and I realized for once that I had on my hands a genuine mourner at the mourner's chair. I let him remain in his devotional attitude until the song was closed, and then touched him and told him to be seated in the chair. I then took occasion to explain the situation, and to show how naturally the old man thought that was the way to proceed as he never knew or heard of any other way. After a scriptural statement of the case, I took his confession. A pool was prepared in a beautiful stream not far from the house, and on Lord's Day night after preaching, we all walked to the place with torches of lightwood, and there, under the tall pines with the moon peeping through their branches, and under the eye of God, the ordinance of baptism was administered. My cousin Virginia assisted in preparing that nice pool, and knew not at the time that she would have the pleasure of seeing her own brother baptized first in it, but thought it was for Uncle

[75]Cf. ante., p. 145.

Archie alone. I shall never forget that beautiful night under Southern skies, and that beautiful scene when two noble young men and the old colored man put on Christ. Six came forward that night at the close of my sermon. After the baptizing we returned to the house, and after necessary preparations partook of the Lord's Supper. . . . After the Supper, the names of the members were signed to the following which I had written in the Bible on a blank leaf between the Old and New Testaments:

"Virginia Hall Church," Lord's Day,

Nov. 15, 1885.

"With the view and for the purpose of uniting as a band of Disciples of Christ, discarding all human names and human creeds, and taking the Bible as our only and sufficient rule of faith and practice, and, thereby forming the nucleus for a Church of Christ in this community, and thus in some measure contribute to the great work of this century begun by our fathers, viz: the restoration of primitive Christianity and the union of God's people, we hereby give our names and pledge our hearts and lives."

Thus closed one of the happiest and best meetings of my life. John Faulk and his son united from the Baptists, and I baptized among others, Lenoir Shannon, the youngest child of James Shannon, and the only one of his children not a disciple of Christ. I felt that it was appropriate and due the faithfulness of Virginia, the wife of Mr. Faulk, that the little church should be named "Virginia Hall," the latter name in memory of the place where the meeting was held.[76]

One can only wonder how long that church existed and how many persons it influenced. Probably it did not survive dissolution of the plantation that was the scene of its creation.

In reporting a revival at Acworth, J. A. Perdue stated, "I did not come here to proselyte. . . . I have learned to preach the gospel and let others alone. Some who have come to us from the denominations, . . . may be saved, doubtless many of them will be."[77] His denial

---

[76]Christian Standard, Dec. 12, 1885, p. 395. Returning to Missouri, Mountjoy died suddenly, Mar. 23, 1886, at the age of 41. In 1949, Disciples reported no congregation in Houston County where Virginia Hall Church was established in 1885.

[77]Ibid., May 28, 1887, p. 174.

of proselytism heralded a new day for Georgia Disciples insofar as their attitude toward other Christians was concerned.

During a revival in 1886 at Atlanta's Third Baptist Church, A. F. Lee, former Baptist, but a minister-member of the Atlanta Christian Church since 1872, clashed with a Baptist preacher named Pickett. Lee explained that Pickett, in a two-hour sermon, referred to him and his brethren as "Campbellites . . . imposters, liars and hypocrites," preaching "false doctrine." Lee publicly claimed he was "maliciously branded" and left the meeting. Pickett reported that all present endorsed his attack, but Lee said not more than one-half did.[78]

Excitement over the Spanish-American War prevented a month's revival at Athens in 1898 because members felt that "they could not pay their part of the expenses," reported Pastor W. A. Chastain. The State Board offered to pay one-half of the expenses, but the meeting was not held because so many members expected to lose their jobs.[79]

Erastus L. Shelnutt, evangelist of the Woman's Society for Georgia Missions, encountered opposition at a meeting he began, Sept. 16, 1899, at Lilburn School in Madison (now Jackson) County, not far from Athens. There were many Primitive Baptists in the community. However, all went well until Oct. 3 when the doors and windows were found nailed shut. Trustees had posted a notice that services must end. Shelnutt had the disappointed group sing, he read a Psalm and offered prayer. The meeting continued at another school three miles away. Enthusiasm was high and a building site was donated. A tabernacle was built and ready for use, Oct. 10. "Preachers began to ridicule and oppose," said Shelnutt, but the meeting continued until Oct. 30 when a congregation of 128 members was organized

---

[78]Report in the Atlanta (Ga.) *Constitution,* reprinted in *Atlantic Missionary,* June 23, 1886, p. 5.

[79]*Missionary Tidings,* Aug., 1898, p. 93.

as the Erastus Church, the name in honor of Shelnutt. It was the longest and largest rural revival ever conducted by the brethren in Georgia, Shelnutt reported.[80] From 1871 through 1899, according to available records, Georgia Disciples organized 134 congregations, including four that were reorganized. Nineteen of the total were Negro and six of those continue in existence. So, a total of 57 churches, white and Negro, were closed by 1949; six others either disbanded or voluntarily decided to have fellowship exclusively with the "anti-organ" Churches of Christ. The founding date of many of the churches is unknown. The list of 70 churches that follows designates Negro churches by the letter "n," and reorganized ones by "r," with name of 1949 county location:

Organized	Church, County	Organized	Church, County
1872 —	New Hope, Gwinnett	1885 —	Union Ridge, Butts
1874 —	rBethany, Paulding	1886 —	Antioch, Cherokee
1875 —	rAcworth, Cobb	1886 —	Bethel, Heard
1875 —	Damascus, Spalding	1886 —	Eastman, Dodge
1875 —	Red Oak, Fulton	1886 —	Hopewell, Gwinnett
1876 —	Athens, Clarke	1886 —	Macon, Bibb
1877?—	Magnolia, Burke	1887 —	Orphans, Dodge
	(reorg. '96 as Corinth)	1888 —	Burnham, Jennings, Fla.
1877?—	Spring Hill, Thomas	1890s?—	Adairsville, Bartow
1877?—	Thomasville, Thomas	1890s?—	Antioch, Butts
1878 —	nAntioch, Lowndes	1890s?—	Antioch, Screven
1878?—	Buckeye, Johnson	1890s?—	nPine Hill, Brooks
1878 —	Lake Park, Lowndes	1891 —	Maxeys, Oglethorpe
1878 —	Mars Hill, Decatur	1891 —	Mt. Zion, Jasper
1878 —	rSavannah, Chatham	1892 —	Halls Chapel, Wash.
1879 —	nAtlanta Rocky Mt.	1892 —	Statham, Barrow
1879 —	Bethany, Pike	1893 —	Tallapoosa, Haralson
1880?—	Ringgold, Spalding	1894 —	Ephesus, Carroll
1880 —	Rocky Ford, Screven	1894 —	Erick, Wheeler
1881 —	Harmony, Jackson	1894 —	Reese, Morgan
1881 —	Wrightsville, Johnson	1895 —	Fitzgerald, Ben Hill
1882 —	Augusta Cent. Richmond	1896 —	Atlanta, West End
1882 —	Union, Fulton	1896 —	rCorinth, Burke
1883 —	Bethany, Carroll	1896 —	nGood Hope, Lowndes
1883 —	Carter Hill, Barrow	1896 —	Hagan, Evans
	(reorganized 1911)	1896 —	Lamar, Banks
1883 —	Sylvania, Screven	1896 —	Meldrim, Effingham
1884 —	Loganville, Walton	1896 —	Rome First, Floyd
1884 —	Winder, Barrow	1896 —	Watkinsville, Oconee
1885 —	Bethel, Rockdale	1897 —	Midway, Barrow
1885 —	Hebron, Oconee	1897 —	Spring Hill, Toombs
1885 —	Tennille, Washington		(reorganized 1917)

[80]*Second Annual Convention, op. cit.,* pp. 19-21.

Organized	Church, County	Organized	Church, County
1897 —	nEvergreen, Lowndes	1899 —	Baldwin, Banks
1898 —	Atlanta, Longley Ave.	1899 —	Bethany, Banks
1898 —	Carrollton, Carroll	1899 —	Erastus, Jackson
1898 —	Dublin First, Laurens	1899 —	Monroe, Walton
1899? —	nBethel, Dodge		

Many of those congregations were in rural areas. Meanwhile, the cause was growing in the towns and cities. In July, 1877, Dr. A. G. Thomas returned to Atlanta from Indianapolis where he taught at Butler College and preached at Greenfield, Ind. He and Mrs. Thomas refused a missionary appointment under the Christian Woman's Board of Missions in 1877 to Jamaica. In 1879, he received a lifetime call from the Atlanta church. However, he relinquished the pastorate to J. S. Lamar, Jan. 1, 1885. Dr. Thomas also preached monthly, except for three years, during 1877-1896 at Acworth, Cobb County. In 1886-87, he was president of the now defunct Burritt College, Spencer, Tenn. Returning to Atlanta, he was president several years of the Georgia College of Medicine and Surgery.

In the spring of 1878, Dr. Thomas participated, as one of four Disciples delegates, in the Second International Sunday School Convention at Atlanta. A report of it said Disciples had "the habit of considering themselves in bad odor with the religious world. . . . This great convention would have done much to dispel such idle notions."[81] During the Atlanta ministry of C. P. Williamson, in the early 1890's, a Christian Endeavor Society, the third one there, was organized at First Christian Church. Miss Louanna Rhodes, later Mrs. L. O. Bricker, was a charter member of the new, popular interdenominational group.[82]

Up to 1900, the Augusta First Christian Church Gothic edifice, dedicated in 1876, was the most handsome structure of the state brotherhood. It was the gift of Mrs. Emily H. Tubman. The site, building, and adjacent par-

---

[81]*Christian Standard*, May 4, 1878, p. 142.
[82]Bolles, *op. cit.*, p. [17].

sonage cost $100,000.[83] Zachary Taylor Sweeney (1849-1926), later a notable minister of the Disciples, held two short pastorates at Augusta. His oratorical ability drew large crowds.

STATISTICS REVEAL GROWTH

In 1871, there were "some 3,000 Disciples in Georgia," Isaac Errett reported.[84] By 1879, Nathan W. Smith estimated there were 50 to 75 congregations and some 25 preachers with about six preaching full time.[85] In 1880, the state had 95 churches, 57 preachers, and 10,890 members.[86] A list of Georgia preachers published that year included names of only 35.[87] In 1884, T. M. Foster, state evangelist, reported 5,400 members, 70 congregations, and 40 preachers in Georgia.[88]

The 1888 *Year-Book of the Disciples of Christ,* issued by the Standard Publishing Co., Cincinnati, contained much statistical data about Georgia brethren. There were 39 preachers listed. The total membership was 8,083. There were 101 churches, white and Negro, in 45 counties, plus an estimated, unreported 30 churches, chiefly Negro, with estimated membership of 1,860. There were 30 Sunday schools with 900 pupils, 125 officers and teachers. The property of the churches was valued at $150,000; annual expenses for churches and schools totaled $21,400 and missionary gifts $1,100.[89]

Those figures were probably more accurate than ones in the 1890 Federal Religious Census of Disciples of Christ, as follows: 64 organizations, 60 edifices with

[83]*Christian Standard,* May 11, 1878, p. 152.

[84]*Ibid.,* Dec. 16, 1871, p. 397.

[85]*Ibid.,* June 7, 1879, p. 182.

[86]*Proceedings, op. cit.,* 1880, p. 15. Lewis, *op. cit.,* p. 143.

[87]Francis Marion Green (Editor), *Preachers of the Churches of Christ in the United States* (Cincinnati: F. M. Green, 1880), p. [2].

[88]*Christian Standard,* Nov. 1, 1884, p. 348.

[89]*Year-Book of the Disciples of Christ* (Cincinnati: Standard Publishing Co., 1888), pp. 7, 8, 50, 51, 64, 68, 69, 70.

seating capacity for 20,805 persons, property valued at $197,925, and 4,676 members.[90] In 1897, a Georgia brotherhood periodical published a list of 68 congregations in the state.[91]

By 1900, the evangelistic Georgia Disciples out numbered Episcopalians in the state and trailed the Presbyterians.[92] J. S. Lamar once described the questionable ethics used by pioneer Disciples to win converts. He said, "men were defeated rather than saved. They were hemmed in and headed off at every turn; . . . and told, 'You have just got to take' it. And when, under these persuasive influences, . . . many of them prudently did, it was heralded as 'another triumph of the gospel.' "[93] Nevertheless, the cause of the Disciples in Georgia had taken root and grown although it had not yet reached full bloom.

Many able preachers and laymen assumed leadership of the brethren during those years. They were living witnesses of statistics that reflected growth and increasing influence. Several prominent persons have been introduced. Two other evangelists who left their mark were Baxter W. Golightly and William Harrison Jones.

Golightly was born at Newnan, Oct. 9, 1853. He was ordained in 1878. The four Georgia churches that he established were Winder, Loganville, Bethel (Rockdale County), and Hopewell. Married to Alice Fullerton in 1880, they had six children. He died at Bay City, Tex., June 16, 1919.[94]

Jones, born Apr. 22, 1843, in Newton County, became a Christian under the preaching of Isham Moody in 1860. Married to Mary E. Cooper in 1865, they had nine children. He was ordained in 1876 by T. M. Harris in

[90]H. K. Carroll, *Religious Forces of the United States.* American Church History Series, 13 vols. (New York: Christian Literature Co., 1893), I, 127.

[91]*The Evangelist*, July 3, 1897, p. 4.

[92]Bedford, *op. cit.*, p. 94.

[93]*Christian Standard*, Apr. 3, 1886, p. 106.

[94]*The Christian-Evangelist*, Aug. 21, 1919, p. 871.

258 DISCIPLES OF CHRIST IN GEORGIA

Liberty Church, Coweta County. He established Bethany Church, Pike County. His main work was in West Georgia and in the Griffin District for 25 years, four as district evangelist. He was pastor of the County Line Church, 1879-1895.[95]

C. S. Lucas was pastor of Augusta's First Church about six years in the 1880's. He was responsible for the organization and building of Central Christian Church (originally Second) and another mission in Augusta. His biography described the growing influence of Disciples in Augusta under his effective ministry.[96]

Laymen, too, were prominent in the state brotherhood, giving of their abilities and leadership without cessation. Joseph Rucker Lamar, who became an Associate Justice of the United State Supreme Court, was a trustee of the Augusta First Church after his father, J. S. Lamar, concluded his pastorate there. Justice Lamar sometimes spoke at weekly prayer meetings, but did not pray in public.[97] His wife, Clarinda, was the daughter of W. K. Pendleton, a president of Bethany College, where Lamar was graduated in 1877.

The Howell family was significant among Georgia Disciples. Judge Clark Howell (1811-1882) was married to Mary D. Hook, daughter of Dr. and Mrs. Daniel Hook, in 1853. She died in April, 1886.[98] She was the third wife of Judge Howell. Their two children were Dr. D. H. Howell and Mrs. A. P. Woodward. Mrs. Mary Howell was the stepmother of Evan Park, Albert, Charlie, Clark II, and William H. Howell.

Evan Park Howell, a son of Clark Howell I, was born at Warsaw, Milton County, Dec. 10, 1839. He was a law

---

95*Southern Evangelist*, Mar. 2, 1901, p. 7.

96B. A. Abbott, *Life of Chapman S. Lucas* (Baltimore, Richmond: Christian Tribune, 1897), pp. 66 f.

97*Cf. ante.*, p. 192 f. Clarinda Pendleton Lamar, *op. cit.*, pp. 60 f.

98*Christian Standard*, May 22, 1886, p. 167. *Atlantic Missionary*, Apr. 21, 1886, p. 5. Judge Clark Howell was born Dec. 28, 1811, in Cabarrus County, N. C., and died in Atlanta on May 14, 1882.

graduate in 1859 and read law at Sandersville with his stepuncle, J. S. Hook. Evan P. Howell served two terms in the Georgia Senate.

Howell bought a half interest in the Atlanta *Constitution* for $10,000 and assumed half of the $27,000 debt. From Oct. 19, 1876, with Henry W. Grady, he edited the paper that began publication on June 16, 1868. After Grady's death in 1889, Howell continued as editor-in-chief until 1897 when he retired. In 1902, he was elected mayor of Atlanta. He married Julia Adelaide Erwin; they had seven children. Evan P. Howell died Aug. 6, 1905, and was buried across the main drive of Atlanta's Westview Cemetery from the Henry W. Grady vault.[99]

Clark Howell II was born at Erwinton, S. C., Sept. 21, 1863. He was graduated from the University of Georgia in 1883, was speaker of the Georgia House of Representatives, and president of the State Senate for two terms. His association with the *Constitution* began in 1884. He succeeded Grady in 1889 and his father in 1897. He was author of a four-volume *History of Georgia*. Howell died on Nov. 14, 1936.[100]

Evan P. Howell and his son, Clark II, were charter members of Atlanta's West End Christian Church, as was Albert Howell, having been formerly affiliated with First Church. Evan P. Howell donated a lot for the first West End building.[101]

Death took two other noted Georgia Disciples in those years. The passing of Mrs. Emily H. Tubman, June 9, 1885, at 91, was memorialized in the 1885 General Convention. The obituary report, read by A. McLean, listed

[99]Reed, *op. cit.*, pp. 71 f. Nixon, *op. cit.*, p. 128. Annie Elizabeth Miller (Compiler), *Our Family Circle* (Macon, Ga.: J. W. Burke Co., 1931), pp. 447, 473. Knight, *op. cit.*, II, 430.

[100]Annie E. Miller, *op. cit.*, pp. 469 ff. Reed, *op. cit.*, p. 410. Clark Howell II married three times. He and his first wife, Hattie Barrett, were parents of Clark Howell III, present publisher of the Atlanta *Constitution*.

[101]Bolles, *op. cit.*, p. [18]. Lenton L. Poss, ''The History of the Christian Church in Georgia'' (Unpublished B. D. Thesis, Brite College of the Bible, Texas Christian University, Fort Worth, 1948), pp. 88 f.

her name first.[102]   Her influence was permanently inscribed in the annals of Georgia Disciples.   Nathan W.
Smith died Aug. 14, 1899, at 85.   The *Gospel Advocate*
said he did more "in pleading for a return to Bible
Christianity than any man in Georgia."   The paper
added that "in his late years," Smith had "affiliated
with those that turned aside from the original purpose"
of the Disciples.[103]

THE WOMEN ORGANIZE THEIR STRENGTH

Behind an enlarging women's program before 1900
were hundreds of devoted Christian women.   The Christian Women's Georgia Missions was organized in the
Atlanta State Convention, Nov. 1, 1882.   It meant "new
elements of strength and activity," Isaac Errett said.[104]
The purpose was to raise funds for Georgia evangelism
through local societies.   Mrs. Mary D. Howell was elected
president.   Mrs. H. W. Fairbanks and Mrs. Alexander
C. Smith were successive secretaries.[105]

By 1884 there were 10 local Georgia auxiliaries.   The
work was already referred to as the C.W.B.M. of Georgia.
The national Christian Woman's Board of Missions was
formed in 1874.   At the 1884 State Convention, $20.05
was given for the national board.   Mrs. Howell was re-
elected president, thus becoming a national vice-president
of the C.W.B.M.[106]   By 1890, Mrs. R. V. Omer was the
Georgia C.W.B.M. president and Miss L. P. Halsted the
secretary.[107]

---

[102]*Missionary Tidings*, Dec. 1885, p. 6.

[103]*Gospel Advocate*, Aug. 24, 1899, p. 537.

[104]*Christian Standard*, Nov. 11, 1882, p. 356.

[105]*Ibid.*, Mar. 3, 1883, p. 108.

[106]*Missionary Tidings*, Dec., 1884, pp. 3, 5.

[107]*Ibid.*, Dec. 1890, p. 17.   Succeeding presidents, to 1900, were: Dora
C. (Mrs. W. C.) Lanier, Mrs. B. O. Miller, Mrs. Eula L. Heade, Mrs. E. B.
Erd.   Other secretaries, before 1900, were: Mrs. E. A. Parker, Miss Bunnie
Love, Mrs. E. E. Smith, Mrs. B. S. McCash, Mrs. J. A. Perdue, Mrs. A. N.
Jenkins.

In 1893, Georgia had 15 C.W.B.M. auxiliaries with a membership of 100; $500 was given for mission work. In the Atlanta Convention that year, Mrs. B. O. Miller was elected Georgia C.W.B.M. president. Miss Bunnie Love was chosen corresponding secretary, succeeding Mrs. E. A. Parker who held the post three years. Mrs. Parker was elected organizer for Georgia.[108]

The 1894 Georgia C.W.B.M. report showed 20 auxiliaries—11 new, one disbanded—with 360 members making contributions of $447.61.[109] Mrs. C. P. Williamson and Miss Bunnie Love attended the national C.W.B.M. Executive Committee meeting at Richmond, Va., Oct. 22, 1894. Mrs. Williamson said that it was the desire of Georgia women "to work in accordance with the plan of the National Board." So $400 of national funds was pledged to Athens as a mission church.[110] The pastor, W. A. Chastain, felt encouraged at having the "noble organization to stand by us."[111]

The National Board regretted that Georgia felt "obligated to aid churches within its borders . . . in such a way that it did not join . . . in the plans long ago arranged for *all* the States."[112] Miss Lois Almira White (1857-1939), a national secretary, who was later Mrs. Neil MacLeod, therefore explained at the 1894 Georgia Convention that the women were not working according to the C.W.M.B. constitution. The Georgia women "thought they could go on raising . . . Georgia mission money along with the C.W.B.M. dues and dispensing the former . . . according to their own discretion."[113] The C.W.B.M constitution stipulated that no money raised by and for it should be diverted to other purposes A resolution to meet the requirement was approved by the Georgia women.

---

[108]*Ibid.*, Dec., 1893, pp. 18, 34, 46.

[109]*Ibid.*, Dec., 1894, p. 5.

[110]*Ibid.*, Dec., 1894, p. 41.

[111]*Ibid.*, Apr., 1895, p. 15.

[112]*Ibid.*, Apr., 1895, p. 14.

[113]*The Evangelist*, Jan. 1, 1898, p. 2.

After that convention action, the women of Augusta's First Christian Church, in order to continue mission aid to several Georgia churches, formed a society for Georgia missions. It operated separately from the C.W.B.M. auxiliary at Augusta, although most women there affiliated with both groups.

That accounted for a proposal at the 1896 State Convention to establish a state women's organization to promote, but not duplicate, evangelistic and educational work. Ministers and lay people opposed such a society, claiming it was not needed. However, the 1897 Sandersville Convention approved the proposal. The new organization was called the Woman's Society for Georgia Missions. Mrs. Albert Howell was chosen president and Mrs. B. O. Miller corresponding secretary. Twenty-eight local societies were organized the first year.

In 1898, Mrs. Eula L. Heade, Georgia C.W.B.M. president, reported that it had "gained a stronger, firmer hold in Georgia." She spent eight months in field work, visiting 47 places. Georgia had 26 auxiliaries that year and contributions for missions totaled $1,079.77. W. A. Chastain, missionary pastor at Athens since 1893, talked on his work at the 1898 General Convention at Chattanooga. The congregation of 90 members was out of debt.[114] He resigned that ministry in 1899. A native Georgian, he was graduated from Bible College, Lexington, Ky., in 1889, and had married Ella Virginia Dobbs, Nov. 30, 1897, at Athens.[115]

During the 1899 Atlanta State Convention, the Woman's Society for Georgia Missions reported three churches organized. There were 34 local societies; 27 gave $677.87; six new ones were reported. E. L. Shelnutt was the organization's evangelist from Apr. 15 to Oct. 31, 1899.[116]

Georgia Christian women thus kept pace with the national tendency to direct their *own* organizations. In

[114]*Missionary Tidings*, Dec., 1898, pp. 186, 194, 196, 197, 206, 235.
[115]*The Evangelist*, Dec. 4, 1897, p. 2. Brown, *op. cit.*, p. 525.
[116]*Second Annual Convention, op. cit.*, p. 24.

doing so, they recovered the vital scriptural sense of every Christian and every church devoted to missions. They also learned parliamentary procedures and recognized the power of their votes long before giving serious consideration to the political ballot.

A YEARNING FOR EDUCATION MANIFESTED

The desire for a trained ministry among Georgia Disciples was evident after the Civil War. The Augusta Church in 1868 appealed for funds with which to train ministers.[117] Preachers then "were for the most part not college men, and seldom did anyone go to college or think of going," said Henry Barton Robison (1866-1953). Indeed, he proved the exception.

Born at Auburn, Jan. 2, 1866, Robison was the youngest of four sons of William Thomas and Elizabeth Elder Robison. In 1876, the family moved to Oconee County. The college-educated T. M. Foster influenced Henry to enter college for ministerial training. Henry's parents feared he would fail, as so many did, but gave him $500.-00. The young man borrowed $25.00 from the new Georgia educational fund of the Disciples and about 1887 started for Lexington, Ky., where he enrolled in Kentucky University, now Transylvania College. By 1894, he had earned two degrees and the classical diploma.[118] In 1907, he received the Ph.D. degree from The University of Chicago and became head of the religion department at Culver-Stockton College, Canton, Mo., in 1910. He died Oct. 11, 1953, at Madison, Wis.

An educational board of Georgia Disciples was formed in 1885. Mrs. A. C. Smith was instrumental in the organization and became corresponding secretary. T. M. Foster was the first president. The board sought a fund to help educate Georgia youth for the Christian ministry.

[117]*Millennial Harbinger,* Dec., 1868, p. 711.

[118]Henry Barton Robison, "A Sketch of Henry Barton Robison" (Unpublished MS., 1941?), pp. 1 f. Typed copy in possession of The Disciples of Christ Historical Society, Nashville, Tenn.

Loans were provided for needy students. Robison realized the need of such aid, so in 1896, he contributed $100.-
00 endowment. The 1897 Georgia Convention approved
by-laws of the Georgia Christian Education Society.
With Dr. A. G. Thomas as president, it was incorporated,
Mar. 3, 1898, and chartered by the Georgia Legislature.[119]

While Ashley Sidney Johnson (1857-1925) was pastor
of Central Church, Augusta, in 1887-88, he operated a
Correspondence Bible College. P. E. Wood and V. P.
Bowers were two of the students. Later, when Johnson
started his School of Evangelists, now Johnson Bible
College, near Knoville, Tenn., Alexander Campbell
Bruce of Atlanta prepared blueprints for the first build-
ing. Albert Theodore Fitts, pastor at Guyton in 1896-97,
later taught at the school.[120]   The proposal of C. P.
Williamson and others, in 1896, to launch a southern
Bible college was not realized.[121]

There was little if any provision for biblical instruction
at state universities at that time. That lack caused the
Christian Woman's Board of Missions to establish a
Bible Chair in 1893.[122]   As a result, Bible lectures for
literary and historical study were given in 1897-99 at the
University of Georgia, Athens, by Dr. Charles Alexander
Young. His textbook was the Bible. He taught about
150 college students, plus hundreds of others, in 1897.[123]

Prof. Young did not teach doctrine, yet there was
opposition to his lectures. Presbyterian and Methodist
ministers shared in the teaching before it was completed.
But the lectures were strongly opposed by W. A. Candler,

---

[119]*Charter and By-Laws of the Georgia Christian Education Society,*
1897-98 (Atlanta: Capital Printing Co., 1898), pp. 1 f. First trustees of
the Society were: W. A. Chastain, T. M. Foster, J. S. Lamar, H. M.
Patterson, E. L. Shelnutt, Mrs. A. C. Smith, Dr. A. G. Thomas, and C. P.
Williamson. By 1919, loans of $3,661.50 had been made to 41 students
(*Christian Messenger,* Year Book Number, Jan.-Feb., 1920, pp. 23, 24, 29).

[120]Robert E. Black, *The Story of Johnson Bible College* (Kimberlin
Heights, Tenn.: Tennessee Valley Printing Co., 1951), pp. 19, 24, 26,
29, 89.

[121]*Christian Standard,* Dec. 12, 1896, p. 1582.

[122]*Missionary Tidings,* Nov. 1897, pp. 131 f.

[123]*The Evangelist,* Mar. 15, 1897, p. 2.

Emory College president, and H. R. Bernard, Mercer University financial agent. Dr. Candler said, ''the establishment of a Bible Chair at the University, can no more impart a christian character to the institution than singing psalms in a side show can sanctify a circus.''[124]

Nevertheless, there was a popular desire for more lectures. Harry Hodson, Baptist alumnus of the University, Chancellor Wm. E. Boggs, and representatives of Athens congregations offered to raise $1,000 for a Bible Chair Lectureship provided the C.W.B.M. duplicated the amount in five years.

Georgia Disciples were gratified with the 1897 lectures. Yet of more than $100 given in cash to support them, only $6.25 came from Disciples.[125] Such lectures were seriously questioned before the first series. They were made possible by four Atlanta women: Mrs. Albert Howell, Miss Bunnie Love, Mrs. John A. Perdue, and Mrs. F. J. Spratling. They raised $300 for the C.W.B.M. Bible Chair Fund.

During the 1898 lectures of four weeks, 118 persons enrolled. There was no opposition that year.[126] The 1898 Chattanooga National Convention recommended the continuance of the Athens lectures since a ''considerable amount was pledged.'' The lectures were repeated for the last time, without opposition, by Dr. Young during eight weeks, January-March, 1899.[127] However, they were then abandoned because of inadequate funds.

Societies and Organs Cause Division

The fellowship of Georgia Disciples was slowly rent asunder by continuing differences of opinion. The controversy was joined mainly over missionary societies and

---

124Atlanta (Ga.) *Constitution* quoted in *The Evangelist,* Apr. 17, 1897, p. 2.

125*The Evangelist,* Apr. 3, 1897, p. 3.

126*Missionary Tidings,* May, 1898, p. 21; Nov., 1898, p. 159; Dec., 1898, p. 189.

127*Ibid.,* Mar., 1899, p. 326; May, 1899, pp. 27 f.

instrumental music in terms of literalism vs. expediency. Debates over those and such matters as Sunday schools and salaried pastors were more or less involved and simultaneous between the Civil War years and 1900. They were all in the area of human judgment where all the brethren met on common ground that was seldom recognized. The issues were not in the realm of doctrine, but they became tests of fellowship.

Records of the struggle in Georgia are scarce. Those available suggest that the situation was similar in many instances to those of their brethren elsewhere. The Georgians were influenced by editors of their favorite brotherhood papers. Up to 1900, in Georgia, the *Christian Standard* was the favorite of those supporting co-operation, missionary societies, and the organ. The *Gospel Advocate,* leading opponent in Georgia against "unscriptural innovations," expressed views of the legalistic, intolerant faction. No one seemed to mind that the periodicals were themselves "unscriptural innovations." Thus, emerging from isolationism and the aftermath of the Civil War, Georgia Disciples slowly took sides even when they did not understand the meaning of the basic issues.

Ability to buy an instrument and esthetic considerations affected many views. J. S. Lamar wrote that instrumental music, "an aid to the worshiper," was the "inevitable consequence of growth and culture."[128] Several Georgia Christian churches used organs before 1900. Perhaps one of the first was introduced in the Gothic building at Augusta in 1875. The Mt. Vernon Church had one in 1890, to the disgust of older members. It caused removal of the three-foot partition dividing men and women at worship.[129] In 1894, when the Guyton church, a rural congregation, had 70 members, the controversies over Sunday schools, women's societies, and organs caused the withdrawal of 23 members.

---

128 James S. Lamar, *Memoirs of Isaac Errett, op. cit.,* II, 25.

129Burson, *et. al., op. cit.,* p. 8.

Before 1900, the new West End Church, Atlanta, had a Story and Clark organ.[130]   The instrument was a "pleasant surprise" for minister and members of Harmony Church, Jackson County, Apr. 11, 1897. "There sat in the middle of the church a beautiful, brand new organ, the gift of friends, with the aid of a few brethren."[131] The Acworth church building burned, Mar. 28, 1899; the organ and some pew cushions were saved.

Many Georgia Christian churches were troubled over the organ or society issues. The Macon congregation had difficulty in 1887 when a year old. James A. Harding (1848-1922) of Winchester, Ky., was evangelizing in Georgia. He was then associate editor of the *Gospel Advocate*. He began a revival at Macon, May 22, preached two sermons, then closed the meeting that night because an organ was used in worship. Dr. J. D. Erwin, Jr., proposed to have the instrument removed for duration of the meeting provided Harding continued preaching. However, the evangelist did not satisfy the congregation with arguments against the organ, so the meeting was cancelled, leaving the Macon group "very much disappointed and mortified." L. M. Erwin, a founder of the congregation, wrote that, "had he informed us of his peculiar views on the organ question *before* he made the engagement and *previous* to his coming," the unpleasant situation could have been prevented.[132]

The report of the disagreement was published in the *Christian Standard,* then reprinted in the *Gospel Advocate,* with Harding adding comment, saying, in part:

. . . We are commanded to withdraw from those that walk disorderly, and I intend to do it most emphatically in regard to these organ users.

My views on the organ question have been published to the brethren for years; but I had no reason to believe that a weak, little church . . . had secured an organ. If they had written

---

[130]*The Evangelist,* Apr. 3, 1897, p. 2.

[131]*Ibid.,* May 1, 1897, p. 3.

[132]*Christian Standard,* June 11, 1887, p. 190. *Gospel Advocate,* July 13, 1887, p. 433.

me that notwithstanding their poverty they had secured an
organ, the trouble would have been obviated, for I would not
have gone.

If the church had been content to walk as did the primitive
churches the trouble would not have arisen; but they chose to
add to their worship a device of the mother of harlots, . . . If
they have any fault to find let them find it with the "scarlet
woman," and with themselves for following her.[133]

Thus did the tensions lead to name-calling. Since the
"antis" felt constrained by Scripture "to withdraw
from those that walk disorderly," and since most of them
regarded the use of an organ in worship as "walking
disorderly," the fellowship was inevitably disrupted.

The Valdosta Church was also disturbed by Harding's
preaching against the organ. Dissension began in 1884
there. One pastor, D. R. Pickens, resigned because of
the dispute. J. S. Lamar became minister in 1887 when
the dissident faction opposed cooperation and a salaried
ministry. No agreement was reached so the minority
group of "antis" withdrew and formed Central Avenue
Church. Nine months later, the majority placed an organ
in the First Christian Church.

However, the difficulties were not completely settled.
There was tension at Valdosta a decade later when J. C.
McReynolds was minister. Nearly every congregation
in that area, he said, had suffered from intolerant strife
over expediencies. Tests of fellowship, "a very creed,"
were instituted. Thus, the New Testament became a
book of mandatory statutes rather than guiding principles. The legalistic brethren insisted that "they understood the Bible as no one else does!" However, the
two congregations met to seek common ground of union
and McReynolds read a paper on "original principles"
of the movement. The assembly refused to admit, "In
essentials, unity; in non-essentials, liberty and toleration," one of the opposition inquiring, "What are the
non-essentials?"

---

[133]*Gospel Advocate*, July 13, 1887, p. 434.

McReynolds said, "Brethren, I am at the end of my string, and I can go no further." It was a sad conclusion and some persons wept, he reported. An observer said, "Brother McReynolds was knocked out by the Central Avenue people the very first round." Yet, he continued to hope that eventually the strife would cease and the division be healed.[134]

At the Rome Church, Mrs. B. Frank Archer stated that one angry member declared "he would rather eat bacon and eggs off the communion table than have an organ in the church."[135]

However, many Georgia brethren doubtless exercised much patience in those disputes. J. S. Lamar indicated that once, saying, "You may belabor our missionary organizations till you tire yourself to death, and we shall be as quiet as little mice; you may even blow our organs for us, or, if you prefer it, *smash* them, and still our fraternal feelings and relations will not be at all disturbed. . . ."[136]

The Berea Church of Henry County illustrated an enlightened way to solve the organ dispute. Christian liberty of opinion, in the best tradition of the Disciples, was extended to all concerned. William S. Fears, founder of the church and its spiritual guide until his death about 1903, opposed instrumental music in worship. The church did not divide, but members differed with Mr. Fears though they respected his convictions. Near the end of his life, unable to attend worship, some elders talked with him about use of the organ. The veteran preacher replied that he could not worship with an instrument, but he did not wish to hinder others by imposing his views

---

[134]*The Evangelist,* Apr. 3, 1897, p. 2. By 1899, the Valdosta "anti" church had established a mission three miles from town "without the aid of a society or board." Harding was one of the preachers (*Gospel Advocate,* Feb. 16, 1899, p. 108).

[135]Quoted in Bedford, *op. cit.,* p. 154. Mrs. Archer, then Miss Scottie Wimbish, and B. Frank Archer (they were married in 1899) were the first members received by confession into the Rome congregation after its organization in 1896. Her parents, Mr. and Mrs. W. G. Wimbish, were charter members.

[136]*Christian Standard,* Dec. 9, 1871, p. 388.

upon them. After his death, the organ was placed in the church.[137] Such Christian forbearance was seldom used in the aggravating situations.

The conflict over missionary societies and music was settled by local congregations, usually, with the minority faction, whatever its views, withdrawing and establishing another church. Each faction claimed to be loyal to the best of New Testament faith and practice. The strategy of separatism that gradually emerged was one of strict, exclusive "restoration" of an apostolic "ancient order."

The prolonged controversy tragically ruptured the fellowship and the new century was to see the climax in a "Waterloo of schism."[138] The end of the conflict, however, did not mean a cessation of brotherhood disputes. They continued over other issues, speculative and practical, into the twentieth century. They became part of a continuing struggle to strike a happy balance between freedom at the local level and more centralized efficiency at state and national levels.

The unprecedented way in which the majority of Georgia's cooperating Disciples worked together interdependently from 1900 through 1914 will be set forth in the next chapter. The despair over division yielded during those years at least to a sense of victorious accomplishment through effective Christian witnessing under the transforming Christ. Thus did the darkness of the old century fade away before the promising light of new, transforming ideas in the twentieth century.

---

[137]Barfield, *op. cit.*, p. 76. In 1870, at the Georgia State Convention, Fears stated, ''There are crushing strifes, contentions, feuds, hair-splittings, among our brethren. The time may come that we will divide'' (*Christian Standard*, Dec. 3, 1870, p. 386).

[138]Quoted by F. D. Kershner, *The Christian-Evangelist*, Feb. 13, 1936, p. 210.

CHAPTER VIII

A New Era of Peril and Promise, 1900-1914

The twentieth century with its portents of change dawned quietly for Georgia Disciples of Christ, but it was not long until opposition again manifested itself. However, despite criticism, the Woman's Society for Georgia Missions continued to evangelize. E. L. Shelnutt, W. A. Chastain, and John Henry Wood conducted revivals and established churches. By 1913 the women had raised more than $11,000 and established 13 congregations.[1]

Mrs. B. O. Miller was unquestionably the W.S.G.M. moving spirit. Elected corresponding secretary in 1897, she held that post until 1904 when she became president where she served until her death in 1926. The Emily H. Tubman Society, formed in Mrs. Miller's Augusta home, was a supporting group. In later years the W.S.G.M. declined in effectiveness and the Georgia women's work was finally unified.[2]

In 1900 Mrs. Miller urged the establishment of a mountain mission school. The proposal received enthusiastic approval. Persons at Baldwin and in Habersham County soon offered land, a house, and some cash to start the

---

[1]*Year Book of the Christian Churches (Disciples of Christ) in Georgia for 1913-1914* (n. p., 1915?), p. 41.

[2]Born Jan. 3, 1850, at Oak Bowery, Ala., Annie Charlotte Jones was the youngest of 11 children of Dr. and Mrs. John Wm. Jones. The family moved to Atlanta in 1855. Annie was married to Bert Olive Miller at Campbellton, Ga., Apr. 14, 1868; they had three children, and became Disciples at Augusta. He died in 1916 after which she moved to Decatur where she died, Oct. 27, 1926.

project, and the 1901 State Convention voted acceptance.[3]
Inadequate finances always proved a handicap. An early
appeal for public support was made by John Temple
Graves in the Atlanta *Journal*.[4]

Mrs. Miller recommended abandonment of the project
in December, 1901, but the school opened at Baldwin,
Jan. 15, 1902, with Miss Bunnie Love as principal. The
school and local Christian church suffered "considerable
[local] opposition" reported G. H. Hinnant, missionary
pastor. In 1903, 64 pupils were enrolled, including Penn
Smith, grandson of Nathan W. Smith.[5] A teacher was
Mrs. Mollie McGee, daughter of R. M. Mitchell of Acworth and granddaughter of Nathan W. Smith. Some
children had to reside at the school.

W. B. Shaw took control of the school, Feb. 13, 1905.
But its upkeep was too much for the women, so, in
December, 1905, the property was deeded to the National
Benevolent Association of St. Louis, Mo., a national
agency of the Disciples.[6] Meanwhile, Shaw opened the
Southeastern Christian Orphanage, Jan. 1, 1906, in a
summer hotel; it became affiliated with the N.B.A. in
1907. Miss Margy English was the first matron[7]; Dr.
J. F. Davis was treasurer until his death in April, 1910.[8]
The Baldwin Home admitted more than 100 children.

However, in November, 1911, Baldwin being considered
unsuitable and the school discontinued, the Southern
Christian Home, with 30 children from five states, was
moved, largely through the influence of Mrs. Lane

[3]*Southern Evangelist*, Jan. 25, 1901; Nov. 28, 1901. Mrs. B. O. Miller, *Mission Work in the North Georgia Mountains* (Atlanta: Evangelist Publishing Co., 1900?), pp. 8 ff. *Annual Report of the Christian Churches in Georgia for 1900* (Atlanta: Evangelist Publishing Co., 1900?), pp. 21 f. *Year Book of the Churches of Christ in Georgia for 1902* (Atlanta: Mutual Publishing Co., 1902), pp. 34 f.

[4]Reprinted in *Southern Evangelist*, Oct. 17, 1901, p. 12.

[5]*Year Book . . . 1902, op. cit.*, pp. 29, 35. *Year Book . . . 1903, po. cit.*, pp. 33, 34, 38.

[6]*Year Book of the Churches of Christ in Georgia for 1905* (n. p., 1905?), p. 37.

[7]Subsequent directors of the Baldwin Home included Mr. and Mrs. L. Gill, Prof. F. E. Ferriss, Miss Bunnie Love, Mr. and Mrs. Ira E. Cowling, Mr. and Mrs. J. F. Green and their son, J. L. Green.

[8]*Christian Philanthropist*, Oct. 1911, p. 50.

Mitchell, to leased quarters at 299 Lee St., Atlanta.[9] She became admissions chairman and held the post many years.

The Georgia Christian Woman's Board of Missions obviously suffered from competition of the W.S.G.M. for women's interest, time, and funds, as well as indifference to *foreign* missions. In 1900, there were 15 auxiliaries with 345 members giving $140.75. By May, 1914, there were 45 local groups and 616 members contributing $1,-311.22.[10] During part or all of 1900-14, financial aid was given to the Athens, Rome, and Columbus churches and to W. H. Smith for Negro evangelism. The Evergreen Auxiliary, Valdosta, had Negro representatives to speak at the 1914 State Convention.[11] The Georgia women received a medal for raising their apportionment of a fund in connection with the 1909 Pittsburgh Centennial Convention that commemorated Thomas Campbell's *Declaration and Address*.[12] They gave $500 for a memorial room in Missions Building, Indianapolis, then C.W.B.M. headquarters, now home offices of The United Christian Missionary Society and other brotherhood agencies.[13]

Mrs. Lydia Hollingsworth was state C.W.B.M. treasurer in 1901-06. However, the length of her service was surpassed by Birdie Farrar (Mrs. L. M.) Omer who was secretary, 1910-18. Her husband, Louis Moses Omer (1859-1944), was pastor at Sandersville, Tennille, Toomsboro, and West Point. Both were missionaries to Mexico briefly beginning in 1900.[14] Miss Mary Irene Orvis did

[9]*Ibid.*, pp. 54 f.

[10]*Annual Report . . . 1900, op. cit.*, pp. 24 ff. *Year Book . . . 1913-1914, op. cit.*, p. 41.

[11]*Year Book of the Churches of Christ in Georgia for 1906* (Atlanta: Byrd Printing Co., 1907), p. 16. *Year Book . . . 1913-1914, op. cit.*, p. 41.

[12]*Year Book of the Christian Churches (Disciples of Christ) in Georgia for 1910* (Atlanta: Lester Book & Stationery Co., 1910), p. 18.

[13]*Year Book of the Christian Churches in Georgia (Disciples of Christ) for 1908* (Atlanta: Byrd Printing Co., 1908), p. 34.

[14]Georgia C.W.B.M. presidents, 1900-14, were: Mesdames A. B. Phillips, Henry Lewis, Eula L. Head, E. B. Erd, H. King Pendleton, Bernard P. Smith, and Nanna Crozier (John H.) Wood. Secretaries were: Mesdames W. A. Chastain, E. B. Erd, W. J. Cocke, G. W. Harlan, J. C. Gentry, and Birdie Farrar Omer.

field work for the Georgia C.W.B.M. prior to becoming a Latin American missionary in 1908. She retired at Ellijay, Gilmer County, in 1938.[15]

Other missionaries from Georgia were Mr. and Mrs. Edward Walker Pease, Wm. M. Taylor, and Miss Gertrude Remington. The Peases—she was a daughter of Dr. and Mrs. A. G. Thomas—were in Norway, 1900-08, under the Foreign Christian Missionary Society. He earned the B.D. degree from Yale Divinity School in 1895 and was pastor of Poplar Springs Church, Washington County, three years. By 1909, he was again a Georgia pastor. In 1901, Mr. Taylor, minister of West End Church, Atlanta, became an evangelistic missionary for the American Christian Missionary Society in Puerto Rico. He returned to the United States in July, 1903, and was appointed southern evangelist for the A.C.M.S.[16] Miss Remington's home was at Thomasville, Ga. She engaged in independent mission work in Japan with John Moody McCaleb. Arriving there Mar. 1, 1904, she returned home in the autumn of 1906 because of tuberculosis.[17]

Clayton W. Plopper left Georgia for Cincinnati in 1900 to become bookkeeper of the F.C.M.S. at $450 a year. Son of Madison H. and Lavinia T. Plopper, he was associated with his father in mercantile business and Fitzgerald assistant postmaster two years. He became F.C.M.S. treasurer in 1910, serving that agency and its successor, The United Christian Missionary Society, until 1945.[18]

[15]They Went to Latin America, Biographies of Missionaries of the Disciples of Christ (Indianapolis: The United Christian Missionary Society, 1947), pp. 11, 12, 85 f.

[16]McLean, op. cit., pp. 133 f. American Home Missionary, Nov. 1903, pp. 260 f. Brown, op. cit., p. 624.

[17]Gospel Advocate, Apr. 2, 1904, p. 246; May 5, 1904, p. 279; Dec. 27, 1906, p. 823. The Christian-Evangelist, June 20, 1907, p. 795.

[18]Southern Evangelist, Jan. 11, 1901, p. 7. Missionary Intelligencer, Nov. 1901, p. 300. The Christian-Evangelist, Jan. 4, 1940, p. 9. World Call, June, 1945, p. 15. McLean, op. cit., pp. 364, 423.

During the ministry of Howard T. Cree, in 1913, Augusta First Church was enlisted by the F.C.M.S. as the state's first missionary living-link. That plan of support, started in 1893, then meant $600 annually to finance a foreign missionary. In 1900, 71 contributing Georgia churches and Sunday schools, plus other sources, gave $925.62 to the F.C.M.S. In 1914 the amount from 70 organizations, plus personal gifts, totaled $2,336.99.[19]

Climactic Encounter and Definitive Schism

The most dramatic encounter of sectarian prejudice and bitter opposition in the history of Georgia Disciples was that suffered by E. L. Shelnutt in 1902. Subsequent brushes with opponents seemed tame indeed by comparison. Some Franklin County Baptists had him arrested and tried on a charge of "disturbing public worship." A revival was scheduled for Unity Academy while a tabernacle was being built. Two of the three trustees approved its use. Enroute, Sunday, Sept. 28, to start the meeting, Shelnutt and a friend met the other trustee, W. C. Culpepper, a Baptist, who said that he and a majority of citizens thereabouts objected to Shelnutt preaching in the school. Shelnutt replied that he would not violate the majority's wishes, but that "it was unjust to condemn a man unheard" and said he would preach in the public road if necessary.

Reaching the Academy, where people had gathered, the doors were found chained and padlocked. Shelnutt decided to preach in a grove, but indignant persons forced open a door. Urged by the people, including one trustee, Shelnutt preached there twice that day. During the following week, with some difficulties, a tabernacle was erected. However, when it was learned that there would be preaching Sunday, Oct. 5, at the nearby New Bethel Baptist Church, Shelnutt recommended worship there.

---

[19]*Missionary Intelligencer,* Nov., 1913, p. 416; Nov. 1900, p. 307; Nov., 1914, p. 451.

The New Bethel Baptist preacher, S. E. Macomson, denounced the "damnable doctrine" of the "Campbell-ites," making Shelnutt the cynosure of those present. All were admonished not to hear Shelnutt, to refuse to feed or shelter him and thus avoid propagating "false doctrine." After the service, Shelnutt introduced himself and invited Macomson to the tabernacle services. Macomson said he was "*not* glad to meet" Shelnutt and that he would not go to the tabernacle. Macomson accused Shelnutt of lying and the latter tried to explain that he was not guilty, but soon realized any explanation was wasted effort. Shelnutt was ordered from the church and outside, after more effort to pacify, he left. Skirmishing followed among angry persons, some with "clenched fists" and "open knives."

On Oct. 8, the sheriff arrested Shelnutt and four others on the charge of "disturbing public worship." Bond was made and the "prisoner preacher" continued the revival, although destruction of the tabernacle was threatened.

The trial was held at Carnesville, county seat, Oct. 14. Testimony of the prosecutors, including Culpepper, plus six witnesses, was "so good for the defense" that no defense witnesses were called. Macomson swore that he "ordered the door locked against" Shelnutt. Judge Little permitted defendants a statement. A plea for a verdict of "malicious prosecution" was withdrawn at Shelnutt's request. The Baptist jury of six men returned a verdict of "not guilty." Shelnutt considered his acquittal the greatest victory of his life.[20]

Shelnutt related his persecutions at the 1902 State Convention of Disciples, Nov. 18. "The great audience was moved to tears" and expressed gratitude for the spirit manifested by the fearless evangelist.[21] The trial

---

[20]E. L. Shelnutt, *Encountering Opposition* (Cincinnati: American Christian Missionary Society, 1902?). The title page erroneously located Franklin County in Tennessee instead of Georgia.

[21]*Year Book . . . 1902, op cit.*, pp. 4, 10, 34. The meeting closed with organization of Union Ground Church. Shelnutt returned in Aug. 1903, with opponents still resisting, but he preached 21 times in a revival (*Year Book . . . 1903, op. cit.*, p. 31).

was the climax of apparent opposition to Disciples by
Baptists in Georgia. Thereafter more amity developed,
with simultaneous state conventions in 1903, 1906, and
1907 exchanging greetings.[22]

The formal recognition of the prolonged defection in
the brotherhood occurred in the 1906 Federal Religious
Census. S. N. D. North, director of the U. S. Bureau of
the Census, asked Editor David Lipscomb of the *Gospel
Advocate* if there was another religious body, separated
from the Disciples of Christ. Lipscomb replied that
there was "a distinct people" who had separated from
the rest of the brotherhood.[23] Earlier, he had stated
that the progressives "have gone out from us and are no
longer of us."[24] Thus, the conservatives or "antis" were
first listed separately as Churches of Christ while the
progressives or "digressives" remained designated Disciples of Christ.

The breach was accompanied by demoralization, much
of it lost to history. In Georgia, the 1906 *Year Book* of
the state missionary organizations, published in 1907,
contained statistical data by districts. The Northern
included the Antioch and Holland Churches of Chattooga
County; both were designated "anti-organ" while
Antioch was also labeled non-cooperative and non-pro-
gressive.[25] A few rural churches were omitted, at their
request, from the 1908 *Year Book* because they were not
cooperative in missionary work.[26] The West End Church
of Christ, Atlanta, was organized in 1903 by a Tennessee
conservative. Apparently, he did not consider uniting
with an existing church because of the sharp cleavage at
that time.[27]

---

[22]*Year Book* . . . *1903, op. cit.,* p. 17. *Year Book* . . . *1906, op. cit.,*
p. 24. *Year Book* . . . *1908, op. cit.,* p. 46.

[23]*Gospel Advocate,* July 18, 1907, p. 457.

[24]*Ibid.,* Mar. 29, 1906, p. 196.

[25]*Year Book* . . . *1906, op. cit.,* p. [39].

[26]*Christian Standard,* Jan. 18, 1908, p. 114.

[27]Bedford, *op. cit.,* pp. 158 f.

So the lines were drawn, individuals having made their choice, and after 1906 the separating churches went their own ways. Nevertheless, the vision of Christian unity persisted in haunting the religious family whose members allowed the miracle of Christian fellowship to be disrupted.

The 1906 Religious Census listed 129 congregations of progressive Disciples with 12,703 members; 110 buildings were valued at $399,620. The 79 Sunday schools with 540 officers and teachers enrolled 4,470 pupils. The conservative Churches of Christ reported 22 churches with 1,046 members and 20 buildings valued at $13,400. Twelve Sunday schools had 46 officers and teachers and 467 pupils.[28]

In 1914, the Disciples reported 142 churches, by districts, as follows: Augusta, 3; Central, 18; Griffin, 16; Northeast, 39; Northwest, 19; Savannah, 14; Southern, 9; and Western, 24 (no Negro churches were indicated; nine were listed in the 1905 *Year Book*, pp. 14, [46] f.). There were 81 Bible schools and 79 preachers.[29] By 1914, 25 senior Christian Endeavor societies were reported with 850 active members and 16 junior groups with 436 members.[30]

NOURISHMENT FOR THE MIND

The *Southern Evangelist* was published by Marion Franklin Harmon at the turn of the century. With the issue of Apr. 19, 1901, Alfred E. Seddon became joint editor of the 16-page weekly and Sept. 13 sole editor and publisher.[31] Harmon moved to Atlanta, Sept. 7, 1898, became pastor of West End Church and helped organize

---

28*U. S. Bureau of the Census . . . Religious Bodies: 1906*, Part II, Separate Denominations (2 vols.; Washington: Government Printing Office, 1910), II, 240 f.; 243 f.

29*Year Book . . . 1913-1914, op. cit.*, pp. 27, 46, 49-52.

30*Year Book of the Christian Churches (Disciples of Christ) in Georgia for 1911* (Athens, Ga.: McGregor Co., 1911), p. 13. Brown, *op. cit.*, p. 674. *Year Book . . . 1913-1914, op. cit.*, p. 23.

Longley Ave. Church. Soon after his arrival, he arranged to publish *The Evangelist*. In three years, circulation of the renamed periodical increased from 500 to 1,500.[32]

Seddon was a colorful figure. Born in London, England, Jan. 30, 1846, he became a Baptist, was a Paris newspaper correspondent, and studied for the Baptist ministry at Regents Park College in London University and then held English pastorates. With his wife, six sons and daughters, he came to the United States in 1888, settling in Philadelphia, then in Florida where he edited the *South Florida Progress* at Fort Meade and Bartow. In September, 1895, he moved to Atlanta and joined the First Christian Church. He helped to organize West End Church in 1897, was its first pastor, and aided in the formation of Longley Ave. Church.[33]

In 1909, Seddon went to France as correspondent of the *Christian Standard* and launched the "Hors de Rome" Mission for conversion of Roman Catholics to Protestantism. The struggling Mission, enthusiastically promoted by the *Standard,* was rent asunder by internal dissension in 1914. By September, after the outbreak of World War I, Seddon left France and the mission was abandoned.[34] Seddon returned to the United States in 1916, resided eight years in Birmingham, Ala., then moved to El Paso, Tex., where he died, Dec. 15, 1939.[35]

At the 1903 Georgia State Convention it was reported that E. L. Shelnutt and Frank L. Adams, grandson of W. S. Fears, had purchased the *Southern Evangelist.*[36] They conducted it until, with the issue of Nov. 1, 1906,

[31]*Southern Evangelist*, Apr. 12, 1901, p. 8.

[32]*Ibid.*, June 9, 1901, p. 8; Aug. 30, 1901, p. 6; Nov. 7, 1901, p. 9.

[33]*Ibid.*, Apr. 12, 1901, p. 9.

[34]*Christian Standard,* Sept. 12, 1914, pp. 1576 f.   Stephen J. Corey, *Fifty Years of Attack and Controversy* (St. Louis: Bethany Press, 1953), pp. 34 f.

[35]*Christian Standard,* Dec. 23, 1939, p. 1224; Jan. 6, 1940, p. 22.

[36]*Year Book . . . 1903, op. cit.,* pp. 16 f.

it was merged with *The Christian-Evangelist* of St. Louis, which was chosen as the Georgia news and promotional medium with Shelnutt the correspondent.[37]

That course apparently did not satisfy Georgians for *The Southland* appeared in 1907 as a private weekly. Issued from Macon with R. W. Simpson as editor and manager, it apparently did not survive the year.[38]

The *Christian Messenger* was initiated in a board meeting of the Georgia Christian Missionary Society in Atlanta's First Church, Dec. 20, 1907. It followed a recommendation of the State Convention that a monthly be issued.[39] The periodical appeared in March, 1908, and was called the *Georgia Christian Messenger* until about 1910. It was first edited by Bernard P. Smith, and during 1910-14 by John H. Wood.[40] In 1908 it had 1,000 subscribers and paid all costs; there were 1,200 in 1909. Lack of funds caused irregular publication in 1912 and four issues appeared in 1913-14 when two-thirds of the subscribers were in arrears.[41]

Publication of Mrs. B. O. Miller's manuscript of a Georgia history of the Christian churches was contemplated in 1901. Four hundred advance orders were sought, but apparently few were placed, for the book never appeared. Indeed, the present volume began with that project.[42] However, her history was not the first projected. The 1878 Washington District Cooperation

---

[37]*The Christian-Evangelist*, Nov. 1, 1906, pp. 1400, 1408.

[38]*Christian Standard*, July 20, 1907, p. 1214. The May 30, 1907, issue of *The Southland*, containing 28 pages, is in possession of the Georgia Christian Missionary Society, Macon.

[39]*Year Book . . . 1908, op. cit.*, p. 47. *Christian Standard*, Feb. 22, 1908, p. 312.

[40]*Ibid.*, Apr. 8, 1916, p. 974.

[41]*Year Book of the Christian Churches (Disciples of Christ) in Georgia for 1909* (Atlanta: Lester Book & Stationery Co., 1909), pp. 8, 10. *Year Book . . . 1910, op. cit.*, p. 6. *Year Book of the Christian Churches (Disciples of Christ) in Georgia for 1913* (Athens, Ga.: McGregor Co., 1913), p. 3. *Year Book . . . 1913-1914, op. cit.*, p. 29.

[42]*Southern Evangelist*, Jan. 25, 1901, p. 10; Feb. 8, 1901, pp. 6, 8; Apr. 10, 1901, p. 10. Mrs. B. O. Miller, *Mission Work . . . op. cit.*, back cover.

asked T. M. Harris to write a history and publish it before expiration of his term as president. Apparently it was not done.[43]

Several "vest-pocket" tracts were published during 1900-14. A popular one was E. L. Shelnutt's *John Sims, Led Into The Light by His Friend, Robert Miller,* printed in 1907 by the Christian Publishing Co., St. Louis. The W.S.G.M. issued several, including two by Mrs. Miller and one by Miss Mamie Harris.[44] There was a dearth of books by Georgia Disciples in those years.

The emphasis of religious education began with election by the 1903 State Convention of Wm. B. Shaw as superintendent of Christian Endeavor (youth) work. On May 1, 1904, he began service as state Sunday school and C. E. evangelist.[45] In 1905, two Negro churches had Sunday schools.[46] In 1909, when Claud M. Mayne was state superintendent, most of the Sunday schools were "uninteresting" and doing "very poor teaching."[47] The 1912 Convention, when T. Olin Hathcock held the state post, suggested use of the term Bible school.[48]

That assembly approved appointment of a regional religious educational director to work with the A.C.M.S. J. Randall Farris served, June 1, 1912, through 1913, when he went to Lexington, Ky. He was succeeded by Frank L. James, Nov. 10, 1914.[49] Farris aided state superin-

---

[43]*Christian Standard,* Nov. 23, 1878, p. 374.

[44]*The Christian-Evangelist,* Aug. 15, 1907, p. 1034. *Year Book . . . 1908, op. cit.,* p. 13.

[45]*Year Book . . . 1903, op. cit.,* p. 17. *Annual Reports of Georgia Christian Missionary Society* (n. p., 1904?), pp. [1, 6, 7]. Succeeding Georgia Sunday school superintendents were: W. H. Roper, Claud M. Mayne, and T. Olin Hathcock. Other Christian Endeavor superintendents were: Mrs. Charles Goodman, Mrs. J. N. Bell, Will Hubbard, and Mrs. Mabel C. (Langford) Mathis.

[46]*Year Book . . . 1905, op. cit.,* p. 47.

[47]*Year Book . . . 1909, op. cit.,* p. 16.

[48]*Year Book . . . 1913, op. cit.,* p. 21.

[49]*American Home Missionary,* Jan. 1914, pp. 17 f.; Nov., 1914, p. 668. William Clayton Bower and Roy G. Ross (Editors), *The Disciples and Religious Education* (St. Louis: Christian Board of Publication, 1936), p. 68.

tendents in Georgia, Alabama, and Mississippi to "pep up nearly every Sunday school." It was a "rich experience," but he just began to meet the need.[50] He conducted the South's first School of Methods at Atlanta First Church in 1913.[51] First Church of Augusta erected the state brotherhood's first religious educational structure.[52]

Miss Mabel C. Langford, now Mrs. Charles Mathis, was a significant leader in the developing Georgia religious educational program. In 1908-10, she was state Jr. Christian Endeavor superintendent; in 1910-14, state superintendent of the Georgia C. E. Union, which she organized, and Georgia field secretary for the United Society of Christian Endeavor. She helped establish over 100 C. E. societies among various religious bodies, including nearly every Georgia Christian church. She also aided formation of city C. E. unions at Athens, Atlanta, Augusta, Macon, and Savannah.

The 1905 Negro State Convention pledged financial support and pupils for Athen's Christian Academy, controlled by trustees elected by the convention. Evangelist W. H. Smith was chairman of trustees for the Negro school.[53]

While Georgia was getting more ministers with college and seminary training, a desire developed for a Christian college in the state. A. E. Seddon proposed the idea in 1904.[54] T. T. G. Linkous did likewise in 1906. In 1907, out of the efforts of H. King Pendleton in Atlanta to

---

[50]Signed letter from J. Randall Farris to J. Edward Moseley, written at Melbourne, Fla., Aug. 21, 1952.

[51]*Ibid.*, Oct. 10, 1952. Barfield, *op. cit.*, p. 132.

[52]Barfield, *op. cit.*, pp. 131 f.

[53]*Year Book . . . 1905, op. cit.*, pp. [45], 48. Other trustees were: C. T. Bowen, secretary, V. M. McLendon, S. M. Price, M. W. Robertson, M. Summers, J. T. Thomas, and M. Yopp.

[54]Bedford, *op. cit.*, p. 277. Perhaps the state's first educational experiment for Disciples was the Jackson Bible School (later Valdosta Christian College?) at Valdosta. Beginning Oct. 13, 1903, there were 82 pupils. Mr. and Mrs. Landon J. Jackson were among five teachers. Whether that was the first session and how long the school operated is unknown (*Gospel Advocate*, Oct. 29, 1903, p. 700).

prepare ministers through Sunday mission preaching, a project developed. The Georgia State Board received suggestions for a joint school with Alabama at West Point. However, lacking a definite proposal from Alabama it was decided to establish a Georgia college at Atlanta. Linkous, volunteer promoter, received $1,000 in pledges on a $25,000 dormitory fund.[55]

It was 1910 before the State Convention took any action to explore the possibilities of a college.[56]   T. O. Hathcock delivered an educational address at the 1911 Convention after which an offer from Josephus Hopwood was considered. President of Virginia Christian (now Lynchburg) College, Lynchburg, Va., he proposed to give $5,000, plus his service, to a Georgia college. The liberal offer was received with appreciation.[57] At the 1912 Convention, Hopwood explained plans and purposes of the college which it was expected would become accredited.[58]

Lamar College opened on a farm near Clarkston, 10 miles from Atlanta, near Stone Mountain, Feb. 4, 1913.[59] It was named in honor of James S. Lamar, preacher and writer. The 305-acre farm cost $40,000 with $10,000 paid in cash. Buildings included a 14-room house that became a dormitory, a woodshed made into a chapel, and a chicken house remodeled into the music studio. The school opened with 15 students, four or more being young women. High school and college courses were offered with manual labor part of the instruction. Forty students enrolled the autumn of 1914.[60]   Hopwood was

---

[55]*Christian Standard,* Jan. 26, 1907, p. 160; Feb. 16, 1907, p. 301; Mar. 2, 1907, p. 396.   *The Christian-Evangelist,* Feb. 14, 1907, p. 215; Feb. 28, 1907, p. 280.

[56]*Year Book . . . 1906, op. cit.,* p. 24.   *Year Book . . . 1911, op. cit.,* p. 6.

[57]*Year Book of the Christian Churches (Disciples of Christ) in Georgia for 1912* (Athens, Ga.: McGregor Co., 1912), p. 8.

[58]*Year Book . . . 1913, op. cit.,* p. 7.

[59]Hopwood indicated in his autobiography, *A Journey Through the Years* (St. Louis: Bethany Press, 1932), that the school opened in 1911. His memory seemed to have tricked him, also, as to the size of the college farm.

[60]*The Christian-Evangelist,* Oct. 15, 1914, p. 1329.

president and a professor. He had served for years as president of Milligan College, near Johnson City, Tenn., and founded Lynchburg College. Dr. L. O. Bricker was chairman of the board of trustes.[61] Eugene Richardson Clarkson was financial secretary. Inadequate financial support caused the school to close in June, 1915.[62]

PLANTING CHURCHES AND PLACING PREACHERS

The brethren constantly employed high-pressure evangelism. Nearly every church held revivals, often with nationally known evangelists and singers. A meeting at West End Church, Atlanta, drew editorial praise from the Atlanta *Constitution* and another meeting there, in 1908, with Herbert Yeuell preaching, forced the transit company to run extra streetcars to accommodate the crowds.[63]

Shortly after Atlanta First Church dedicated its new building in 1907, a revival packed the building night after night and resulted in 309 new members, including 91 male adults. Allen Wilson was the preacher.[64] Those additions boosted the total membership to about 1,000, the largest of any congregation in Georgia. Only others with more than 300 members then were the two Augusta churches, Antioch of Oconee County, and Corinth.

Many revivals conducted when and where possible resulted in the organization of new churches. Georgia, however, made mistakes like those elsewhere when little thought was given to location, or adequate leadership. Consequently, many churches did not grow, some closing soon after establishment. H. C. E. Combs described the situation thus:

[61]Other trustees in 1913 were: J. Hopwood, T. O. Hathcock, C. G. Hannah, Morgan Head, Clem Jolly, T. T. G. Linkous, A. R. Moore, T. C. Pitman, F. G. Power, E. L. Shelnutt, Charles T. Smith, J. H. Taylor, and John H. Wood.

[62]*Prospectus Lamar College* (Clarkston, Ga.; Lamar College, 1913). Hopwood, *op. cit.*, pp. 115-118.

[63]Barfield, *op. cit.*, pp. 129 f.

[64]*Ibid.*, pp. 127 f.

. . . We sent out evangelists who organized churches, wherever they could, and then left them to themselves. Many of these churches were very weak or isolated and unable to secure the care of a minister. . . . Our mistake was in organizing more work than we could take care of. . . . The present policy to strengthen what we have, seems to me the wiser plan.[65]

During 1900-14 at least 100 congregations were organized in Georgia. Two-thirds, or 68, of that number did not live, including six Negro churches.[66] The list of 32 churches that survived, with the dates of founding where known, present names ("r" indicating reorganization) and county locations, follows:

Organized	Name	County	Organized	Name	County
1900	—	Atlanta Cap. View, Fulton	1908?	—	Hall's Chapel, Washington
1900	—	College Pk. First, Fulton	1908	—	Jefferson First, Jackson
1901	—	New Franklin, Franklin	1909	—	Brooklet, Bulloch
1901	—	Pembroke, Bryan	1909	—	Lawrenceville, Gwinnett
1902?	—	Atlanta Central, Fulton	1909	—	Columbus Cen., Muscogee
1902	—	Union Ground, Franklin	1909	—	Centennial, Hancock
1902	—	Unity, Jackson	1910	—	East Pt. First, Fulton
1903	—	Ray City, Berrien	1910	—	Oak Grove, Decatur
1905	—	Fitzgerald Cen., Ben Hill	1911?	—	Canton, Cherokee
1905	—	High Shoals, Oconee	1911	—	rCarter Hill, Barrow
1905	—	rWest Point, Troup	1912	—	Savannah Cen., Chatham
1906	—	Brooks, Fayette	1913	—	Community (E. Atlanta)
1906	—	Mt. Carmel, DeKalb	1913	—	Good Hope, Walton
1907	—	Americus, Sumter	1914	—	Bishop First, Oconee
1907	—	Lowell, Carroll	1914	—	Harvest, Habersham
1908?	—	Atlanta Grove Pk., Fulton	1914	—	Hilltonia, Screven

The only adequate church buildings Georgia Disciples had before 1900 were at Augusta, Macon, and Rome. Therefore, the entire state brotherhood rejoiced when First Church, Atlanta, dedicated its new edifice, the best in Georgia, near the State Capitol, July 28, 1907, with 2,000 persons present. The structure cost $55,000. Under the leadership of the minister, H. King Pendleton, a brother of Mrs. Joseph Rucker Lamar, the congregation left the Hunter Street building, which was then surrounded by livery stables, for the new site at Trinity

---

[65]*Southern Evangelist*, Jan. 18, 1901, p. 6. Bedford, *op. cit.*, pp. 119 f.
[66]*Year Book . . . 1905, op. cit.*, pp. [45]-48.

and Pryor, that cost $10,000. Sixty-three gifts of $100 each were made on dedication day.[67]

It was a time of much church construction. Fitzgerald Central, Griffin, Mt. Vernon, Sandersville, Savannah, Valdosta, Atlanta West End, West Point, and Winder all erected new structures, useful and with some measure of architectural attractiveness. Several buildings burned, including Valdosta in 1901, Mt. Vernon in 1905, and Savannah in 1910, but new edifices soon replaced them.

There were many obscure, unsung heroes in the ministry of the Georgia Disciples before World War I. A state Ministerial Association was formed, Nov. 3, 1910, during the Dublin State Convention. W. A. Chastain was elected the first president of the fellowship group.[68]

Native Georgians became prominent in the state's ministerial leadership. The number included E. L. Shelnutt, who established more Christian churches in the state than any other person, W. A. Chastain, John Henry Wood, William Benjamin McDonald, O. A. Moore, Thomas F. Yarbrough, and Frank L. Adams.

The list of other able preachers during 1900-14 was a long one. Among the more conspicuous were the following: A. T. Autry, Victor P. Bowers, Howard J. Brazelton, Dr. L. O. Bricker, D. A. Brindle, R. Lin Cave, E. R. Clarkson, Howard T. Cree, Gerald Culberson, L. A. Cunningham, George F. Cuthrell, Wm. E. Daugherty, H. C. Dodson, T. H. Fitts, Wm. O. Foster, O. E. Fox, Stanley R. Grubb, Robert Alexander Helsabeck, A. B. Herring, J. J. Langston, T. T. G. Linkous, J. M. Mason, N. D. Meadow, P. H. Mears, Dr. Allen Rice Moore, Sherman B. Moore, John Wm. Moody, W. F. Mott, G. W. Neal, L. M. Omer, E. G. Orahood, E. W. Pease,

---

[67]*The Christian-Evangelist*, Aug. 15, 1907, p. 1051. *Christian Standard*, Aug. 24, 1907, p. 1414. Several Chinese were members of First Church, Atlanta, for a decade or more. They were received into the fellowship through a special class taught by Miss Rosebud Archer and others. Racial prejudice flared, however, and forced their withdrawal from the church about 1910 (Bolles, *op. cit.*, p. [17]. Bedford, *op. cit.*, p. 110).

[68]*Year Book . . . 1911, op. cit.*, p. 12. *Year Book . . . 1912, op. cit.*, p. 20.

H. King Pendleton, E. T. Porter, J. E. and O. P. Spiegel, Dr. Richard W. Wallace, Belt White, and Allen Wilson.

Among outstanding lay members were E. B. Hook, an editor of the Augusta *Chronicle,* and Justice and Mrs. Joseph Rucker Lamar of Augusta. Hook and Mrs. Lamar were Bible school teachers. The Lamars moved to Atlanta when he was appointed a Justice of the Georgia Supreme Court, Jan. 1, 1902. He resigned that post, Apr. 10, 1905, and returned to Augusta. He left Augusta again when appointed to the United States Supreme Court by President Wm. H. Taft. Lamar, a Democrat, was confirmed without opposition by the Senate, Dec. 15, 1910.[69]

By World War I Georgia's staunch, pioneer Disciples had died, along with other prominent brethren, Mrs. B. S. McCash, state C.W.B.M. secretary for a time before 1900, died May 16, 1901. A. B. Phillips died suddenly, Dec. 28, 1903, while pastor of First Church, Augusta. Dr. A. G. Thomas passed away the same month, Dec. 14, 1903. His long-time colleague, James S. Lamar, died at Augusta, Jan. 30, 1908. Mrs. Mary G. Moore, charter member of the reorganized Acworth Church in 1875 and grandniece of Thomas Jefferson, died Feb. 13, 1907, in Atlanta.[70]

COOPERATION THE KEYNOTE OF MISSIONS

The Georgia Christian Missionary Society was incorporated at Athens on Nov. 7, 1905. By-laws, ratified by

---

[69]*Christian Standard,* Mar. 7, 1903, pp. 323 f. Clarinda Pendleton Lamar, *op. cit.,* pp. 118, 134. Justice Lamar died in his Washington home, Jan. 2, 1916. Frank Mason Robinson (1846-1923), long-time elder and Bible school teacher of First Church, Atlanta, who was secretary of the Coca-Cola Co., from its organization in 1892 until about 1912, designed the famous Coca-Cola trademark (Clark Howell, *op. cit.,* II, 10).

[70]The deceased Disciples also included the following: J. A. Dasher, Mrs. R. Lin Cave, Dr. Francis Jackson, W. S. Fears, Capt. R. M. Mitchell, Capt. Evan P. Howell, Mrs. Wm. B. Shaw, W. T. Lowe, Miss Irene Dasher, Mrs. James S. Lamar, Dr. M. B. Doster, Dr. C. C. Stockard, T. M. Foster, Dr. J. F. Davis, and Mrs. James S. Mayne, state C.W.B.M. treasurer, 1909-14.

the 1905 State Convention, provided for delegates from the churches and remained in effect in 1914.[71] During 1900-14, the state organization had five executives.

At the turn of the century, Harry Charles Ellison Combs (1866-1922) was corresponding secretary and state evangelist. In 1892, a new graduate of The College of the Bible, Lexington, Ky., he became pastor at Macon. He was born at New Franklin, O., Oct. 8, 1866.[72] Combs was succeeded in the state post, Apr. 1, 1902, by R. Lin Cave who served more than a year. On Sept. 1, 1903, his successor was W. J. Cocke.

During Cocke's term, which closed Feb. 6, 1906, when he went to Kentucky, the title became state secretary. Bernard P. Smith held the post from Feb. 10, 1906, through the 1909 State Convention. Under him E. R. Clarkson of Red Bluff, Calif., was called as state evangelist, beginning July 1, 1907.[73] Most years, student evangelists were employed in the summers.

In 1910, John Henry Wood began his terms as state secretary. They continued beyond 1914. Born at Covington, Newton County, Sept. 23, 1865, he was graduated in 1891 from The College of the Bible, Lexington, Ky., and became Northeast District evangelist. Pastor of several churches, particularly Winder, in that area, he rendered years of sacrificial service.[74] He died at Rome, Mar. 19, 1939.

W. H. Smith, Moses Yopp, and D. V. N. Abney were evangelists who served under the Georgia Negro Convention. Smith was president of the 16th Annual Negro Convention, Oct. 19-22, 1905, at Eastman, attended by 27 persons. A. J. Edmondson, Wrightsville, was the white speaker. Yopp spoke about Negro work at the

---

71Year Book . . . 1905, op. cit., pp. [3, 4, 9]. Year Book . . . 1913-1914, op. cit., p. 54.

72Southern Evangelist, Jan. 18, 1901, p. 9.

73Year Book . . . 1908, op. cit., p. 38.

74Brown, op. cit., p. 527. J. C. Flanigan, Gwinnett Churches, A Complete History of Every Church in Gwinnett County, Georgia, With Short Biographical Sketches of Its Ministers (Lawrenceville, Ga.: n. p., 1911), p. 326.

white State Conventions. Abney organized three churches in 1905. His evangelism was supervised by the Georgia Christian Missionary Society which contributed $225 that year to his work.[75]

Georgia's Golden Jubilee Convention was held at First Church, Augusta, Nov. 21-23, 1900. More than 100 persons attended from outside that city, making the assembly the largest held until then. There were 230 persons registered for the 1902 convention. Succeeding conventions to World War I apparently did not exceed that enrollment. There were 42 congregations represented at the 65th assembly in 1913 by 154 delegates.

The social conscience of Georgia Disciples expressed itself in 1903, and at nearly every convention thereafter through 1914, against the liquor traffic. After state prohibition became law, Jan. 1, 1908, later conventions reaffirmed loyalty to it and deplored lack of enforcement. The Negro brethren were urged by their convention to be "temperate in all things." Efforts of the Anti-Saloon League and the W.C.T.U. were encouraged and at the request of the Georgia Baptist Temperance Committee, Disciples in 1906 authorized a similar group to help secure passage of a state prohibition law. T. M. Foster, Northeast District preacher until his death in 1910, was elected a Prohibition member of the Georgia Legislature in 1900.

During 1900-14, the American Christian Missionary Society generously aided 38 churches and otherwise assisted financially the Georgia missionary program. Contributions totaled $26,426.91 for the years, 1897-1920.[76] The national and state societies jointly employed the Georgia secretary and each paid one-half of his salary. While all mission monies for home and state missions raised in Georgia were sent to the national offices, then in Cincinnati, the A.C.M.S. at one time returned 90 per cent of all such funds to the Georgia State Board.

[75]*Year Book* . . . *1905, op. cit.,* pp. 12 f.; 23 f.; [45] f. *Year Book* . . . *1906, op. cit.,* p. 23.
[76]Lewis, *op. cit.,* p. 42.

The International Convention of Disciples of Christ met in Atlanta's Auditorium Armory, Oct. 7-14, 1914. It was the first time the assembly met in the Southeast. Twelve agencies made annual reports. Governor John Marshall Slaton and the Atlanta Mayor welcomed the delegates. Hill M. Bell, president of Drake University, Des Moines, Ia., was convention president.

Operating on a delegate basis, the convention reaffirmed the principle of equitable representation from local churches. There were 321 churches represented by 580 certified delegates. Total enrollment of visitors and delegates was about 2,500. After publication of the convention minutes in 1915, the *Christian Standard* challenged the genuineness of the delegates' certificates and called the delegate convention a "monumental fake." Graham Frank, convention secretary, discussed the charges in a reply published in *The Christian-Evangelist.*[77]

Luther Otterbein Bricker, minister of First Christian Church of Atlanta since 1911, was local convention general chairman. He presided at the communion service attended by 4,000 or more, and was elected third vice-president of the A.C.M.S. He had presided at the 1911 Georgia State Convention. In 1913, he led First Church to have the brotherhood's largest Sunday school and had introduced the observance of decision days for church membership.[78] As local chairman, he was assisted by 16 sub-committee chairmen.[79]

A four-page *Daily Bulletin,* edited by Secretary Frank, was published by the convention. Newspapers were commended for "fair reporting" of the sessions. F. D.

[77]*Christian Standard,* May 29, 1915, p. 1150; June 5, 1915, p. 1180. *The Christian-Evangelist,* July 1, 1915, p. 826.

[78]*The Christian-Evangelist,* June 8, 1913. *A Memorial Booklet* Honoring the Rev. L. O. Bricker, D.D. . . . (Atlanta: Donaldson-Woods Co., 1942?), p. 13.

[79]They were: H. E. Bailey, A. M. Beatty, John Cooper, M. F. Downing, W. O. Foster, C. G. Hannah, T. O. Hathcock, R. S. Hook, Harry A. Jones, B. S. McCash, F. W. Patterson, H. M. Patterson, L. F. Rogers, F. J. Spratling, Dr. Cecil Stockard, and John H. Wood.

Kershner, then president of Texas Christian University, wrote convention sidelights for the Atlanta *Constitution* and E. B. Bagby, a minister, did the same for the Atlanta *Journal.*[80]

Allen Rice Moore, Savannah pastor, was elected a convention vice-president. C. S. Lucas, while minister at Augusta, had received the honor at the 1884 Convention. Dr. Moore conducted devotions one morning and presented a resolution for a restudy of the Scriptures that was adopted. He spoke half a dozen times in business meetings. He had just published a booklet, *Alexander Campbell and the General Convention,* that endorsed a delegate convention. He was Savannah pastor, 1912-19, and president of the 1913 State Convention.

Children of the Southern Christian Home sang at the benevolent session. The sons of Mr. and Mrs. L. M. Omer of West Point sold "missionary cotton," which they grew, for the benefit of the C.W.B.M., during the sessions.[81] The boys' mother, Mrs. Birdie Farrar Omer, Georgia C.W.B.M. secretary, directed a Sunday afternoon prayer service at First Church. Mrs. John H. Wood was chairman of the C.W.B.M. nominating committee.

Thirteen resolutions reflecting the mind of Disciples were adopted by the convention. Howard T. Cree, Augusta pastor, was a member of the resolutions committee of 10 persons.

World War I had begun and its shadow, resting upon the convention, found "expression in nearly all the addresses," wrote Dr. J. H. Garrison, editor-emeritus of *The Christian-Evangelist,* in his famous "Easy Chair" column.[82] The assembly regarded the war "with deep sorrow" and called "upon Christian people everywhere to note the futility of preserving peace by preparedness for war."

---

[80]*The Christian-Evangelist,* Oct. 22, 1914, p. 1366.

[81]*Loc. cit.*

[82]*Ibid.,* Oct. 22, 1914, p. 1358.

The brethren rejoiced in the "Christian statesman-
ship" of President Woodrow Wilson and commended
him for maintaining peace between the United States
and Mexico. That expression was approved even though
the convention also was supposed to represent Canada,
a matter usually overlooked in the assemblies with the
preponderance of delegates from the United States.

The convention acknowledged the "impotence of a
divided church" and called upon the brethren to work,
plead, and pray for "restoration of the lost unity of
the church." Delegates felt "pleased and blessed" by
the "talent from other communions" that took part in
the convention and considered such participation a demonstration of Christian unity.

"We are so much alike," declared the epigrammatic
Shailer Mathews, president of the Federal Council of
the Churches of Christ in America, "that we cannot tell
each other apart except by magnifying each others'
faults."[83] He was one of eight or more speakers of
national reputation from other religious bodies to address the convention.

The last session, Wednesday night, Oct. 14, with the
convention's largest attendance except for the communion service, "was marked by brotherly love and a great
spirit of hopefulness for the future."[84] The closing
address, by Col. John Temple Graves, was preceded by
a concert from 600-800 voices of Atlanta Negro college
students. After the singing of "God Be With You Till
We Meet Again," Dr. L. O. Bricker pronounced the
final benediction on the assembly that brought incom-
parable recognition to Georgia Disciples.[85]

"No convention . . . had better preparation and han-
dling" was an editorial judgment. It was considered a

---

[83]*Ibid.*, Oct. 15, 1914, p. 1351.

[84]*Ibid.*, Oct. 22, 1914, p. 1355.

[85]*Minutes*, General Convention of Churches of Christ, Atlanta, Georgia,
October 7-14, 1914 (Typed document of the International Convention
Archives in custody of The Disciples of Christ Historical Society, Nash-
ville, Tenn.), pp. 55, 67, 68, 71 ff.

"milestone" in cooperation.   A. McLean, beloved foreign missions executive of the brotherhood, observed,
"I do not see how a convention committee could have
done better. . . . The end of the convention is the beginning of the conquest."[86]

However, the years of cooperation were ending.   The
subsequent sweat and tears over difficult issues will be
discussed next.

[86]*The Christian-Evangelist,* Oct. 22, 1914, pp. 1355, 1366; Oct. 29, 1914, p. 1394.

CHAPTER IX

Dissension Disrupts the Fellowship, 1915-1929

Reflecting Civil War valor, Georgia Disciples of Christ faced the emergency situations of World War I with a courage that knew no retreat. Church honor rolls displayed names of those called to service. A few ministers entered the chaplaincy while many engaged in field work with the Y.M.C.A. Rank-and-file members enlisted in the Red Cross. Convention resolutions expressed the concern over international affairs.

Through the War Emergency Committee of the American Christian Missionary Society, Georgians helped to provide aid to churches adjacent to camp cantonments. Their contributions to the Society during the war period totaled $2,946.51. The war-emergency services cost the national brotherhood $14,331.21.[1] The 1917 State Convention endorsed the Federal Food Administration, urged reduction of excessive food consumption, and recommended that the Army provide one chaplain for each 1,200 men enlisted.[2]

The A.C.M.S. established a committee to endorse competent Disciple chaplains and to provide some equipment and service during tours of duty.[3] The Georgia Christian Missionary Society raised a chaplaincy fund with Gilbert H. Fern, Macon pastor, as treasurer. Apparently money he raised was given to Chaplain James A. Moore, 121st Regiment, son of Dr. Allen Rice Moore,

---

[1]Lewis, *op. cit.*, p. 145.

[2]*Christian Messenger*, Jan.–Feb., 1918, p. 22.

[3]*American Home Missionary*, Oct., 1918, p. 673. Willard M. Wickizer, *A Brief Organizational History of the Committee on Military and Veterans Services and Its Predecessor Committees* (Indianapolis: United Christian Missionary Society, Feb., 1953), p. 1. Lewis, *op. cit.*, p. 145.

and pastor at Sandersville, then Griffin before the latter church granted him war leave. He was in the Mexican border fighting and went to France with the famous Rainbow Division. In the fighting zone, he was transferred to the 29th Division. He was struck on his helmet by shrapnel and received a shock that led to his death at Hagan, Ga., June 24, 1924. His last pastorate was at Macon.[4]

Other Georgia chaplains included Wright T. Moore, another son of Dr. A. R. Moore; Russell M. Bythewood, product of Savannah First Church; Prof. Garland J. Parrish of Southeastern College; Wm. Paul Reagor, born in Winder, the son of Pastor Wm. Franklin and Emily S. (Elder) Reagor; and Robert M. Bell, Thomas County native who joined Spring Hill Church there in 1908 and became president of Johnson Bible College in 1941. Those engaged in Y.M.C.A. field work were: Wm. A. Bradley, E. R. Clarkson, Rayborn C. Foster, Clebourne E. Gregory, Stanley R. Grubb, Landon J. Jackson, Harry A. Jones, Adolph O. Jordan, James L. Leggett, and Robert L. Sharpe.[5] Howard T. Cree left the ministry of Augusta First Church to become a director of war camp community service.[6] In 1919, Mrs. Maria Reynolds Ford was overseas with the Red Cross. She later resided at Albany. A missionary to Puerto Rico and Argentina, 1902-07 and 1909-14, she taught at the College of Missions, Indianapolis, in 1916, and later was an executive of the Christian Woman's Board of Missions there.[7]

The honor rolls in church buildings reflected the concern of all with the war. The Maxeys congregation had 12 of 150 members enlisted. So many preachers aided the war that the Savannah District had no evangelist in

---

[4]*Christian Messenger*, Jan.–Feb., 1918, p. 6. *The Christian-Evangelist*, July 3, 1924, p. 857.

[5]*American Home Missionary*, Dec., 1918, pp. 92 ff.

[6]John T. Brown and E. W. Thornton (Editors), *Who's Who in Churches of Christ* (Cincinnati: Standard Publishing Co., 1929), p. 65.

[7]*They Went to Latin America, op. cit.*, pp. 63 f.

1918. A Red Cross chapter was organized in 1917 at Southeastern Christian College by Prof. Howard S. Hilley with 25 members. The majority of the students enlisted in the 1919 drive. The school went "over the top" in united war work subscriptions, part of the fund being raised by cotton picking.[8]

The 1918 State Convention met in Atlanta, Nov. 12-15. Topics of messages reflected concern with the war, as follows: "Building an International Church," "Our Plea and Changing World Conditions," "The Minister and the War," "The Present Crisis," and "The Church and the Soldier." The session of the Woman's Society for Georgia Missions convened under unusual circumstances. It followed just after the parade that celebrated Atlanta's rejoicing and thanksgiving for the Armistice. The celebration caused small attendance at a late hour for an abbreviated program.[9]

Enlarging Opportunities for Cooperation

On the basis of success sparked by teamwork in World War I's drives, the Inter-Church World Movement was launched. After surveying the world's Christian needs, the major Protestant forces of the United States planned to meet them by discovering and developing necessary personnel and funds. Disciples of Christ endorsed their participation at the 1919 International Convention. The campaign failed and expenses exceeded receipts, leaving Disciples morally obligated to pay more than $600,000 of the debt. That was done with some congregations that opposed participation paying apportionments of the "debt of honor."

---

[8]*Christian Messenger*, Jan.–Feb., 1918, pp. 5 f. [50]; Dec., 1918–Jan., 1919, pp. 3 f., 33.

[9]*Ibid.*, pp. 5 f., 22. Alexander Stephens Boone, Toomsboro, Ga., Postmaster, sold $40,000 of War Savings Stamps during World War I. His father, Joshua Minton Boone, native of the state, was a Disciple minister. A. S. Boone's grandfather, Daniel Boone, was a nephew of D. Boone, famous pioneer explorer (Clark Howell, *op. cit.*, III, 417 f.).

The Georgia brethren endorsed the cooperative project and agreed to underwrite it "to the extent of two and one-half per cent of their askings." Dr. L. O. Bricker was representative on the Georgia Advisory Council. Howard T. Cree, former Augusta minister, was assistant Southern field work director. Failure of the movement resulted in a tendency for each church to withdraw into narrow exclusiveness. The future of every cooperative program was clouded with uncertainty for Disciples as the fence-builders of "Restorationism" swung into concerted action.[10]

The Men and Millions Movement was a brotherhood interagency committee formed in 1913 to raise $6,000,000 for expanded missionary and educational work. World War I delayed completion of the campaign, but $6,018,-063.52 was received, including $1,000,000 from R. A. Long, Kansas City lumberman. Georgians pledged $23,932.80, actually gave $8,057.55 through their churches. The largest amounts were: Valdosta, $1,285; Atlanta First, $1,120.84; Sandersville, $604.17; Conyers, $566.00; Augusta First, $390.[11] It was a significant demonstration of the value of teamwork in the solicitation of missionary and educational funds.

The 1919 International Convention in Cincinnati approved the organization of The United Christian Missionary Society. It was the first Protestant agency in the United States to combine education, home, and foreign missions into one administrative board. Benevolence was added too for good measure. In addition to more efficient coordination, the new Society reduced administrative expenses and competition for missionary dollars. Mrs. Stanley R. Grubb and Judge T. O. Hathcock were the first Georgia members of the United Society's 120-person Board of Managers.

[10]*1920 Year Book, Disciples of Christ,* pp. 19 ff., 38. W. R. Warren (Editor), *Survey of Service* (St. Louis: Christian Board of Publication, 1928), pp. 15 f. Brown and Thornton . . . *op. cit.,* p. 65.

[11]*1929 Year Book, Disciples of Christ,* p. 137. *Christian Messenger,* Dec., 1918–Jan., 1919, pp. [43-47]. *World Call,* Sept., 1919, p. 57.

The Georgia Christian Missionary Society had no organic union with the United Society. Nevertheless, that State Board suffered with other brotherhood cooperative agencies when hostile critics of the United Society hurled charges of centralized control, ecclesiasticism, and theological liberalism at the organized work. During the turbulent 1920's, when debates waxed furiously and frequently, the fellowship of the brethren in Georgia was sadly disrupted. However, the majority of the Georgia Disciples continued to support the cooperative program.[12]

Opposition to the organized agencies and their leaders reached a climax at the 1926 Memphis International Convention. In 1927, when no assembly was scheduled, conservative opponents organized the North American Christian Convention in Indianapolis. Signers of the call included T. O. Hathcock, L. L. LaBoon, and J. E. Skelton, the latter of Athens. Judge Hathcock was elected on the continuation committee in 1929.[13]

On Oct. 1, 1919, Dr. A. R. Moore closed his seven-year Savannah pastorate to become Southeastern superintendent for the A.C.M.S., and its successor, the United Society. He served from an Atlanta office until the fall of 1921 when it was closed.[14]

Frank L. James, of Little Rock, Ark., graduate of Drake University, became Southeastern Bible school superintendent, Nov. 10, 1914. He resigned, Apr. 1, 1916, and a few weeks later Homer F. Cooke succeeded him. Cooke had the office in Jacksonville, Fla., since he was also Florida state secretary. Cooke was succeeded,

---

[12]Dr. L. O. Bricker, Atlanta, in 1917-20, and Dr. Richard William Wallace, Valdosta, in 1926-29, were members of the International Convention Executive Committee. Dr. Wallace also signed the 1926 Memphis Convention resolution endorsing a representative, delegate convention. Valdosta pastor through 1929, Dr. Wallace received the honorary D.D. degree that year from the University of Georgia.

[13]*Christian Standard*, Mar. 19, 1927, p. 268; Oct. 19, 1929, cover p. [985].

[14]*Christian Messenger*, Oct., 1919, p. 2. *Second Annual Report of the United Christian Missionary Society*, July 1, 1921–June 30, 1922 (St. Louis: United Christian Missionary Society, 1922), p. 105.

Apr. 1, 1919, by Oliver Alvin Smith who kept the office in Jacksonville. A graduate of Texas Christian University, Smith served only until Jan. 1, 1920. The office was returned to Atlanta, Nov. 1, 1920, when Errett Burgess Quick, graduate of Yale Divinity School in 1913, began regional service under the United Society.[15]

Under supervision of the regional director, Bible schools slowly improved their instruction and lessons. By 1929, Peachtree in Atlanta, Savannah First, Americus, and Griffin had erected or provided educational buildings. Youth summer training conferences were urged in Georgia by 1923. The first accredited conference under Mr. Quick's direction met at Camp Smyrna, Presbyterian grounds at Conyers, Aug. 8-14, 1927, with 28 students and 11 instructors. Dr. Myron T. Hopper was dean and Miss Cammie Gray the missionary; Edward T. Small was elected student president.[16]

The conferences grew rapidly. The second one met at Tocca Falls in the Piedmont section, June 25–July 1, 1928, with 57 students and 14 instructors. The third, July 8-14, 1929, had 83 students and a faculty of 16.[17]

Georgia Christian churches contributed through their Bible schools a total of $890.92 for missions and benevo-

15American Home Missionary, Nov., 1914, p. 668; Oct., 1916, p. 681. World Call, June, 1919, p. 53. Fire destroyed the home of Clyde E. Pickett, Georgia Bible school superintendent in 1917, with his library and the state records (American Home Missionary, July, 1917, p. 576); he was maintained full time, Feb. 15, 1917–Apr. 1, 1918, by Mrs. Wm. S. West, of Valdosta (Christian Messenger, Jan.–Feb., 1918, p. 8; Dec., 1918–Jan., 1919, p. 7). The 1925 State Convention approved a Georgia director to work with Mr. Quick. Edgar R. Craighead was elected, but apparently never assumed office (The Christian-Evangelist, Nov. 26, 1925, p. 1537).

16Youth's Conference Call, Oct., 1927, pp. 4 ff. Separate, independent forces first rallied in camp at Toccoa Falls, 93 miles northeast of Atlanta, Aug. 4-13, 1924, with 86 registrations. The faculty of the 1925 camp, attended by 102 persons, included E. B. Quick and Miss Mary Irene Orvis, missionary of the United Society (Christian Standard, June 7, 1924, p. 921; Sept. 5, 1925, p. 2076).

17Youth's Conference Call, Oct., 1928, p. 14; Oct., 1929, pp. 5, 16. Lawton G. Hatcher, Augusta First Church, was president of the 1929 Georgia Christian Endeavor Convention when 80 of 170 delegates were Disciples (Christian Messenger, Dec., 1929, pp. 2 f.). Mrs. W. F. Mott was Georgia Christian Endeavor superintendent for Disciples many years.

lence during Oct. 1, 1914–Sept. 30, 1915. Thirty-two of
98 schools gave $3,279.63 for those causes represented by
the United Society for the year ending June 30, 1929.[18]

When the C.W.B.M. united with the United Society in
1920, Mrs. C. N. Downey was Southeastern women's
secretary, the office having been established in Atlanta
in 1919. From 1921 to 924, she was also Georgia secretary, resigning because of the regional work.[19] The regional post was dissolved in 1929 when Mrs. Downey
became a general field representative of the United Society.

In 1915 there were 52 local women's missionary groups
that had 930 members in Georgia churches; they gave
$2,057.34 to state and national funds. There were 74
organizations in 1923 with 1,849 members. By June 30,
1929, there were 1,610 members in 55 organizations giving $6,535.83 that year.[20]

In 1919 the Southern Christian Home in Atlanta removed to Cleburne Ave., N.E. The attractive five-acre
site contained a historic house that was used until 1927.
In 1919, $75,000 was pledged for a new home and South-
eastern College. Belt White, the benevolent representative, continued to solicit funds for the home. Women
of Georgia, Florida, and South Carolina pledged $25,000
as their Golden Jubilee gift to celebrate a half century
of organized women's work among Disciples. By Nov.
1, 1924, receipts totaled $23,799.91, including $16,992.08
from Georgia.[21]

---

[18]*1916 Year Book, Disciples of Christ*, p. [26]. *1929 Year Book, Disciples of Christ*, pp. 18 f., 697.

[19]*World Call*, Nov., 1919, p. 45. *Christian Messenger*, Feb., 1925, p. 17.
Birdie Farrar (Mrs. L. M.) Omer was succeeded as Georgia women's
secretary in 1918 by Mrs. J. A. Perdue, who was followed through 1929
by Miss Mattie Mitchell, Mrs. J. I. Allman, Mrs. C. N. Downey, Mrs.
Leonard O. Turner, and Mrs. E. B. Quick. Presidents, 1915-29, were:
Mrs. J. H. Wood, Mrs. W. C. Knopf, Mrs. S. R. Grubb, Mrs. H. C. Phipps,
and Mrs. W. R. Lang. State treasurer all that time was Mrs. J. W.
Ferguson.

[20]*Missionary Tidings*, Nov., 1915, p. 302. *Christian Messenger*, Feb.,
1924, p. 14. *1929 Year Book, Disciples of Christ*, p. 105.

[21]*World Call*, Oct., 1919, p. 48; Dec., 1924, p. 50.

On July 19, 1927, the executive committee of the United Society, then supervising the brotherhood benevolent program, authorized construction of the new home. The old house was razed and the cornerstone laid Oct. 20, 1927, during the State Convention with Leroy E. Rogers, local board president, directing the program.[22] The building was occupied in 1929 by 36 children. The site, building, and equipment cost $125,000. Miss Sue Steiner Hook, granddaughter of Dr. Daniel Hook, became home superintendent, June 15, 1922. Mr. and Mrs. J. C. Gentry lived there for several years and cared for the children at much personal sacrifice until the coming of Miss Hook. The 1929 operating budget of the home was $11,000.

At the end of 1915, John H. Wood concluded the state secretaryship, having become founding president of Southeastern Christian College. He had also been half-time field representative for the National Benevolent Association. Claude C. Jones succeeded him in the state post, June 1, 1916, and served until Dec. 31, 1918. W. H. Roper held the office during 1919-22 with George H. Ramsey the state evangelist in 1920-21. There was no incumbent in 1923. J. Arthur Taylor served June 1, 1924-26. A. F. DeGafferelly worked in Georgia and the Carolinas during some of that time as an evangelist of the United Society. While Winder pastor, J. H. Wood was acting secretary, then office secretary, in 1927-28. Max C. Deweese was field secretary-state evangelist, with aid of the United Society, until Nov. 1, 1928, when he went to St. Paul, Minn.

Bruce Nay was chosen state secretary Nov. 20, 1928, and began his work Jan. 1, 1929, with an office in First Church, Atlanta. He had preached in Georgia 14 years, the last seven at Central Church, Fitzgerald. Educated at Johnson Bible College in Tennessee, he preferred to

---

[22]*Christian Messenger,* Nov., 1927, p. 2. *The Christian-Evangelist,* Nov. 3, 1927, p. 1472.

evangelize, particularly in rural areas.[23] Hence, the program of the Georgia Christian Missionary Society under him was traditional, as it had been. Many revivals were conducted, several new churches organized and others revived, missionary pastors sustained at Columbus, Rome, and Waycross most of that time, and brotherhood causes promoted. The state periodical, the *Christian Messenger,* appeared nearly every month, edited by the state secretary or some minister who was assigned the task. Circulation was small: 246 in 1917, 600 in 1929, with 40 of 58 preachers subscribing.[24] Although not a paid executive, Claud Mayne, Winder, completed a decade as G.C.M.S. treasurer in 1929.[25] Missionary gifts from Georgia totaled $11,187.32 in 1915 and $25,981.98 in 1929, the latter amount from 72 churches; 80 churches made no gifts in 1929 to the organized agencies.[26]

Numerically small in churches and membership, Georgia Negro Disciples did not work together, it was reported in 1925 by I. C. Franklin, regional evangelist.[27] Their 1918 State Convention registered 44 persons, the one in 1927 only 16. While 18 churches made reports in 1918, only 10 did so in 1929. Regular State Sunday School Conventions met each summer.

The yearning for "better understanding" led to organization of the Negro National Christian Missionary Convention in Nashville, Tenn., in 1917. M. Summers, Georgia Negro evangelist several years, and George T. White, Valdosta Negro minister, were two of 40 white and Negro delegates. Summers became a member of the first com-

---

[23]*1916 Year Book, Disciples of Christ,* p. 14. *Christian Standard,* Dec. 25, 1915, p. 415; Apr. 20, 1921, p. 2193; Nov. 27, 1926, p. 646. *The Christian-Evangelist,* May 13, 1915, p. 600; Nov. 4, 1926, p. 1402.

[24]*Christian Messenger,* Dec., 1918–Jan., 1919, pp. 7, 20; Dec., 1929, pp. 7 f.

[25]*Ibid.,* Dec., 1930, p. 10.

[26]*1916 Year Book, Disciples of Christ,* p. 71. *1929 Year Book, Disciples of Christ,* pp. 692, 699.

[27]*Minutes of the Ninth Annual National Christian Missionary Convention of the Churches of Christ of the United States, Cincinnati, Ohio, Aug. 24-30, 1925* (n. p., n. d.), p. 17.

mittee on permanent organization, later the advisory committee.[28]

In 1919, Mrs. A. T. Autry and Mrs. Griner, white Disciples of Guyton, were guest speakers at the Negro State Convention. The 1917 white State Convention recommended aid by the G.C.M.S. for the Negro work. Little was done, however, due to lack of funds.[29]

The 1920 Negro State Convention accepted I. C. Franklin as regional evangelist for Georgia, Florida, South Carolina, and Alabama. J. H. Griffith and R. B. Tucker were state evangelists in 1920 with the aid of the United Society.[30]   In 1920, Mrs. Laura Pittman, Thomasville, was president of the state Negro women's work. During nearly all of 1915-29, W. H. Smith, Negro state evangelist in 1916-17, was chairman of the Negro State Convention and State Board.

There were 31 Negro churches in Georgia and 685 Bible school pupils in 1915. In 1929, there were 22 churches and 12 preachers.[31]

Statistical data from Federal Religious Censuses of 1916 and 1926 revealed the growth of Georgia Disciples. In 1916 there were 144 congregations, 16,885 members, 108 edifices; 98 churches had property valued at $704,650; indebtedness on 19 totaled $60,604; 11 parsonages were valued at $37,050; the average salary of 21 preachers was

[28]*Report of the First General Convention of Christian (Colored) Churches in the U.S.A. Held at Nashville, Tenn., Aug. 5-9, 1917* (n. p., n. d.), pp. 5, 17, 26.

[29]*Christian Messenger,* Dec., 1918–Jan., 1919, p. 15; Jan.–Feb., 1918, p. 23.

[30]*Minutes of the Thirty-Second Annual State Convention of the Churches of Christ of the Colored Christian Brotherhood in Georgia, Held With Evergreen Church in Valdosta, Ga., From October 21st to 24th, 1920* (Sandersville, Ga.: Sandersville Progress Print, 1920), p. 5. *1921 Year Book and Annual Reports (October 1, 1920–June 30, 1921) . . . Organizations of Disciples of Christ . . .* (St. Louis: United Christian Missionary Society, 1921?), p. 254.

[31]*1916 Year Book, Disciples of Christ,* pp. 87-93. *Christian Messenger,* Dec., 1929, p. 38.

$1,679. There were 119 Bible schools, 878 officers and teachers, and 8,946 pupils.[32]

By 1926, Disciples reported 149 churches (43 urban, 106 rural) with 17,328 members (8,456 urban, 8,872 rural). That represented steady growth in urban areas. There were 137 church structures; 134 reported property valued at $1,943,400; 23 had debts of $91,542; 18 parsonages were valued at $108,900, five being indebted for $23,017. In one year, 139 churches raised $656,936—$35,374 for missions and benevolences, the balance of $621,562 for current expenses and improvements. The Bible schools numbered 115 with 967 officers and teachers and 9,115 pupils.[33]

By June 30, 1929, statistical data about the Georgia Disciples revealed the following:

Churches		Members	B. S. Pupils	Local Expenses	Gifts to Missions
White	129	17,741	8,840	$153,388.55	$25,011.53
Negro	23	838	295	1,321,51	12.30
Totals	152	18,579	9,135	$154,710.06	$25,034.83[34]

THE RISK AND ROMANCE OF NEW CHURCHES

During 1915-29, Dr. L. O. Bricker of Atlanta emerged as the most audacious and adamantine minister among Georgia Disciples. He was pastor of the First Christian Church until 1925 when it became embroiled in controversy and a division created Peachtree Christian Church. By 1920, First Church had 1,642 members, making it the largest brotherhood congregation anywhere south of the Mason-Dixon Line.

Dr. Bricker's ministry attracted many prominent people. After World War I, socially prominent families of

---

32U. S. Bureau of the Census. *Religious Bodies: 1916.* Part II. Separate Denominations, History, Description, and Statistics (Washington: Government Printing Office, 1919), pp. 248 ff.

33U. S. Bureau of the Census. *Religious Bodies: 1926.* Vol. II. Separate Denominations. Statistics, History, Doctrine, Organization and Work (Washington: Government Printing Office, 1929), pp. 468 ff.

34*1929 Year Book, Disciples of Christ,* pp. 368, 370, 693.

Atlanta moved northward, away from the downtown area near the State Capitol where First Church was located. Dr. Bricker's proposal that First move north started controversy and the opposition temporarily delayed action.

In 1924, Dr. Bricker, a widower, was married to Louanna Rhodes, daughter of A. G. Rhodes, wealthy furniture store owner of Atlanta. Soon thereafter, Dr. Bricker proceeded with the organization of another congregation, the founding and building being extraordinarily colorful.

Faced with the choice of remaining with First Church or helping to establish the new congregation, more than half of the active members followed Dr. Bricker. Peachtree Christian Church was organized on Mother's Day, May 10, 1925, by 420 constituent members from persons present in the Atlanta Woman's Club.

Only 284 active members stayed in First Church. Many inactive ones apparently made no choice. John Knox of Emory University preached for the downtown congregation during that summer.[35] Dr. C. R. Stauffer, already a noted minister in the national brotherhood of Disciples, became pastor of the First Church in September, coming from Ninth Street Christian Church, Washington, D. C.

The situation was further complicated by a lawsuit. Peachtree, claiming to be the majority, sought the right to use the name First and the property. The case was compromised, with the old church retaining the name First and the property but paying the new church $50,000. The money was borrowed, indorsed by both Peachtree and First men. . . .[36]

Under Dr. Stauffer's leadership, First reported 600 members by Easter, 1926, with many inactive members

[35]Bolles, *op. cit.*, p. [19]. Dr. John Knox, who married Miss Lois Adelaide Bolles, granddaughter of Dr. A. G. Thomas, is now a professor in Union Theological Seminary of New York City.

[36]Bedford, *op. cit.*, p. 196.

resuming an active relationship with the church. By June 30, 1929, First had 1,057 resident members while Peachtree enrolled 754.[37]

Peachtree's first service in an incompleted assembly room at Peachtree and Spring Streets was on Easter Sunday, 1926. With financial resources exhausted, the congregation faced a most difficult taks to finish the Gothic cathedral envisioned by Dr. Bricker.

Then the faithful and prosperous Amos Giles Rhodes (1850-1928) proposed to provide $150,000 for the main structure if other members would raise $50,000 to complete the educational unit and buy furnishings and equipment. Later, he added $50,000 more for chimes and gave frontage, valued at $30,000, on Spring Street. He died, June 16, 1928, before the dedication, leaving $10,000 for landscaping.[38] The Woman's Council raised $24,000 for the pipe organ.

In the magnificent Peachtree building, an unmodified, fifteenth century English Gothic was adapted to ideals of the Disciples. The white marble chancel with an altar instead of the traditional communion table was made the focus of the sanctuary. In the altar's base there was placed a symbol of Judaism, a six-pointed star, cut from a blood-red Palestinian stone.[39] Explaining it, Dr. Bricker said, "No unkind word will ever be said here of anybody's race or religion. No uncharitable judgment will ever be passed here upon any fellow human being."[40]

The main speaker at dedicatory services, Oct. 7-14, 1928, was Dr. Charles Clayton Morrison, Chicago, editor of *The Christian Century*, influential Protestant periodical. A. F. Wickes, for many years architect of the Disciples' Board of Church Extension, listed Peachtree as one of 10 representative brotherhood churches.[41]

[37] *1929 Year Book, Disciples of Christ*, p. 366.

[38] *A Memorial Booklet . . . op. cit.*, p. 14. *The Christian-Evangelist*, Nov. 18, 1926, p. 1459; Nov. 1, 1928, p. 1405.

[39] *The Christianity Century*, Oct. 25, 1928, p. 1279.

[40] *The Christian-Evangelist*, Nov. 1, 1928, p. 1405.

[41] *Shane Quarterly*, Oct., 1943, p. 227.

A preacher of "strong spiritual force," Dr. Bricker drew large crowds. One Sunday night in the spring of 1915, for instance, nearly 2,000 persons heard him discuss Christian unity and there were 70 responses to the gospel invitation in First Church that day.[42] Possessed of holy boldness, he preached in words charged with the deep timbre of his convictions. He always stood up to be counted when the issue was important to him. He was convinced of the innocence of Leo M. Frank in the sensational case of 1913-15 for which the Texas-born Jew was finally hanged by an incited mob for an atrocious crime.[43] He courageously defended his friend, John Marshall Slaton, then Governor of Georgia, for commuting the death sentence to life imprisonment. The Governor's clemency was called a "courageous act" by the Atlanta *Journal* and "devotion to the law and order" by *The Christian-Evangelist*.[44]

Dr. Bricker's concern for prisoners led, in 1922, from a Bible class at the Atlanta Federal Penitentiary, to organization of the "First Christian Church in Prison." Wm. M. Jones, ordained to the ministry by Dr. Bricker at First Church, taught the class that began with six men. Attendance grew to 160 in 1922 when 23 prisoners confessed their faith. The U. S. Justice Department issued an unprecedented order permitting their baptism in

[42]*Christian Standard*, May 15, 1915, pp. 1080 f.

[43]Frederick D. Kershner, then president of Texas Christian University, like Dr. Bricker, convinced of Frank's innocence, wrote an unpublished book, "The Martyr," about the Frank case. After Dr. Kershner became editor of *The Christian-Evangelist* in December, 1915, he was unable to find a reputable publisher who would issue the book because of intense prejudice against Frank in Georgia (F. D. Kershner, letter to J. Edward Moseley, written in Indianapolis, Ind., dated Oct. 20, 1952).

[44]Atlanta (Ga.) *Journal*, June 21, 1915. *The Christian-Evangelist*, July 1, 1915, p. 817. Coulter, *op. cit.*, p. 400. Francis X. Busch, *Guilty or Not Guilty?* (Indianapolis; New York: Bobbs-Merrill Co., 1952), pp. 67 f. In his book, Busch, objectively reviewing the case, concluded (pp. 73 f.) that Frank "may have been guilty, and he may have been innocent." Slaton, however, stated in 1953 that if he "had been compelled to act and could not have commuted the sentence," he would have "granted an absolute pardon to Frank" (John M. Slaton, signed letter to J. Edward Moseley, written in Atlanta, Ga., dated Nov. 19, 1953).

First Church, Sept. 20. The prisoners then formed the prison congregation with 49 charter members. It was the only church of its kind anywhere.[45]

The ministry for the 3,000 prisoners received $726.15 in 1923 from the United Society. However, by 1925, the work was identified with the Prison Evangelism Commission of the Christian Restoration Association and Jones had left First Church for the Grant Park Church.[46]

About 1920, when Judge T. O. Hathcock was president of Georgia's Western District, he proposed establishing new congregations with a "schoolhouse brigade."[47] Dr. Bricker opposed the plan. Judge Hathcock and his friends proceeded with their evangelism proposals, probably not realizing that they were beginning to enclose the churches following their leadership behind a barrier of exclusiveness. In thus circumscribing the ecumenical witness of the Disciples, while suspicious of ecclesiastical control, they became ready subjects of conservative editorial influence.

Dr. Bricker, meanwhile, dreamed of a beautiful church structure on Peachtree. His attitude toward struggling congregations prejudiced their leaders against the organized missionary program symbolized by First and Peachtree Churches. The distressing conflict that ensued over this divergence of opinion profoundly affected the unity of Georgia Disciples.

In 1919 the Western (formerly Atlanta) District of 10 counties approved organization of three churches annually for five years. Joel B. Hardigree, Oconee County native, became district evangelist. He was succeeded by Owen Still, product of the Winder Church. His wife, Shirley, was youth worker with the evangelistic team.

---

[45]*Christian Standard*, Oct. 7, 1922, pp. 1 f.; Oct. 21, 1922, p. 73; June 2, 1923, p. 1070. Bolles, *op. cit.*, p. [19].

[46]*1924 Year Book, Disciples of Christ*, p. 76. *Restoration Herald*, Sept., 1925, p. 26; Nov., 1925, p. 26.

[47]*Christian Standard*, Apr. 22, 1922, p. 3457.

Still addressed the 1918 State Convention and was elected convention secretary. In 1927, he was Western District president.[48]

Rallies, under various names, promoted the threat to cooperative missions in Georgia. The first Southeastern Group Evangelism Congress, sponsored by the *Christian Standard,* met at East Point, Apr. 4-6, 1922. C. J. Sharp of the paper's staff helped raise 400 for Still's back salary. However, a cooperative missionary spokesman shared in the fellowship. E. B. Quick, regional Bible School superintendent of the United Society, addressed the meeting, as he did the 1922 autumnal Western District Convention.[49] The East Point meeting "set in motion latent forces" for evangelism throughout Georgia. Actually, the program filled the void created by the lack of effective evangelism then by organized state missions.

Judge Hathcock, district "permanent president" then, reported that "no word of criticism of any agency was heard" during the rally. He had been a State Board member, 1910-22, and was then a member of the Board of Managers of the United Society. It was thought he was becoming a loyal supporter of the views of the *Christian Standard,* hostile opponent of the Society and most other International Convention agencies. At the same time, the periodical gave editorial and financial support to

[48]*Christian Standard,* Nov. 18, 1922, p. 102; Oct. 28, 1923, cover p. [889]; July 26, 1924, p. 1093; Oct. 24, 1925, p. 2253; Dec. 24, 1927, p. 1050. *Christian Messenger,* Dec., 1918–Jan., 1919, pp. 4, 6, 17. Still studied at Johnson Bible College in Tennessee, 1911-13, then, returning to Georgia attended Lamar College, 1913-15, and Southeastern Christian College, 1915-19. He received the A.B. degree from the latter. The Cincinnati (O.) Bible Seminary opened in 1924, consolidating McGarvey Bible College, Louisville, Ky., and Cincinnati Bible Institute, both of which opened in 1923 as independent, loyal, ministerial training schools. Still, continuing his conservative education, received the A.M. degree from C.B.S. in 1925. That seminary and Johnson Bible College are still in existence.

From 1917 until about 1929, Still was pastor of East Atlanta, Ellenwood, College Park, Carrollton, and Atlanta Capitol View Christian Churches.

[49]*Christian Standard,* Apr. 22, 1922, p. 3458; Nov. 18, 1922, p. 209.

independent home and foreign missions, virtually becoming a missionary agency itself.

The organization of conservative "Restoration"
churches in the Western District especially occupied
much of Judge Hathcock's time. He was a charter member of Capitol View Church, organized in 1920, and
provided financial backing to help the congregation buy
a building site. He aided in many ways to establish
Grant Park Church in 1924-25 when the congregation
was known as Central, then South Blvd. Church.

Grant Park Church was formed in February, 1924, by
John Sidney Raum, evangelist of the Sidney Smith
Clarke Fund that functioned in Cincinnati as an outreach
of the "loyal" brethren. Agitation for the new congregation began when it was expected that First Church
would move from its downtown location. When First
split in 1925, Grant Park members did not return to the
"mother" church. That "would have meant their support of the U.C.M.S. They would not bow the knee."
The Clarke Fund, organized in 1921, was succeeded in
1925 by the Christian Restoration Association, formed
with aid of the *Christian Standard*.[50]

In 1923, the independent forces spread into Northeast
Georgia which then had 47 churches in 14 counties. Roy
Linton Porter (1878-1938) became Athens minister in
1921. He served until May, 1923, when he resigned to
become a field representative of the Loyal Movement of
the Standard Publishing Co., of Cincinnati. Martin
Benjamin Miller (1890-1953) succeeded Porter in Athens,
Sept. 1, 1923. Miller became pastor in 1926 of Tabernacle Church, Columbus, Ind., where Z. T. Sweeney, another former Georgia minister, preached many years.
Still later, Miller became an evangelist of the Christian
Restoration Association and engaged in other independent home missions.[51]

[50]*Restoration Herald*, Sept., 1925, p. 24; Oct., 1925, p. 25; Oct., 1929,
p. 8. *Christian Standard*, Mar. 22, 1924, cover p. [625]; July 18, 1925,
p. 1001. Corey, *op. cit.*, p. 5.

[51]*Christian Standard*, Apr. 20, 1921, p. 2193; May 15, 1923, p. 940.
The Christian-Evangelist, Aug. 19, 1926, p. 1043. *Restoration Herald*,
June, 1934, p. 5.

Miller was chairman of a Group Evangelism Congress in Athens, May 1, 2, 1924. He was aided in promoting it by C. J. Sharp, Harvey Bream, and Roy L. Porter of the Standard Publishing Co. Miller's close associate was G. L. (Jerry) Johnson, zealous Christian Endeavor worker who became Northeast District evangelist, Jan. 1, 1924, and in September, 1925, youth worker of the Standard's Loyal Movement.[52]

A dispute in Athens First Church over public issues caused some members to withdraw and form Central Christian Church. The latter was first listed in the *1927 Year Book, Disciples of Christ,* with 25 members and F. L. Adams as minister. The breach was finally healed in 1942. Stanley Roberts Grubb was the Athens pastor, 1909-1921; a new building was dedicated in 1915. After the congregational dispute, he returned for a second pastorate with Athens First Christian Church on Mar. 7, 1926, serving until 1936.[53]

Savannah became an influential independent center. A. R. Adams suggested how the disruption developed in Second Christian, now Central Church of Christ of that city. In 1922, the building was in poor condition, attendance was small, and there was a 4,000 debt. When Adams became pastor, he was informed that the church did not support the United Society. He felt that he "had no right to dictate to them as to how they should give," he said, and continued:

. . . I did write the United Society, and asked them to send a man to explain things to our congregation, with the hope that we could co-operate with them, but they ignored my request,

---

[52]*Christian Standard,* May 17, 1924, pp. 823 f., 827; June 14, 1924, p. 944; Sept. 5, 1925, p. 2077. In 1925, after an appeal by Owen Still, $61.33 was given on the debt of the LaGrange Church of Troup County by the Standard Publishing Co., its president, Wm. R. Errett, and Miss Jane Errett, sister of Russell Errett, the firm's principal owner and manager at that time (*Christian Standard,* Aug. 8, 1925, p. 1090).

[53]*The Christian-Evangelist,* Mar. 4, 1926, p. 275. Grubb died May 3, 1939, during his third pastorate at Columbia, S. C. (*The Christian-Evangelist,* Aug. 31, 1939, p. 926.)

and their representatives likewise ignore the Second Church when they visit our city.[54]

United Society officials seldom answered their critics in print during those years. Doubtless both factions were at fault in building barriers that denied Christian fellowship.

It was reported at a Western District Convention in 1925 that the district then had 12 full-time ministers, every closed church had been re-opened, and several new churches formed. The district was then publishing a paper, *The Christian;* Samuel A. Strawn (1864-1933), pastor of Longley Avenue Church, was editor. The paper was being published in 1922.[55]

The increasing dissension among Georgia's Disciples meant the raising of barriers and creation of distrust when separatism prevented or broke off the fellowship. The ranks eventually solidified into hostile separatists practicing exclusive independency and determined supporters of cooperative missionary endeavor always amenable to religious change. Lay views were shaped by influential preachers and the inevitable struggle for control of congregations and property usually occurred when pulpits were vacant.

Georgia's "great field," said John H. Wood in 1928, desperately needed "close, harmonious cooperation between all our forces, local, District, State and National."[56] Yet little was being done to arrive at compromise solutions in order to bring the diverging brethren together again. More and more, by 1929, each group went its own way.

Altogether, 60 or more Christian churches, including 25 Negro ones, were established in Georgia during 1915-

---

[54]*Christian Standard,* Nov. 29, 1924, p. 223. Cuthrell W. Lipsey and Grover Lee Hardison entered the ministry from Savannah Central. Lipsey was pastor of First Christian Church, Muskogee, Okla., when it split in 1947 over support or nonsupport of the United Society and ecumenical work. He died in 1949 while enroute to San Antonio, Tex., to join the faculty of Southern Christian College, independent ministerial school of which Hardison was president (Corey, *op. cit.,* pp. 211-217).

[55]*Christian Standard,* Aug. 15, 1925, p. 1992; Dec. 5, 1925, p. 2395.

[56]*Christian Messenger,* Nov., 1928, p. 4.

29.[57]   The 22 that survived are listed below with founding years, present names ("n" for Negro and "r" for
reorganized) and county locations as follows:

Organized	Name	County	Organized	Name	County
1915?—	nMcClendon Gr.,	Treutlen	1921 —	Decatur First,	DeKalb
1915 —	Palmetto,	Oglethorpe	1921 —	Glennville,	Tattnall
1915?—	nWelcome Hope,	Brooks	1922 —	rAtlanta Grove Pk.,	Fulton
1916 —	Hardwick Ox. Mem.,	Bald-	1922 —	Whitesburg,	Carroll
		win	1923 —	Atlanta Lakewood,	Fulton
1916 —	Waycross First,	Ware	1924 —	Atlanta Grant Pk.,	Fulton
1917 —	rSpring Hill,	Toombs	1924 —	Albany First,	Dougherty
1917 —	Tusculum,	Effingham	1925 —	Atlanta Peachtree,	Fulton
1919 —	Bainbridge,	Decatur	1926 —	Cross Plains,	Carroll
1919 —	Williamson,	Pike	1928 —	rReese,	Warren
1920 —	Atlanta Cap. View,	Fulton	1928 —	rSylvania,	Screven
1921 —	rAmericus,	Sumter			

In 1917, only 13 of 56 reporting churches had full-time
preaching. That was a real danger for the state brotherhood. Yet in 1929 there were still 20 to 25 churches without pastors and some had not heard a single sermon during the year.[58]   In spite of the growing breach in the
state brotherhood, many ministers and lay people contributed to the work. In addition to those already mentioned in this chapter, the number included the following:

A. T. Autry, James H. Barfield, Gerald Culberson,
Ophir Kirk Cull, L. A. Cunningham, W. A. Everhart, J.
Randall Farris, O. E. Fox, Duke C. Jones, E. C. Lacy,
W. R. Lang, Edgar C. Lucas, T. T. G. Linkous, W. F.
Mott, Gerald Y. Smith, A. D. Strobhar, David F. and
John W. Tyndall, brothers, Charles S. Van Winkle, and
Allen Wilson.[59]

---

[57]According to the Federal Religious Censuses, the anti-organ, conservative Churches of Christ had 58 churches in 1916 and 64 in 1926. A
prominent Atlanta preacher was Samuel Henry Hall, West End Church
of Christ, 1906-20, when it reached 350 members and he organized several
congregations. He was followed in 1920 by B. C. Goodpasture, who served
until 1927, and beginning in 1928 at Seminole Avenue Church of Christ,
Atlanta (Batsell Barrett Baxter and M. Norvel Young [Editors], *Preachers
of Today* [Nashville: Christian Press, 1952], pp. 136 f., 145).

[58]*Christian Messenger,* Jan.-Feb., 1918, p. 2; Dec., 1929, p. 9.

[59]Prominent Disciples who died during 1915-29 included Alexander
Campbell Bruce, Nathan T. Elder, C. G. Hannah, Mr. and Mrs. Albert
Howell, Miss Bunnie Love, Mrs. B. O. Miller, A. R. Moore, John Albert
Perdue, Mr. and Mrs. A. G. Rhodes, Mrs. A. C. Smith, W. H. Smith,
and George White.

The Struggle for Education

Simultaneously in 1915, two Georgia educational institutions opened. One was Dasher Bible School, seven miles south of Valdosta, and the other, Southeastern Christian College at Auburn.

Announcement of the Dasher School was made in the *Gospel Advocate* by anti-organ brethren of the Church of Christ. They proposed to teach the Bible and public school courses.[60] Twenty-two pupils enrolled for classes in the Dasher Church. A two-story frame school was ready in 1916. The county contributed support money since most of the pupils were from the local area. However, county aid was withdrawn in 1928. The first unit of an administration building was erected the same year.

Southeastern Christian College opened, Sept. 7, 1915, at Auburn, a village 45 miles northeast of Atlanta and 28 miles southwest of Athens, in Barrow County. It was launched, with aid of the G.C.M.S., to train Christian leaders. Eighty-eight high school and collegiate students, including 14 ministers, enrolled the first year.

The Auburn school had been operated since 1892 by Baptists and was last known as Perry-Rainey Institute. Hiram N. Rainey, lay preacher, had been expected to endow it. There was a brick administration building and two frame dormitories on an 11-acre campus.[61] The vacant campus and low price appealed to the Disciples; E. L. Shelnutt pithily described the situation thus:

> . . . Perry-Rainey walked out, leaving college building, dormitory, everything from student's patched breeches to the presidency, for little less than $11,000, . . . The Baptists made a failure at Perry-Rainey, due, it is claimed, to location and to their multiplicity of schools in the State. As it will be our only school in the Southeast, there is hope of making it a success.[62]

---

[60]*Gospel Advocate*, Sept. 9, 1915, p. 908.

[61]Flanigan, *op. cit.*, pp. 296-298, 363. Apparently, a Presbyterian school existed in that vicinity in 1832-35 (Orr, *op. cit.*, p. 138).

[62]*Christian Standard*, May 29, 1915, p. 1165.

With Lamar College still in existence at Clarkston, two mass meetings of Disciples were held in Atlanta First Church, to consider the proposed new school. The Baptist offer was accepted, Mar. 2, and a committee authorized to complete the transaction.[63] That property was transferred May 11, 1915, in the Fulton County Court House. John H. Wood, state secretary, was elected president in June. The first faculty included W. A. Chastain, dean, and Henry R. Garrett, once president of Milligan College, near Johnson City, Tenn., and Midland (Tex.) College. T. O. Hathcock was chairman of the executive committee.[64]

Presumably the largest student enrollment, 108, was during 1918-19 when there were 15 preachers with one-half ministering to about 20 churches. Associated with other brotherhood colleges through membership in the Board of Education, Southeastern participated in the Men and Millions Movement and up to Mr. 31, 1919, received 7,671.03 from it.[65] President Wood termed that a "great forward step," but added:

It has been intimated to me that a few people believe that the schools receiving aid from the Men and Millions Movement surrender their liberty to become amenable to others in regard to courses of study, teachers, etc. . . . this is a mistake. A school does not give up its freedom in any way, is permitted to manage its affairs untrammeled and free from all "red tape."[66]

Nevertheless, that was an ominous rumbling of increasing opposition to come from dissident Georgia brethren.

[63]The committee included John H. Wood, chairman, S. R. Grubb, T. O. Hathcock, Claud Mayne, H. M. Patterson (*Christian College, Auburn, Ga. [Co-Educational], First Announcement. Prospectus, 1915-1916* [n. p., 1915], p. 13).

[64]Mayor W. O. Perry, Winder, was vice-chairman; John W. Crenshaw, secretary; J. F. Whitehead, treasurer, and S. R. Grubb, the other member. Other trustees were: L. O. Bricker, W. A. Chastain, M. J. Head, Josephus Hopwood, Claud Mayne, A. R. Moore, H. M. Patterson, C. T. Smith, John H. Wood, and S. H. Wood (*Christian College . . . Prospectus . . . op. cit.,* p. 6).

[65]*World Call,* Sept., 1919, p. 59.

[66]*Christian Messenger,* Jan.-Feb., 1918, p. 5.

By January, 1919, Henry R. Garrett was co-president with John H. Wood. *The Cherokee,* first student annual published in 1920, was dedicated to Garrett who returned to Tennessee in 1921. The girls' dormitory burned in 1920. Dr. Allen Rice Moore, a trustee, who held the Ph.D. degree from Dexter College of Missouri, became president about October, 1921. He resigned the next summer to become a professor in Atlanta Theological Seminary (Congregationalist). He died Sept. 22, 1922.[67]

George A. Hubbell succeeded Dr. Moore as president of Southeastern College.[68] Shortly after his election, the 1922 State Convention voted to pay the college debt, to complete the dormitory, to operate "an Academy or Junior College" at Auburn, and to proceed with establishment of a "standard Christian College in a strategic" Southeastern center. One educational headache was not sufficient, it seemed! Approval was voted to solicit $175,000 for the educational work and pledges of $10,124 were received at the convention. *Pledges,* however, did not pay bills already overdue.[69] The college trustees voted, Dec. 27, 1922, to authorize $20,000 in seven per cent, 10-year bonds to aid the school's desperate financial situation.[70]

Erastus Lamar Shelnutt was the last president of the Southeastern Christian College at Auburn, apparently beginning his term in the summer of 1923.[71] At the end of 1921, the college had only 50 students. In another year, with five teachers, total income was $3,000, the deficit, $7,000. The 1924 receipts totaled $10,800, including $6,000 from the churches. Fourteen ministerial

---

[67]*Ibid.,* Dec., 1918–Jan., 1919, p. 3. *The Christian-Evangelist,* Dec. 2, 1920, p. 1275; Oct. 5, 1922, p. 1283. Moore's son, Wright T. Moore, in 1923, taught Bible and sociology at the seminary.

[68]*World Call,* Oct., 1922, p. 55.

[69]*Christian Messenger,* Jan., 1923, pp. 23, 25, 27, 34.

[70]*Ibid.,* p. 4.

[71]*World Call,* Aug., 1923, p. 54.

students registered during the last year, 1924-25, when total enrollment was only 32.[72]

The closing of the Auburn school was due to its poor location, lack of academic accreditation, dissatisfaction of a minority of Georgia Disciples with the college's participation in the Men and Millions Movement and affiliation with the Board of Education of Disciples of Christ. Then, too, in 1920 proposals were being considered for establishment of a regional School of Religion adjacent to the University of Alabama at Tuscaloosa.[73]

Southeastern trustees met Sept. 23 and Nov. 5, 1924, and endorsed the proposed School of Religion, electing Dr. L. O. Bricker, John H. Wood, and Claud Mayne as trustees. The 1924 Georgia State Convention at Rome, Nov. 6, approved the regional project, being the last state to do so. On Jan. 6, 1925, Southeastern trustees met in Atlanta and voted to close the college. When the struggling institution concluded its work, May 17, 1925, the proposed regional School of Religion was expected to open in 1926. By the summer of 1926, $100,000 was reported pledged on a goal of $300,000. Insufficient pledges and funds caused abandonment of the regional School of Religion before it ever opened. In 1927, John H. Wood still sought a way to liquidate the Southeastern debt so as to hold the property for future secondary school use.[74]

Atlanta Christian College originated with W. Glenn Carter as a Bible institute or preparatory school for

---

[72]*1922 Year Book, Disciples of Christ*, p. 70. *1923 Year Book, Disciples of Christ*, pp. 260 ff. *1924 Year Book, Disciples of Christ*, p. 213. *1925 Year Book, Disciples of Christ*, pp. 234 ff. Prominent alumni of the school included: Elmer Napoleon Anthony, James Harkness Barfield, Carl R. Cheek, Thomas Olin Slaughter, Percy Doyle Snipes, Owen Still, J. Luther Stone, and Clarence W. Thomas.

[73]*World Call*, June, 1922, p. 18. *Christian Messenger*, July, 1930, p. 2.

[74]*1925 Year Book, Disciples of Christ*, pp. 9, 31. *The Christian-Evangelist*, July 1, 1926, p. 820; Nov. 4, 1926, p. 1402; Nov. 17, 1927, p. 1539. *Christian Messenger*, Feb., 1925, pp. 8 f.; Aug., 1930, pp. 2, 5. *World Call*, Mar., 1925, pp. 23 ff.; Sept., 1925, p. 42. *Christian Standard*, Oct. 10, 1925, p. 2197.

Christian service volunteers unable to attend college. Pastor at East Point, suburb of Atlanta, he had the East Point Bible Institute operating in October, 1922.[75]

By 1925 the school became a more formalized reversion to the pioneer manual labor school and adopted the name, "The Christian School." At a Western District rally, Carter announced that the district had obtained use of a 100-acre farm for the project. Training and experience were provided for preaching, farming, teaching, and construction. The farm home was soon filled and additional applicants were denied admittance because of inadequate equipment and funds. Carter taught the Bible and pupils attended public school for regular academic work. Every pupil was required to "pledge himself to some form of Christian service"; several continued their training in various colleges and became effective church leaders. Outstanding among these is Duke C. Jones, now pastor at Reidsville, N. C.

When the school opened, Sept. 1, 1925, there was a $5,000 house on the grounds. The site, two miles from East Point, was the birthplace and early home of Nora Head (Mrs. T. Olin) Hathcock. Members then of East Point Christian Church, Judge and Mrs. Hathcock not only provided the farm site, but contributed to the school's financial support. Having been concerned with the school from its beginning, they were considered founders of Atlanta Christian College.[76]

Announcement was made in 1928 of a "new school," named Atlanta Christian College. Hathcock was re-

---

[75]*Christian Standard,* Nov. 18, 1922, p. 209. Born at Newnan, Coweta County, Ga., Carter became a member of Liberty Church, entered Johnson Bible College, near Knoxville, Tenn., in 1913. After preaching for four years in Tennessee and Oklahoma, he returned to Georgia, Jan. 1, 1921, as pastor of East Point Christian Church, where he served until September, 1925. Then he became superintendent of The Christian School there, serving for two years in that capacity. Also, during 1923 and 1924, he taught in Atlanta Theological Seminary (Congregationalist) which in 1929 became affiliated with the Vanderbilt School of Religion, Nashville, Tenn.

[76]*Restoration Herald,* Oct., 1925, p. 19. *Christian Standard,* June 20, 1925, p. [906].

ported to have given 100 acres of farm land, with buildings for 30 students, to the school corporation. John S. Raum, general evangelist of the Christian Restoration Association, who had, during 1927-28, been founding president of Northern Bible College at Pierre, S. D., became president of the reorganized Atlanta school.[77]

Maurice Bertrand Ingle, professor at Milligan College in Tennessee, 1921-28, became dean and served until 1930. Carter, Owen Still, and S. A. Strawn were other faculty members.[78] Carter, however, continued to support organized missionary work and became pastor in nearby College Park in 1926.

Atlanta Christian College thus became a ministerial training school of the independent forces "without any taint of destructive criticism or ecclesiasticism." Needed to "spread the plea," it was intended "to check the inroads of modernism in the Southland."[79]

"May this new institution do great good," was the greeting extended by John H. Wood, then concluding his long tenure as state secretary of the G.C.M.S.[80] How much good it did became a matter of controversy in Georgia and elsewhere.

Certainly the brethren in Georgia had their share of difficult issues during 1915-1929. Whether they liked it or not, the interpretations of the teachings of the fathers were changing as were the attitudes of succeeding generations of Disciples of Christ. A majority of the state brotherhood continued, however, as had been true across the years, to adhere to the principle of cooperation in extending the Kingdom of God.

[77]Born in Holland, Raum studied for the Dutch Reformed ministry. After several Christian church pastorates, he was Montana mission superintendent for the C.W.B.M., and the A.C.M.S. in 1909-13.

[78]*Restoration Herald*, Oct., 1928, p. 13. *Christian Messenger*, Sept., 1930, p. 1. A.C.C. trustees were T. O. Hathcock, E. H. Bryant, M. W. Fodrie, Dr. J. H. Hodges, S. A. Strawn, and Wm. Trailor.

[79]*Restoration Herald*, Oct., 1928, p. 13. *Christian Standard*, Dec. 24, 1927, p. 1050.

[80]*Christian Messenger*, July-Aug., 1928, p. 2.

The next two decades, 1930-1949, brought acute problems, caused by the financial depression and World War II. Their effects and the resultant rising expectations of Georgia Disciples of Christ will be chronicled from stalemate to advance in the next and concluding chapter.

CHAPTER X

Challenging Obligations and Opportunities, 1930-1949

The financial depression and World War II affected all that Georgia Disciples of Christ did in 1930-1949. Church indebtedness accumulated as preachers and laymen struggled valiantly with poverty until war-induced prosperity made payment possible.

Nearly every full-time congregation was burdened with debt when the depression struck.[1] Some church property, like East Atlanta and West End, Atlanta, was lost.[2] Numerous applications were submitted for the vacant pulpits. "We hope," wrote State Secretary Bruce Nay in 1936, "all the vacant Georgia pulpits will soon be filled with good men so that our postage expense may be reduced."[3] Missionary offerings decreased sharply and donations of supplies to the Southern Christian Home tumbled as did their estimated cash value.

The impact of World War II caught Georgians unprepared to cope with terrific military and civilian problems. The State Convention in 1936 was "unalterably opposed to the entire war system." In 1938 the convention expressed horror at the persecution of German Jews and Christians, opposed the sale of munitions to Japan, and favored government ownership of munition factories. E. G. Orahood surprised the 1939 Convention "with an attack on the recent lifting of the Arms Em-

[1]*Christian Messenger,* Dec., 1929, p. 8.
[2]*Ibid.,* Jan., 1941, p. 3 Feb., 1945, p. 1.
[3]*Ibid.,* Mar., 1936, p. 5.

321

bargo.'"[4] Yet by Pearl Harbor Day, Georgia Disciples were patriotic supporters of the war. Georgia ministers rendered meritorious service with the American military chaplaincy in nearly every war theatre.[5]

A brotherhood Committee on War Services, formed in 1941, met needs arising from the war. Dr. Willard M. Wickizer was the executive secretary. Resources came from the Emergency Million, War-Time Service, and Week of Compassion Funds.[6] Field representatives aided churches to meet needs of the service personnel. Local service men's clubs were formed by several churches and Christian youth groups gave programs at military hospitals.[7]

The Mt. Vernon Church in Walton County was unable to entertain the 1942 State Convention in its new building because of gasoline and tire rationing. Abbreviated sessions were held in Atlanta First Church.[8] All other state conventions were held.

In 1943, the Athens Church, like most others, had more than one tenth of its members in the armed services (65

---

[4]*The Christian-Evangelist*, Dec. 10, 1936, p. 1619; Jan. 26, 1939, p. 115; Dec. 7, 1939, p. 1339. *Christian Messenger*, Dec., 1938, pp. 6 f. In 1947, Charles F. Schwab and Mrs. James R. Beach attended the first Washington World Order Workshop of the Social Welfare Department of The United Christian Missionary Society. Mrs. Beach was also one of 100 persons at the first United Nations Seminar the same year. Atlanta was host in 1948 to a brotherhood World Order Conference.

[5]The number included: Harry J. Berry, Fred W. Carlock, Carl R. Cheek, Luther M. Cole, Orvel Calhoun Crowder, Lorenzo J. Evans, Richard H. Gear, Howard Henry Groover, Jr., Grover Lee Hardison, LeRoy S. Hulan, Maury Hundley, Robert A. Preston, Hartwell M. Ramsey, Edward S. Reese, Benjamin O. Sims, Werdie S. Van Arsdale, Jr., Charles S. Van Winkle, William N. Weaver, and Hayes H. Webster. George O. Tease, who began a pastorate at Fitzgerald in 1948, had been an Australian Army chaplain. Verval Lloyd Smith and Ernest E. Thompson were on active duty other than chaplaincy, although they were ministers.

[6]Gifts from Georgia to the War-Time Service and Week of Compassion Fund were as follows: in 1944, 23 churches gave $2,329.21; in 1945, 38 gave $3,701.51; in 1946, 40 gave $3,667.11; in 1947, 45 gave $5,688.19; in 1948, 64 gave $56,149.88; in 1949, 85 gave $41,900.80.

[7]*Christian Messenger*, Apr., 1943, p. 5; Oct., 1943, pp. 3, 8; Nov., 1943, p. 4; Apr., 1944, p. 5.

[8]*Ibid.*, Sept., 1942, p. 8; Oct., 1942, p. 4.

persons out of a membership of 503). Many other members moved to work in defense industries.[9] Women in the state promoted a fellowship of absentee-active members, the home society maintaining an active relationship with those for whom the national emergency meant enforced absence.[10] Honor rolls and service flags with stars for those in the service were displayed in nearly every church. Military and civilian defense personnel received Christian literature, local bulletins, many letters. Memorial services were conducted for those who made the supreme sacrifice for their country.

At least 21 congregations were formed in Georgia during 1930-49, including six reorganizations. Four had closed by 1949, or before. The procedure of organizing new churches under state auspices changed with the Marietta congregation. If, after a survey, a church was needed, the building site was purchased and a building provided before organization. Aid was given by a sponsoring church and/or the State Board; in 1948 the latter decided to organize only churches it could aid until self-support was assured.[11]

The names of 17 new churches that survived, with years of founding ("r" meaning reorganized, "n" for Negro) and county locations, follow:

Organized	Name County	Organized	Name County
1931 —	Brunswick, Glynn	1942 —	Toccoa, Stephens
1932 —	nAtlanta Second, Fulton	1944 —	rnGreston, Dodge
1934 —	Diamond Hill, Madison	1944 —	rMarietta First, Cobb
1935 —	East Pt. Jefferson Park, Fulton	1945 —	rCanton, Cherokee
		1947 —	rBrunswick, Glynn
1935 —	Palmetto, Fulton	1948 —	Brookhaven, DeKalb
1935 —	Savannah S. Garden, Chatham	1948 —	Whistleville, Barrow
		1949 —	Macon Houston Av., Bibb
1938 —	rBaldwin, Banks		
1939 —	Savannah Pineh't, Chatham	1949 —	rMarietta First, Cobb

[9]Ibid., Mar., 1943, p. 3; Nov., 1943, p. 6. When Camp Stewart was built in Liberty County, the town of Willie was eradicated. Last services of the Willie Christian Church were held in December, 1940.

[10]Ibid., Aug., 1944, p. 5.

[11]Ibid., June, 1948, p. 8.

By 1949, end of a century of organized work, statistics of Georgia Disciples, incomplete as always, reflected growth despite the wrangling that disrupted their ranks. In that year, 154 churches were reported (141 white, 13 Negro) with 27,167 members (26,316 white, 851 Negro). The 154 Bible schools reported enrollment of 12,429 (12,198 white, 231 Negro). There were 104 preachers. Gifts for local expenses totaled $436,607.24 and for missions and benevolences, $83,759.92.[12]

Comparative statistics of Georgia Disciples and the anti-organ Churches of Christ which went their separate way in 1906 follow. No Federal Religious Census was taken in 1946 so the figures for 1949, taken from denominational year books, were substituted. The survey revealed[13]:

Year	Number of Churches		Membership	
	Disciples of Christ	Churches of Christ	Disciples of Christ	Churches of Christ
1906	128	22	12,703	1,046
1916	144	58	16,885	2,671
1926	149	64	17,328	4,039
1936	100	38	17,315	4,976
1949	154	80	27,167	6,000 (?)

Benton Cordell Goodpasture, minister of two Churches of Christ in Atlanta for 18 years, left the city in 1939 for Nashville, Tenn., where he became editor of the *Gospel Advocate,* weekly anti-organ periodical. While in Atlanta, he helped form several congregations.[14] During

---

[12]*1949 Year Book, Disciples of Christ,* pp. 361, 690, 695.

[13]U. S. Bureau of the Census. *Religious Bodies: 1926 . . . op. cit.,* pp. 397, 469. U. S. Bureau of the Census. *Religious Bodies: 1936.* Vol. II, Part 1. Denominations A to J. Statistics, History, Doctrine, Organization and Work (Washington: Government Printing Office, 1941), pp. 465, 536. *1949 Year Book, Disciples of Christ,* pp. 361, 694. *Church Directory and List of Preachers of Churches of Christ, 1949* (Austin, Tex.: Firm Foundation Publishing House, 1949), pp. 55 f.; 123 f.

[14]*Gospel Advocate,* Mar. 2, 1939, pp. 197, 205. Baxter and Young, *op. cit.,* pp. 136 f. The *Georgia Christian,* Church of Christ periodical, edited by E. H. McGaha, was issued at Summerville, Chattooga County, about 1940 (Claude E. Spencer [Compiler], *Periodicals of the Disciples of Christ and Related Religious Groups* [Canton, Mo.: Disciples of Christ Historical Society, 1943], p. 68).

1930-1949, probably a few Christian churches in rural districts became identified temporarily with the anti-organ churches.

Offerings increased with war-time prosperity and many churches accumulated building funds. The post-war years reflected the state's most significant era of church construction. Macon First Church erected an imposing edifice while Cecil A. Denney was pastor. A sanctuary, youth center, and educational unit were built on an 11-acre site. The $300,000 structure was made possible through generous gifts of over $200,000 by Charles O. McAfee, candy manufacturer and State Board treasurer. When dedicated in 1948, indebtedness was only $40,000. Construction began in 1949 on the $300,-000 building of Decatur First Church, Charles F. Schwab, minister. The youth center of the Georgian colonial structure of Savannah First Church, Harry J. Berry, pastor, was dedicated in 1949. The brick Mt. Vernon Church, constructed in 1941 along simple Gothic lines, became the loveliest rural building of the Disciples in Georgia. M. G. Aldridge, Macon contractor, assisted generously in building several churches.[15]

The leading Christian churches of Georgia during 1930-1949 were First and Peachtree of Atlanta. Dr. L. O. Bricker, Peachtree minister, suffered poor health from 1928 until his death. On July 1, 1930, when Peachtree had 470 members, Robert W. Burns became resident pastor. Almost immediately, he was elected to the executive committee of the State Board.[16] Dr. Bricker soon retired unofficially and moved to Miami Beach, Fla. However, he kept in touch with the church and returned for important occasions. He died at the age of 68 on

[15]Other church buildings erected before the end of 1949 included: Albany, Atlanta Capitol View, Community, and Grant Park, Augusta Central, Bogart, Carrollton First, Columbus Central, East Point First, Hardwick, Harmony near Commerce, Lakewood, Lawrenceville, Ludville, Macon Houston Ave., Marietta, Oak Grove near Bainbridge, Palmetto, Pembroke, Union near Watkinsville, Waycross, and Wrightsville. By the middle of 1945, 36 churches in the state owned parsonages.

[16]*Christian Messenger*, Dec., 1930, p. 18.

Aug. 13, 1942. The erection of Peachtree Christian Church was undoubtedly the crowning event of his ministry. Dr. Frederick D. Kershner termed him "one of the most colorful and imposing figures of our contemporary religious history."[17]

Robert Whitehall Burns, born at Merchantville, N. J., on Jan. 20, 1904, became resident minister at Peachtree when he was 26 years old.[18] They matured together. He was educated at Drake University, Washington University (A.B., 1928), and Eden Theological Seminary (B.D., 1930). Oglethorpe University conferred the hononary Doctor of Divinity degree upon him in 1938. He began preaching in 1923. The 1928 brotherhood Youth Convention elected him president and he presided over the frank youth features of the Seattle International Convention in 1929 and the Washington, D. C., Convention the following year.[19]

While Dr. Burns gained influence in Georgia Discipledom, Dr. Clarence Roy Stauffer, minister of First Church, was the most significant leader of the state brotherhood and a tower of strength for cooperation. Chairman of the State Board nearly 18 years, he was chairman of the first State Religious Education Committee named in 1930, was twice (1930, 1938) president of the Atlanta Christian Council, and of the Family Welfare Society. He was a member of the national Baptist-Disciple unity committee and a vice-president of the International Convention. In 1937, he and Mrs. Stauffer were fraternal delegates from the International Convention (representing both Canadian and American Disciples) to the annual British Conference of Churches of Christ at Glasgow, Scotland. First Church made it

---

[17]*The Christian-Evangelist*, Sept. 17, 1942, p. 1017.

[18]John Burns (1825?-1911), grandfather of Dr. Robert W. Burns, operated a book publishing firm in St. Louis, Mo. The business was finally sold to the Christian Publishing Co., now the Christian Board of Publication there (*Discipliana*, Oct., 1943, pp. 27 f.).

[19]*Youth's Conference Call*, May-June, 1928, pp. 5 ff.; Oct., 1929, pp. 9, 13.

possible for them to tour the Holy Land afterward. Their two sons, Clarence C., and Paul S., became ministers.

By 1942 First Church had paid the last of the $50,000 debt incurred when Peachtree Church was established. All principal and interest payments were met when due and for years the church was the state's largest contributor to missions. After Dr. Stauffer's last sermon, preached over a national radio network, Sunday, Mar. 19, 1944, he was stricken and died Mar. 21 when 62 years old. The *Atlanta Constitution* called him "one of Atlanta's most influential ministers" who was "inseparably connected with every good feature of Atlanta life." The Atlanta Federation of Trades resolved that he "consistently raised his voice in behalf of those who toil and the ideals of the labor movement."[20]

Dr. Stauffer was succeeded by Harrison McMains of West Point, Ga., in September, 1944, when First Church had 1,378 members. Born in Baltimore, he was graduated from Lynchburg (Va.) College and received the B.D. degree from the Vanderbilt School of Religion. A glee club member in college, he later sang in two Broadway shows, the "New Moon" and "Rio Rita." With sympathy for the plight of minority peoples, he was an excellent choice for First Church which was losing strength because of its downtown location.[21] First's building was remodeled at a cost of about $40,000 in 1946.

During 1936, when Peachtree Church had no indebtedness, Mr. and Mrs. Lindsay B. Hopkins, non-Disciples, gave the church adjoining property, with a 15-room mansion, valued at $35,000 for a parsonage. In 1940 lots were purchased to the rear of the church structure, where in 1942, a $20,000 youth center, with a two-story Chapel in the Woods, was dedicated. The Annie Laurie Warren

20Quoted in *The Christian-Evangelist*, Apr. 5, 1944, p. [339].
21Bedford, *op. cit.*, p. 256.

Chapel, open 24 hours of every day, was dedicated in 1949. Commodore and Mrs. Virgil P. Warren contributed $62,000 of the $104,000 cost.

Peachtree Christian Church became widely recognized for having one of the largest and finest collections of treasured stained glass windows in existence.[22] All but two were installed during 1930-49. Every window represented an original design. Those in the sanctuary were created in England by William Glasby and his daughters, Misses Barbara and Dulcima Glasby. The lovely gospel in glass, depicting significant events in the life of Christ, cost $60,000. The window showing the institution of the Lord's Supper was the gift of Dr. and Mrs. L. O. Bricker.[23]

After addition of the Warren Chapel in 1949, the Peachtree property was estimated to be worth at least $1,000,000. One of the Disciples' most generous congregations, by 1949 more than $250,000 had been given to various missions and benevolences.

The Georgia Christian Ministers' Fellowship was reorganized in 1935 by Bruce Nay, state secretary. Annual midwinter meetings were held thereafter in Atlanta, Macon, or Griffin. E. Guy Orahood was the first president. Wilbur T. Wallace served as secretary-treasurer for several years.[24]

An intensive summer ministerial training program grew out of the brotherhood Crusade for a Christian World at Peachtree Church. It sought to strengthen the Christian ministry in the South. The program began in 1948 when students enrolled for supervised study under the direction of James Lane Hooten. Georgia congregations thus had leaders available for vacation Bible schools, preaching, evangelistic campaigns, and commu-

---

[22]*Shane Quarterly*, Oct., 1943, p. 259.

[23]*Christian Messenger*, Mar., 1939, p. 5.

[24]Prominent ministers who died in 1930-49 included the following: Frank L. Adams, Daniel Abram Brindle, William Allen Chastain, Hamilton C. Dodson, A. B. Herring, M. B. Ingle, Wm. M. Jones, W. S. Martin, M. S. Moser, W. F. Mott, Wm. L. Reese, T. W. Salter, John V. Thomas, and Eli Simeal Clee Webb.

nity surveys. Other youth, too, were inspired to consider a life calling of Christian service. The students received honoraria from Peachtree with which to continue their academic work.

Three Negroes were the principal leaders of Georgia's Negro Christian churches during 1930-49. They were Lorenzo J. Evans, D. T. Williams, and H. J. Johnson.

Evans, state secretary-evangelist, 1935-1941, was supported by Negro churches and The United Christian Missionary Society cooperating with the Georgia State Board.[25] A graduate of Southern Christian Institute in 1932, while in Atlanta he received the B.A. degree in 1939 from Clark University and took graduate studies at Gammon Seminary. He enlisted in the Army chaplaincy, Mar. 17, 1942, spent two years overseas, and was discharged in October, 1945. He returned to his Atlanta home, purchased in 1944, and preached for Rocky Mount Church. He later became national director of Christian education for the National Christian Missionary Convention in Indianapolis, Ind.

Second Church, Atlanta, was organized by D. T. Williams, Apr. 14, 1932, and he became minister. He reorganized Christian Hope Church near Greston, Dodge County, in 1944. He was elected president of the Negro State Convention in 1935 and re-elected in 1948 and 1949. He was chosen one of the state evangelists in 1941.[26] H. J. Johnson, Valdosta, by 1946 had served one South Georgia congregation for 25 years, and preached for several others. He was president of the Negro State Convention a number of years, being re-elected in 1941 for a four-year term.[27]

---

[25]In 1930-31, perhaps longer, O. Zollar of Valdosta was Georgia state evangelist for Negro churches under The United Christian Missionary Society (*Christian Messenger*, Dec., 1930, p. 41).

[26]*Christian Messenger*, June, 1942, p. 1; Jan., 1945, p. 4; Dec., 1935, p. 8. *Minutes of the 53rd Annual State Convention of the Colored Christian Churches of Georgia, Held at McLendon Grove Church near Soperton, Georgia, From October 23 to 26, 1941* (Sandersville, Ga.: Progress Print, 1942?), p. 6.

[27]*Christian Messenger*, Nov., 1946, p. 8; Jan., 1943, p. 2. *Minutes . . . 1941, op. cit.*, p. 6.

D. D. Davis, another Valdosta preacher, was chairman of the 1930 Negro State Convention when there were 20 Negro churches in the state. A major action of the 1935 convention was electing a State Board to work in cooperation with the United Society.[28] The 1941, 1942, 1944, 1947, and 1948 conventions, and perhaps others, voted: "We believe in and support the program of Missions and urge each church to send a missionary offering to the United Christian Missionary Society . . . for each special day, Thanksgiving, Christmas, Easter and Children's Day."[29] The 1948 white Georgia State Convention voted to assist the Negro churches "in whatever way possible."[30] That was always the expressed policy, but apparently little was ever done, mainly because of inadequate finances.

THE GROWTH OF SEPARATISM

The dissension among Georgia Disciples that began in the turbulent twenties over doctrinal and organizational questions developed into a plague of distrust and discord during 1930-1949. More and more two separate groups emerged in the state brotherhood.

Actually there were always two types of Disciples, in Georgia and elsewhere. One sought to exemplify the spirit of Christ with reasonable expedients by means of which the church was able to meet changing conditions. However, strict constructionists tried to duplicate an absolute blueprint of the church which they sincerely believed the New Testament contained. Conflict and separatism appeared inevitable with such irreconcilable at-

---

[28]*Christian Messenger*, Dec., 1935, p. 8.

[29]*Minutes* . . . 1941, *op. cit.*, p. 10.

[30]*Christian Messenger*, Jan., 1949, p. 3. Among white Disciples at some Georgia Negro State Conventions, where they were always welcomed, were: Grant K. Lewis of The United Christian Missionary Society, Mr. and Mrs. Bruce Nay, Mr. and Mrs. John R. Chatfield (later missionaries under The United Christian Missionary Society to the Philippines and to the Belgian Congo), Miss Sue Steiner Hook, L. A. Cunningham, Wilbur T. Wallace, and Dr. and Mrs. T. L. Harris.

titudes. Jointly supported programs of missions, evangelism, and education, which strengthened the bonds of fellowship, yielded to separate, competing programs. Both types gradually developed aggressive, well-disciplined forces.

Through congregational autonomy local churches decided which group to support. A struggle, not always apparent when it began, occurred in several congregations. In the showdown of such tests of strength the leaders who were aware and alert and consequently moved first usually obtained control of local church properties.

Some independent preachers insisted on congregational officers signing creedal statements of opposition to The United Christian Missionary Society and Unified Promotion. Those who resisted, strong supporters of the organized work, then usually withdrew and formed another congregation. If independents failed to get control in a given church, then that faction would withdraw. Seldom was anyone expelled.

Strangely, open membership—the reception of other Christians by transfer of membership without immersion—was not the apparent cause of congregational division in Georgia as it was in other areas. Open membership seemed to have been practiced in Georgia about 1917, or before, the custom probably being introduced in the East Atlanta Church which later became the Community Christian Church. Owen Still discussed the matter in an article, "I Served an Open-Membership Church."[31] He was the pastor of the congregation for several years while a student at Southeastern Christian College. About 35 non-immersed persons, first called "associate members," were on the church roll when he took the pastorate.

Atlanta Christian College, reorganized in 1937, became a rallying center for the independents. Trustees and faculty met rigid creedal tests. The school had closed in

_____
[31]*Christian Standard*, May 9, 1925, pp. [763] f.

June, 1930, when M. B. Ingle was president.[32] George
W. BonDurant became president in 1939 after a year as
dean. He was a graduate of Cincinnati Bible Seminary.
His wife was formerly Sarah Presley of Capitol View
Church, Atlanta. In 1948 he became president of Roa-
noke Bible College, Elizabeth City, N. C.[33]

In 1943, Judge T. O. Hathcock promised to give the
school property valued at $10,000 which had been used
for seven years through the generosity of his wife. Mrs.
Hathcock, member of Jefferson Park Church, East Point,
was fatally wounded, Sept. 8, 1943, by a hit-and-run
motorist's automobile.[34] The property consisted of 15
acres of land and several small, frame buildings. A
boys' frame dormitory was built in 1945 when 45 students were enrolled.[35]

Early in 1948,[36] Orvel Calhoun Crowder became president of A.C.C. He received the A.B. degree, in 1937,
from Hiram (O.) College, an accredited liberal arts
school affiliated with the Board of Higher Education of
Disciples of Christ. He had taught for three years at
C.B.S., and held the M.A. degree from that conservative school. He also studied at Oberlin College and the
University of Cincinnati.[37]

There were eight resident teachers in 1949 and about
70 students. The group preached for 18 churches.
Robert O. Weaver, East Point minister, became chairman of the trustees in June, 1949, when Judge Hathcock
was named chairman-emeritus.[38] A frame dormitory

---

[32]*The Christian,* periodical of the Western District independent churches
had Paul V. Scott of Atlanta Christian College as editor in 1930 (*Christian
Messenger,* Apr., 1930, p. 3).

[33]*Horizons,* June, 1953, p. 20.

[34]*Christian Standard,* Sept. 18, 1943, p. 801; Oct. 2, 1943, p. 836.

[35]*Ibid.,* Dec. 18, 1943, p. 1083; Aug. 17, 1946, p. 567.

[36]John W. Eynon, another C.B.S. graduate, was president pro tem in
1948. He later became vice-president of the Winston-Salem (N. C.) Bible
College for Negroes (*Horizons,* June, 1953).

[37]*Restoration Herald,* Feb., 1948, p. 5.

[38]Trustees at the end of 1949 were: W. F. Aldridge, James Allgood,
Roy Davis, Horace H. Dunn, T. O. Hathcock, J. H. Hodges, J. E. Lipscomb,
Hugh D. Morgan, B. F. Morris, Aubrey L. Payne, Fred William Smith,
William Traylor, Robert O. Weaver, and Oren H. Whitton.

was built in 1949, but the non-accredited school possessed an extremely small library of limited range and debts continued to delay proposed expansion.[39]

Another manifestation of separatism was direct-supported missionaries. Competition for scarce missionary dollars was thus increased in many of the small and weak churches. Among the most prominent of these independent missionaries were Owen and Shirley (Swetnam) Still.[40] A native Georgian, Still was a home missionary of the American Christian Missionary Society in 1914 and subsequently minister of several Georgia churches. He became an evangelist for the Christian Restoration Association of Cincinnati in 1935, receiving $70.00 a month from that organization then.[41] In 1937, he reported, "During the last twelve months C.R.A. has only been able to pay its part on my salary for six months." His average monthly salary was then $136.67.[42]

The Stills and their four children left Atlanta, Sept. 25, 1937, for missionary work in Japan with the Yotsuya Mission of Emily B. (Mrs. W. D.) Cunningham. Mrs. Still was co-author, with Mrs. Cunningham, of *The Flaming Torch, The Life Story of W. D. Cunningham,* published in 1939. The Stills returned to the United States on furlough in June, 1941. The Cunningham Mission was incorporated in 1943; Judge T. O. Hathcock and George W. BonDurant were two incorporators.[43]

Mr. and Mrs. Still returned to Japan when post-war ocean travel was possible, but came back to the United States in 1948 for a year's sick leave "with salaries and

---

[39]*Christian Standard,* June 4, 1949, p. 358; Aug. 6, 1949, p. 500.

[40]Others from Georgia included: Harold and Lois Sims, Stanley R. and Mabel Buttray, serving in Japan, and James and Carol Herget in Jamaica.

[41]*Restoration Herald,* Sept., 1935, p. 3. Leon L. Myers succeeded Still as minister of Capitol View Church, Atlanta, and on Apr. 15, 1933, Myers became C.R.A. evangelist with headquarters in Atlanta. On May 1, 1934, he became president of the C.R.A. and editor of the *Restoration Herald* (*Restoration Herald,* Apr., 1933, p. 12; May, 1933, p. 4; May, 1934, cover).

[42]*Ibid.,* Sept., 1937, pp. 2, 4.

[43]*Christian Horizon,* Jan., 1944, p. 2.

house rent provided'' by vote of their mission colleagues in Japan. When Mrs. Still's illness prevented their return to Japan, they were dropped from the Cunningham Mission payroll on June 30, 1949.[44] They subsequently engaged in evangelistic work in the Hawaiian Islands.

The Georgia independents also used other means to express their separatism. Christian service camps were held in the summers, for a long period at Toccoa Falls. By 1949, the Georgia Christian Assembly, Crawfordville, was for older youth one week and young children another. In addition, a church workers' week was conducted at Atlanta Christian College.

In the late 1940's the independent ministers, under the leadership of Hugh D. Morgan, a Georgian who was graduated from the Cincinnati Bible Seminary, formed the Georgia Christian Ministerial Association. John W. Eynon was elected president with Morgan the secretary. J. Paul Morgan was president in 1949.[45]

Independent rallies and conventions under various names were conducted regularly. After a Savannah rally in 1946, R. O. Weaver, East Point minister who led the singing at the 1943 State Convention, said that the East Point brethren were ready ''to join in a movement under Christ to go forward in Georgia. We can't reform the Disciples denomination within or without.''[46] That decision reflected the increasing growth of separatism among Georgia Disciples. The first Southern Christian Convention met in Atlanta, Apr. 19-21, 1949, with 960 persons registered.[47]

Many independents apparently deplored the drift toward separatism as did a number of Disciples who supported the agencies of the organized brotherhood forces. Yet virtually nothing was being done in 1949 to halt its rapid spread.

[44]*Christian Standard*, June 4, 1949, pp. 358 f.

[45]*Restoration Herald*, Feb., 1950, p. 7.   Beford, *op. cit.*, pp. 240 f. *Christian Standard*, June 4, 1949, p. 358.

[46]*Restoration Herald*, Apr., 1946, p. 6.

[47]*Christian Standard*, Apr. 16, 1949, p. 243; Apr. 30, 1949, p. 277.

EXTENSION OF THE COOPERATIVE OUTREACH

Georgia Disciples gradually began to support, financially and otherwise, Christian unity as expressed by inter-church agencies. For the year ending June 30, 1949, six churches gave $157.50 to the Federal Council of the Churches of Christ in America.[48] The World Council of Churches, formally organized in 1948, also began to receive some support.

The Georgia Council of Churches was being formed by the end of 1949. The 1948 Macon State Convention of Disciples voted to participate in formation of the new inter-church group. The 1949 Centennial Convention approved a proposed constitution. A revised constitution, drafted by a committee of which Dr. Charles W. Ross, state secretary-director, was chairman, was adopted in 1951.[49]

After serving eight years as secretary of the Atlanta Christian Council, Maurice W. Marling resigned June 30, 1949. While holding the inter-church position, he was also pastor of the Acworth and Liberty (near Newnan) Churches. He took the pastorate of the Jasper, Ala., First Church. Harrison McMains, minister of Atlanta First Church, was president of the Council when Mr. Marling concluded his service.

The brotherhood's first World Convention met in Washington, D. C., in 1930 with 93 delegates present from 18 Georgia churches. The second assembly, in 1935 in Leicester, England, was attended by six Georgians: Mrs. Ida L. Chamberlin, Mr. and Mrs. Bruce Nay of Atlanta; Mr. and Mrs. A. D. Strobhar of Savannah and their niece, Miss Carolyn Salter.[50] The 1940 World Convention was postponed because of war, finally meeting

---

[48]The churches were: Community, First, and Peachtree of Atlanta, Poplar Springs near Sandersville, First of Savannah, and First of Valdosta (1949 *Year Book, Disciples of Christ*, p. 708).

[49]*Christian Messenger*, Jan., 1949, p. 3; Feb., 1952, p. 4.

[50]*Ibid.*, Nov., 1930, p. 5; July, 1935, p. 6; Aug., 1935, p. 4.

in Buffalo, N. Y., in 1947 with 41 present from Georgia.

A number from Georgia shared in the activities of the International Convention of Disciples of Christ which met nearly every year. A full-time staff opened headquarters in Indianapolis in 1946. The convention increasingly became the representative voice of Discipledom. Eighty from 26 Georgia churches were at the Cincinnati Centennial Convention of 1949. That year 14 churches of the state gave $353.50 for support of the convention.

During 1884-1949, Georgia Christian churches received 66 loans from the Board of Church Extension of Disciples of Christ totaling $315,680; several received more than one loan. Columbus Central Church was the only congregation in the state to receive a grant loan ($2,500) with no interest charges. During depression years the Board canceled past due interest amounting to $4,173.25 for seven Georgia churches. Charles O. McAfee, Macon, was elected a trustee of the Board in 1946.[51]

The Southern Christian Home's new building, completed in 1930, housed 32 children on June 30 that year. It was filled to capacity of 42 boys and girls in 1949, a staff of nine persons was required, and many children had to be refused admission. Approximately 500 children lived in the home from its founding to the end of 1949. The Bible school of First Christian Church provided transportation fare for the children to and from services every Sunday morning.

Contributions from many persons and churches in the Southeast supported the home. An outstanding supporter was Edwin Gould, New York Episcopalian who died in 1933. He visited the home twice and gave it more than $15,000 in less than two years. He said the home was one of the three best in the world. The White-

[51] *1951 Blue Book.* Annual Report for 1950 (Indianapolis: Board of Church Extension of Disciples of Christ, 1951), p. 12.

head Foundation contributed $2,000 in 1938. Operating
receipts for the year ending June 30, 1930, totaled
$11,594.44 while the 1949 budget amounted to $32,250.

In 1937 the Southern Christian Home became the first
children's home in the state to be licensed by the then
new Georgia Public Welfare Department. The home's
standards were above the state's minimum requirements. A. R. Mayfield was then president of the home's
Board of Supervisors. Irene J. (Mrs. H. A.) Watts in
December, 1948, completed 15 years as secretary of the
board. Mrs. Paul Weir was chairman of the board in
1949 when Paul Weir was representative on the National Benevolent Association's Board of Trustees.[52]

On Sept. 1, 1938, E. H. Koch became Southeastern
field representative for the benevolent work. He was the
first to hold the post since Belt White, representative for
20 years, relinquished it. Mr. Koch served until October,
1943. He was succeeded by H. E. Steele, born and reared
near Concord, on Feb. 1, 1944, when he concluded a ministry at Fitzgerald. Mr. Steele made his home in Macon
and continued to hold the post in 1949.

Illness forced Miss Sue Steiner Hook to retire as the
superintendent of the home on June 15, 1947. Born in
Augusta, she was the daughter of Judge James Schley
and Emily Jane (Harris) Hook. An oil painting of Miss
Hook by Louis Gregg was presented to the home by the
Preachtree women when she retired. About $5,000 for
the boys' building fund was received from three silver
teas. The first was in Miss Hook's honor in 1947 when
the fund totaled $32,000. It exceeded $45,000 at the 1949
Centennial State Convention. Plans for the Sue Steiner

---

[52]Georgia's 1949 ''Front Line Churches'' (giving $300 or more annually
for benevolence) were: $1,000 or more, Atlanta Peachtree; $500 or more,
Atlanta and Savannah First Churches; $300 or more, Augusta Central,
Macon First, Rome First. The churches that gave $1.00 or more per
member for benevolence that year were: Albany First; Peachtree; Bethesda,
Tennille; Guyton; Hall's Chapel; Lake Park; Liberty, Newnan; Loganville; Rome First; and Sylvania (*N.B.A. Family Talk*, Feb., 1950, pp.
14, 15, 16, 21).

Hook Boys' Building to provide living quarters for 24
boys were drawn that year and construction scheduled.
Over $30,000 from Georgia Crusade offerings went into
this building.

Miss Ida McMillan was Miss Hook's successor. Born
at Fitzgerald, she had resided 28 years in Washington,
D. C., where she was admitted to practice law and worked
with the Federal Treasury and the General Accounting
Office. She was the Crusade benevolence speaker at the
Centennial International Convention in Cincinnati in
1949.

The Georgia brethren gave nearly $40,000 to help erect
the National City Christian Church on Thomas Circle in
Washington, D. C.[53] That brotherhood campaign for
$1,500,000 was followed as the depression settled over
the nation by a drive for $8,000,000 to set up a minis-
terial Pension Fund. W. R. Lang, Sandersville layman,
was Georgia chairman of the Pension Fund committee.
Sixty-two churches gave to the state goal of $61,000.
Though slow to enlist, Georgia became the first state
to enroll the minimum number of churches with 45 committed by Sept. 15, 1930, and more than 40 preachers
enlisted. Georgia's first death benefit from the Pension
Fund occurred in 1939 when John H. Wood passed
away.[54]

Inflation and war-time needs brought about the Emergency Million for Life and Work during 1941-43. The
state goal was $12,000 with 42 churches contributing
$13,737.27. The State Board received $1,828.12 of the
fund for its program.[55]

---

[53]*Christian Messenger*, Dec., 1930, p. 8. A 1945 campaign to eliminate
the National City Church debt was for $150,000. Georgia's goal was
$1,712 with $1,341.10 contributed by Feb. 1, 1946 (*Christian Messenger*,
June, 1945, p. 1; Mar., 1946, p. 2).

[54]Bedford, *op. cit.*, p. 199. *Christian Messenger*, Dec., 1930, p. 7; Apr.,
1939, p. 1.

[55]*Christian Messenger*, Aug., 1943, p. 1; Sept., 1943, p. 3. *1943 Year
Book, Disciples of Christ*, p. 73.

"A Crusade for a Christian World," launched in 1946, focused attention of Disciples on urgent post-war religious needs. There were general objectives, specific program goals, and a financial aim of $14,000,000. When completed, 115 Georgia churches had contributed $153,-750.61 to reach 90.4 per cent of the state goal of $170,-049.16. The state thus ranked second in the nation, Utah with only two churches placing first. It was a real triumph of co-operation, one of the most outstanding achievements in the state brotherhood's history.[56]

Cecil A. Denney, Hugh T. Holland, and Luther M. Cole were annual Georgia Crusade chairmen. The state's success in raising funds was due undoubtedly to the use of annual specific projects, as follows: 1) $55,000 for establishing the Christian College of Georgia, 2) $30,000 for one wing of the boys' building at the Southern Christian Home, and 3) $30,000 for about 30 reconstruction projects in The United Christian Missionary Society Mission in the Philippine Islands. In addition, $20,000 was for Week of Compassion relief needs, $6,000 for the Georgia Council of Christian Women's special project, and $29,049.16 for undesignated work. Forty-seven churches completed or went beyond their financial goals.[57]

The same number of churches accepted the dozen or more comprehensive program goals.[58] Georgia goals that were exceeded included three pastoral unities instead of two—Griffin served by Wm. A. Everhart, Screven by H. E. Smith, and Poplar Springs-Tennille by Christie M. Harp. Then four instead of three new congregations were organized—Marietta, Brunswick, Brookhaven, and Macon Houston Ave.—by the end of 1949. The Thomasville church property was purchased by the State Board, Dec. 5, 1949.

---

[56]*Crusade Report: Prelude to a Decisive Decade* (Indianapolis: A Crusade for a Christian World, 1953), p. [17].

[57]*Christian Crusader*, Oct., 1950.

[58]*Ibid.*, Sept., 1949, p. 8.

Early in the Crusade, in 1947, Mr. and Mrs. John R. Chatfield left their effective ministry in Georgia to engage in missionary rebuilding labors in the Philippines for the United Society. He became Peachtree's third missionary link while she was the link of Decatur First Church.[59] Miss Leila Laman Callender was a pre-Crusade missionary to Mexico. She went out in 1944 after being ordained in Valdosta First Church and commissioned at Graham Chapel of Missions Building, Indianapolis. Savannah First built a church in the Philippines at Rizal City, just outside of Manila. The "Little Peachtree" Chapel was dedicated at San Luis Potosi, Mexico, Feb. 15, 1948. It was the gift of Commodore and Mrs. Virgil P. Warren with furnishings provided by other Atlanta Peachtree members.

Nationally, the Crusade results were disappointing since only $8,410,090.77 was finally raised. Non-cooperating Disciples maintained that the movement was just another raid on local church treasuries. Yet in Georgia only a few of the rigidly independent churches of the Atlanta and Savannah areas failed to participate in the Crusade.[60] The Crusade brought a greater concern to Disciples for evangelism, missions, education, benevolence, and stewardship. The cooperative forces of the state brotherhood were aggressively expectant because the seemingly impossible had been accomplished.

Attendance at the State Conventions, held annually by the Georgia Christian Missionary Society,[61] increased during 1930-1949. For instance, there were 143 dele-

---

[59]By 1950 Georgia churches supporting missionary links through The United Christian Missionary Society were: Atlanta First and Peachtree, Decatur First, Griffin First, Macon First, Savannah First, and Valdosta First.

[60]Bedford, *op. cit.*, p. 267.

[61]The legal charter of the G.C.M.S., was renewed in 1945 to expire on Apr. 22, 1980. Edgar R. Craighead, president of the Christian Men of Georgia, handled legal details (*Christian Messenger*, Feb., 1945, p. 5; May, 1945, p. 1).

gates from 28 churches in the 1930 Griffin sessions; 477
from 56 churches in 1944 at Atlanta Peachtree. The
Centennial State Convention met Nov. 14-16, 1949, with
the Griffin First Church, Nelson Schuster, minister, as
did the first one in 1849. Charles F. Schwab, Decatur
minister, was president. There were more than 500 registrations with 1,000 persons in attendance. A 10-year
program of advance was heartily recommended. A com-
memorative booklet was in demand as a souvenir. During those years the various district conventions continued to meet regularly.

A new national promotional plan began operation in
1935. Its origin was explained by Dr. Charles W. Ross
thus:

. . . Unified Promotion came into being in 1934, as a result of
the feeling that there was necessity for a unified and unifying
approach to the churches, and for elimination of both the
spirit and fact of competition for support from the churches
between different agencies.[62]

Dr. C. O. Hawley, executive director of Unified Promotion when it began to function on July 1, 1935, continued
in that capacity in 1949. The G.C.M.S. became a participating agency, Jan. 1, 1936, following approval of the
1935 Athens State Convention. Unified Promotion
slowly strengthened the spirit of cooperation inherent
in Discipledom. However, as always, income of the
State Board from U. P. ($4,919.38 in 1948-49) was never
enough for the needs.

Georgia's contributions through Unified Promotion to
brotherhood causes increased from $9,097.05 in 1935-36
to $25,037.63 in 1948-49. In addition, gifts to benevo-
lence in 1948-49 amounted to $8,484.16. By 1949 there

[62]*Biennial Meeting of the Home and State Missions Planning Council
of Disciples of Christ,* Hotel Claridge, St. Louis, Missouri, December 2-4,
1952 (n. p., n. d.,), p. 58.

were 10 Georgia churches giving more than $1,000 annually to Unified Promotion.[63]

The G.C.M.S. established a permanent fund in 1935 with a $3,000 annuity gift from Mrs. Ida L. Chamberlin of Atlanta.[64] On Dec. 31, 1946, when State Secretary Bruce Nay retired, the fund totaled $5,046.35. The money was later invested in the G.C.M.S. headquarters building at 1063 High St., Macon.[65] Claud Mayne was treasurer of G.C.M.S. funds, 1919-1938.[66] He was succeeded in November, 1938, by Charles O. McAfee, Macon manufacturer, who continued to hold the post in 1949.

State missionary aid helped to keep many Georgia Christian churches alive. In Jan., 1931, the *Christian Messenger* listed 63 such congregations. Some died, others are now non-cooperative. Increasingly, ministers, trained in accredited seminaries and supporters of the organized agencies, occupied town and city pulpits. The *Christian Messenger* had readers in 103 churches in 1939. Bruce Nay was editor through the Jan., 1947, issue; Charles F. Schwab was editor pro tem for the Feb.–Apr., 1947, numbers; Dr. Charles W. Ross was editor after the issue of May, 1947.[67] Charles B. Holder succeeded Dr. C. R. Stauffer as State Board chairman in

[63]A. T. Autry became minister at Guyton, near Savannah, Jan. 1, 1916, and was still there Dec. 31, 1949. For more than 30 years his congregation ranked first in the state for per capita giving to missions and benevolences (*Christian Messenger*, Jan., 1943, p. 3. Bedford, *op. cit.*, p. 187).

[64]Born at Watkinsville, Ga., Apr. 8, 1863, Mrs. Chamberlin was a charter member of the Athens First and Peachtree Churches. She gave nearly $50,000 to causes of the Disciples, including the Athens, Peachtree, and Brunswick churches, benevolence, the Pension Fund, Board of Church Extension, and the Christian College of Georgia (Mrs. Ida L. Chamberlin. Letter to J. Edward Moseley, written in Atlanta, Ga. Dated May 4, 1953. A. L. S.).

[65]*Christian Messenger*, Dec., 1947, p. 3.

[66]About 1939 Claud Mayne was named official chaplain of the Georgia State Prison at Reidsville, Tattnall County. He died Mar. 18, 1948, in Atlanta. For a few years, prior to 1942, another Disciple, Robert A. Preston, was the Federal Prison chaplain in Atlanta.

[67]*Christian Messenger*, Feb., 1947, p. 5. A Northeast Georgia News Letter, C. M. Driskell, Athens, editor, was announced in 1944 (*Christian Messenger*, Aug., 1944, p. 5; Oct., 1944, p. 2).

Nov., 1943. He served until Nov., 1947, when J. R. Farris was elected. Luther M. Cole was named chairman in 1948 and held the post at the end of 1949.

After 18 years as state secretary, Bruce Nay retired, Dec. 31, 1946, having held the position longer than any other person. He conducted revivals in 86 Georgia churches. His salary was often in arrears during the depression. He and his wife resided in Atlanta's Marion Hotel and when there was not enough cash to pay for meals, they cooked food over a gas burner in their one room that also doubled as a state office. He paid the rent and travel and postage expenses out of a salary that was only $2,400 at its highest level. He wrote frankly about these matters in an article that answered misleading charges about state missions' overhead costs.[68]

Nay was a vice-president and secretary of the brotherhood's National Association of State Secretaries. When he retired friends presented him with gifts of $1,100. He became pastor at Americus on Feb. 1, 1947,[69] going to Belvedere, S. C., on Oct. 1, 1948.

Dr. Charles William Ross became secretary-director of the G.C.M.S. in April, 1947, coming from the pastorate of the McLemore Avenue Christian Church, Memphis, Tenn. Former property of Macon First Church was bought for state offices. He immediately began administering an aggressive program of state missions, evangelism, church development, and Christian education. The state religious education commission was dissolved[70] and the Committee on Christian Education of the G.C.M.S. was organized. A state planning committee met annually with simultaneous and joint sessions of the state groups.

---

[68]*Ibid.*, Apr., 1943, p. 3.

[69]Former state secretaries who died, 1930-1949, were: John H. Wood, Mar. 19, 1939; Bernard P. Smith, Nov. 27, 1940; and Erastus Lamar Shelnutt, Mar. 28, 1941.

[70]Dr. C. R. Stauffer was chairman of the first commission appointed in 1930; other members were: Miss Estelle Bowles, Edgar R. Craighead, Olin E. Fox, Mrs. W. R. Lang, and Bruce Nay (*Christian Messenger*, Dec., 1930, p. 30). Through 1949 other chairmen included A. D. Strobhar, Edward T. Small, Charles F. Schwab, and Harry J. Berry.

The summer religious educational training program showed substantial growth. By 1949 the state had two accredited youth conferences and two Chi Rho (intermediate) camps. The first of the latter in 1946 enrolled 78 pupils from 23 churches. The first advanced youth conference met in 1948 with Florida participating in 1949. The first Southeastern adult conference was held in 1942.

The depression-caused decline in religious educational offerings forced a readjustment in the area leadership. While continuing the area program, E. B. Quick was also Florida secretary-evangelist, 1931-35. In 1940 he preached for the Red Oak and Corinth Churches while continuing as the Georgia and South Carolina director of religious education. He then became the South Carolina secretary-director, concluding his Georgia work on June 30, 1941.[71]

At the 1944 State Convention the Christian Men of Georgia elected Edgar R. Craighead of Peachtree Church their first president. The group sponsored projects and sought to correlate their work with that of the G.C.M.S., not to duplicate or overlap it. Charles O. McAfee, Macon, was named a charter member of the National Laymen's Advisory Commission of the Disciples when it was formed in 1946. Bernard S. Ramsey of Atlanta was elected president of the Christian Men of Georgia in 1949. The Centennial State Convention that year approved a recommendation that originated with Knowles Youngblood, a Peachtree layman, to call a full-time state director of men's work.[72] D. L. Havens and Wilbur T. Wallace were supported as district evangelists in Northeast Georgia.

---

[71]*Christian Messenger*, Jan., 1940, p. 5. *The Christian-Evangelist*, Feb. 13, 1941, p. 220.

[72]*World Call*, Feb., 1946, p. 4. *The Christian-Evangelist*, Feb. 2, 1950. Prominent Georgia laymen who died during 1930-1949 included: B. Frank Archer, C. M. Bailey, Capt. Fred A. Beach, John Cooper (chairman of the official board of Atlanta First Church for 37 years), J. R. Dasher, J. P. Downing, Ferdinand S. Drewry, L. M. Erwin, Thomas Belton Fullilove, J. C. Gentry, Dr. T. L. Harris, J. J. Jordan, Albert G. Lamar, and W. R. Lang.

The name of Mrs. Beach became familiar in Georgia women's work. Edith Rowley (Mrs. Fred A.) Beach, Savannah, served six years (1932-38) as president of the Georgia Women's Christian Missionary Society.[73] Then her daughter-in-law, Anne J. (Mrs. James Rowley) Beach, became state secretary on the customary part-time basis in November, 1941, continuing through 1949. Nancy B. (Mrs. L. O.) Turner was secretary during 1930-1941, resigning because of her husband's illness.

In 1945 the women changed the name of their state group to the Georgia Council of Christian Women since the organization had outgrown strictly missionary endeavor.[74] Therefore, the State Board was organized on a functional basis representative of the wide range of Christian women's personal and service outreach interests. On May 13, 1949, the first Georgia Christian Women's Fellowship was organized at Marietta First Church with Mrs. C. M. Roberts elected president. The new name was later widely adopted throughout the state and internationally for Disciple women's organizations.[75]

Mrs. C. R. Stauffer was the first president of the Georgia Council of Ministers' Wives when it was formed

[73]Presidents of the state women's board during 1930-1949 were: Mrs. W. R. Lang, 1930-32; Mrs Fred A. Beach, 1932-38; Corinne Berry (Mrs. Harper A.) Tucker, 1938-1944; Mrs. Homer R. Hulse, 1944-45; Elizabeth (Mrs. D. John) Brodmann, 1945-49. Secretaries were: Mrs. E. B. Quick, 1930; Mrs. L. O. Turner, 1930-1941; Mrs. James R. Beach, 1941-49. Treasurers were: Mrs. J. W. Ferguson, 1914-31; Mrs. L. E. Anthony, 1931-36; Mrs. R. H. O'Kelley, 1936-1944; Mrs. Estelle Crossfield, 1944-45; Mrs. Luther M. Cole, 1945-49.

[74]In 1930, 48 Georgia missionary organizations with 1,593 members gave $6,190.35 to the United Society (*1930 Year Book, Disciples of Christ*, p. 115). By June 30, 1949, the women had 99 organizations with 2,638 members contributing $11,501.34 through Unified Promotion (*1949 Year Book, Disciples of Christ*, p. 72).

[75]*Christian Messenger*, June, 1949, p. 7. Women of the Atlanta area organized for fellowship at Peachtree Church on Mar. 23, 1943, with 100 present from nine churches (*Christian Messenger*, Mar., 1943, p. 1).

Prominent Christian women who died during 1930-1949 included: Mrs. Fred A. Beach, Mrs. Jennie Darnell, Miss Eugie Dasher, Mrs. W. H. Hayes, Mrs. Joseph Rucker Lamar, Mrs. Lane Mitchell, Miss Mattie Mitchell, Mrs. W. L. Reese, Mrs. Flora S. Swetnam, and Nanna Crozier (Mrs. John H.) Wood. Mrs. Wood died Feb. 23, 1939. She was once a field worker for the C.W.B.M. Mrs. Lamar died in 1943 and Miss Mitchell on Oct. 17, 1944.

in 1930. The National Council had been organized in
Atlanta in 1914 by Mrs. Walter M. White. Agnes Neff
(Mrs. Robert W.) Burns was honored with the national
presidency in 1947 and presided at sessions in San Fran-
cisco, Calif., during the 1948 International Convention.[76]

Georgia Disciple women brought outstanding recognition to the state brotherhood and exercised considerable influence through interdenominational positions
they held. Mrs. C. R. Stauffer was re-elected president
of both the Georgia and the Atlanta Councils of Church
Women. Mrs. Chester E. Martin also held the position
with both Councils. Mrs. L. O. Turner was a president
of the State Council. Mrs. James R. Beach organized
and was first president of the Savannah Council. Mrs.
Charles Mathis organized the observance of the World
Day of Prayer in Macon in 1933, from which came the
Macon Council, and was twice president of that Council.
Mrs. John H. Wood was a founder of the Rome Council.

Mrs. James F. Whitehead, Athens, was Georgia's
1949 Mother-of-the-Year. Mrs. Frances Craighead
Dwyer was the 1946 Atlanta Woman-of-the-Year. Member of Peachtree Church, she is the daughter of Mr.
and Mrs. Edgar R. Craighead. An attorney-at-law herself, she is the wife and daughter of lawyers. She was
Georgia chairman of the Association of Southern Women
for the Prevention of Lynching.[77]

The 1940's witnessed increased participation of
Georgia Disciple youth in the United Christian Youth
Movement, organization of the Georgia Christian Youth
Fellowship, the first State C.Y.F. Convention, and the
gradual extinction of Christian Endeavor societies.[78]

The State C.Y.F. was organized in 1944 and Miss
Camille Jackson, shortly afterward to become Mrs.
Donald Harp, was elected the first president. Charles

[76]*Christian Messenger,* Dec., 1930, p. 21. *The Christian-Evangelist,*
Oct. 29, 1944, p. 1394.

[77]*Christian Messenger,* Apr., 1935, p. 2; June, 1947, p. 4.

[78]Disciple presidents of the Georgia Christian Endeavor Union during
1930-1949 included the following: Carl Cooper, Miss Helen Cox, Edward
Kicklighter, Roy Miller, Bruce Nay, and Miss Florence Williams.

O. McAfee, Jr., Macon, and Miss Martha Whitehead, Athens, were chosen vice-presidents and Miss Dorothy Weatherly, Atlanta, secretary. Miss Whitehead was elevated to the presidency in 1947.[79] The first Georgia C.Y.F. Convention met at Griffin, Feb. 5-6, 1949, with 206 persons present. Newton B. Fowler, Jr., of Atlanta, later quite prominent in brotherhood youth and student work, presided.[80]

AN EMPIRICAL APPROACH TO EDUCATION

If the task of a minister be difficult—and it was no bed of roses in Georgia—how much more so was the struggle to get an adequate ministerial education. Many Georgia congregations had closed for lack of trained preachers. Fortunately, the Disciples were not lacking when their day of educational opportunity arrived. Without hesitation they met the need for an accredited educational institution. The establishment of the Christian College of Georgia at Athens, adjacent to the University of Georgia, was to prove a quickening influence to the state brotherhood.

A half century before, Georgia Disciples dreamed of an educational institution in the state to educate ministers. In the late 1890's, loyal women struggled in vain because of inadequate funds to launch the Georgia Bible Chair.[81] The founding of the Christian College of

---

[79]*Christian Messenger*, Dec., 1944, p. 5; Dec., 1947, p. 2. On Dec. 27, 1949, Miss Whitehead began her professional Christian educational career with The United Christian Missionary Society in Indianapolis, Ind. (*Christian Messenger*, Jan., 1950, p. 3.)

[80]*Ibid.*, Mar., 1949, pp. 4 f.

[81]Schools started after 1900 were: Jackson Bible School at Valdosta, Christian Academy (for Negroes) at Athens, Lamar College, Southeastern Christian College, Dasher Bible School that developed into Georgia Christian Institute, and Atlanta Christian College. Only the last two survived in 1949.

In 1949 Georgia Christian Institute continued under the sponsorship of anti-organ Churches of Christ near Valdosta. Irven Powell Lee was principal, 1938-1942; W. O. Norton was superintendent in 1942. Also, Lacy H. Elrod served as president and Prewitte Copeland as dean. The original building burned in 1932. Additions to existing structures were built in 1940 and 1946. New dormitories were erected in 1941 and 1943 and three other buildings in 1947 and 1949.

Georgia as an accredited undergraduate school meant that after 50 years the Disciples were returning to Athens. That type of school was succeeding on several American campuses.

In 1928, and perhaps before, Stanley R. Grubb, twice minister at Athens, sensed the need for an educational program in connection with the University of Georgia. Lack of funds prevented a student program in the 1920's and he was prevailed upon to yield hope for an Athens school for other experiments. Seeing the failure of other schools because of competing interests and personality clashes, among other factors, he realized anew the need for the Athens project. He then declared:

> . . . It is my conviction that here in this city, taking advantage of all that the State offers, we can, for a comparatively small sum of money, do a great work in preparing young men for the ministry and other religious work. We have a large group of churches which could be served by students from such an institution. Many of these churches are almost without preaching under present conditions.
>
> . . . .
>
> . . . To our mind this is the outstanding need of our cause in this section now. The sum of $200,000 would enable us to make a good beginning.[82]

Such a prophet ought not to be without honor among his own brethren. It was fitting that his wife should be privileged to turn the first spade of earth at groundbreaking ceremonies for the Christian College of Georgia in 1948.[83]

The idea of establishing a Bible Chair and student center was proposed by Elmer N. Anthony in the autumn of 1945 at a meeting in Atlanta First Church. Approval came in 1946 from the Christian ministers meeting in Macon. Then, in the spring of 1946, the State Board appointed a committee to locate a building site. The Georgia Christian Missionary Society purchased a lot

[82]*Christian Standard,* Oct. 27, 1928, p. 1110. Mr. Grubb concluded his last ministry with Athens First Church in 1936. He died at Columbia, S. C., May 3, 1939, at the age of 63.

[83]*The Christian-Evangelist,* Aug. 4, 1948.

on Hull Street, Athens, in September, 1946. On Nov. 8, 1946, the State Board voted to set aside $50,000 of Georgia receipts from the brotherhood Crusade for the project. The 1946 State Convention heartily favored establishing the chair of religion and student center. The educational project enlarged as it matured and it was decided to name it the Christian College of Georgia.

Edgar R. Craighead, Atlanta layman, gave enthusiastic leadership to raising the necessary funds. His address before the 1947 State Convention at Waycross inspired M. M. Monroe of that city to hand him a check for $1,000. W. Clare Harris gave $1,000 on the cost of the lot and at least $5,000 for the building. Elmer N. Anthony contributed $5,000 with credit to his churches, Mt. Vernon and Monroe. C. O. McAfee, Macon, later gave $9,798.04 in a challenge that led others to give amounts sufficient to complete the dormitory facilities.

President Harmon White Caldwell of the University encouraged the Christian College of Georgia. After opening, the new school became affiliated with the Board of Higher Education of Disciples of Christ. Dr. Robert W. Burns and Dr. Woodrow W. Wasson were the first members of the Board in behalf of Georgia Disciples.

Twelve trustees were elected at the 1947 State Convention. In 1949 the board was expanded to a membership of 24. The first trustees were the following: Elmer N. Anthony, chairman; Paul C. Howle, vice-chairman; W. Clare Harris, treasurer; Edgar R. Craighead, executive secretary, and Harry J. Berry, D. John Brodmann, Robert W. Burns, W. Glenn Carter, Walter B. Hearn, Charles O. McAfee, C. B. Mankin, and E. Guy Orahood.[84]

About 300 persons attended the ground-breaking for the Christian College of Georgia, July 4, 1948, on the South Hull Street lot, one block from the main campus.

[84]*Christian Messenger*, Dec., 1947, p. 2. The 12 other trustees elected in 1949, upon authorization of the State Convention, were: W. H. Artley, George East, Fletcher Findley, W. R. Hutchison, W. A. Joyner, Harrison McMains, M. M. Monroe, J. Glover Morris, Edward S. Reese, Nixon O. Taylor, John Park Winkler, and Knowles Youngblood (*The Christian-Evangelist*, Dec. 7, 1949, p. 1224. *Christian Messenger*, Dec., 1949, p. 6).

United States Senator Richard B. Russell was the speaker. The new building was dedicated, July 3, 1949, with an address by Dr. Robert W. Burns. It was the persistence and labors of Elmer N. Anthony, Edgar R. Craighead, Paul C. Howle, and Dr. Burns, more than any others, who brought the dream to realization.

The incomplete, two-story structure provided the dean's residence and a men's dormitory. The rooms for 18 students were quickly rented when the new building was opened. Preference was given to Disciples taking classes in the new Christian College of Georgia. However, rooms were available to men of all denominations on a first-come, first-served basis.

Chartered by the Superior Court of the State of Georgia, Nov. 14, 1947, the Christian College had a three-fold purpose: 1) to provide leadership for Disciple students; 2) to house Disciple men and train those preparing for the ministry; and 3) to offer religious instruction to any student, with university credit, without extra tuition. Up to 15 quarter hours of credit were to be accepted by the University of Georgia for any student.

Dr. Woodrow Wilson Wasson, formerly identified with the conservative, anti-organ Churches of Christ, was chosen as dean to direct activities and to teach classes. He held the A.B. and A.M. degrees from Vanderbilt University and the B.D. and Ph.D. degrees from The University of Chicago. He came to Georgia from the University of Houston where he was professor of religion. His book, *James A. Garfield, His Religion and Education,* was based on his doctoral dissertation.[85]

When the Christian College of Georgia opened in September, 1949 (classes began on Sept. 26), the University of Georgia had 7,700 students. James Lane Hooten, aspiring preacher reared in Atlanta Peachtree Church, enrolled as the first student in Christian College. He was in the U. S. Navy, 1945-46, and studied at the Georgia Institute of Technology two years before decid-

---

[85]*Christan Messenger,* Dec., 1949, p. 7. *World Call,* July-Aug., 1953, p. 4.

ing for the ministry in 1948. He was the preacher in 1949 for the Bogart and Statham churches. He thus represented the high type of ministerial student which the founders of the Christian College of Georgia knew were necessary to meet the needs of Georgia Christian churches.

The first course, "The Origin and Early History of Christianity," enrolled seven students, including Miss Martha Whitehead, the only young woman in the class. The Disciples' Student Fellowship was formed in November "to relate religion to the problems and interests of students at the University." Its representative to the University Religious Association was Miss Whitehead. Miss Carolyn Newton was elected the first D. S. F. president. During the first year, there were 13 students enrolled, six of them being ministerial.

The churches contributed $9,051.35 to the Christian College of Georgia its first year, 1949-1950. Total income and expenditures amounted to $17,183.39 and gross assets were $102,000. There was a $40,000 indebtedness when the school opened, since paid in full. From the beginning of the project, however, the churches and their leaders seemed determined that the new educational program would be undergirded with adequate and regular financial support.

The Christian College of Georgia offered the means of formidable advance for Georgia Disciples. Realization of the long-cherished educational dream indicated a better day for those cherishing a glorious heritage. A century of cooperation was completed and for better or for worse the Georgia Disciples of Christ faced the unknown future with its continuing challenges and opportunities.

Appendix

Georgia State Conventions, 1849-1949

Date	Church	President
Date	*Church*	*President*
1849 Sept. 15	Griffin (School)	
1850 Sept. 13-14	Griffin First	
1851 Oct. 10-12	Griffin First	
1852-1853 Data unavailable		
1854 Oct. 6-8	Griffin First	
1855 Oct. 11-14	Clarke County	Dr. Daniel Hook
1856 Oct. 10-12	Atlanta First	Dr. Daniel Hook
1857 Oct. 16-18	Atlanta First	
1858-1869 Data unavailable		
1870 Nov. 4-6	Atlanta First	James S. Lamar
1871 Sept. 20-21	Atlanta First	James S. Lamar
1872		James S. Lamar
1873-1878 Data unavailable		
1879 Nov. 20-21	Atlanta First	Nathan W. Smith
1880 Nov. 10-12	Atlanta First	James S. Lamar
1881 Nov. 9-11	Augusta First	James S. Lamar
1882 Nov.1-3	Atlanta First	Dr. A. G. Thomas
1883 Oct. 10-12	Atlanta First	Dr. A. G. Thomas

Date	Church	President
1884 Oct. 7-10	Atlanta First	Dr. A. G. Thomas
1885 Nov. 4-5	Augusta First	Dr. A. G. Thomas
1886	Atlanta	
1887	Atlanta Central	
1888 Oct. 17	Griffin First	Dr. A. G. Thomas
1889	Acworth First	R. M. Mitchell
1890		
1891 Nov.	Atlanta First	
1892 Nov.	Atlanta First	
1893 Oct. 24-26	Atlanta First	T. H. Blenus
1894	Augusta First	C. P. Williamson
1895		
1896 Nov.	Athens First	
1897 Nov. 14-18	Sandersville First	Wallace Tharpe
1898 Nov. 14-17	Macon First	
1899 Nov. 15-?	Atlanta First	
1900 Nov. 21-23	Augusta First	W. A. Chastain
1901 Nov. 18-21	Atlanta West End	E. L. Shelnutt
1902 Nov. 17-19	Winder First	A. B. Phillips
1903 Nov. 16-19	Macon First	S. B. Moore
1904 Nov. 15-18	Savannah First	R. Lin Cave
1905 Nov. 6-9	Athens First	J. H. Hughes
1906 Nov. 19-22	Valdosta First	Howard T. Cree
1907 Nov. 18-21	Atlanta First	Howard T. Cree
1908 Nov. 9-11	Fitzgerald Central	H. King Pendleton
1909 Nov. 2-5	Winder First	Thomas E. Patterson
1910 Nov. 1-3	Dublin First	Thomas E. Patterson

Date	Church	President
1911 Nov. 7-9	Augusta First	L. O. Bricker, *v-p*
1912 Nov. 5-8	Rome First	Thomas E. Patterson
1913 Nov. 10-14	Macon First	Allen Rice Moore
1914 May 5-7	Valdosta First	Stanley R. Grubb
1915 May 3-6	Griffin First	W. H. Roper
1915 Nov. 1-4	Winder First	W. O. Perry
1916 Nov. 14-16	Athens First	W. F. Mott
1917 Nov. 13-15	Fitzgerald Central	L. M. Omer
1918 Nov. 12-15	Atlanta First	Allen Wilson
1919 Nov. 17-19	West Point	R. W. Wallace

(Joint Convention with Alabama)

Date	Church	President
1920 Nov. 9-11	Augusta First	J. Randall Farris
1921 Nov. 1-3	Sandersville First	E. Guy Orahood
1922 Nov. 13-15	Macon First	L. O. Bricker
1923 Nov. 13-15	Athens First	B. F. Foster
1924 Nov. 4-6	Rome First	Wright T. Moore
1925 Nov. 3-5	Fitzgerald Central	J. Randall Farris
1926 Oct. 19-21	Savannah First	Bruce Nay
1927 Oct. 18-20	Atlanta First	E. C. Lucas
1928 Oct. 23-25	Winder First	C. R. Stauffer
1929 Nov. 12-14	Waycross First	E. C. Lacy
1930 Nov. 18-20	Griffin First	W. R. Lang
1931 Nov. 17-19	Atlanta Peachtree	A. Douglas Strobhar
1932 Nov. 15-17	Macon First	Robert W. Burns
1933 Nov. 14-16	Savannah First	T. W. Bowen
1934 Nov. 13-15	Valdosta First	W. Glenn Carter
1935 Nov. 12-14	Athens First	Edward T. Small

Date	Church	President
1936 Nov. 17-19	Atlanta First	W. A. Joyner
1937 Nov. 16-18	Fitzgerald Central	Charles B. Holder
1938 Nov. 15-17	Dublin First	Hoke S. Dickinson
1939 Nov. 15-17	Winder First	Vere H. Rogers
1940 Nov. 13-15	Rome First	W. Clifford Foster
1941 Nov. 12-14	Savannah First	Charles L. Garrison
1942 Nov. 11-13	Atlanta First	Robert S. Bennett
1943 Nov. 16-18	Athens First	L. A. Cunningham
1944 Nov. 14-16	Atlanta Peachtree	George D. West
1945 Nov. 19-21	Macon First	J. Glover Morris
1946 Nov. 18-20	Mount Vernon near Monroe	Elmer N. Anthony
1947 Nov. 17-19	Waycross First	Paul C. Howle
1948 Nov. 15-17	Macon First	Emmett A. McNabb
1949 Nov. 14-16	Griffin First	Charles F. Schwab

NEGRO STATE CONVENTIONS, 1889-1949

1889-1904 Data unavailable		
1905 Oct. 19-22	Eastman	W. H. Smith
1906	Mullis Grove near Cadwell	
1907-1917 Data unavailable		
1918 Nov. 21-24	Eastman	W. H. Smith
1919 Oct. 23-25	Springfield Mount Olive	W. H. Smith
1920 Oct. 21-24	Valdosta Evergreen	W. H. Smith
1921 Oct. 19-23	Atlanta Rocky Mount	W. H. Smith
1922-1926 Data unavailable		

Date	Church	President
1927 Oct. 20-23	Eastman	W. H. Smith
1928 Oct. 25-28	Welcome Hope near Barney	W. H. Smith
1929 Oct. 24-27	Valdosta Evergreen	C. E. Edwards
1930 Oct. 23-26	Bethesda near Oconee	D. D. Davis
1931-1934 Data unavailable		
1935 Oct. 24-27	Bethesda near Oconee	D. T. Williams
1936 Oct. 22-25	Pine Hill near Cadwell	
1937 Oct. 21-24	Welcome Hope near Barney	
1938 Oct. 18-23	Bethesda near Oconee	
1939 Data unavailable		
1940 Oct. 24-27	Welcome Hope near Barney	
1941 Oct. 23-26	McLendon Grove near Soperton	H. J. Johnson
1942 Oct. 22-26	Welcome Hope near Barney	H. J. Johnson
1943 Oct. 21-24	Pine Hill near Cadwell	H. J. Johnson
1944 Oct. 19-22	Bethesda near Oconee	H. J. Johnson
1945 Oct. 25-28	Welcome Hope near Barney	H. J. Johnson
1946 Oct. 24-27	Eastman	H. J. Johnson
1947 Oct. 23-25	Bethesda near Oconee	H. J. Johnson
1948 Oct. 21-24	Welcome Hope near Barney	D. T. Williams
1949 Oct. 20-23	Pine Hill near Cadwell	D. T. Williams

A Selected Bibliography

BOOKS

COULTER, ELLIS MERTON. *Georgia: A Short History*. Rev. and enlarged ed.; Chapel Hill: University of North Carolina Press, 1947. xii + 510 pp.

DAVIDSON, ROBERT. *History of the Presbyterian Church in the State of Kentucky*. New York: Robert Carter; Lexington, Ky.: Charles Marshall, 1847. xii + 371 pp.

GARRISON, WINFRED ERNEST. *Religion Follows the Frontier;* A History of the Disciples of Christ. New York: Harper & Brothers, 1931. xiv + 317 pp.

—— and ALFRED THOMAS DEGROOT. *The Disciples of Christ: A History*. St. Louis: Christian Board of Publication, 1948. 592 pp.

History of the Baptist Denomination in Georgia. With Biographical Compendium and Portrait Gallery of Baptist Ministers and Other Georgia Baptists. Compiled for the *Christian Index*. Atlanta: Jas. P. Harrison & Co., 1881. viii + 613 + iv pp.

HOWELL, CLARK. *History of Georgia*. 4 vols.; Chicago-Atlanta: S. J. Clarke Publishing Co., 1926.

JONES, JOHN WILLIAM. *Christ in the Camp;* or, Religion in Lee's Army. Supplemented by a Sketch of the Work in the Other Confederate Armies. Richmond, Va.: B. F. Johnson & Co., 1887. 624 pp.

KNIGHT, LUCIAN LAMAR. *Georgia's Landmarks, Memorials and Legends.* 2 vols.; Atlanta: Byrd Printing Co. Vol. I 1913, xi + 1065 pp. Vol. II, 1914, x + 1190 pp.

LAMAR, CLARINDA PENDLETON. *The Life of Joseph Rucker Lamar, 1857-1916.* New York: G. P. Putnam's Sons, 1926. vii + 284 pp.

LAMAR, JAMES SANFORD. *Memoirs of Isaac Errett,* With Selections From His Writings. 2 vols.; Cincinnati: Standard Publishing Co., 1893.

LOVE, E. K. *History of the First African Baptist Church;* from its organization, January 20th, 1788, to July 1st, 1888. Savannah, Ga.: Morning News Print, 1888. 360 pp.

MCNEMAR, RICHARD. *The Kentucky Revival* . . . Cincinnati: Printed; Albany: Reprinted by E. & E. Hosford, 1808. 119 pp.

MARTIN, THOMAS H. *Atlanta and Its Builders.* A Comprehensive History of the Gate City of the South. 2 vols.; Atlanta: Century Memorial Publishing Co., 1902. I, xii + 718 pp; II, x + 723 pp.

MILLER, ANNIE ELIZABETH (Compiler). *Our Family Circle.* Macon, Ga.: J. W. Burke Co., 1931.

Mudge, Enoch. *History of American Missions to the Heathen,* From Their Commencement to the Present Time. Worcester, Mass.: Spooner & Howland, 1840. 726 pp.

Nixon, Raymond B. *Henry W. Grady, Spokesman of the New South.* New York: Alfred A. Knopf, 1943. x + 360 + xiv pp.

Oats, Sergeant [John Beverly Vawter]. *Prison Life in Dixie.* Giving a Short History of the Inhuman and Barbarous Treatment of Our Soldiers by Rebel Authorities. . . . Chicago: Central Book Concern, 1880. 209 pp.

Orr, Dorothy. *A History of Education in Georgia.* Chapel Hill: University of North Carolina Press, 1950. xiv + 463 pp.

Ragsdale, B. D. *Story of Georgia Baptists.* Vol. I. Atlanta: Foote & Davies Co., 1932. 361 pp.

Reed, Wallace P. *History of Atlanta, Georgia,* With Illustrations and Biographical Sketches of Some of Its Prominent Men and Pioners. Syracuse, N. Y.: D. Mason & Co., 1889. 491 + 211 pp.

Robinson, Gil. *Old Wagon Show Days.* Cincinnati: Brockwell Co., 1925. 250 pp.

Rogers, John. *The Biography of Eld. Barton Warren Stone,* Written by Himself: With Additions and Reflections. 5th ed.; Cincinnati: J. A. and U. P. James, 1847. 404 pp.

Sabin, Joseph. *A Dictionary of Books Relating to America,* From Its Discovery to the Present Time. 29 vols.; New York: J. Sabin's Son, 1885. Vol. XV, 582 pp.

Simms, James M. *The First Colored Baptist Church in North America.* Constituted at Savannah, Georgia, January 20, A.D. 1788, With Biographical Sketches of the Pastors. Philadelphia: J. B. Lippincott & Co., 1888. 264 pp.

Spencer, Claude Elbert (Compiler). *An Author Catalog of Disciples of Christ and Related Religious Groups.* Canton, Mo.: Disciples of Christ Historical Society, 1946. 367 pp.

Stacy, James. *A History of the Presbyterian Church in Georgia.* Elberton, Ga.: Press of the *Star,* 1912. 404 pp.

Starr, Emmet. *History of the Cherokee Indians and Their Legends and Folklore.* Oklahoma City: Warden Co., 1921. 680 pp.

Stevenson, Dwight Eshelman. *Walter Scott: Voice of the Golden Oracle.* St. Louis: Christian Board of Publication, 1946. 240 pp.

Strickland, Reba Carolyn. *Religion and the State in Georgia in the Eighteenth Century.* New York: Columbia University Press, 1939. 211 pp.

Strobel, P. A. *The Salzburgers and Their Descendants;* Being the history of a colony of German (Lutheran) Protestants who emigrated to Georgia in 1734, and settled at Ebenezer, twenty-five miles above the city of Savannah. Baltimore: T. Newton Kurtz, 1855. 308 pp.

SWEET, WILLIAM WARREN. *Religion on the American Frontier: The Baptists, 1783-1830*. Vol. I. New York: Henry Holt & Co., 1931. ix + 652 pp.

———. *Religion on the American Frontier: The Presbyterians, 1783-1840*. Vol. II. Chicago: University of Chicago Press, 1936. xii + 939 pp.

TIERS, M. C. *The Christian Portrait Gallery;* Consisting of Historical and Biographical Sketches and Photographic Portraits of Christian Preachers and Others. Cincinnati: Author, 1864. 254 pp.

WARE, CHARLES CROSSFIELD. *Barton Warren Stone;* Pathfinder of Christian Union, A Story of His Life and Times. St. Louis: Bethany Press, 1932. xiv + 357 pp.

WHITE, GEORGE. *Historical Collections of Georgia*. 3rd ed.; New York: Pudney & Russell, 1855. xvi + 4 + 688 + 41 pp.

———. *Statistics of the State of Georgia*. Savannah: W. Thorne Williams, 1849. 624 + 77 pp.

Year Book of Disciples of Christ. 1888, 1916, 1920, 1921, 1922, 1923, 1924, 1925, 1929, 1930, 1943, 1949.

PAMPHLETS

Annual Reports of Georgia Christian Missionary Society. n. p., 1904. [12] pp.

Annual Report of the Christian Churches in Georgia. For 1900. Convention Minutes of the State Society, Woman's Society for Georgia Missions, Christian Woman's Board of Missions, North East Georgia Co-operation, and Educational Society. Atlanta: Evangelist Publishing Co., 1900? 32 pp.

BOLLES, MR. AND MRS. H. D. "A History of the First Christian Church, Atlanta, Georgia, 1851-1951," in *One Hundred Years of the First Christian Church, Atlanta, Georgia*, Centennial Celebration, 1851-1951. Edited by Marie Townsend. Atlanta: Cullom & Ghertner Co., 1951. [48] pp.

BROOKES, IVESON L. [A Southern Clergyman]. *A Defence of Southern Slavery. Against the Attacks of Henry Clay and Alex'r. Campbell.* In which much of the false philanthropy and mawkish sentimentalism of the abolitionists is met and refuted. In which it is moreover shown that the association of the white and black races in the relation of master and slave is the appointed order of God, as set forth in the Bible, and constitutes the best social condition of both races, and the only true principle of republicanism. 2nd ed.; Hamburg, S. C.: Robinson and Carlisle, 1851. 48 pp.

BURSON, MARY WRIGHT, ARLEVIA BURSON, AND BELLE WRIGHT PHILLIPS. *One Hundred Years at Mt. Vernon Christian Church (Near Monroe, Ga.) 1842-1942.* n. p., 1942? 16 pp.

DARSIE, GEORGE. *Twenty-Five Years at Kentucky's Capital.* A Sermon Preached at Frankfort, Ky., December 7th, 1902. St. Louis: Christian Publishing Co., 1902? 16 pp.

DOWLING, LEVI H. (Compiler). *The Christian Almanac.* Indianapolis: L. H. Dowling, 1867. 60 pp.

The General Convention of Churches of Christ. The Report of
the Executive Committee. Presented to the General Convention, Atlanta, Georgia, October 6, 1914. n. p., 1914.
8 pp.

GREEN, FRANCIS MARION. *Preachers of the Churches of Christ
in the United States.* Cincinnati: F. M. Green, 1880.
[56] pp.

HALL, ALEXANDER WILFORD (Compiler). *The Christian Register,*
containing a statistical report of the Christian churches
in Europe and America. Loydsville, Belmont County,
Ohio: Alexander Hall, 1848. [50] pp.

*In Memoriam. Mrs. Emily H. Tubman, born March 21st, 1794.
Died June 9th, 1885.* n. p., n. d. 27 pp.

KING, WILLIAM. *A Discourse Concerning the Inventions of Men
in the Worship of God.* Philadelphia: Jesper Harding,
1828. 94 pp.

LAMAR, JAMES SANFORD. *Recollections of Pioneer Days in Georgia.* n. p. 1906? 64 pp.

————. *What Is the Christian Church? or, Who Are the Dis-
ciples of Christ?* Reprinted from *Frank Leslie's Sunday
Magazine.* Cincinnati: Tract Committee of the General
Christian Missionary Convention, 1883. 12 pp.

MARSHALL, ROBERT, DUNLAVY, JOHN, MCNEMAR, RICHARD,
STONE, BARTON W., THOMPSON, JOHN. *An Abstract of An
Apology, For Renouncing the Jurisdiction of the Synod of*

Kentucky. Being a Compendious View of the Gospel, and a Few Remarks on the Confession of Faith. Lexington, Ky.: n. p., 1804? 72 pp.

MILLER, ANNIE CHARLOTTE (Mrs. Bert O.). *"Antioch" the Mother Church of the Disciples in Georgia.* Atlanta: E. W. Allen and Co., 1904. 16 pp.

Report of the Proceedings of the General Convention of the Christian Churches of the U.S.A. For 1849, 1856, 1858, 1859, 1860, 1861, 1863, 1865, 1866, 1867, 1868, 1869, 1870, 1871, 1872, 1873, and 1874. Issued by various publishers in Cincinnati. For a number of years the convention operated as the American Christian Missionary Society. Appeared as *Proceedings* for the conventions of 1875, 1876, 1878, 1879, 1880, 1881, 1882, 1883, 1884, and 1889. During those years the organization functioned as the General Christian Missionary Convention.

SHELNUTT, ERASTUS LAMAR. *Encountering Opposition.* Cincinnati: American Christian Missionary Society, 1902? 24 pp.

VON RECK, Commissary and John Martin Bolzius. *An Extract of the Journals of Mr. Commissary Von Reck, Who Conducted the First Transport of Saltzburgers to Georgia: and of the Reverend Mr. Bolzius, One of Their Ministers.* London: Society for Promoting Christian Knowledge, 1734. 38 pp.

Year Book of the Churches of Christ, Christian Churches or Disciples of Christ in Georgia. For 1902, 1903, 1905, 1906, 1908, 1909, 1910, 1911, 1912, 1913, and 1913-1914. (The 1900 and 1904 publications appeared as *Annual Reports,* which see.) The volumes generally had reports of the

Women's groups, the State Board and its missionary pastors and evangelists, religious education, convention proceedings, and sometimes, one or more reports of district conventions. The 1905 issue also included Minutes of the 1905 Negro State Convention. Most were issued by Atlanta or Athens publishers. In succeeding years, the *Year Book* generally appeared as an issue of the *Christian Messenger,* monthly periodical of Georgia Disciples of Christ.

PERIODICALS AND NEWSPAPERS

American Home Missionary, Cincinnati, O., 1896, 1914, 1917, 1918.

Atlanta Constitution, Atlanta, Ga., 1886, 1893, 1897.

Atlanta Journal, Atlanta, Ga., 1915.

Atlantic Missionary, Cuckoo, Va., 1886.

Bible Advocate, Paris, Tenn., 1845, 1846.

The Christian-Evangelist, St. Louis, Mo., 1884, 1892, 1893, 1906, 1907, 1914, 1915, 1919, 1920, 1922, 1924-1926, 1927, 1928, 1936, 1939, 1940-1942, 1944, 1948-1950.

Christian Friend, Goldsboro, N. C., 1854.

The Christian Index, Washington, Ga., 1838, 1856.

Christian Journal, Harrodsburg, Ky., 1843.

Christian Magazine, Nashville, Tenn., 1848-1852.

368   BIBLIOGRAPHY

Christian Messenger, Georgetown, Ky., and Jacksonville, Ill., 1828-1833, 1835.

Christian Messenger, Macon, Ga., 1918-1920, 1923-1925, 1927-1930, 1935, 1936, 1938-1940, 1942-1950, 1952.

Christian Philanthropist, St. Louis, Mo., 1911.

Christian Preacher, Cincinnati, O., 1837.

Christian Review, Nashville, Tenn., 1844, 1845, 1847.

Christian Standard, Cincinnati, O., 1867, 1869-1871, 1873, 1875, 1876, 1878-1887, 1891-1893, 1896, 1897, 1903, 1907, 1908, 1910, 1914-1916, 1921-1929, 1939-1941, 1943, 1946, 1949.

The Christian Union, Augusta, Ga., 1856.

Discipliana, Canton, Mo., 1943, 1944.

The Evangelist, Carthage, O., 1834.

The Evangelist, Atlanta, Ga., 1897, 1898.

Georgia Historical Quarterly, Savannah, Ga., 1917.

Gospel Advocate, Nashville, Tenn., 1855-1857, 1861, 1866-1873, 1883, 1899, 1904, 1906, 1907, 1915, 1939.

Gospel Proclamation, St. Clairsville, O., 1847, 1848.

Millennial Harbinger, Bethany, W. Va., 1832, 1833, 1835, 1836, 1838-1840, 1842, 1845, 1846, 1848-1851, 1854-1861, 1866-1868, 1870.

Missionary Intelligencer, Cincinnati, O., 1900, 1901, 1913, 1914.

Missionary Tidings, Indianapolis, Ind., 1884, 1890, 1893-1895, 1897-1899, 1915.

Missionary Weekly, Cuckoo, Va., 1888.

Morning Watch, Evergreen, S. C., 1837-1839.

The Primitive Baptist, Tarboro, N. C., 1838.

Religious Historian, Nashville, Tenn., 1872.

Restoration Herald, Cincinnati, O., 1925, 1928, 1929, 1933-1935, 1937, 1946, 1948, 1950.

The Shane Quarterly, Indianapolis, Ind., 1943.

Southern Christian, Atlanta, Ga., 1894.

Southern Evangelist, Atlanta, Ga., 1901.

World Call, Indianapolis, Ind., 1919, 1922-1925, 1945, 1946, 1953.

Youth's Conference Call, St. Louis, Mo., 1927-1929.

UNPUBLISHED MATERIAL

BARFIELD, JAMES HARHNESS. "A History of the Disciples of Christ in Georgia, 1819-1914." Unpublished B.D. Thesis, School of Religion of Vanderbilt University, Nashville, Tenn., 1938. [v] + 136 + 4 pp.

Bedford, A. Goff. "The Emergence and Growth of the Christian Church (Disciples of Christ) in Georgia." Unpublished A.M. Thesis, University of West Virginia, Morgantown, W. Va., 1953. 291 pp.

Daniell, Jack Mathews. "The Disciples of Christ in Northeast Georgia." Unpublished B.D. Thesis, The College of the Bible, Lexington, Ky., 1950. iii + 90 pp.

Darsie, George. Unpublished diary for 1885, one of more than 30 of his annual, longhand journals in the Philip Fall Memorial Library of the First Christian Church, Frankfort, Ky.

Gum, Mrs. Robert Richardson and Mrs. M. C. Darnell. "History of the First Christian Church, Frankfort, Kentucky." Dedicated to the Memory of Mrs. Emily H. Tubman. Unpublished MS., 1947. One copy in possession of the Philip Fall Memorial Library of the First Christian Church, Frankfort, Ky.

Hook, Edward. "Dr. Daniel Hook." Unpublished MS., Memorial Address, 1878? 8 pp. Typed copy in possession of The Disciples of Christ Historical Society, Nashville, Tenn.

Howell, Mrs. Mary D. "The Life of Dr. Daniel Hook." Unpublished MS., 1875? iii + 91 pp. Typed copy in possession of The Disciples of Christ Historical Society, Nashville, Tenn.

Miller, Annie Charlotte (Mrs. Bert O.). "The First Christian Church of Augusta." Unpublished MS., 1904? In possession of The Disciples of Christ Historical Society, Nashville, Tenn.

Minutes, General Convention of Churches of Christ (Disciples of Christ), Atlanta, Georgia, October 7-14, 1914. 80 pp.

typed. In the International Convention of Disciples of
Christ Archives at The Disciples of Christ Historical
Society, Nashville, Tenn.

Poss, LENTON L. "The History of the Christian Church in
    Georgia." Unpublished B.D. Thesis, Brite College of
    the Bible, Texas Christian University, Fort Worth, Tex.,
    1948. v + 145 pp.

ROBISON, HENRY BARTON. "A Sketch of Henry Barton Robi-
    son." Unpublished MS., 1941? 5 pp. Typed copy in
    possession of The Disciples of Christ Historical Society,
    Nashville, Tenn.

Index

DATE DUE

DEMCO 38-297